Restoration and Reclamation of Boreal Ecosystems

Attaining Sustainable Development

Boreal ecosystems contain one-third of the world's forests and stored carbon, but these regions are under increasing threat from both natural and anthropogenic disturbances. Written by leaders from the forefront of private, public, and academic sectors, *Restoration and Reclamation of Boreal Ecosystems* emphasizes a broad, conceptual approach to the specific application of empirical research into development planning, restoration, and modeling of these ecosystems, the importance of which is highlighted at a time of global climate change as they act as carbon sinks. There is a focus on the reclamation of exploited ecosystems from a holistic standpoint, ranging from environmental and edaphic variables to the restoration of foundational flora. Recent advances in quantification of ecosystem services, such as habitat suitability and carbon storage modeling are also detailed. The book contains case studies that address how both historical and novel assemblages can provide ecosystem stability under projected climatic and land-use scenarios.

DALE H. VITT is Professor Emeritus of Plant Biology, former Chair of the Department of Plant Biology and University Outstanding Scholar at Southern Illinois University, Carbondale.

JAGTAR S. BHATTI is a research scientist and project leader with Natural Resources Canada, Canadian Forest Service, Northern Forestry Centre in Edmonton, Canada.

Restoration and Reclamation of Boreal Ecosystems

Attaining Sustainable Development

DALE H. VITT
*Department of Plant Biology
and Center for Ecology,
Southern Illinois University,
Carbondale, IL, USA*

JAGTAR S. BHATTI
*Canadian Forest Service,
Northern Forestry Centre,
Edmonton, AB, Canada*

CAMBRIDGE UNIVERSITY PRESS
Cambridge, New York, Melbourne, Madrid, Cape Town,
Singapore, São Paulo, Delhi, Mexico City

Cambridge University Press
The Edinburgh Building, Cambridge CB2 8RU, UK

Published in the United States of America by
Cambridge University Press, New York

www.cambridge.org
Information on this title: www.cambridge.org/9781107015715

First published 2012

Printed and bound in the United Kingdom by the MPG Books Group.

A catalogue record for this publication is available from the British Library

Library of Congress Cataloguing in Publication data
Restoration and reclamation of boreal ecosystems : attaining sustainable
development / [edited by] Dale Vitt, Jagtar Bhatti.
p. cm.
Includes bibliographical references and index.
ISBN 978-1-107-01571-5 (hardback)
1. Taiga ecology.   2. Rain forest ecology.   3. Rain forest conservation.
4. Taiga conservation.   5. Forest ecology.   I. Vitt, Dale H. (Dale Hadley), 1944–
II. Bhatti, J. S. (Jagtar S.)
QH541.5.T3V55   2012 577.3'7–dc23   2012015310

ISBN 978-1-107-01571-5 Hardback

Contents

      The colour plates will be found between page 178 and 179.

Contributors

EDITORS

Dale H. Vitt Department of Plant Biology and Center for Ecology, Southern Illinois University, Carbondale, IL 62901, USA

Jagtar S. Bhatti Canadian Forest Service, Northern Forestry Centre, 5320–122 St., Edmonton, AB T6H 3S5, Canada

ASSISTANT EDITOR

Juliet Caviness Department of Plant Biology and Center for Ecology, Southern Illinois University, Carbondale, IL 62901, USA

CONTRIBUTORS

Roxane Andersen The James Hutton Institute, Craigiebuckler, Aberdeen AB15 8QH, UK

Paul Arp Faculty of Forestry and Environmental Management, UNB, Fredericton, NB, Canada

Caroline Bampfylde Oil Sands and Clean Energy Policy Branch, Alberta Environment, 12th floor, 10025–106 St. NW, Edmonton, AB T5J 1G4, Canada

Vicky Bérubé Laval Université, Québec City, QC G1V 0A6, Canada

Juan Blanco Forest Ecosystem Simulation Group, Department of Forest Sciences, University of British Columbia, Vancouver, BC V6T 1Z6, Canada

Rosemary Bloise Department of Plant Biology, Southern Illinois University, Carbondale, IL 62901, USA

Erin Brault Department of Biology, Villanova University, Villanova, PA 19085, USA

Christine Daly Suncor Energy Inc., Fort McMurray, AB T9H 3E3, Canada

Joyce Gould Parks Tourism, Parks and Recreation, Edmonton, AB, Canada

Martha D. Graf Institute of Environmental Planning, Leibniz Universität, Hannover, Germany

Michelle Harris Department of Biology, Villanova University, Villanova, PA 19085, USA

Doug Hiltz Faculty of Forestry and Environmental Management, UNB, Fredericton, NB, Canada

Melissa House Department of Plant Biology, Southern Illinois University, Carbondale, IL 62901, USA

Pavel Juruš Department of Electrical and Computer Engineering, ECERF, 2nd floor, 9107–116 St., University of Alberta, Edmonton, AB T6G 2V4, Canada and Institute of Computer Science, Academy of Sciences of the Czech Republic, Prague, Czech Republic

Sara Koropchak Department of Plant Biology, Southern Illinois University, Carbondale, IL 62901, USA

Simon Landhäusser Department of Renewable Resources, University of Alberta, Edmonton, AB, Canada

Yaqiong Li Department of Electrical and Computer Engineering, ECERF, 2nd floor, 9107–116 St., University of Alberta, Edmonton, AB T6G 2V4, Canada

Ellen Macdonald Department of Renewable Resources, University of Alberta, Edmonton, AB, Canada

Gord McKenna BGC Engineering, 500–1045 Howe St., Vancouver V6Z 2A9, BC, Canada

Randy Mikula Kalium Research, 12515–39 Ave., Edmonton, AB T6J 0N1, Canada

Stephen B. Mowbray Department of Biology, Villanova University, Villanova, PA 19085, USA

Petr Musilek Department of Electrical and Computer Engineering, ECERF, 2nd floor, 9107–116 St., University of Alberta, Edmonton, AB T6G 2V4, Canada

Jae Ogilvie Faculty of Forestry and Environmental Management, UNB, Fredericton, NB, Canada

Rémy Pouliot Université Laval, Québec City, QC G1V 0A6, Canada

Jonathan Price University of Waterloo, Waterloo, ON N2L 3G1, Canada

Sylvie Quideau Department of Renewable Resources, University of Alberta, Edmonton, AB, Canada

Fereidoun Rezanezhad University of Waterloo, Waterloo, ON N2L 3G1, Canada

Line Rochefort Université Laval, Québec City, QC G1V 0A6, Canada

James Rodway Department of Electrical and Computer Engineering, ECERF, 2nd floor, 9107–116 St., University of Alberta, Edmonton, AB T6G 2V4, Canada

Kimberli D. Scott Department of Biology, Villanova University, Villanova, PA 19085, USA

Brad Seely Forest Ecosystem Simulation Group, Department of Forest Sciences, University of British Columbia, Vancouver, BC V6T 1Z6, Canada

Maria Strack Department of Geography, University of Calgary, 2500 University Dr. NW, Calgary, AB T2N 1N4, Canada

Rob Vassov Syncrude Canada Ltd., Research and Development, 9421–17 Ave., Edmonton, AB T6N 1H4, Canada

Melanie A. Vile Department of Biology, Villanova University, Villanova, PA 19085, USA

Mike Vitt 3GreenTree Ecosystem Services Ltd., 3960 Marine Ave., Belcarra, BC V3H 4R9, Canada

James M. Waddington McMaster Centre for Climate Change and School of Geography and Earth Sciences, McMaster University, 1280 Main St. W, Hamilton, ON L8S 4K1, Canada

Clive Welham Forest Ecosystem Simulation Group, Department of Forest Sciences, University of British Columbia, Vancouver, BC V6T 1Z6, Canada

Barry White Alberta Sustainable Resource Department, Edmonton, AB, Canada

R. Kelman Wieder Department of Biology, Villanova University, Villanova, PA 19085, USA

Carla Wytrykush Syncrude Canada Ltd., Research and Development, 9421–17 Ave., Edmonton, AB T6N 1H4, Canada

Preface

The boreal forest, or taiga, is a mosaic of lakes, peatlands, and upland forests, all placed on a mostly topographically flat, featureless landscape having strong hydrological connectivity. The climate is harsh, with long, cold winters and fairly dry, cool summers. Water is at a premium and species diversity is low. Community succession is largely driven by disturbance, especially wildfire; however, in recent decades anthropogenic disturbances have become increasingly prevalent. Disturbances related to resource development such as forestry practices, reservoir creation, peat harvesting, and oil and gas production most recently from bitumen extraction from oil sands are especially frequent. Both open-pit and SAGD operations produce either large scale or frequent disturbances and the science of reclaiming these areas is still in its infancy.

This book is composed of chapters that reveal our current state of knowledge on reclamation and restoration of these boreal ecosystems. The chapters in this book were selected from presentations, discussions, and posters that were presented during a three-day symposium held at the Matrix Hotel in Edmonton, Alberta on March 25–27, 2010. This symposium, *Reclamation and Restoration of Boreal Peatland and Forest Ecosystems: Toward a Sustainable Future*, addressed problems and recent research being carried out in North America on the topic.

The chapters in this book emphasize the use of natural regimes as models for reclamation and present the resulting challenges of reclaiming boreal ecosystems. In addition, the importance of the boreal forest as a carbon store has implications for global climate and several chapters focus on this global concern.

This book was partially funded by the Canadian Sphagnum Peat Moss Association (CSPMA), Natural Resources Canada (CFS), Northern Alberta Institute of Technology Boreal Research Institute (NAIT), Oil Sands Research and Information Network (OSRIN), and PEATNET, a NSF (US) funded RCN Peatland Ecosystem Analysis and Training Network grant to Dale Vitt and R. Kelman Wieder. This book was edited by Juliet Caviness. We gratefully acknowledge the support of Chris Powter (OSRIN), Hugh Seaton (NAIT), and Paul Short (CSPMA).

Dale H. Vitt   Jagtar Bhatti
Carbondale, June 18, 2012

Part I Utilizing natural regimes as models for reclamation and restoration

1

The changing boreal forest
Incorporating ecological theory into restoration planning

INTRODUCTION

Boreal ecosystems dominate the landscape across much of Canada, Fennoscandia, and Russia. In Canada, they comprise 35% of the total land area and about 77% of Canada's forestland (NRC 2011). These boreal ecosystems are highly variable and consist of lakes, wetlands – especially peatlands – and a variety of upland forest types, all adapted to long, cool winters and short, cool and humid summers. Uplands and peatlands form a mosaic of community types across the landscape, with bogs and fens often forming large peatland complexes, and uplands varying from aspen-dominated deciduous forest to spruce–fir–pine-dominated conifer forests. In the oil sands region of Alberta, peatlands compose 29% of the landscape (Lee and Cheng, 2009) and are an integral part of the functioning landscape. The underlying bedrock, surficial materials, hydrological connectivity, and soils are highly variable within the boreal landscape, and climate is the major controlling factor.

In general, the plant communities of the boreal forest are young in age, and have developed from species northward immigrations since the retreat of the Wisconsinan glaciers – some 12,000 years ago. Across this evolving landscape, the plant and animal communities have continually been influenced by recurring disturbance events. Wildfire has been the most important natural disturbance. In Canada, 2.1 million hectares of boreal forest are burned annually (NRC 2011); however, much has changed over the last century. Disturbances have become larger and more severe. During the early 1900s, the disturbance regime of Canada's boreal forest was dominated by natural disturbances, with human

Restoration and Reclamation of Boreal Ecosystems, ed. Dale Vitt and Jagtar Bhatti. Published by Cambridge University Press. © Cambridge University Press 2012.

influences playing only local roles. Agricultural expansion, escaped local fires, and high-grade logging were the predominant human disturbances. During the latter half of the 1900s, and continuing today, these human disturbances have changed remarkably and include clearing for roads, energy extraction, clear-cutting, peat harvesting, and reservoir creation, set against a backdrop of increasing insect outbreaks, wildfires, and climatic change (Timoney, 2003). The result is two-fold: the disturbances are more severe and larger in scale or occur at higher frequency, and these result in a highly fragmented landscape. As disturbances increase across the boreal landscape, our ability to rehabilitate these disturbed areas also becomes more important, and the principles of ecological succession must guide our actions (Walker and del Moral, 2003). These actions and interventions need to be built around a framework of natural succession. In particular, we must build on restoration theory in order to develop methodologies appropriate for the boreal forest and its unique characteristics. We need to better understand the set of natural ecosystems and recognize that the prevailing disturbance regime of the boreal region has changed.

The change in disturbance regimes for these boreal ecosystems may be a response to the larger-scale phenomenon of global change, resulting from human-induced changes in the physical climate system, land use, and atmospheric pollution (IGBP, 2010). Changes in the disturbance regime, and the resulting ecosystem response, are the consequence of both direct (e.g., oil and gas extraction) and indirect (e.g., climate change) effects of human activity, which vary over time and with local conditions. Understanding the complex relationship between landscape change and ecosystem processes is necessary to predict both the feedbacks to global change and the future resource availability and ecosystem services.

Feedback mechanisms associated with interactions of altered disturbance regimes, vegetation structure and function, and biospheric carbon (C) pools all contribute to the linkages with the atmosphere that are presented in Figure 1.1. Climatic variables and atmospheric deposition of nutrients are important ecosystem-driving variables that affect processes such as plant distribution, composition, and growth. Site-specific conditions and small-scale processes determine the relative importance of these variables. Of particular importance are the changes in: (1) vegetation composition and distribution; (2) net C fluxes via plant production and decomposition (Houghton, 2003); and (3) water and energy fluxes altered by precipitation, evapotranspiration (Amiro et al., 2010), and runoff (Lal, 2008). The processes controlling these factors are highly sensitive to

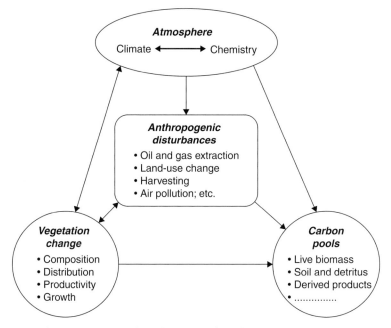

Figure 1.1. The relationship between forest/peatland ecosystem components, their interactions, and atmospheric-climate feedbacks. (Modified from Bhatti et al., 2001.)

environmental change and response at leaf, tree, and stand levels and occur within days to decades (Shugart and Smith, 1996).

A key factor affecting vegetation structure and function is the natural or anthropogenic disturbance regime (Yade et al., 2011b). This regime alters processes that affect ecosystem structure and function at large, and spatial and temporal scales. Alterations in resource availability and its partitioning among biotic components, changes in ecosystem structure, and changes in disturbance regimes are three ways by which changes at the stand or biome level occur. These changes may not be immediately observed and instead may occur over an extended period of time–from years to decades or centuries. Changes in forest structure, both in terms of age–class structure (Kurz et al., 2008, Yade et al., 2011b) and spatial distribution can modify the local, regional, and global scale climate through alteration of albedo, humidity, and ground level wind patterns (Canadell et al. 2007). Yade et al. (2011a) have shown that stand-replacing disturbances play a complex, but very important role in determining the annual exchange of CO_2 with the atmosphere.

As expected, the impact of global change is a significant alteration of the frequency and timing of disturbance events in northern forests (Flannigan et al., 2009). Metsaranta et al. (2010) demonstrated that frequent large-scale forest disturbances such as wildfires could accelerate forest biome adaptation to changing climate conditions. With increased frequency of stand replacement disturbances recently, it is important to understand what are the principal ecological processes governing variability of boreal ecosystems and their inhabitants, as well as their resilience to disturbances; how do we maintain resilience in boreal ecosystems and still maintain viable resource extraction industries? Successful restoration is a key component to the future of this complex boreal landscape and restoration is dependent on understanding how ecosystems and communities change over time.

Biological science has also changed. As Keddy (1999) has described, we have reached the end of an era of exploration and description. The era of discovering the diversity of life and documenting species richness set the stage for our understanding of the species pools from which communities are composed. It also set the stage for relating the patterns of species occurrence to environmental gradients. Biomes were described, species distributions related to elevational and latitudinal gradients, and many of our theories in community and ecosystem ecology proposed. In comparison, the present focus is the search for mechanisms and interrelationships of a multitude of ecosystem components. Unfortunately, ecology is complicated and patterns are often messy, leaving one dissatisfied and wondering if rules do, indeed, exist. Even though they may be disguised, they do exist, and furthermore, they are important for our understanding of natural patterns. As we explore the rules for structure and function of natural communities and ecosystems, we also need to recognize that these same rules govern the restoration of disturbed areas, and in particular, we must utilize these rules to rebuild communities on the boreal landscape.

Ecologists have long been interested in how communities change over time (Pickett et al., 2008). Perhaps the earliest studies were those of Henry Cowles, who observed floristic changes from lakeshore inland along Lake Michigan and interpreted these as representing community change through time (Cowles, 1899). Somewhat later, Frederick Clements (1916) and Henry Gleason (1917) provided a foundation of competing ideas on community succession and laid the groundwork for modern successional theory. Clements' view of discrete assemblages of species arriving, assuming dominance, and shifting in discrete phases until a final "climax" community was attained in a predictable manner was quite different from Gleason's view of individual species arriving and responding dynamically to their environments, with a variable, nonpredictable successional progression and endpoint. In 1977, Connell and Slatyer proposed three general models of succession focusing on life history traits of species. In general, they argued that the interactions of resource availability and site history provide a set of circumstances for a set of species arrivals; these arrival species establish, grow, and interact with one another. The result of these events is: (1) facilitation, whereby species modify their surroundings and make conditions suitable for the next group of species; (2) tolerance, whereby late-arrival species are not affected by early arrivals; or (3) inhibition, whereby early arrivals suppress or exclude late-arriving species.

A FRAMEWORK

From a reclamation/restoration point of view, we can utilize many of these ideas to build a theoretical framework for reclamation and restoration in the western boreal forest. This framework encompasses four ecological filters, and each can be translated into a set of operational protocols necessary for successful restoration planning (Figure 1.2).

- **Site history and resource availability:** disturbed sites have basic resource levels, determined by position on the landscape, local and regional hydrology, and chemical and physical limits of the substrate. Additionally, sites are varied in size and positioned along unique portions of resource gradients. Sites are strongly affected by regional climate and its annual variation. Our detailed understanding of the key environmental drivers at each restoration site is the first step in developing operational protocols and engineering the site for species arrivals.
- **Species availability:** the availability of arriving species is controlled by the abilities of diaspores to be dispersed from surrounding areas and the available regional species pool. Size of the disturbance, number of potential contributing species, and resource limitations of the recipient site are all-important thresholds to be crossed. Seed, spore, and bud banks are important determinants that have the potential to limit the arriving species pool. Operationally, it may not be sufficient to depend on species arrivals from natural existing donor sites; species may need to be selected and introduced (Brudvig and Mabry, 2008). In applied contexts, it is critical to understand how species respond to important environmental gradients (Gignac et al., 1991).

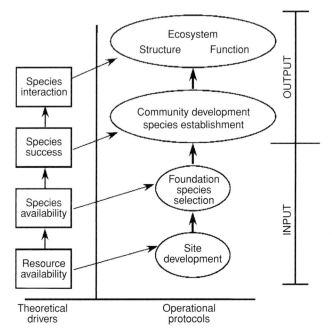

Figure 1.2. Four ecological filters taken from successional theory (left side) and the resulting actions and findings required for restoration of large-scale or frequent disturbances.

Both site preparation and species selection are inputs to successful restoration and lead to a series of potential results or outputs (Figure 1.2).

- **Species performance:** arriving species must establish, grow, and reproduce. Establishment and growth are important early stage indicators of species success, while reproduction, both sexual and asexual, is important later on. Early regeneration dynamics such as seedling mortality and narrow environmental requirements may form a "bottleneck" for successful establishment (Poorter, 2007). The initial establishment and success of foundation species leads to early community development. Species success is manifested in the development of community structure, wherein species are sorted into a variety of vegetational layers. Operationally, the system must be carefully monitored for individual species responses and also for structural complexity and development.
- **Interspecific interactions:** once species are established and structural attributes begin to form, biotic interactions such as competition, herbivory, and invasions of aggressive species are factors that determine the eventual outcome of species succession.

These biotic interactions determine the eventual success of individual species, but do not determine the functional integrity of the community. If the correct foundation species are present, then, with time, additional species arrivals will increase the species diversity. These complex species interactions provide the backdrop for the return of ecosystem function, and successful restoration requires the assessment of both community richness and ecosystem functions.

In summary, this framework outlines four key processes that act as ecological filters and that must be recognized in any reclamation or restoration project. These translate to: (1) site development utilizing natural analogues; (2) species selected from comparative natural situations; (3) species performances based on clear natural benchmarks; and (4) development of community stabilization, species richness, and ecosystem function, again based on natural analogues.

These four ecological filters and associated operational protocols form the framework for restoration of boreal disturbances. The chapters in this book provide answers and background to some of these. Much of what we have learned and presently utilize in boreal restoration is practically based. It is time that we develop these operational protocols from ecological theory, theory that has resulted from decades of exploration and experimentation. The chapters in this book attempt to provide insights into a number of key areas. In particular, the stage is set by a series of chapters exploring the use of natural regimes as baselines for site and species inputs. Second, several authors review what we have learned over the past few decades about implementing successful planting regimes, introducing regional species, and early site development. Third, we learn how successful some of the restorations have been, and how we can attempt to manage C in a changing world of C offsets. Having read these reviews of what we know of restoration across the boreal regime, we are left with many questions; some of these are presently being answered by research programs already in place, while others remain for the future.

POSSIBLE FUTURE SURPRISES AND THE PATH FORWARD

Five research themes would strengthen scientific understanding of future restoration efforts.

- **Significant data and knowledge gaps exist**. Although we have cleverly engineered sites for control of water and chemistry, we still know little about how species and the system as a whole will respond. We have just scratched the surface of understanding community development or how species diversity can be installed into restoration plans. The surprise may be that we can, indeed, restore (not reclaim) landscapes.

- **Histories**, or developing a series of meaningful benchmarks to know if we are successful, have been a nagging problem for a decade. Is it correct to compare our three- to five-year-old "fen" with one that has been functional for millennia? Unlikely, but where are the correct benchmarks on the landscape? The surprise may be that adequate function may be achieved before we know that we have it.

- **Hydrology** provides the necessary conditions for both wetlands and uplands to function; however, climate also plays a key role. There are clear research needs to quantify the roles of temperature and precipitation under a changing climatic regime and to learn more of how these relate to regional hydrology. Unfortunately, the surprise is that global climate change may have an overriding local effect.

- **Carbon cycles** must be better understood. We need to better quantify C fluxes and sequestration at early stages of restorations. We know much about C stocks and C fluxes, and we need to better develop C offset baselines–we may be surprised by what we learn about C management.

- **Models** are needed to better predict how our short-term restoration efforts will play out over the next decades. These models need to be climate-linked and able to detect threshold dynamics as well as internal feedbacks.

The message from chapters in this book is clear: reclamation and restoration cannot be afterthoughts to operations. Operational protocols that are in line with the limiting ecological filters must be in place in the early planning stages of operations. We have learned that the addition of organic material to help develop the soils and introduce diaspores is extremely beneficial, but the timing of this introduction is also critical to the long-term site development and C cycling. Time is of the essence in restoration, and the development of reclamation protocols that incorporate ecological theory into site engineering is the key to success. Finally, peatlands have their own set of ecological services and play a pivotal role on the landscape. As such, peatlands are equal partners in achieving landscape restoration.

REFERENCES

Amiro, B. D., Barr A. G., Black T. A., et al. (2010). Ecosystem carbon dioxide fluxes after disturbance in forests of North America. *Journal of Geophysical Research*, **115**, G00K02.

Bhatti, J. S., Apps M. J., Jiang, H. (2001). Examining the carbon stocks of boreal forest ecosystems at stand and regional scales. In R. Lal, J. M. Kimble, R. F. Follett, B. A. Stewart, eds., *Assessment Methods for Soil C Pools*. Boca Raton, FL: CRC Press LLC, pp. 513–532.

Brudvig, L. A. and Mabry, C. M. (2008). Trait-based filtering of the regional species pool to guide understory plant reintroductions in midwestern oak savannas, USA. *Restoration Ecology*, **16**, 290–304.

Canadell, J. G., Le Quéré, C., Raupauch, M.R., et al. (2007). Contributions to accelerating atmospheric CO_2 growth from economic activity, carbon intensity, and efficiency of natural sinks. *Proceedings of the National Academy of Sciences*, **104**, 18866.

Clements, F. E. (1916). *Plant Succession: an Analysis of the Development of Vegetation*. Washington, DC: Carnegie Institution of Washington.

Connell, J. H. and Slatyer, R. O. (1977). Mechanisms of succession in natural communities and their role in community stability and organization. *American Naturalist*, **111**, 1119–1144.

Cowles, H. (1899). The ecological relations of the vegetation on the sand dunes of Lake Michigan. Part I. Geographical relations of the sand dune floras. *Botanical Gazette*, **27**, 95–117.

Flannigan, M., Stocks, B., Turetsky, M., Wotton, M. (2009). Impacts of climate change on fire activity and fire management in the circumboreal forest. *Global Change Biology*, **15**, 549–560.

Gignac, L. D., Vitt, D. H., Zoltai, S. C., Bayley, S. E. (1991). Bryophyte response surfaces along climatic, chemical and physical gradients in peatlands of western Canada. *Nova Hedwigia*, **53**, 27–71.

Gleason, H. A. (1917). The structure and development of the plant association. *Bulletin of the Torrey Botanical Club*, **44**, 463–481.

Houghton, R. A. (2003). Revised estimates of the annual net flux of carbon to the atmosphere from changes in land use and land management 1850–2000. *Tellus*, **55B**, 378–398.

IGBP (International Geosphere–Biosphere Programme). (2010). Developing an integrated history and future of people on earth (IHOPE): research plan. IGBP Report No. 59, IGBP Secretariat, Stockholm.

Keddy, P. (1999). Epilogue: from global exploration to community assembly. In E. Weiher and P. Keddy, eds., *Ecological Assembly Rules Perspectives, Advances, Retreats*. Cambridge: Cambridge University Press, pp. 393–402.

Kurz, W. A. G., Stinson, G., Rampley, G. J., Dymond, C. C., Neilson, E. T. (2008). Risk of natural disturbances makes future contribution of Canada's forests to the global carbon cycle highly uncertain. *Proceedings of the National Academy of Sciences*, **105**, 1551–1558.

Lal, R. (2008). Carbon sequestration. *Philosophical Transactions of the Royal Society (B)*, **363**, 815–830.

Lee, P. and Cheng, R. (2009). *Bitumen and Biocarbon: Land Use Conversions and Loss of Biological Carbon due to Bitumen Operations in the Boreal Forests of Alberta, Canada*. Edmonton, AB: Global Forest Watch Canada.

Metsaranta, J. M, Kurz, W. A., Neilson, E. T., Stinson, G. (2010). Implications of future disturbance regimes on the carbon balance of Canada's managed forest (2010–2100). *Tellus*, **62B**, 719–736.

NRCan. (2011). _HYPERLINK http://www.NRCan.gc.ca_www.NRCan.gc.ca_ (Accessed July 22, 2011).

Pickett, S. T. A., Cadenasso, M. L., Meiners, S. J. (2008). Ever since Clements: from succession to vegetation dynamics and understanding to intervention. *Applied Vegetation Science*, **12**, 9–21.

Poorter, L. (2007). Are species adapted to their regeneration niche, adult niche, or both? *The American Naturalist*, **169**, 433–442.

Shugart, H. H. and Smith, T. M. (1996). A review of forest patch models and their application to global research. *Climatic Change*, **34**, 131–154.

Timoney, K. P. (2003). The changing disturbance regime of the boreal forest of the Canadian prairie provinces. *The Forestry Chronicle*, **79**, 502–516.

Walker, L. R. and del Moral, R. (2003). *Primary Succession and Ecosystem Rehabilitation*. Cambridge: Cambridge University Press.

Yade, P., Birdsey, R. A., Fang, J., et al. (2011a). A large and persistent carbon sink in the world's forests. *Science*, 1201609, Published online July 14, 2011 [DOI:10.1126/science.1201609].

Yade, P., Chen, J. M., Birdsey, R., et al. (2011b). Age structure and disturbance legacy of North American forests. *Biogeosciences*, **8**, 715.

R. KELMAN WIEDER, MELANIE A. VILE, KIMBERLI D. SCOTT,
DALE H. VITT, ERIN BRAULT, MICHELLE HARRIS,
AND STEPHEN B. MOWBRAY

2

Disturbance and the peatland carbon sink in the Oil Sands Administrative Area

INTRODUCTION

The Oil Sands Administration Area (OSAA) covers 14,042,214 ha of the northern Alberta boreal forest. Within the OSAA, peatlands cover 4,123,554 ha, or 29% of the total area, and 461,838 ha of these peatlands potentially could be changed/converted under a scenario of full development of the oil resource (Lee and Cheng, 2009). One of the critical ecological services delivered by boreal peatlands is their function as a net sink for atmospheric CO_2, accumulating and storing carbon (C) as peat (Vitt and Wieder, 2006). As oil sands development continues in northern Alberta, recent studies have begun to assess the broader impacts of land use change from a C source/sink perspective where peatlands play a prominent role (Lee and Cheng, 2009; Schneider and Dyer, 2006; Yeh et al., 2010). Although the peatlands in the OSAA function as an ongoing net sink for atmospheric CO_2, the strength of this C sink is affected by the wildfire regime, periodic drought, and anthropogenic activities, most notably oil sands development. Here, we discuss natural variation in the regional peatland C sink, as related to wildfire and drought, to provide a context for assessing the present and potential future effects of oil sands development.

PEATLAND CARBON AND WILDFIRE

Wildfire in the boreal forest of northern Alberta represents a disturbance to ecosystem structure and function. Across all of Alberta, from 2002–2011, an average of 1541 fires per year burned 220,875 ha; 54% of the fires

Restoration and Reclamation of Boreal Ecosystems, ed. Dale Vitt and Jagtar Bhatti. Published by Cambridge University Press. © Cambridge University Press 2012.

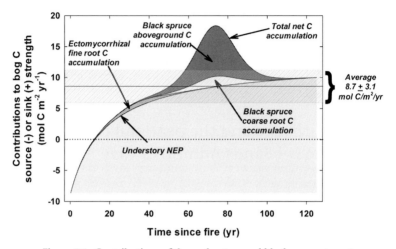

Figure 2.1. Contributions of the understory and black spruce trees to changing carbon (C) balance of Alberta bogs after fire. (Adapted from Wieder et al., 2009.)

were human-caused and 46% were lightning-caused (Alberta Sustainable Resource Development; http://www.srd.alberta.ca/Wildfire/Wildfire Status/HistoricalWildfireInformation/10-YearStatisticalSummary.aspx). A historical analysis of fire over a 12,000 km² area near Wabasca, AB, indicated that between 1950 and 2000, an average of 18.4±3.9 km² of bog and 24.0±3.8 km² of fen burned annually, corresponding to fire return intervals of 123±26 yr and 105±17 yr for bogs and fens, respectively (Turetsky et al., 2004). Hence, the peatlands of northern Alberta persist as a mosaic of sites across the landscape that represents different lengths of time since fire.

Across a 102-year time-since-fire bog chronosequence in northern Alberta, the C source/sink function changes predictably (Figure 2.1), with an average net C sink strength along the 102-year chronosequence of 8.7±3.1 mol/m²/yr (104±37 g C/m²/yr) (Wieder et al., 2009). When coupled with direct losses of C to the atmosphere via direct combustion during bog fire, the net C sink becomes 77±28 g C/m²/yr. Applying this value to the 412 km² of peatland in the OSAA indicates a regional peatland net C sink of 3.2±1.2 Tg/yr in the absence of oil sands development.

The C sequestration function of peatlands of northern Alberta has considerable potential to be diminished because of changing climate. An increase of non-winter air temperatures of only 2°C would decrease the net C sink strength from 77±28 g C/m²/yr to 35±12 g C/m²/yr. Such a change would decrease the OSAA regional peatland C sink to 1.4±0.5 Tg/yr in the absence of oil sands development, and to 1.0 ± 0.2 Tg/yr under the scenario of full development of the oil resource.

One of the consequences of ongoing climate change is an increase in the number of fires and the area burned annually across the North American boreal forest (Flannigan et al., 2005; Krawchuk et al., 2009) and across northern Alberta (Krawchuk and Cumming, 2011; Tymstra et al., 2007). For bogs, a shortening of the fire return interval not only increases direct losses of CO_2 to the atmosphere by direct combustion, but also decreases the regional net bog C sink strength as the average age (time-since-fire) of bogs on the landscape shifts toward younger sites (Figure 2.1). For the 12,000 km^2 study area of Turetsky et al. (2004), a shortening of the fire return interval from 123 to 61 years would result in the region's peatlands functioning overall as neither a sink nor a source of atmospheric CO_2 (Wieder et al., 2009).

PEATLAND CARBON AND DROUGHT

Peatlands of continental western Canada persist at the dry end of the climatic regime for boreal peatlands globally, with total annual precipitation of less than 500 mm and with potential evapotranspiration approximately equal to annual precipitation (Wieder et al., 2006). Episodic drought in the southern grassland/agricultural areas of southern Alberta, Saskatchewan, and Manitoba has received considerable attention (Bonsal and Regier, 2007; Bonsal and Wheaton, 2005; McGinn, 2010; Schindler and Donohue, 2006; Wilson et al., 2002); however, drought conditions can extend northward into the OSAA. Peatland net ecosystem exchange can be severely compromised by drought and attendant desiccation of mosses (Alm et al., 1999; Vile et al., 2011).

To experimentally examine the effects of drought on bog C cycling, we established a rainfall exclusion study at Utikuma Lake Bog, Alberta (55°48.358′N; 115°10.977′W). In 2007, in each of two sections of Utikuma Lake Bog (one section had most recently burned in 1914, and the other in 1951), we placed clear, acrylic rainfall exclusion roofs (1.2 m × 1.2 m) over 12 aluminum collars (60 cm × 60 cm) that had been installed for quantification of understory net ecosystem production (NEP_U, as indicated by net CO_2 exchange) using the static chamber approach; 12 other collars served as unroofed controls (Vile et al., 2011; Wieder et al., 2009). We reported previously that over the first year, surface peat moisture increased in response to rain events, but roofing prevented this response; however, roofing had no clear measureable effects on bog NEP_U (Vile et al., 2011).

The roofs remained in place, and in 2009, we continued NEP_U measurements under a range of PAR conditions from full sunlight to complete darkness by placing different-density shade cloths on the static chambers while measuring CO_2 fluxes. We characterized NEP_U as a function of PAR and near-surface air temperature (Wieder et al., 2009):

$$NEP_U = \frac{P_{MAX} \times PAR \times \alpha}{PAR \times \alpha + P_{MAX}} - A \times Q_{10}^{T/10} \qquad [2.1]$$

The parameters of the equation are P_{MAX} (maximum gross CO_2 capture at infinite PAR; μmol CO_2 m^{-2} s^{-1}), α (photosynthetic quantum efficiency; μmol CO_2 m^{-2} s^{-1} per μmol PAR m^{-2} s^{-1}), A (total understory respiration from both vascular plants within the chambers and decomposition in the underlying peat column at 0°C; μmol CO_2 m^{-2} s^{-1}), and Q_{10} (the temperature dependence of total understory respiration; dimensionless) (Bubier et al., 2003; Vile et al., 2011; Wieder et al., 2009).

Effects of roofing were more evident in 2009 than in 2007, with roofed plots showing substantially lower estimates of P_{MAX}, α, and A (Table 2.1). A weather station (WatchDog® 2800; Spectrum Technologies, Plainfield, IL) in both sections of the bog indicated that the older section of the bog (1914 burn) was shadier than the younger section (1951 burn), although air temperatures were similar in both sections of the bog in both years (Figure 2.2). Using the parameters estimated for the NEP_U equation and hourly PAR and air temperature values from the weather stations, we calculated hourly NEP_U values. When summed to provide weekly NEP_U estimates (Figure 2.2), it is evident that roofing had little influence on NEP_U in 2007, but led to substantially decreased NEP_U in both sections of the bog. Over the June–September interval in 2009, rainfall exclusion by roofing reduced NEP_U by 12% and 43% in the older and younger sections of the bog, respectively (Table 2.1).

We quantified net primary production (NPP) of *Sphagnum fuscum* in roofed and unroofed plots over the 2010 growing season using the cranked wire method, in which vertical growth of the mosses is multiplied by the bulk density of the 3-cm length of *Sphagnum* stems immediately below the capitula (Clymo, 1970; Vitt, 2007). Bulk densities did not differ between roofed and unroofed plots, averaging 0.010±0.001 g cm^{-3}. Net primary production did not differ between the two sections of the bog (P = 0.1056), but was affected by roofing (P < 0.0001), with a non-significant interaction (P = 0.6723). In the unroofed plots, NPP averaged 155±9 g m^{-2} yr^{-1} (Figure 2.3), which is within the range of variation that we have measured at other sites across Alberta (Vitt et al., 2003; Wieder et al., 2009). However, in the roofed plots, the moss surface decreased

Table 2.1. *Parameter estimates (± approximate standard errors) from fitting rectangular parabola to relationships between understory net ecosystem production and photosynthetically active radiation*

	Year	Bog last burned in 1914		Bog last burned in 1951	
		No roof	Roof	No Roof	Roof
P_{MAX} (μmol CO_2 m^{-2} s^{-1})	2007	8.84±0.47	8.72±0.53	10.65±0.57	9.46±0.44
	2009	12.43±0.85	10.02±0.72	17.10±0.90	10.29±0.77
α (μmol CO_2 m^{-2} s^{-1} per μmol PAR m^{-2} s^{-1})	2007	0.0476±0.0068	0.0373±0.0058	0.0428±0.0064	0.0441±0.0065
	2009	0.0572±0.0078	0.0382±0.0055	0.0435±0.0042	0.0305±0.0043
A (μmol CO_2 m^{-2} s^{-1})	2007	1.112±0.164	0.794±0.144	1.290±0.198	1.324±0.185
	2009	1.649±0.251	0.977±0.167	1.597±0.199	1.262±0.194
Q_{10}	2007	1.54±0.06	1.65±0.07	1.58±0.05	1.52±0.05
	2009	1.55±0.07	1.73±0.09	1.66±0.06	1.60±0.07
n	2007	750	749	745	748
	2009	425	415	395	445
Pseudo R^2	2007	0.75	0.45	0.56	0.58
	2009	0.57	0.57	0.75	0.60
June 1–September 30 NEP_U (g m^{-2})	2007	131	149	160	140
	2009	122	107	121	69

P_{MAX}, maximum gross photosynthetic CO_2 capture at infinite photosynthetically active radiation (PAR); α, photosynthetic quantum efficiency; A, total understory respiration from both vascular plants within the chambers and decomposition at 0°C; Q_{10}, temperature-dependence of total understory respiration; n, the number of observations. Pseudo-R^2 values were calculated as 1 − (the ratio of the residual sum of squares to the corrected total sum of squares); NEP_U, understory net ecosystem production (Lindquist, *et al.*, 1994). All regressions were significant at P < 0.0001. Results from 2007 have been published previously (Vile, et al. (2011)).

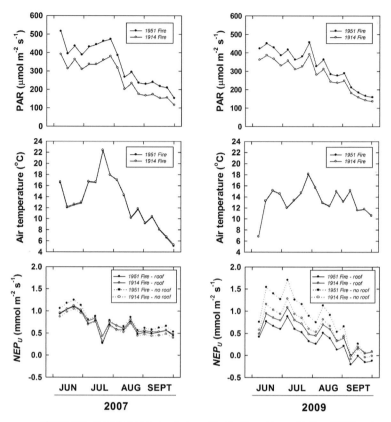

Figure 2.2. Growing season photosynthetically active radiation (PAR) and air temperature data from the two sections of Utikuma Lake bog (most recent fires in 1914 and 1951), from weather stations and weekly understory net ecosystem production (NEP_U) in the roofed and unroofed plots of each section of the bog for 2007 and 2009.

during the growing season, reflecting the stressed condition of the *Sphagnum fuscum* plants, which visually had turned from a normal dark, greenish-brown color to tan, coupled with decomposition of the near-surface peat.

Results of experimental rainfall exclusion studies are consistent with findings of other studies of drought in peatlands. At a rich fen near Perryvale, Alberta, using the closed chamber approach, Vile et al. (2011) showed greatly diminished NEP_U under natural drought conditions, but recovery after three years of normal rainfall. Mosses such as *S. fuscum* on peatland hummocks seem to be especially susceptible to desiccation (Bragazza, 2008; Vile et al., 2011). While the mosses at the Perryvale

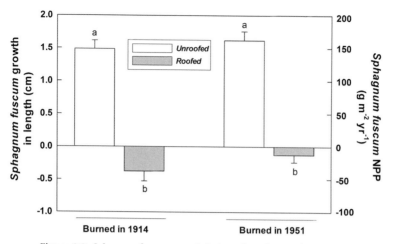

Figure 2.3. *Sphagnum fuscum* growth in length and net primary production (NPP) in the roofed and unroofed plots of each section of Utikuma Lake bog over the May–October 2010 growing season. Mean values with the same letter do not differ significantly (two-way analysis of variance).

rich fen recovered after three years of normal rainfall, Bragazza (2008) reported no signs of recovery of *Sphagnum* mosses after four years of drought at a peatland in the Italian Alps.

Drought represents a natural, recurring disturbance to peatlands of northern Alberta. If we apply our observed reduction in July–September NEP_U of 12%–43% in roofed versus unroofed conditions, drought has the potential to decrease the C sink of 3.2 ± 1.2 Tg/yr in the absence of oil sands development to 1.8–2.8 Tg C/yr. It appears that in northern Alberta, the peatland C sink function recovers after several years of normal precipitation, thus the influence of drought on the regional C balance is both episodic and ephemeral.

PEATLAND CARBON AND OIL SANDS DEVELOPMENT

Lee and Cheng (2009) estimated that 461,838 ha of peatlands within the OSAA could potentially be affected under a scenario of full development of the oil resource. Using a value for long-term net rate of C accumulation in peat of 19.4 g $C/m^2/yr$ (Vitt et al., 2000), Lee and Cheng (2009) estimated that full development of the oil resource would decrease the regional peatland sink for atmospheric CO_2 by 85 Gg/yr, from 800 to 715 Gg/yr. The 19.4 g $C/m^2/yr$ represents long-term net C storage in peat over thousands of years (Vitt et al., 2000), determined by radiocarbon dating of deep peats, and is a crude estimator of present-day peatland function. If we use Lee and Cheng's (2009) peatland disturbance areas and our estimate of the peatland net C sink of 77 ± 28 g C/m^2/yr, we can estimate that the regional peatland net C sink would be decreased by 12.5%, from 3.2 ± 1.2 Tg C/yr to 2.8 ± 1.1 Tg C/yr under the full development scenario.

Of the estimated 461,838 ha of peatlands that potentially could be affected, 59,767 ha may be lost to bitumen mining operations (Lee and Cheng, 2009). In addition to the elimination of the natural C sink, the 116.2 Gg of C stored as peat will undergo decomposition, ultimately releasing this C back to the atmosphere as CO_2 (Lee and Cheng, 2009). The remaining peatlands within the OSAA are potentially altered by *in situ* approaches to oil sands development. Lee and Cheng (2009) based their estimate that 42.3 Gg of C will be released by alteration of peatlands in *in situ* development areas on C releases from peat mines undergoing restoration (Cleary et al., 2005). However, if the disturbance to peatlands in *in situ* development areas is mostly removal of trees during the construction of seismic lines in winter, mosses and ericaceous shrubs may survive. In Alberta bogs recovering naturally after fire, when the moss and ericaceous shrub cover is reestablished, but black spruce cover remains low, the net C sink is approximately zero (Wieder et al., 2009). Estimating the effects of *in situ* development on the peatland C sink requires further research to link the scope of the disturbance to the magnitude of the C sink change.

With ongoing climate change, both fire frequency and area burned are expected to increase across Canada's northern boreal forest (Stocks et al., 2002; Turetsky et al., 2004). A decrease in the peatland fire return interval from 120 to 100 years or an increase in non-winter air temperatures of 0.5°C would lower the regional peatland C sink by 12.5% (Wieder et al., 2009). In drought years, a diminished regional C sink can be of a greater magnitude than the effects of full development of the oil sands resource, but such events are episodic in nature. In contrast, both oil sands development and a changing fire regime represent disturbances that will lead to a progressive and potentially substantial decrease in the strength of the peatland C sink in the Oil Sands Administrative Area.

Reclamation/restoration of peatland areas disturbed by oil sands development offers some potential in beginning to counteract the effects of disturbance, if such efforts can restore the net C accumulating function of peatlands. Research in this area is in its infancy. However, a large experiment designed to assess different treatments (fertilization, water level, soil amendments, cultivation of amendments into the mineral soil, and initial planting approach) on the potential to reclaim decommissioned mineral oil pads initially constructed within bogs has shown success in the establishment of *Carex aquatilis* and *Salix lutea* (Vitt et al., 2011) (see Chapter 5). Although all plots were sources of CO_2–C over the first two years, in the third summer, plots exhibited positive NEP_U (Mowbray, 2010; Wieder et al., 2010). Implementing large-scale peatland reclamation/restoration in the OSAA presents research and technological challenges, while providing opportunities for potentially offsetting decreases in the regional peatland C sink that are associated with oil sands development.

REFERENCES

Alm, J., Schulman, I., Walden J., et al. (1999). Carbon balance of a boreal bog during a year with an exceptionally dry summer. *Ecology*, **80**, 161–177.

Bonsal, B. and Regier, M. (2007). Historical comparison of the 2001/2002 drought in the Canadian prairies. *Climate Research*, **33**, 229–242.

Bonsal, B. R. and Wheaton, E. E. (2005). Atmospheric circulation comparisons between the 2001 and 2002 and the 1961 and 1988 Canadian prairie droughts. *Atmosphere-Ocean*, **43**, 162–172.

Bragazza, L. (2008). A climatic threshold triggers the die-off of peat mosses during an extreme heat wave. *Global Change Biology*, **14**, 2699–2695.

Bubier, J. L., Bhatia, G., Moore, T. R., Roulet, N. T., LaFleur, P. M. (2003). Spatial and temporal variability in growing season net ecosystem CO_2 exchange at a large peatland, Ontario, Canada. *Ecosystems*, **6**, 353–367.

Cleary, J., Roulet, N. T., Moore, T. R. (2005). Greenhouse gas emissions from Canadian peat extraction, 1990–2000: a life-cycle analysis. *Ambio*, **34**, 456–461.

Clymo, R. S. (1970). The growth of *Sphagnum*: methods of measurement. *Journal of Ecology*, **58**, 13–49.

Flannigan, M. D., Logan, K. A., Amiro, B. D., Skinner, W. R., Stocks, B. J. (2005). Future area burned in Canada. *Climatic Change*, **72**, 1–16.

Krawchuk, M. A. and Cumming, S. G. (2011). Effects of biotic feedback and harvest management on boreal forest fire activity under climate change. *Ecological Applications*, **21**, 122–136.

Krawchuk, M. A., Moritz, M. A., Parisien, M.-A., Van Dorn, J., Hayhoe, K. (2009). Global pyrogeography: the current and future distribution of wildfire. *PLoS ONE*, **4**, e5102.

Lee, P. and Cheng, R. (2009). *Bitumen and Biocarbon: Land Use Conversions and Loss of Biological Carbon due to Bitumen Operations in the Boreal Forests of Alberta, Canada*. Edmonton, AB: Global Forest Watch Canada.

Lindquist, J. L., Rhode, D., Puettmann, K. J. & Maxwell, B. D. (1994) the influence of plant population spatial arrangement on individual plant yield, *Ecological Applications*, **4**, 518–524.

McGinn, S. M. (2010). Weather and climate patterns in Canada's prairie grasslands. In J. D. Shorthouse and K. D. Floate, eds., *Arthropods of Canadian Grasslands. Vol. 1: Ecology and Interpretations of Grassland Habitats*. Ottawa, ON: Biological Survey of Canada, pp. 105–119.

Mowbray, S. B. (2010). *Evaluating Early Functional Success of Reclaiming Decommissioned Oil Wellsites Constructed in Peatlands in Alberta, Canada Through CO_2 Flux Measurements*. M.S. thesis, Villanova University, Villanova, PA.

Schindler, D. W. and Donahue, W. F. (2006). An impending water crisis in Canada's western prairie provinces. *Proceedings of the National Academy of Sciences of the USA*, **103**, 7210–7216.

Schneider, R. and Dyer, S. (2006). *Death by a Thousand Cuts: Impacts of in situ Oil Sands Development on Alberta's Boreal Forest*. Edmonton, AB: Canadian Parks and Wilderness Society and The Pembina Institute.

Stocks, B. J., Mason, J. A., Todd, J. B., et al. (2002). Large forest fires in Canada, 1959–1997. *Journal of Geophysical Research*, **108**, 8149.

Turetsky, M. R., Amiro, B. D., Bosch, E., Bhatti, J. S. (2004). Historical burn area in western Canadian peatlands and its relationship to fire weather indices. *Global Biogeochemical Cycles*, **18**, GB4014.

Tymstra, C., Flannigan, M. D., Armitage, O. B., Logan, K. (2007). Impact of climate change on area burned in Alberta's boreal forest. *International Journal of Wildland Fire*, **16**, 153–160.

Vile, M. A., Scott, K. D., Brault, E., Wieder, R. K., Vitt, D. H. (2011). Living on the edge: the effects of drought on Canada's western boreal peatlands. In Z. Tuba and N. G. Slack, eds., *Bryophyte Ecology and Climate Change*. Cambridge: Cambridge University Press, pp. 277–297.

Vitt, D. H. (2007). Estimating ground layer net primary production in tundra, peatlands, and forests. In T. Fahey, ed., *Principles and Standards for Measuring Net Primary Productivity in Long-term Ecological Studies*. Oxford, UK: Oxford University Press, pp. 82–105.

Vitt, D. H., Halsey, L. A., Bauer, I. E., Campbell, C. (2000). Spatial and temporal trends in carbon storage of peatlands of continental western Canada through the Holocene. *Canadian Journal of Earth Sciences*, **37**, 683–693.

Vitt, D. H. and Wieder, R. K. (2006). Boreal peatland ecosystems: our carbon heritage. In R. K. Wieder and D. H. Vitt, eds., *Boreal Peatland Ecosystems*. Amsterdam: Springer, pp. 423–427.

Vitt, D. H., Wieder, K., Halsey, L. A., Turetsky, M. (2003). Response of *Sphagnum fuscum* to nitrogen deposition: a case study of ombrogenous peatlands in Alberta, Canada. *The Bryologist*, **106**, 235–245.

Vitt, D. H., Wieder, R. K., Xu, B., Kaskie, M., Koropchak, S. (2011). Peatland establishment on mineral soils: effects of water level, amendments, and species after two growing seasons. *Ecological Engineering*, **37**, 354–363.

Wieder, R. K., Scott, K. D., Kamminga, K., et al. (2009). Postfire carbon balance in boreal bogs of Alberta, Canada. *Global Change Biology*, **15**, 63–81.

Wieder, R.K., Vitt, D. H., Benscoter, B. W. (2006). Peatlands and the Boreal Forest. In R. K. Wieder and D. H. Vitt, eds. *Boreal Peatland Ecosystems*. Amsterdam: Springer, pp. 1–8.

Wieder, R. K., Vitt, D. H., Mowbray, S. (2010). Can decommissioned oil pads in boreal Alberta be reclaimed to carbon-accumulating peatlands? San Francisco, CA: American Geophysical Union Annual Meeting, Poster B13A-0458.

Wilson, B. I., Trepanier, I., Beaulieu, M. (2002). *The Western Canadian Drought of 2001 – How Dry was it?* Catalogue no. 21-004-XIE, Vista on the Agri-Food Industry and the Farm Community, Canada: Agriculture Division, Statistics Canada, Ottawa, ON.

Yeh, S., Jordaan, S. M., Brandt, A. R., et al. (2010). Land use greenhouse gas emissions from conventional oil production and oil sands. *Environmental Science and Technology*, **44**, 8766–9772.

PAVEL JURUŠ, PETR MUSILEK, YAQIONG LI, AND JAMES RODWAY

3

Regional-scale modeling of greenhouse gas fluxes

INTRODUCTION

Boreal ecosystems are the world's largest terrestrial store of carbon, and their present and future evolution has important consequences for the climate. They hold almost 50% of the estimated 1146 Pg global carbon pool of forest ecosystems (Dixon et al., 1994). Observation and modeling of CO_2 concentrations and surface fluxes in regions with a high level of industrial activity are important for detecting and localizing ecosystem disturbances, and for evaluating results of reclamation and restoration efforts. A sophisticated modeling system can also be used to examine alternative development scenarios in such regions.

Mathematical models, based on our observation of the environment and its changes, can improve our understanding of natural processes in these ecosystems and how they are affected by human activities. In order to make effective use of such models, the role of mathematical modeling and its close relationship to observations must be well understood. Temporal and spatial patterns found through modeling serve as the underlying evidence upon which rules and mechanisms affecting the ecosystem can be deduced.

A mathematical model is a quantitative formulation of particular mechanisms. When such a formulation is transformed into an algorithm, and finally into an executable code, the resulting computer model can accept input data (e.g., weather and soil moisture) and produce outputs (e.g., concentrations of atmospheric gases). The practical applicability of a model depends, among other factors, on the type of required input data, as each potential type (e.g., solar radiation, soil composition, vegetation

Restoration and Reclamation of Boreal Ecosystems, ed. Dale Vitt and Jagtar Bhatti. Published by Cambridge University Press. © Cambridge University Press 2012.

classification, vegetation indices, soil temperature) differs in availability. To be useful, a model must be validated to ensure that the output data is either directly or indirectly comparable to observations.

Transforming a set of rules into computer code usually includes a number of simplifications that can be divided into several broad categories:

- reduction and/or simplification of the number of mechanisms;
- an approximation of the original mathematical formulation, as solved by a computer algorithm;
- reduction and simplification of the data serving as an input for the computer model.

These simplifications are generally inevitable due to limited knowledge of underlying mechanisms, computational complexity, excessive amounts of data, or limited availability and/or quality of input data. Simplifications are important, but not exclusive, sources of error. Other types of error include representativeness errors and errors caused by the inability to precisely characterize initial conditions.

Representativeness errors reflect discrepancy between the spatial and temporal extent of the modeled quantities and observations. Typically, values from the model and observed values are either instantaneous point values or averages over time or area. Averaging occurs not only on the model side. For example, satellite observations can be spatial averages for areas extending up to hundreds of kilometers depending on the satellite instrument. Another example is flux towers that measure fluxes using eddy-covariance techniques at one point, but are assumed to represent fluxes over the so-called tower footprint, which has a typical radius of around 1 km. In an illustrative case, a model produces hourly outputs of instantaneous concentrations of NO_2 in the atmosphere and concentrations are averaged over the grid cells with a horizontal spacing of 1 km and a vertical extent of 0–20 m above the ground. When we compare these model values with observations from an *in situ* station measuring the one-hour average NO_2 concentration in one spot, we compare two variables representing different quantities. Our error will depend on temporal variability and spatial homogeneity of NO_2 observations. This problem of different support sizes appears in many different disciplines, and methods have been developed to treat such cases (Gelfand et al., 2001).

Atmospheric modeling is particularly susceptible to error due to imprecision in initial conditions. Sensitive dependence of weather on the initial conditions (popularly known as the butterfly effect) means that a small error in the initial conditions can cause large prediction errors degrading the weather forecast over the course of several days. For horizons longer than 15 days, it is generally impossible to obtain a useful deterministic forecast (Lorenz, 1982; Straus and Paolino, 2009). The combination of meteorological modeling and atmospheric chemistry compounds these problems, as this requires that initial conditions be specified for the weather and for the concentrations of the trace gases of interest. Initial and boundary conditions for the meteorological part of the model are easy to obtain from coarse resolution global forecasts. On the other hand, determining initial and boundary conditions for trace gas concentrations may involve combining *in situ* and remotely sensed measurements, anthropogenic emissions inventories, and biogenic flux model information, all of which have the potential to introduce considerable error. The model's sensitivity to these errors may be largely determined by processes inside the domain; for example, large anthropogenic emissions in the interior may hide many small initial/boundary condition effects.

Chemical transport modeling, an essential part of modeling of greenhouse gas fluxes in the atmosphere, is prone to error in the description of turbulent mixing within a planetary boundary layer (PBL). The description of PBL comes from numerical models of weather and the differences between various PBL parameterizations can be substantial (Zhang and Zheng, 2004). An error in the height of the mixing layer is directly projected onto the error of modeled chemical concentrations, as incorrect amounts of chemical species are mixed into a layer of incorrect thickness. A number of studies have examined the connection between error in the numerical weather model (especially the description of PBL) and chemical transport simulations (Han, et al., 2009; Misenis and Zhang, 2010; Nowacki, et al., 1996).

SPECIFICS OF BOREAL AREAS AS SEEN BY MODELERS

Boreal forests in Alberta are one of the fastest changing ecosystems worldwide (Potapov et al., 2008). The rate of change is thought to be driven less by deforestation than by the impact of human activities and industrial development (Isaacs, 2007); however, very little is known about the impact of this development on ecosystem productivity. It is expected that, coupled with observed climate change and forest management practices, anthropogenic activities will produce a new boreal ecosystem of unknown properties (Taggart and Cross, 2009).

Remote sensing data indicate that northern ecosystems respond to climate change with an extended growing season and increased absorption of photosynthetically active radiation (PAR), but not necessarily with increased net primary production (NPP) or carbon sequestration. Biologically meaningful interpretation of satellite data remains very difficult without complementary ground-based observations linked to key components of net ecosystem production (NEP). Over the last decade, acquisition of ground-based data suitable to correlate biological processes with remote sensing data has enabled ground-breaking research in dynamic vegetation modeling and carbon accounting; however, this integration of advanced technologies for environmental monitoring progress has only been applied in temperate regions with dense networks of biological monitoring facilities and meteorological stations. Boreal forests represent critical geographical areas that could be monitored and supported with the help of advanced modeling technologies.

Canada's boreal ecosystems present unique challenges. Elsewhere, research teams are able to calibrate plant "green-up" dates derived from satellite data with actual dates of bud flush on deciduous species. For boreal areas, accurate comparisons cannot be made due to insufficient ground-based data. Yet, satellite remote sensing is the only way that scientists will be able to monitor such vast areas and develop models of ecosystem change. To provide the missing data, advanced modeling systems must combine data from inventories, forest research sites, and newly installed carbon flux towers. Modeling of CO_2 distribution and its changes in the atmosphere is the cornerstone of any such advanced modeling tool. It can provide the data needed for identification of spatiotemporal patterns and trends, or for discovery of species associated with industrial activities, and their relationship to ecosystem health.

Models of atmospheric behavior are currently available. Some use temporal and spatial scales suitable for modeling of CO_2 which is, beside water vapor, the most important greenhouse gas. The remainder of this chapter focuses on the modeling of CO_2 on a horizontal scale of 2–20 km (called the "meso-gamma" scale in the context of atmospheric science). This class of models has many specific properties that distinguish it from both fine-scale and local models and continental/global models.

OBSERVATIONS: THE FIRST PREMISE OF MODELING

Observations are essential for the formulation, calibration, and evaluation of a model. The two basic types of observation are *in situ* and remote measurement. *In situ* measurements use instrumentation located directly at the point of interest and in contact with the observed subject. In the case of CO_2, they include flask measurements (gas is collected in a flask for detailed analysis later), flux tower measurements, and basic sensor measurements. This type of measurement usually provides more precise and complex information than remote measurement, but scarce population and limited infrastructure in higher latitudes generally means that a very small number of available *in situ* measurements can be made. Remote sensing of CO_2 usually measures the full profile of CO_2 in the atmosphere. Instruments for remote sensing can be mounted on ground structures, aircraft, or earth orbiting satellites. Satellite-based remote sensing instruments require no infrastructure in the observed region. The convenience of such systems often makes satellite measurements the main source of evidence for atmospheric CO_2 models.

Infrared (IR) spectroscopy is the technique most widely used for CO_2 measurements. Infrared is used for remote sensing, for aircraft campaigns, for *in situ* measurements, and for laboratory analysis of flask samples. In this approach, IR radiation is passed through a gas sample and the transmitted radiation is examined for wavelengths that have been absorbed by the sample. The resulting spectra are compared with reference data to estimate the types of gas and the amount of each type present in the sample. Results of IR analysis can be affected by atmospheric scattering, temperature, humidity, and surface pressure (Dufour and Breon, 2003). These factors are better controlled and accounted for with *in situ* measurements. Due to the long life of CO_2 in the atmosphere and the resulting need for very accurate measurements, *in situ* measurements are the most valuable.

Another benefit of *in situ* measurements is that CO_2 flux models can use measurements from flux towers. These towers measure concentrations of CO_2 at one or more vertical levels of atmosphere, and surface fluxes of CO_2 can be estimated using eddy covariance techniques. Information about surface fluxes is particularly valuable for model calibration and verification.

There is increasing interest in the measurement of ^{13}C and ^{18}O isotopes in the atmosphere. Because photosynthesis discriminates against the use of the ^{13}C isotope, the ratio of ^{13}C to ^{12}C in the atmosphere can be used to estimate the amount of carbon being taken up by plants, a vital link in the carbon cycle (Ciais et al., 1995). Less attention has been given to the ratio between ^{18}O and ^{16}O in atmospheric carbon dioxide. However, it is another potential source of valuable information with respect to vegetative carbon uptake (Flanagan and Ehleringer, 1998). While techniques are available for estimating the $^{13}C/^{12}C$ ratio from high resolution satellite images, they require prior determination of the relationship between the $^{13}C/^{12}C$ ratio and the vegetation structure present (Wang et al., 2009). Currently, no direct remote measurements of this relationship can be made, making *in situ* observations the only way to retrieve this data.

There are several satellite instruments capable of remote measurements of CO_2 concentrations through analysis of the spectral bands sensitive to CO_2 concentrations, so-called CO_2 retrievals. These instruments include HIRS (high-resolution IR sounder, flown on various satellites), AIRS (atmospheric IR sounder, flown on the Aqua satellite), SCIAMACHY (scanning imaging absorption spectrometer for atmospheric chartography, flown on ENVISAT), IASI (IR atmospheric sounding interferometer, flown on the METOP series of satellites), and TANSO-FTS (thermal and near IR sensor for carbon observations–Fourier transform spectrometer, flown on GOSAT, the greenhouse gases observing satellite). However, only the SCIAMACHY and TANSO-FTS instruments observe the atmosphere in the near-infrared band, which is also sensitive to CO_2 concentrations in the lower troposphere. The other instruments measure only within the thermal IR band, which has maximal sensitivity for CO_2 in the upper troposphere, but almost no CO_2 sensitivity for lower layers. This means that only near IR measurements can capture diurnal variations of CO_2 in the lower troposphere caused by changes in atmospheric mixing height, by regional-scale transport, and by regional-scale sources and sinks.

Although both the SCIAMACHY and TANSO-FTS instruments are mounted on polar-orbiting satellites, their spatial resolutions and sampling strategies differ. The SCIAMACHY provides full coverage of the earth's surface by coarse resolution observations (1 pixel represents on average 30×60 km^2), while TANSO-FTS provides samples with finer resolution (1 pixel has a diameter of about 10.5 km), but with pixels 88–280 km apart. GOSAT is the first mission dedicated to greenhouse gas observation, and it is the first satellite to provide CO_2 measurements in resolutions comparable to regional scale models. The CO_2 observing satellites now in planning or preparation stages (e.g., OCO-2, CarbonSat) will have even better resolution and/or coverage.

Observations of other quantities are also useful for modeling of CO_2, especially in cases where we are interested in incorporating biogenic sources and sinks. One classic source of remotely sensed environmental data is MODIS (moderate-resolution imaging spectroradiometer), mounted on both the Aqua and Terra Earth observing satellites. These satellites continuously monitor earth in 36 spectral bands between 0.405

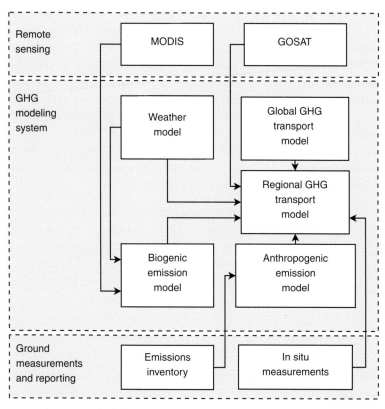

Figure 3.1. Block diagram of a typical greenhouse gas (GHG) modeling system.

and 14.385 μm. The observations serve as the basis for a number of important ecosystem and land cover indices, including the EVI (enhanced vegetation index), the NDVI (normalized difference vegetation index), the LSWI (land surface water index), and the LAI (leaf area index). As indicators of vegetative activity, these indices are important for modeling ecosystem carbon uptake.

A GREENHOUSE GAS MODELING SYSTEM

A typical greenhouse gas modeling system (GHGMS) uses remotely sensed data on greenhouse gas (GHG) concentrations and vegetation phenology, ground-based data on carbon concentrations and fluxes, and information on anthropogenic emissions from inventories and reports. A possible structure of such a system is shown in Figure 3.1.

The system consists of several blocks, each responsible for a specific part of CO_2 modeling. The blocks selected for simulation of meteorological conditions, chemical transport, and biogenic surface fluxes depend on the choice of transport model and available couplings between the models. However, the choice of initial and boundary conditions for both meteorology and CO_2 concentrations is largely open, and depends on the particular application and also on the model used for anthropogenic fluxes.

In the GHGMS described in this chapter, the principal building block is the chemical transport model WRF–VPRM (Ahmadov et al., 2007). It consists of two main components:

- meteorological weather research and forecasting (WRF) model with extension WRF-Chem for modeling of transport and chemical reactions of various components of the atmosphere (currently, only transport is used for modeling of CO_2);
- model of biogenic surface fluxes VPRM (vegetation photosynthesis and respiration model).

Weather research and forecasting model

The WRF model is one of the most widely used regional-scale meteorological models (Skamarock et al., 2008). Typical horizontal resolutions of this model range from several hundreds of meters to tens of kilometres, depending on the type of application. The WRF-Chem model (Grell et al., 2005) is an extension of the WRF model that allows modeling of chemical species in the atmosphere. Depending on the chemical component, such modeling may require the physical description of a number of processes: gas phase chemistry of the atmosphere, aqueous phase chemistry, aerosol chemistry, photochemical processes, advection and diffusion of chemical tracers, dry and wet deposition and eventual resuspension, and models of both biogenic and anthropogenic surface fluxes. For simulations of CO_2, only advection and diffusion parts of the WRF-Chem model are used. Biogenic surface fluxes are provided by the VPRM, and anthropogenic surface fluxes are modeled based on emission inventories.

The WRF-Chem model allows for concurrent simulation of atmospheric emission, transport, and mixing by applying meteorological information (Grell et al., 2005). Both facets (chemical and meteorological) are simulated with the same timesteps, grid spacings, and physics and transport schemes within the model. This consistency removes the need for the spatial and temporal interpolations that may be required for other models.

Vegetation photosynthesis and respiration model

The VPRM provides biogenic surface fluxes (Mahadevan et al., 2008) of CO_2 to be used in the WRF model as a passive tracer. It uses several input variables from the WRF model and satellite data to calculate hourly vegetation photosynthesis and respiration of CO_2 from different vegetation types. These time series are then provided back to the WRF model along with meteorological variables at each timestep. The land cover data used by the VPRM is usually generated by mapping a high resolution land cover map, SYNMAP (Jung et al., 2006), to eight land use classes, including evergreen and deciduous trees.

The photosynthesis of vegetation is calculated as a function of the EVI and LSWI from MODIS satellite data at 500-m resolution. These calculations use air temperature at 2 m (T2) and shortwave downward radiation (SWDOWN) data generated by the WRF model. Respiration fluxes are evaluated as a linear function of T2 from WRF, while the net ecosystem exchange (NEE) is a sum of vegetation photosynthesis and ecosystem respiration. This is a great simplification of the complex processes of vegetation respiration and photosynthesis, and the resulting model is necessarily somewhat mechanistic. However, this simplification makes it possible to use this model in almost any part of the world, and makes calibration using *in situ* measurements more feasible.

Initial and boundary conditions

As the WRF–VPRM is a regional model, the initial and boundary conditions for both meteorological variables and atmospheric CO_2 concentrations must be provided. Meteorological fields are usually obtained from outputs of coarser simulations. These large-scale or global simulations may originate from an operational forecast for up-to-date simulations or, preferably, from an analysis; that is, a combination of forecast with observations. Alternatively, for modeling past concentrations and fluxes, reanalysis can be used; that is, a retrospective estimation of atmosphere state that takes into account observations that were not available at the time of operational analysis.

In setting the boundary and initial conditions for CO_2 concentrations, options are more limited. This becomes even more challenging when simulating recent years, as availability of global model outputs usually lags by 1–2 years. In some situations, empty or constant boundary and/or initial conditions can provide satisfactory simulation results. However, such simplification is more justifiable for chemical species with shorter lifetimes in the atmosphere; its use for CO_2 would require thorough verification.

Anthropogenic emissions

Anthropogenic CO_2 emissions are very small compared to biogenic fluxes, especially on short-time scales of hours or days. Their significance is further reduced in boreal areas that generally have low population density and little industry. Nevertheless, they usually cannot be completely neglected as shown in an example presented later. In addition, anthropogenic emissions are important in the overall annual CO_2 budget. An unbalanced budget causes interannual increases of CO_2 concentrations in the atmosphere, and plays an important role in climate forcing (e.g., Hansen et al., 1981).

Sources of information about anthropogenic emissions of CO_2 range from global inventories, through more refined national inventories, to full emission models. The dividing line between emission inventories and emission models is fuzzy. Examples of classical emission inventories are the national reports to the UNFCCC (United Nations Framework Convention on Climate Change) provided by the signatory countries, in accordance with the Climate Change Convention. These reports contain annual emissions of CO_2 for an entire country, divided into several sectors of economy. These inventories, however, cannot be directly used for modeling of CO_2 fluxes.

Gridded inventories, usually based on the original national reports, are more suitable for modeling CO_2 fluxes. They commonly use other sources of information as proxies for spatial disaggregation. Typical representatives of this category describe total annual emissions at each point of a regular grid. Examples include the EDGAR (version 4.0) inventory with a $0.1° \times 0.1°$ grid, and the more specialized ODIAC inventory (Oda and Maksyutov, 2011) with a 1 km $\times$ 1 km grid; both inventories are defined for the entire planet. Spatial disaggregation can be based, for example, on population density, databases of large point sources, or even on satellite views of earth nightlights.

Emission models go even further – they attempt to describe fully resolved emission profiles, in both space and time. Such spatiotemporal disaggregation is usually based on auxiliary input data. The amount and

Table 3.1. *A contingency table*

	Event observed	Event not observed	
Event forecast	Hits	False alarms	Total forecast
Event not forecast	Misses	Correct negatives	Total not forecast
	Total observed	Total not observed	Total

quality of data required to create such a model is relatively high. The first national scale models appeared only recently (see project VULCAN, Gurney et al., 2009).

MODEL VERIFICATION AND INVERSE MODELING

Model verification

The model values and measurement values are tightly connected. Perhaps the most important area where such connections exist is model evaluation. Comparing model results with measurement results can be as simple as displaying two time series. However, the most important outcome of model evaluation is the assessment of its accuracy. Such an assessment process can be quite complex.

The simplest way to quantify differences between model and observation is to use traditional error statistics such as:

root mean square error

$$RMSE = \sqrt{\frac{\sum_{i=1}^{n}\left(x_i^f - x_i^o\right)^2}{n}}, \qquad [3.1]$$

mean absolute error

$$MAE = \frac{\sum_{i=1}^{n}|x_i^f - x_i^o|}{n}, \text{ and} \qquad [3.2]$$

and mean percentage error

$$MPE = \frac{\sum_{i=1}^{n}\frac{x_i^f - x_i^o}{x_i^o}}{n}, \qquad [3.3]$$

where x_i^f is the i-th modeled (forecast) value and x_i^o is the i-th observation.

Another type of traditional error measure is based on the so-called contingency tables (Table 3.1). A contingency table is created by stratification of observed phenomena into two categories (a stratification criterion could be, for example, exceedance of a threshold concentration of CO_2).

The most widely used categorical skill scores are:

critical success index

$$CSI = \frac{hits}{hits + misses + false\ alarms} \quad \text{and} \qquad \text{[3.4]}$$

equitable threat score

$$ETS = \frac{hits - hits\ expected\ by\ chance}{hits + misses + false\ alarms - hits\ expected\ by\ chance}, \qquad \text{[3.5]}$$

where

$$hits\ expected\ by\ chance = \frac{total\ observed \times total\ forecast}{total}. \qquad \text{[3.6]}$$

The CSI quantifies how well an event was forecast: CSI = 0 means no forecasting skill, while CSI = 1 indicates a perfect forecast. When the fraction of observed events is high, it is easier to predict the event by chance and CSI is generally higher than it is for events with lower frequencies. The ETS is an adjustment of CSI that discounts random hits: ETS = 0 indicates no forecasting skill (the same as a random forecast), while ETS = 1 is a perfect forecast; ETS can be negative when the results are worse than a random forecast.

Interpretation of resulting numbers should always take all circumstances into account. An example is the aforementioned problem of representativeness. Reducing the question of model accuracy to a single number is always a simplification that inevitably hides most details and that can easily be misleading when not used with care. A typical example of undesirable behavior of an error measure is the preference for smoothed quantities in most traditional error measures (e.g., for all the statistics defined earlier). Such statistics give better results for models that are smoothed with "washed-out" details, than for models with features that better reflect reality, where the error is in the location (in space or time) of the feature. Advancing to a model with more features and with better spatial resolution can thus, paradoxically, lead to worse error statistics. This behavior is known in literature as the "double penalty issue" (Rossa et al., 2008).

Error statistics can be either dimensionless, where the ordering of pairs of model and measurement values is not important, or they can take into account the spatiotemporal ordering and extent of observation and model grid. The first category includes RMSE, MAE, CSI, and ETS. The same statistics can be used for either time series at one spatial point or for an arbitrary subset of full time space. The second category contains more sophisticated skill scores based on neighborhood search, hierarchical trees, object matching, image warping techniques, etc. A recent overview of such measures can be found in Gilleland et al., (2009). A typical case of evaluation has two or three spatial dimensions and zero or one temporal dimension (although two temporal dimensions are possible; for example, in operational forecasts, the first time dimension can express model times for which the model values are valid, and the second dimension can be model times when different simulations started).

Although error statistics describe model accuracy, they provide only static information. They are usually applied to a portion of model and observational data, commonly collected from a test case. The purpose of evaluation is to obtain information about errors that can be expected in future model simulations. If this information is based on error statistics obtained from a test case, it is important that the test case (time period, area coverage, climatic conditions, etc.) represents the intended area of application well. Estimation of general model performance should thus use as much testing data as possible. Ideally, the testing data should include simulations for a number of diverse situations and conditions. On the other hand, it is possible to evaluate model accuracy for particular model conditions, or to compare different accuracies for different conditions. An example is the evaluation of weather forecasts–weather is usually more regular and predictable in tropical rain forests compared to mid-latitude continental areas, and expected error statistics (of a good universal weather model) will be significantly different for each area.

The idea of different predictabilities based on particular situations is employed in probabilistic forecasts. In contrast to traditional deterministic forecasts, probabilistic forecasts predict not only the quantities themselves, but also their expected error statistics (uncertainty). Predicted error statistics can be expressed in many forms, including full probability distribution, confidence intervals, probability of exceeding a threshold, etc. Limiting factors include the theoretical and technical difficulties in making such predictions and the challenge in communicating complex concepts of uncertainty to end-users. By far the most popular probabilistic forecast is the quantitative precipitation forecast, which can be understood as a probabilistic categorical forecast. Another well-established type of probabilistic forecast is the ensemble forecast, comprising several different (deterministic) forecasts. Each member of the ensemble can be seen as a possible scenario of evolution, and the spread of the ensemble provides an estimate of forecast uncertainty.

A deterministic forecast can usually be made from a probabilistic forecast by taking an expected value; for example, the ensemble mean for the ensemble forecast, although the situation gets complicated when the probabilistic distribution of errors is strongly non-Gaussian and averaging (e.g., for multimodal distribution) does not give realistic results. Traditional error statistics are therefore applicable to probabilistic forecasts in that they work with expected values of the probabilistic forecast.

A different approach is needed to evaluate predictions of uncertainty. In other words, error statistics of error statistics prediction are required. The most used indicator for categoric variables is the Brier score (BS) defined for binary events (e.g., rain, no-rain) as:

$$BS = \frac{1}{n} \sum_{i=1}^{n} (p_i - o_i)^2, \qquad\qquad [3.7]$$

where p_i is forecast probability of the i-th event, and o_i is 1 if the event occurs and 0 otherwise. The best Brier score, 0, is acquired when the prediction of the probability of an event is always 0% or 100% (meaning, in fact, deterministic prediction), and it is always correct. The worst Brier score, 1, means that predicted probabilities were always 0% or 100%, and always incorrect. An important property of the BS is that incorrect estimation of skill of forecast is penalized, meaning that the BS is, for example, worse for overly sharp estimates (close to 0% or 100%) when forecasting skill is, in reality, low. For example, when there is no forecasting skill at all, the best BS is achieved when the (constant) forecast probability is the same as the relative climatological frequency of the event.

The Brier skill score (BSS) is an adjustment of the BS similar to the ETS adjustment of CSI to discount random "climatological" hits.

$$BSS = \frac{BS_{clim} - BS}{BS_{clim}}. \qquad\qquad [3.8]$$

The climatological BS is the Brier score where all probabilities are constant and equal to the relative frequency of the event. The best value for the BSS is 1, meaning a perfect forecast. BSS equals 0 for a climatological forecast and it can have an arbitrarily low negative value when the results are worse than the climatological forecast.

Data assimilation

Thus far, the observations were considered the indisputable truth, while the model was deemed erroneous and responsible for the discrepancy between the model and observations. Observation errors can, however, be quite significant. For example, in the case of aircraft measurements above a boundary layer (relayed through the Aircraft Communications,

Addressing, and Reporting System, ACARS), Benjamin et al., (1999) found observation errors of 0.5 K and 1.1 m s^{-1}, respectively, for temperatures and a single component of wind vector. This error was even larger for the lower troposphere (because of its higher variability of atmosphere), where the estimated errors (including representativity error for a 10-km scale) were 0.5 K and 1.8 m s^{-1}. Modern observing systems use complex instrumentations and algorithms for retrieval of often indirect observations. In many cases of satellite measurements, the relative errors can be as high as 100% (Boersma et al., 2004).

These facts diminish the role of observations as the absolute evidence of truth. Instead, a framework of data assimilation has been created to estimate the true state of the modeled system. Data assimilation uses a state space approach, where the whole state of a system at a particular time is contained in the mathematical vector x (components of the vector can be, for example, CO_2 concentrations at all grid points in a case of CO_2 modeling, or values of all prognostic meteorological values at all grid points in a case of numerical weather prediction). Several versions of x can be differentiated by superscripts, for example, x^f, x^t, and x^a, may denote "forecast," "true," and "analysis," respectively (the term "analysis" is the legacy of the first applications in meteorology, where the best estimate called "subjective analysis" was created by a human expert). The true state x^t is inaccessible as it is not possible to know the exact state of the system. Even with the huge observation machinery of the worldwide weather network, it is not possible to obtain exact information about the weather at a given time. The best approximation is an estimate x^a, based on all available information, including observations, model simulations, physical assumptions, and knowledge of the statistical behavior of errors involved in the estimation.

Observations at a given time can be captured into a mathematical vector y containing the observed values of all measurements. This vector belongs to the so-called observation vector space, which differs from the model space containing vectors x. The relation between model space and observation space can be made by an observation operator, H, which translates model quantities into (simulated) observations. For instance, H can be a simple spatial interpolation of model grid values to a particular location in the case of single *in situ* measurement of CO_2 concentration. Alternatively, H can contain a complex formula transforming state space atmospheric variables (pressure, temperature, surface albedo, and atmospheric composition including CO_2 concentrations) into observed infrared intensity, as it might be formulated in the case of a satellite measurement of CO_2.

Differences between model vectors and observation vectors can be measured in observation space as:

$$|H(x^f) - y|. \qquad [3.9]$$

The choice of the norm for the distance of the two vectors is discussed later. As mentioned previously, part of the responsibility for the difference belongs to model error and part belongs to observational error, so it is not advisable to minimize only the difference between model and error-burdened observations. The true state generally lies somewhere between model and observations and our estimate of the truth must have, in some sense, minimal distance from both model and observations.

The sum of those distances can be expressed as:

$$J(x) = |(x - x^f)|_B + |(y - H(x))|_R, \qquad [3.10]$$

where the first term corresponds to the difference between estimate x and the model forecast, and the second term is the difference between estimate x and observations. The goal of data assimilation is to find the best possible estimate x^a that minimizes $J(x)$. Subscripts B and R represent the choice of norms for the distances. The distance is normalized in such a way that less erroneous observation and model components have larger weights in distance computation. Thorough mathematical treatment of model and observation errors leads to norms based on model and observation error covariance matrices (denoted as B and R). Functional $J(x)$ can be then written as:

$$J(x) = (x - x^f)^T B^{-1} (x - x^f) + (y - H(x))^T R^{-1} (y - H(x)) \qquad [3.11]$$

Minimization of functional $J(x)$ is the fundamental problem of data assimilation. It is worth noting that matrix B, in particular, can have dimensions up to $10^8 \times 10^8$ in real-life applications. This means that B does not fit into the memory (or even the hard disk) of contemporary conventional computers. Problems with computation and minimization of $J(x)$ lead to different variants of data assimilation, including variational data assimilation and ensemble data assimilation techniques.

Inverse modeling

The data assimilation framework is a good basis for formulation and solution of many kinds of inverse modeling problems. The classical forward model can be described as operator M, which produces a new state based on a previous state and some input parameters a (subscripts denote time):

$$x_t^f = M\left(x_{t-1}, a_{t-1}\right) \qquad\qquad [3.12]$$

Input parameters can have both time-dependent and time-independent components; a previous state, x_t, does not have a superscript because it can be either a model forecast or model analysis depending on the situation. Inverse modeling, on the other hand, starts from observations and tries to find a model state or model parameters that can lead to observed quantities. A typical example is an estimation of anthropogenic emissions based on measured concentrations. The main challenge is that concentrations are measured at differing locations and times. All processes separating the two events (including atmospheric transport, diffusion, chemical reactions, deposition, etc.) must somehow be tracked from measurement backward to emission. A data assimilation framework offers a formulation of the inverse problem, which is almost the same as a search for the best x^a in data assimilation. The cost function, which should be minimized, looks very similar to the cost function of data assimilation. The vector x, however, is augmented to include desired input parameters and matrix B is redesigned accordingly. When inverse modeling is performed for estimation of time-independent parameters, minimization of cost function $J(x)$ is done not for one instant, but for a longer time window. This estimation is thus done in both physical space and time and corresponds to the so-called 4D-Var data assimilation. The first part of $J(x)$ now stands for the distance of the estimate from some starting (often called first-guess or a priori) estimate and the second part of $J(x)$ denotes the distance of the model, with given input parameters, from the observations.

A CASE STUDY: SIMULATION FOR NORTHERN ALBERTA

This case study illustrates typical model outputs and features. The area used for the simulation contains most of Alberta and extends to parts of Saskatchewan and British Columbia, Canada. The entire modeled area of 990×990 km^2 is covered by a grid with 99×99 grid cells of 10×10 km^2 size. A number of points of interest in this particular domain illustrate the behavior of the model:

- cities of Edmonton and Calgary represent large urban areas with large-scale anthropogenic activities;
- large coal-fired electricity generation plants;

- Athabasca oil sands as a remote area with intensive industry related to oil extraction;
- part of Lake Athabasca to the northeast of the domain.

The time period covered by the simulation is the month of August, 2009.

The initial and boundary conditions for the meteorological part of the WRF–VPRM were obtained from the North American Regional Reanalysis data set (NARR, http://dss.ucar.edu/pub/narr/). The NARR data covers the entire North American continent, with spatial resolution of 32 km, and temporal resolution of 3 hr. The initial and boundary conditions for CO_2 concentrations were obtained from the six-hourly 3D fields of the global tracer model TM3, which has horizontal resolution of approximately $3.83° \times 5°$ (latitude $\times$ longitude) and contains 19 vertical levels up to the tropopause. The TM3 fields were provided by the authors of a global CO_2 inversion study (Rödenbeck et al., 2003). The TM3 version of the tracer model assimilates concentrations from 63 measurement stations located around the world.

The anthropogenic CO_2 emissions are based on the Emission Database for Global Anthropogenic Research (EDGAR, version 4.0) data sets (European Commission, 2009). They provide annual CO_2 emissions with resolution of $0.1° \times 0.1°$ (latitude $\times$ longitude). Because the latest published EDGAR inventory is for year 2005, it was extrapolated for 2009 using national annual reports. The temporal disaggregation of annual emissions was based on electrical load profiles, as they should reflect both the changes in CO_2 emissions from power generation facilities and changes in the relative levels of human activity. Resulting anthropogenic emissions have typical daily and weekly shapes capturing diurnal and weekday/weekend cycles. The anthropogenic emissions from EDGAR and the biospheric fluxes from the VPRM are integrated into the lowest model level at each timestep.

The meteorological component of the modeling system, the WRF model, has a wide selection of configuration options and physical schemes, each suitable for a different type of simulation. The domain configuration and choice of physical parameterizations used for this study are specified in Table 3.2.

Comparison of the model with tower measurements

The observation site used for the comparison of modeled and measured values is denoted by a star in Figure 3.2. This western peatland flux station is located close to Lac La Biche and Athabasca rivers in Alberta,

Table 3.2. *Overview of the weather research and forecasting model physics/dynamics options used for simulations*

Domain configuration	One domain with horizontal resolution of 10 km, 99*99 grids; 45 vertical levels
Timestep	1 hour
Physics schemes	Radiation – RRTM longwave, Goddard shortwave
	Microphysics – Single-moment five-class scheme
	PBL – Yonsei University scheme
	Surface layer – MM5 similarity
	Land surface – Noah land surface model
Dynamics schemes	Diffusion – simple diffusion

PBL, planetary boundary layer.

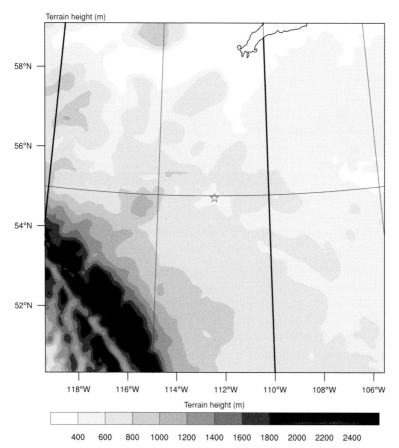

Figure 3.2. Topography of the weather research and forecasting (WRF) model domain; the star indicates the western peatland site location.

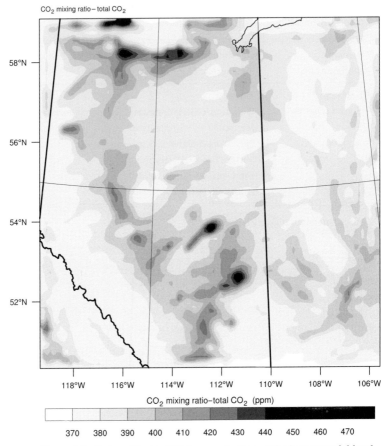

CO$_2$ mixing ratio – total CO$_2$

CO$_2$ mixing ratio–total CO$_2$ (ppm)

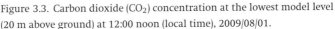

370   380   390   400   410   420   430   440   450   460   470

Figure 3.3. Carbon dioxide (CO$_2$) concentration at the lowest model level (20 m above ground) at 12:00 noon (local time), 2009/08/01.

Canada (Syed et al., 2006). The location belongs to the central mixedwood subregion of the Boreal region of Alberta (Vitt et al., 1998). The elevation of the station is 626 m, and the dominant cover type is treed fen, with stunted black spruce and larch trees.

The results of the simple forward simulation shown in Figure 3.3 provide information about both anthropogenic and biogenic surface fluxes and about CO$_2$ concentrations in the atmosphere. The modeled day and night vertical profiles of CO$_2$ are shown in Figure 3.4. Some limitations of this particular approach are obvious; for example, the biogenic surface fluxes over Lake Athabasca are always zero. This is because the biogenic fluxes are provided entirely by the VPRM, which does not consider water/atmosphere fluxes. A specific model for lake CO$_2$ fluxes could

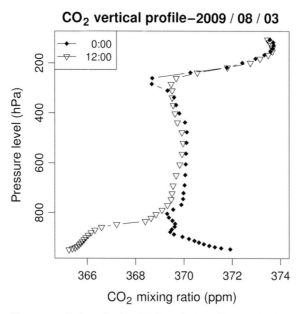

Figure 3.4. Carbon dioxide (CO_2) vertical profiles at midnight and noon.

be used to complement the system if these fluxes are important for a particular application. A similar problem arises when the modeled area is not landlocked as in our case, but contains an ocean.

Another limitation stems from the properties of data used as the inputs for the model. For example, the anthropogenic CO_2 emissions in our case study were derived from the EDGAR global CO_2 inventory, with some refinements based on the updated national GHG inventory of Canada. Many assumptions and simplifications were used in the creation of the emission profiles, involving both the spatial and temporal disaggregation of aggregate estimates. The spatial allocation, for example, depends on such factors as locations of energy and manufacturing facilities, situation of road networks, and human population density. These assumptions can introduce inaccuracies. For example, EDGAR was created with global coverage, and exact facility location may not be as important on a global scale as it is in this much smaller regional domain. The methods of spatially allocating anthropogenic emissions continue to improve (Oda and Maksyutov, 2011). This, in turn, will improve the accuracy of results from models like WRF-VPRM.

The only way of testing the validity of the emission model is a systematic measurement campaign (preferably including measurement of the carbon isotopes used to determine the fossil or biogenic origin of the carbon). Models like WRF–VPRM would be an excellent aid for the preparation of such campaigns, and for interpretation of their results.

The case presented in this study uses a model with horizontal grid cells of 10×10 km^2 and the lowest vertical layer has a height of around 20 m. This model works with concentrations and fluxes above the canopy level and all input and output variables are averaged for the volume (10 km $\times$ 10 km $\times$ 20 m) of one 3D grid cell. When comparing model results with *in situ* observations, one has to be aware of the different representativities of the model and measurements. For example, flux towers usually have assumed footprints. Information about the footprint, along with homogeneous biome and geographic conditions around the measurement site, can be used to improve the representativity of local measurements. This makes observations easier to compare to the model.

To illustrate the accuracy of the weather model that drives the CO_2 modeling system, Figure 3.5 shows a comparison of modeled and observed temperatures. The hourly CO_2 concentrations from the modeling system output are compared with measurements from the tower made at 30 minute intervals. Figure 3.6 shows this comparison in terms of the CO_2 mixing ratio and the net ecosystem exchange (NEE).

The comparison of modeled and observed concentrations shows that the high-resolution, regional-scale model is able to predict daily variations in CO_2 concentration. However, the nighttime model output is much lower than nighttime observations. This is partly due to the representativity errors mentioned earlier. More importantly, the underestimated concentrations are likely caused by the model overestimating turbulent mixing during calm nights. Numerical models often have artificial lower limits for turbulent diffusivity. To prevent numerical instabilities and physical singularities that would occur in atmosphere without any diffusive processes, the diffusivity cannot reach values close to zero. A calm night is, however, one instance when the turbulent mixing in the model is overestimated, and the CO_2 produced by vegetation respiration at the canopy level is vertically diffused into higher layers of the modeled atmosphere. This discrepancy can be resolved to some extent by postprocessing of model outputs.

The second plot in Figure 3.6 shows that the model provides NEE values that agree well with observed data. The model results are smoother than observed data due to the spatial and temporal averaging that occurs in the model. Short-scale variability of the observations is caused by the noisy character of turbulence, and subsequently, of the data measured

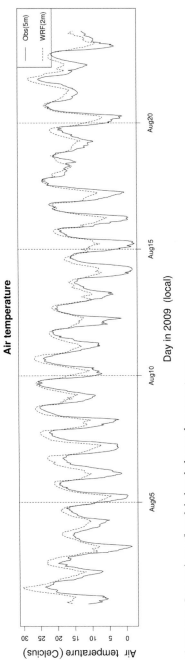

Figure 3.5. Comparison of modeled and observed temperatures.

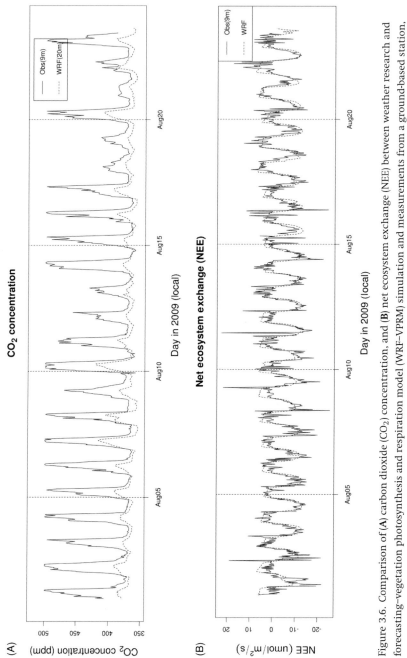

Figure 3.6. Comparison of (A) carbon dioxide (CO_2) concentration, and (B) net ecosystem exchange (NEE) between weather research and forecasting–vegetation photosynthesis and respiration model (WRF–VPRM) simulation and measurements from a ground-based station, Lac Labiche.

by the eddy covariance technique. The morning spikes in the observed data are likely a result of emerging turbulent mixing in the morning, which causes release of CO_2 that was entrapped in the canopy during the night.

Comparison of the model with satellite measurements

The GOSAT (the GHG observing satellite) data sets (Yokota et al., 2009) provide two types of quantities related to CO_2 concentrations. The first variable is the total column of CO_2, a vertical sum of CO_2 at the point of measurement. The second is the column-averaged molar fraction of CO_2 (XCO2), computed as the total column of CO_2 divided by the total column of dry air. Dry air columns are based on the operational analysis data provided by the Japan Meteorological Agency (JMA).

In order to compare the GOSAT observations with the WRF–VPRM simulation results, CO_2 total columns are calculated from the model output by summing over all vertical levels. The dry air columns are computed in similar fashion. The XCO2 is a simple ratio of those two quantities. The dry air columns assumed in GOSAT data are not available directly, but can be derived simply as the ratio of CO_2 column and XCO2, provided by GOSAT.

The comparisons of model versus GOSAT observations for the CO_2 columns and the dry air columns are shown in Figure 3.7. For each observation point at a specific location and time, corresponding variables from the model were calculated using inverse distance weighted interpolation horizontally, and linear interpolation temporally.

The simulation is clearly highly correlated with the GOSAT observations, but biased for both CO_2 and dry air columns. The model values are about 10% lower than the GOSAT observations. This is likely caused by the limited vertical height of the model. The model simulates up to 100 hPa, close to the height of the tropopause, which is usually sufficient for meteorological simulations. However, the highest (100 hPa) layer still accounts for about 10% of the atmosphere mass.

We performed corrections to compensate for the air above 100 hPa. The dry air columns were modified by adding the amount of total air mass above 100 hPa. The small amount of water vapor was not considered, as the air in the stratosphere is much drier than in the troposphere. Without weather forcing, the CO_2 concentrations above the tropopause are relatively invariant with respect to time and location. In the top vertical layer of the WRF model, the CO_2 mixing ratio shows a small

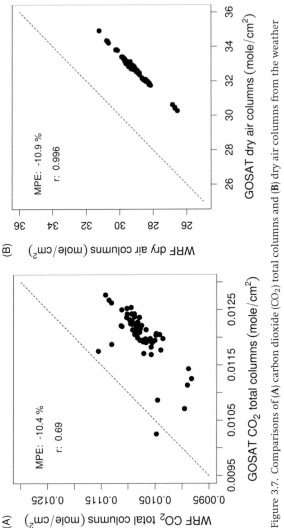

Figure 3.7. Comparisons of (A) carbon dioxide (CO_2) total columns and (B) dry air columns from the weather research and forecasting–vegetation photosynthesis and respiration model (WRF–VPRM) and the GOSAT (the GHG observing satellite).

variance with time, ranging from 372.7 ppm to 373.6 ppm. Thus, the average value (373 ppm) of CO_2 mixing ratio in the top layer was used as the CO_2 mixing ratio above 100 hPa to correct the CO_2 total columns. The vertical variation of CO_2 in the stratosphere was neglected.

After this correction, the value of MPE changed from -10.4% to -0.482% for the CO_2 columns, and from -10.9% to -0.17% for the dry air columns. Figure 3.8 shows the comparison between GOSAT and WRF–VPRM outputs after the correction.

After the correction, both CO_2 and dry air column abundances calculated from WRF–VPRM outputs show good agreement with GOSAT observations. Surprisingly, the situation is different for the XCO2–GOSAT comparison, as shown in Figure 3.9. Division of the CO_2 column by the dry air column results in much higher variance for observed values than for modeled values.

A likely reason for this difference is the fact that the XCO2 in the model is computed by dividing a modeled CO_2 column by a modeled dry air column. Quantities of CO_2 and dry air are highly correlated (because CO_2 is well mixed in higher layers of the atmosphere), as are errors in CO_2 and dry air quantities. Most of the error in both CO_2 and dry air quantities is not due to the incorrect concentration of CO_2, as that is almost constant, especially in higher layers of the model. Rather, an incorrect distribution of air mass is likely to contribute significantly to the errors. It affects both the CO_2 column and the dry air column proportionally. As a result, division of the two quantities leads to a reduction in the overall variance. The results obtained by the WRF–VPRM in this study comply with a study of XCO2 distribution by Olsen and Randerson (2004).

In the case of GOSAT, the CO_2 columns are observed, but the dry air columns originate from the meteorological model. Errors in those two quantities can therefore be considered uncorrelated (although some hidden correlation is still possible due to the retrieval algorithms, which often use a number of model-derived atmospheric variables). The error in the distribution of air mass is thus amplified: the CO_2 column based on a real air mass distribution is divided by a dry air column based on a modeled air mass distribution. Division in this case causes further nonlinear propagation of errors and larger overall variance.

SUMMARY AND CONCLUSIONS

Boreal forests play an important role in the global carbon cycle, and a better understanding of this role may allow for the mitigation of the impact

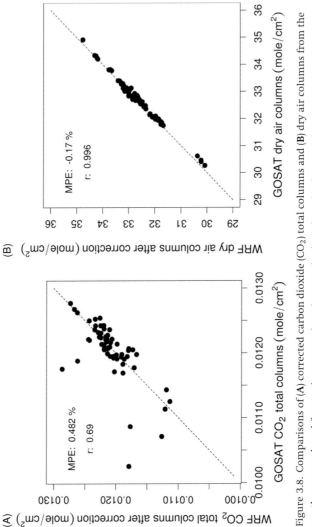

Figure 3.8. Comparisons of (**A**) corrected carbon dioxide (CO_2) total columns and (**B**) dry air columns from the weather research and forecasting–vegetation photosynthesis and respiration model (WRF–VPRM) and the GOSAT (the GHG observing satellite).

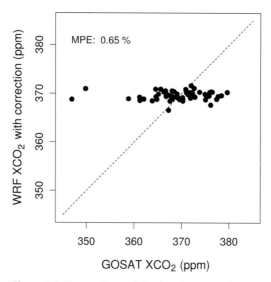

Figure 3.9. Comparisons of the dry air averaged carbon dioxide (CO_2) (XCO2) columns from the weather research and forecasting–vegetation photosynthesis and respiration model (WRF–VPRM) and the GOSAT (the GHG observing satellite).

of human activities on boreal ecosystems. One way to improve this understanding involves measuring the concentration of atmospheric CO_2, gas that is important to vegetation photosynthesis and respiration. Atmospheric CO_2 measurements may be taken *in situ* or remotely. Although both methods have limitations, difficulty in making a large number of spatially distributed *in situ* measurements in boreal forests makes a strong case for the use of remotely sensed data.

However, measurements alone cannot provide a full insight into the boreal ecosystem. They can be used to create mathematical models to examine the causes and effects of environmental changes and assess various development scenarios. During model development, a number of assumptions must be made to balance model accuracy with the availability of input data, limited process knowledge, computational complexity, and the inherent limitations of the computer systems used to execute the models.

Resulting models can be evaluated using a variety of error statistics, including both numerical and categorical measures of different complexities. While these are very important for model verification, they cannot be blindly applied and may require some interpretation. With the high relative errors of some observations, resulting from complex acquisition methods, some error measures should not be used at all. In such cases, data assimilation can be used to estimate the true state of the variable by combining observations and model values. Data assimilation can also be used to create inverse models, which use observations to work in the reverse direction and find the previous state that produced the observed values. This may allow for the determination of more exact locations of anthropogenic as well as biogenic emission sources. These locations could be used as a basis for planning *in situ* measurement campaigns, which in turn could be used to improve emissions models.

In this work, we present a relatively simple forward model based on a numerical weather prediction model with support for the modeling of atmospheric transport, combined with a model of biogenic fluxes. The model was applied to boreal areas of northern Alberta. The simulation domain contained a number of interesting features of both biogenic and anthropogenic natures. The initial and boundary conditions for both the weather and CO_2 concentrations were obtained from coarser scale models. Remotely sensed data were used to provide the necessary information about vegetative activity for the biogenic flux model, and information about anthropogenic emissions was also included, based on publicly available emission inventories.

Comparisons with the simulation results were made between both *in situ* flux tower measurements and remotely sensed satellite data. The flux tower comparison shows that the model is able to capture some of the daily variations in CO_2 concentration, but underestimates the measured data. This difference, more profound during nights when the atmosphere is not well mixed, can be attributed to the representativeness error and the difference in height between model and measurements. Comparison of model and satellite measurements showed a high correlation, with a negative bias of about 10%. This bias was largely caused by the limited representation of the atmosphere in the model, and was easily corrected.

Despite some limitations, the simulation using the proposed GHGMS captures a number of interesting characteristics of the diurnal variations in the atmospheric CO_2 concentration in this area. As more measurements become available from newly launched satellites or *in situ* monitoring networks, the creation, improvement, and validation of emissions models and GHGMS will advance. The use of such models will help to elucidate the role of boreal forests in the global carbon cycle and the impact of human activities on these forests, and will suggest ways in which this ecosystem can be protected.

The GHGMS, introduced in this chapter, combines several available tools to model CO_2 on a regional scale (1–100 km) and with a high temporal resolution. Outputs of the modeling system can be directly compared with measured CO_2 concentrations that have site-specific spatial and temporal characteristics. In regions with a high level of industrial activity, such as the oil sands development areas in northern Alberta, this system can help to detect and localize ecosystem disturbances, and to evaluate the results of reclamation and restoration efforts. Ultimately, the modeling system can be used to assess the impact of industrial development on ecosystems, and to examine alternative development scenarios.

However, the model itself is not sufficient to obtain a full picture of CO_2 concentrations and their evolution in space and time. It must be supplemented by *in situ* and satellite measurements and cross-validated. Availability of all this information will provide a solid basis to corroborate and enhance reports provided by industry and government organizations.

REFERENCES

Ahmadov, R., Gerbig, C., Kretschmer, R., et al. (2007). Mesoscale covariance of transport and CO_2 fluxes: evidence from observations and simulations using the WRF-VPRM coupled atmosphere-biosphere model. *Journal of Geophysical Research-Atmospheres*, **112**, D22107.

Benjamin, S., Schwartz, B., Cole, R. (1999). Accuracy of ACARS wind and temperature observations determined by collocation. *Weather and Forecasting*, **14**, 1032–1038.

Boersma, K., Eskes, H., Brinksma, E. (2004). Error analysis for tropospheric NO2 retrieval from space. *Journal of Geophysical Research-Atmospheres*, **109**, D4311.

Ciais, P., Tans, P., White, J., et al. (1995). Partitioning of ocean and land uptake of CO_2 as inferred by delta-C13 measurements from the NOAA climate monitoring and diagnostics laboratory global air sampling network. *Journal of Geophysical Research-Atmospheres*, **100**, 5051–5070.

Dixon, R. K., Soloman, A. M., Brown, S., et al. (1994). Carbon pools and flux of global forest ecosystems. *Science*, **263**, 185–190.

Dufour, E. and Breon, F.-M. (2003). Spaceborne estimate of atmospheric CO_2 column by use of the differential absorption method: error analysis. *Applied Optics*, **42**, 3595–3609.

European Commission, Joint Research Centre (JRC)/Netherlands Environmental Assessment Agency (PBL). (2009). *Emission Database for Global Atmospheric Research (EDGAR)*, release version 4.0. Address: http://edgar.jrc.ec.europa.eu.

Flanagan, L. B. and Ehleringer, J. R. (1998). Ecosystem-atmosphere CO_2 exchange: interpreting signals of change using stable isotope ratios. *Trends in Ecology and Evolution*, **13**, 10–14.

Gelfand, A. E., Zhu, L., Carlin, B. P. (2001). On the change of support problem for spatio-temporal data. *Biostatistics*, **2**, 31–45.

Gilleland, E., Ahijevych, D., Brown, B., Casati, B., Ebert, E. E. (2009). Intercomparison of spatial forecast verification methods. *Weather and Forecasting*, **24**, 1416–1430.

Grell, G., Peckham, S., Schmitz, R., et al. (2005). Fully coupled 'online' chemistry within the WRF model. *Atmospheric Environment*, **39**, 6957–6975.

Gurney, K., Mendoza, D., Zhou, Y., et al. (2009). High resolution fossil fuel combustion CO_2 emission fluxes for the United States. *Environmental Science and Technology*, **43**, 5535–5541.

Han, Z., Zhang, M., An, J. (2009). Sensitivity of air quality model prediction to parameterization of vertical eddy diffusivity. *Environmental Fluid Dynamics*, **9**, 73–89.

Hansen, J., Johnson, D., Lacis, A., et al. (1981). Climate impact of increasing atmospheric carbon dioxide. *Science*, **213**, 957–966.

Isaacs, E. The Canadian Oil Sands in the Context of the Global Energy Demand. *Extended Abstracts for 17th Convocation of the International Council of Academies of Engineering and Technological Sciences (CAETS)*. Tokyo, October 2007.

Jung, M., Henkel, K., Herold, M., Churkina, G. (2006). Exploiting synergies of global land cover products for carbon cycle modeling. *Remote Sensing of Environment*, **101**, 534–553.

Lorenz, E. (1982). Atmospheric predictability experiments with a large numerical-model. *Tellus*, **34**, 505–513.

Mahadevan, P., Wofsy, S. C., Matross, D. M., et al. (2008). A satellite-based biosphere parameterization for net ecosystem CO_2 exchange: vegetation photosynthesis and respiration model (VPRM). *Global Biogeochemical Cycles*, **22**, 17.

Misenis, C. and Zhang, Y. (2010). An examination of sensitivity of WRF/Chem predictions to physical parameterizations, horizontal grid spacing, and nesting options. *Atmospheric Research*, **97**, 315–334.

Nowacki, P., Samson, P., Sillman, S. (1996). Sensitivity of urban airshed model (UAM-IV) calculated air pollutant concentrations to the vertical diffusion parameterization during convective meteorological situations. *Journal of Applied Meteorology*, **35**, 1790–1803.

Oda, T. and Maksyutov, S. (2011). A very high-resolution (1 km × 1 km) global fossil fuel CO_2 emission inventory derived using a point source database and satellite observations of nighttime lights. *Atmospheric Chemistry and Physics*, **11**, 543–556.

Olsen, S. and Randerson, J. (2004). Differences between surface and column atmospheric CO_2 and implications for carbon cycle research. *Journal of Geophysical Research-Atmospheres*, **109**, D02301.

Potapov, P., Yaroshenko, A., Turubanova, S., et al. (2008). Mapping the world's intact forest landscapes by remote sensing. *Ecology and Society*, **13**, 2.

Rödenbeck, C., Houweling, S., Gloor, M., Heimann, M. (2003). CO_2 flux history 1982–2001 inferred from atmospheric data using a global inversion of atmospheric transport. *Atmospheric Chemistry and Physics*, **3**, 1919–1964.

Rossa, A., Nurmi, P., Ebert, E. (2008). Overview of methods for the verification of quantitative precipitation forecasts. In S. Michaelides, ed., *Precipitation: Advances in Measurement, Estimation and Prediction*. Heidelberg: Springer Berlin, pp. 419–452.

Skamarock, W. C., Klemp, J. B., Dudhia, J., et al. (2008). *A Description of the Advanced Research WRF*, Version 3. Technical Report, NCAR/TN475+STR, NCAR.

Straus, D. and Paolino, D. (2009). Intermediate time error growth and predictability: tropics versus mid-latitudes. *Tellus Series A-Dynamic Meteorology and Oceanography*, **61**, 579–586.

Syed, K., Flanagan, L., Carlson, P., Glenn, A., Van Gaalen, K. (2006). Environmental control of net ecosystem CO_2 exchange in a treed, moderately rich fen in northern Alberta. *Agricultural and Forest Meteorology*, **140**, 97–114.

Taggart, R. and Cross, A. (2009). Global greenhouse to icehouse and back again: The origin and future of the boreal forest biome. *Global and Planetary Change*, **65**, 115–121.

Vitt, D. H., Halsey, L. A., Thormann, M. N., Martin, T. (1998). *Peatland Inventory of Alberta. Phase 1: Overview of peatland resources in the natural regions and subregions of the Province*. University of Alberta, Edmonton, AB, pp. 117 and digital database.

Wang, L., Okin, G., Macko, S. (2009). Satellite prediction of soil delta C-13 distributions in a southern African savanna. *Journal of Geochemical Exploration*, **102**, 137–141.

Yokota, T., Yoshida, Y., Eguchi, N., et al. (2009). Global concentrations of CO_2 and CH_4 retrieved from GOSAT: first preliminary results. *SOLA*, **5**, 160–163.

Zhang, D. and Zheng, W. (2004). Diurnal cycles of surface winds and temperatures as simulated by five boundary layer parameterizations. *Journal of Applied Meteorology*, **43**, 157–169.

DOUG HILTZ, JOYCE GOULD, BARRY WHITE, JAE OGILVIE,
AND PAUL ARP

4

Reclamation and restoration of boreal ecosystems: attaining sustainable development

Modeling and mapping vegetation type by soil moisture regime across boreal landscapes

INTRODUCTION

Modeling and mapping vegetation changes across the landscape is of considerable importance to sustainable land use planning, including reclamation and restoration across boreal plains and elsewhere. This chapter demonstrates how high-resolution vegetation changes from hydric to xeric can be inferred from LiDAR-derived digital elevation models (DEM). This demonstration involves two contrasting case studies in Alberta: the Willmore Wilderness Park within the Alberta Rocky Mountains and Foothills, and one section of the well-studied EMEND ("Ecosystem Management Emulating Natural Disturbance") forest area (EMEND, 2006), representing the boreal dry mixedwood natural subregion near Peace River (Figure 4.1). Technically, the work proceeds from:

1. a plot-based indexing of vegetation type according to species-specific soil moisture requirements (referred to as vegetation index, or VI);
2. establishing the relationship between the plot-based VI and the topographically derived depth-to-water index (DTW, Murphy et al., 2011); and
3. using that relationship to model and map VI across the two study areas, with DTW as the main VI predictor, with and without local slope and aspect corrections.

Restoration and Reclamation of Boreal Ecosystems, ed. Dale Vitt and Jagtar Bhatti. Published by Cambridge University Press. © Cambridge University Press 2012.

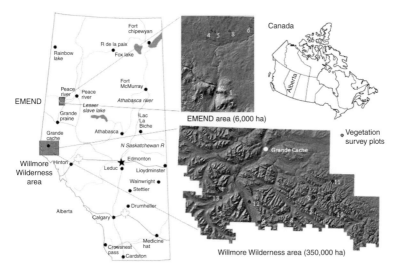

Figure 4.1. Locator map for the EMEND and Willmore Wilderness Park study areas (hill-shaded LiDAR-derived digital elevation models), with vegetation survey locations detailed in Table 4.1.

For the purpose of reclaiming and restoring boreal ecosystems, maps thus generated provide a high-resolution benchmark of the pre-disturbance vegetation-type distributions from depressions to ridge top and along flow channels. As such, these maps serve as informative data layers for delineating the reintroduction of desired habitats, earmarking locations for the reintroduction of common and rare native species, determining the direction and spread of invasive species across the landscape, locating wildlife corridors, choosing least-impact access roads and control points, and planning associated field operations in considerable detail. The maps may also become useful benchmark and research tools for addressing vegetation and soil–water interactions on reclaimed areas (Naeth et al., 2011), and along roads (active or abandoned), trails, seismic lines, pipe lines, power lines, dikes, and other linear and nonlinear structures (Nash, 2010).

The methods described in this chapter build on earlier research, using coarse- and fine-gridded DTMs for the derivation to VI, DTW, and the topographic wetness index (TWI). For details and references to preceding work of a similar type, see Kopecký and Čížková (2010) regarding TWI–VI analyses, and Murphy et al. (2011) on the subject of DTW versus TWI comparisons aimed at mapping and modeling of soil, drainage, and vegetation type. With reference to the VI literature, the results presented here only refer to vegetation type by moisture regime, and therefore do not inform about species-specific preferences regarding nutrient and light availability, acidity, salinity, or temperature (Humbert, et al., 2007; Schmidtlein, 2005; Woodward, 1987). In addition, the VI projections are based solely on digitally derived variations in topography, and therefore do not inform about vegetation indices that can be derived for the same areas based on spectral image analyses (Halounová, 2008; Yilmaz, et al., 2008). In spite of these limitations, it would appear that the methods described constitute a major advance in vegetation modeling and mapping (Anderson et al., 2006; Austin, 1980; Franklin, 1995; Goward et al., 2002; Tappeiner et al., 1998; Venterink and Wassen, 1997).

METHODOLOGY

Field calibrations and mapping

Calibrating the slope- and aspect-corrected VI equations proceeded by indexing vegetation type per 1 m × 1 m plots nested within larger survey plots across the Willmore Wilderness Park (85 plots) and along transect lines within the EMEND Park (90 plots; Figure 4.1; Table 4.1). The plots within the Willmore Wilderness area were accessed by helicopter, while the plots within the EMEND area were accessed by ground travel and transect walking. All plots were GPS referenced to within ±4 m. Vegetation indexing per plot was done by: (1) listing all species within each 1 m × 1 m plot; (2) ascertaining the species-specific soil moisture preferences from xeric to hydric by number, from 0 to 8, guided by the available vegetation field guides for the general area; and (3) weight-averaging the resulting numbers across the species by plot, abundance, (Willmore), or absence/presence alone (EMEND).

Delineating flow channels, wet areas, and the cartographic depth-to-water index

The wet areas and associated DTW delineation process from digital elevation data are illustrated in Figure 4.2. Several GIS algorithms were used to perform the task. First, a LiDAR-derived DEM for the study area is acquired, and a digital surface free of depressions is generated using the ArcGIS FILL function (Tarboton, 1997; Tarboton et al., 1991). The filled DEM is then used to comprehensively determine flow direction, slope gradient, and flow accumulation across the study area with the D_8 and D_∞ flow algorithms (Hornberger and Boyer, 1995; O'Callaghan and Mark, 1984). Doing so results in: (1) the slope gradient grid; (2) the DTW = 0 defining the flow−channel grid based, for example, on 4-ha flow

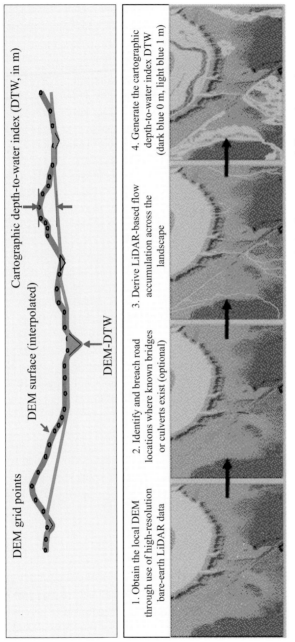

Figure 4.2. Overview and principles of the GIS-based flow channel and cartographic depth-to-water modeling and mapping processes. (See color plate section for colored image.)

Table 4.1. *Transect locations of vegetation survey plots (eastern-most points)*

Area	Transect	Number of survey plots	Latitude	Longitude
EMEND	1	11	56 45 15.76N	118 20 42.28W
	2	26	56 45 18.47N	118 21 40.94W
	3	10	56 44 55.43N	118 24 59.92W
	4	11	56 50 01.91N	118 23 18.83W
	5	9	56 49 59.13N	118 22 54.14W
	6	8	56 50 28.91N	118 17 37.50W
	7	7	56 44 37.84N	118 20 39.63W
	8	7	56 50 04.88N	118 20 44.42W
Willmore	1	4	53 36 38.25N	118 29 57.22W
	2	4	53 32 38.30N	118 37 54.73W
	3	4	53 59 02.66N	119 29 36.01W
	4	11	53 38 40.47N	119 35 53.41W
	5	5	53 32 08.75N	119 34 23.87W
	6	10	53 27 40.87N	119 10 31.34W
	7	6	53 31 47.95N	119 24 27.64W
	8	9	53 29 07.89N	118 49 13.58W
	9	9	53 36 46.80N	118 38 51.65W
	10	6	53 31 00.04N	118 26 22.24W
	11	5	53 42 30.21N	118 27 38.96W
	12	5	53 34 31.76N	119 16 56.76W
	13	4	53 35 39.17N	119 33 42.01W

EMEND, ecosystem management emulating natural disturbance.

initiation threshold values to signal perennial surface flow (Murphy et al., 2009); and (3) a least-elevation (least-cost) grid between any grid cell and the nearest open-water cells with DTW = 0. The resulting DTW grid was formally obtained from:

$$\text{DTW [m]} = \left[\sum \frac{dz_i}{dx_i} a \right] x_c, \qquad [4.1]$$

where dz/dx is the slope gradient at each cell i along the path, a is 1 m when the path crosses the cell parallel to the cell boundaries and $2^{0.5}$ m when it crosses diagonally, and x_c is cell size. By definition, there is therefore a strong dependence between the DTW- and the DEM-derived flow–channel network and the adopted flow initiation threshold. For forested areas, dry-weather initiation for permanent streams depends on: (1) catchment slope, increasing from 1 to 4 ha or more as the slope decreases from 100% toward zero; and (2) geological substrate, depending on flow allocation to surface and subsurface drainage channels (Jaeger et al.,

2007). Decreasing this threshold from 4 ha to smaller areas increases the areas mapped to be wet, thereby simulating the change in soil moisture status from generally dry (e.g., end of summer) to wet (e.g., after the snowmelt season or prolonged precipitation events). Hydrographic DEM corrections (Figure 4.2) are needed: (1) when the DEM data do not conform with the exact locations of open-water surfaces, shorelines, and streams; and (2) when surface structures such as roads and bridges, as well as DEM artifacts, obscure flow continuity along streams (Garbrecht et al., 2001; Murphy et al., 2007).

For comparison, the widely used TWI given by:

$$\text{TWI} = \ln[\text{flow-accumulated area/tan}(\pi \text{ slope\_angle}/180)]. \qquad [4.2]$$

was also mapped for the two study areas and for each plot location in particular, using the same DEM and flow direction, slope gradient, and flow accumulation algorithms.

The quality of the wet-area delineation process was checked by: (1) overlaying the DTW map on the aerial photograph mosaic and the bare-ground DEM for the study areas; and (2) profiling the LiDAR-generated data layers across the study areas by scanning along straight lines and displaying the resulting cross-sections involving: (a) the first and last pulse returns corresponding to canopy height and bare-ground elevation, respectively, and (b) the corresponding DTW line below the bare-ground elevation, as illustrated in Figure 4.3. Doing so revealed a close location correspondence between mapped and actual flow channels and wet areas, including wetlands.

Vegetation index modeling

Previous DEM-based analyses (Murphy et al., 2011) revealed closer relationships between soil type, drainage type, vegetation type, and a variety of soil properties and $\log_{10}\text{DTW}$ than with TWI. Hence,

$$\text{VI} = (a_{\text{VI}} + b_{\text{VI}}\log_{10}\text{DTW}) \qquad [4.3]$$

where a_{VI} and b_{VI} are calibration coefficients. This formulation is adjusted to account for local variations in slope and aspect, as follows:

$$\text{if VI} \leq 4: \text{VI}_{\text{adj}} = \text{VI} + 0.5\,\text{VI}\,[1 - \exp(-a_{\text{slope}}\text{slope})]$$
$$\times \sin[\pi(\text{aspect} - a_{\text{aspect}})/180]; \qquad [4.3a]$$

$$\text{if VI} > 4: \text{VI}_{\text{adj}} = \text{VI} + 0.5\,(8 - \text{VI})\,[1 - \exp(-a_{\text{slope}}\text{slope})]$$
$$\times \sin[\pi(\text{aspect} - a_{\text{aspect}})/180]. \qquad [4.3b]$$

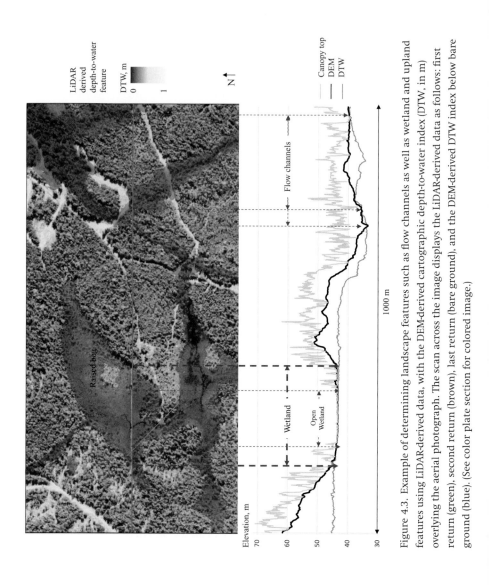

Figure 4.3. Example of determining landscape features such as flow channels as well as wetland and upland features using LiDAR-derived data, with the DEM-derived cartographic depth-to-water index (DTW, in m) overlying the aerial photograph. The scan across the image displays the LiDAR-derived data as follows: first return (green), second return (brown), last return (bare ground), and the DEM-derived DTW index below bare ground (blue). (See color plate section for colored image.)

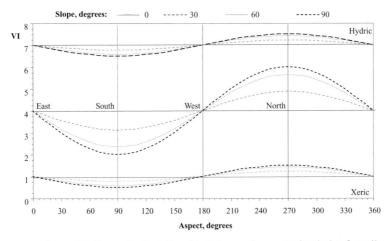

Figure 4.4. Conceptual relationship between the vegetation index for soil wetness (VI) modified by slope and aspect slope and aspect according to Eqs. 4.3a and 4.3b with VI = 1, 4, and 7 for flat conditions as base lines.

with slope = tan(slope_angle), slope_angle and aspect in degrees (northern aspect: 0°), and with a_{slope} and a_{aspect} as additional calibration coefficients. For the cell-by-cell mapping purpose, DTW, slope, and aspect were averaged through cell-centered neighborhood smoothing, because the elevational precision of LiDAR-generated DEMs generally varied by ±15 cm from cell to cell. The slope and aspect contributions to VI implied by Eq. 4.2 are illustrated in Figure 4.4 for three $a_{VI} + b_{VI} \log_{10} DTW$ levels: 1, 4, and 7, with $a_{slope} = 1$ and $a_{aspect} = 90°$. Accordingly, greatest slope and aspect contributions would occur for the mesic VI levels, and these contributions would diminish toward extreme dry and wet conditions.

The plot-generated VI numbers were used to calibrate the coefficients in Eq. 4.2 using the map-derived $\log_{10} DTW$, slope, and aspect values. This calibration was optimized through least-squares regression fitting, and the model thus calibrated was subsequently used to map VI across the two study areas, with the LiDAR-derived $\log_{10} DTW$, slope, and aspect values for each grid cell as VI predictor variables.

RESULTS AND DISCUSSION

Plot-based surveys and VI mapping

The species encountered within the survey plots for the two study areas are listed in Table 4.2 along with their field-guide suggested soil moisture

Table 4.2. *Species-specific xeric to hydric vegetation index for the groundflora of the EMEND and Willmore Wilderness Park*

Species	EMEND	Willmore	Ref.	Species	EMEND	Willmore	Ref.	Species	EMEND	Willmore	Ref.
Abies lasiocarpa	5	5	b,d	Equisetum arvense	–	8	a	Picea mariana	6	6	b,d
Achillea millefolium	2	2	a	Equisetum hyemale	–	2	a	Pinus contorta	3	3	b
Aconitum delphinifolium	–	3	e	Equisetum pratense	5	–	a	Platanthera hyperborea	–	8	c
Actaea rubra	4	4	b	Equisetum scirpoides	5	5	a	Pleurozium schreberi	5	5	a
Agropyron sp.	3	3	a	Equisetum sylvaticum	4	4	e	Poa palustris	–	5	a
Alnus crispa	3	3	a	Equisetum pratense	–	7	c	Polemonium caeruleum	7	7	b
Alnus tenuifolia	6	6	d,g	Erigeron peregrinus	–	2	e	Polygonum viviparum	–	5	b
Amalanchier alnifolia	3	3	a,c	Festuca altaica	–	1	b,c	Polytrichum sp	5	5	g
Anemone multifida	–	3	b	Festuca brachyphylla	–	2	c	Populus balsamifera	5	5	b
Antennaria alpina	–	3	c	Festuca occidentalis	–	2	c	Populus tremuloides	4	4	b
Antennaria umbrinella	–	2	b	Festuca rubra	–	3	c,e	Potentilla diversifolia	–	4	b,c
Apocynum androsaemifolium	3	3	a	Festuca sp	–	2	a,b	Potentilla nivea	–	4	e
Aquilegia flavescens	–	3	b,c	Fragaria vesca	3	3	a	Ptilium crista-castrensis	6	6	g
Aralia nudicaulis	3	3	a	Galium boreale	3	3	b,c	Pyrola asarifolia	4	4	b,c
Arctostaphylos rubra	–	2	e	Galium trifidum	7	7	b,c	Pyrola grandiflora	–	3	c
Arctostaphylos uvi-ursi	–	2	a	Galium triflorum	5	5	a	Pyrola secunda	–	4	c
Arnica angustifolia	–	4	c,e	Geocaullon lividum	5	5	a	Pyrola virens	4	4	a
Arnica cordifolia	3	3	c,e	Geum macrophyllum	7	7	a	Ranunculus lapanicus	5	5	a
Artemsia norvegica	–	2	e	Goodyera repens	4	4	a	Ranunculus macounii	7	7	b
Artemisia frigida	–	2	b	Gymnocarpium dryopteris	5	5	f	Ribes glandulosum	–	6	a
Aster ciliolatus	3	3	a	Habenaria hyperborea	6	6	a	Ribes lacustre	7	7	a
Aster conspicuus	4	4	g,f	Habenaria obtusata	6	6	a	Ribes oxyacanthoides	5	5	b
Astragalus americanus	3	3	b,c	Habenaria orbiculata	5	5	b,c	Ribes triste	5	5	a

Species	1	2	3
Astragalus vexilliflexus	–	3	c,e
Athyrium filix-femina	4	4	c
Betula glandulosa	8	8	a
Betula papyrifera	5	–	b
Betula pumila	6	–	b
Bizzania trilobata	–	7	f,g
Bromus sp.	3	3	a
Calamagrostis canadensis	6	6	a
Caltha leptosepala	–	7	b
Calypso bulbosa	5	5	c
Campanula rotundifolia	–	2	b,c
Campanula uniflora	–	2	e
Cardamine pensylvanica	5	5	c
Carex aquatilis	–	7	c
Carex scirpoidea	–	5	c
Carex sp.	5	5	c
Cassiope mertensiana	–	4	b,e
Cassiope tetragona	–	4	b,e
Castilleja occidentalis	–	5	b
Chimaphila umbellata	–	3	c
Circaea alpina	5	5	a
Cirsium arvense	–	7	c
Cladina rangifera	1	1	a
Climacium dendroides	7	7	a
Hedysarum alpinum	–	2	a
Hedysarum boreale	–	4	b
Heracleum lanatum	4	4	b
Hieracium umbellatum	1	1	b
Hierochloe odorata	–	4	c
Hylocomium splendens	5	5	a
Impatiens capensis	7	7	c,f
Juncus sp.	7	7	a
Juniperus communis	–	2	a
Kalmia polifolia	6	6	a
Larix laricina	3	–	b,d
Lathyrus ochroleucus	7	3	a
Ledum groenlandicum	4	7	a
Linnaea borealis	6	4	a
Lonicera caerulea	4	6	a,c
Lonicera dioica	4	4	a
Lycopodium annotinum	–	4	a
Lycopodium complanatum	3	2	a
Maianthemum canadense	7	3	b,c
Mentha arvensis	–	7	a
Menziesia ferruginea	4	4	b
Mertensia paniculata	5	4	a
Mitella nuda	–	5	a
Moehringia lateriflora	7	4	a
Rosa acicularis	–	3	a
Rubus alleghaniensis	–	4	g
Rubus arcticus	6	6	b
Rubus chamaemorus	7	7	a
Rubus idaeus	5	5	a
Rubus pedatus	–	5	b
Rubus pubescens	4	4	a
Salix arctica	–	4	a,c
Salix barrattiana	–	5	a,c
Salix glauca	–	5	a,c
Salix nivalis	6	4	a,c
Salix sp.	–	6	a
Salix vestita	–	3	a,c
Saxifraga bronchialis	–	2	c
Saxifraga oppositifolia	–	5	c
Senecio pauperculus	7	7	a
Sheperdia canadensis	2	2	a
Silene acaulis	–	3	g
Smilacina trifolia	8	8	b
Solidago canadensis	3	3	b
Sphagnum sp.	8	8	a
Stellaria longifolia	–	5	a
Taraxacum officinale	4	4	g
Thalictrum sparsiflorum	5	5	c

(cont.)

Table 4.2 (cont.)

Species	EMEND	Willmore	Ref.
Corallorhiza maculata	3	3	a
Cornus canadensis	4	4	a
Cornus stolonifera	5	5	a
Dasiphora floribunda	–	2	e
Delphinium bicolour	–	2	b
Delphinium glaucum	4	4	b
Dicranum scoparium	3	3	g
Dicranum sp.	3	3	f,g
Drepanocladus uncinatus	6	6	a
Dryas integrifolia	–	3	e
Dryas octopetala	–	3	e
Dryopteris carthusiana	5	5	f
Elymus canadensis	–	2	b
Empetrum nigrum	–	6	e
Epilobium angustifolium	3	3	b,c
Epilobium ciliatum	5	5	b
Moneses uniflora	5	5	a
Monotropa hypopitis	3	3	c
Myosotis asiatica	–	5	c
Orthilia secunda	3	3	e,f
Oxycoccus microcarpus	8	8	b
Oxyria digyna	–	4	c
Oxytropis podocarpa	–	3	g
Parnassia palustris	7	7	a
Pedicularis arctica	–	4	c
Pedicularis capitata	–	4	c
Pedicularis lanata	–	3	c
Petasites palmatus	4	4	a
Petasites sagittatus	8	8	a
Phleum pratense	–	4	c
Picea engelmannii	–	4	b
Picea glauca	4	4	b
Tofieldia glutinosa	–	7	c
Trifolium pratense	–	4	c
Trifolium repens	–	4	c
Urtica dioica	5	5	c
Vaccinium cespitosum	–	2	a
Vaccinium myrtilloides	3	3	a
Vaccinium oxycoccos	–	7	a
Vaccinium scoparium	–	3	c
Vaccinium vitis-idaea	4	4	a
Veronica americana	7	7	e
Veronica wormskjoldii	–	5	e
Viburnum edule	5	5	a
Viburnum opulus	–	5	a,c
Vicia americana	3	3	a
Viola canadensis	5	5	b
Viola renifolia	4	4	a
Zigadenus elegans	7	7	b

- absent

a Gerling et al. (1996)
b Rowe (1956)
c Moss and Packer (1983)

d Farrar (1995)
e Kershaw et al. (1998)
f Beckingham and Archibald (1996)

g UBC E-flora BC (2009)

0 Very xeric
1 Xeric
2 Sub-xeric

3 Sub-mesic
4 Mesic
5 Sub-hygric

6 Hygric
7 Sub-hydric
8 Hydric

UBC, University of British Columbia, 2009 [30].

Table 4.3. *Best-fitted regression results for VI, based on Eq. 2, 2a, and 2b and the two study areas*

	a_{VI}		b_{VI}		a_{slope}		a_{aspect}		r^2	RMSE
EMEND	4.04	±0.07	−0.99	±0.05	0.35	±0.17	85	±18	0.68	0.54
Willmore	4.85	±0.08							0.77	0.58

r^2, coefficient of determination; RMSE, root mean square error.

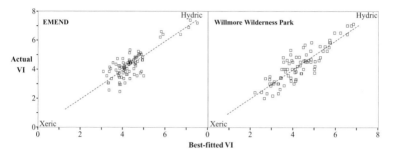

Figure 4.5. Actual versus Eq. 4.2-calibrated vegetation index VI from xeric to hydric using $\log_{10}$DTW as well as slope and aspect (Eq. 4.2, 4.3a, and 4.3b) as VI predictor variables.

preferences. Many species are common to both areas, but there are more species registered for the Willmore Wilderness Park than for the EMEND area. This is likely due to: (1) the difference in the overall survey areas (350,000 ha for the former, and 6,000 ha for the latter); and (2) the differences in location, topography, and climate (boreal to alpine versus boreal only). The vegetation classes are fairly equally represented across the soil moisture range at both locations, but there were no plots centered on very wet spots, on dry to very dry spots, on barren or near barren spots, or on slopes >25°. Nevertheless, the resulting field-assessed VI values were well correlated with the map-derived $\log_{10}$DTW values (Eq. 4.2; EMEND: $r^2 = 0.68$, Willmore: $r^2 = 0.77$ by species abundance, $r^2 = 0.57$ by species presence; Figure 4.5; Table 4.3), and did not require the suggested slope and aspect adjustments. In contrast, the corresponding r^2 values for the VI–TWI correlations were quite weak for both study areas (r^2 about 0.3; details not shown). Similarly weak VI–TWI correlations were reported by Kopecký and Čížková, (2010) for another study area and using various TWI-determining algorithms.

While DEM-based TWI derivations vary strongly by DEM resolution, grid-point interpolation methods, and local slope gradient derivations, DTW is affected by DEM resolution, grid-point interpolation methods, and cell-to-cell slope derivations in minors ways only (Murphy et al., 2011). In addition, mapped areas with DTW ≤1 m (with DTW referenced to all flow channels with a flow initiation threshold of 4 ha) mimic the position of the water table below the ground considerably better and more consistently than TWI, especially in low-lying areas and along flow channels. The close-up examples in Figure 4.6 further attest to the general conformance between the actual and $\log_{10}$DTW-generated VI values. Applying the plot-calibrated model to the two study areas resulted in the maps displayed in Figures 4.7 and 4.8. In each case, these maps conform to the expected hydric to xeric VI gradations from valley bottoms to ridge tops in considerable detail.

Reclamation and restoration applications

In reclaiming and restoring previously disturbed surface areas, it is important to map the influence of local topographic controls on pre-disturbance, existing, and desired variations in local soil moisture regime and vegetation patterns. While LiDAR DEMs may not yet be available for mapping pre-disturbance moisture conditions across the entire boreal forest with the LiDAR-afforded precision, it is nevertheless possible to approximate the preexisting patterns based on coarser resolution DEMs where available. To assess disturbed situations in their current conditions, one could use the approach described in this chapter and the resulting maps to: (1) predict the pathways of invading vegetation based on the species-specific dispersal modes and moisture requirements according to "do-nothing" scenarios; (2) reengineer the current flow and water retention patterns to achieve more desirable VI patterns; or (3) enhance overall ecosystem services in the same area to improve upon preexisting conditions (e.g., to allow for deeper soil percolation to promote greater vegetation productivity, cleaner water and air, reductions in temperature extremes and hydrological risks, etc.). An example of how the approach can be used for general vegetation assessment and management within and along linear structures such as seismic lines is shown in Figure 4.9. This example establishes the procedural context by which the proposed methods can be used for line-specific restoration planning, through, for example, producing or enhancing lineal inventories, determining revegetation, browse and forage goals and targets, or improving corridor-specific line-of-sight and trafficability conditions (Nash, 2010).

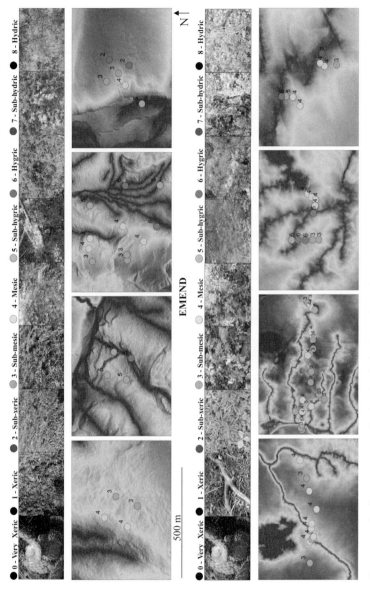

Willmore Wilderness Park

● 0 - Very Xeric ● 1 - Xeric ● 2 - Sub-xeric ● 3 - Sub-mesic ● 4 - Mesic ● 5 - Sub-hygric ● 6 - Hygric ● 7 - Sub-hydric ● 8 - Hydric

N

500 m

EMEND

● 0 - Very Xeric ● 1 - Xeric ● 2 - Sub-xeric ● 3 - Sub-mesic ● 4 - Mesic ● 5 - Sub-hygric ● 6 - Hygric ● 7 - Sub-hydric ● 8 - Hydric

Figure 4.6. Conformance examples for plot-derived VI values with the corresponding LiDAR-derived VI map for the EMEND area (lower images), and the Willmore Wilderness Park (upper images), also showing xeric to hydric ground vegetation images. (See color plate section for colored image.)

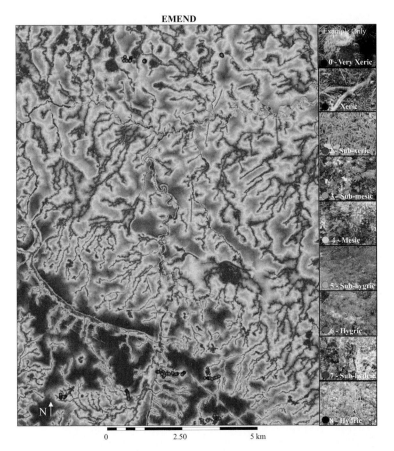

Figure 4.7. Vegetation index for the EMEND area. (See color plate section for colored image.)

The VI mapping approach discussed here can also be used to predict disturbance impacts on vegetation and soils ranging from absent and weak to severe (Latofovic et al., 2005; Sitters et al., 2012). For previously or currently undisturbed scenarios, the approach allows for ready visualization of likely encroachment pathways taken by invasive species, and delineating the vulnerable areas of specific habitats for plants and animals to anticipated physical or biological disturbances. For severely disturbed areas, this approach lends itself to mapping locations that may contribute to or detract from achieving desired revegetation goals on account of excessive soil wetness or dryness at high resolution.

Model generalizations

The maps displayed in Figures 4.7 and 4.8 may become important filters in mapping the distribution of plant and animal species and communities

Willmore Wilderness Park

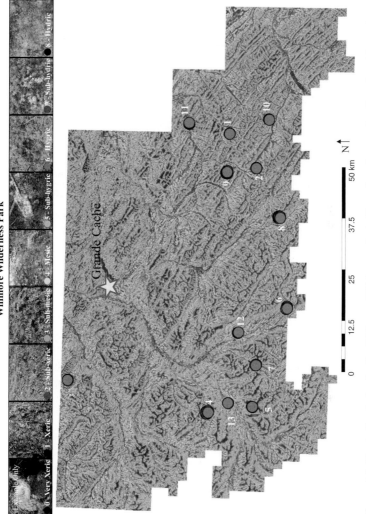

Figure 4.8. Vegetation index for the Willmore Wilderness Park. (See color plate section for colored image.)

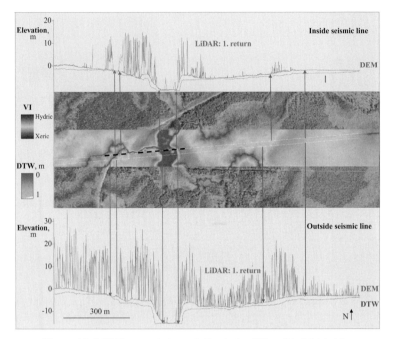

Figure 4.9. LiDAR-generated vegetation index (VI) and height (m) in relation to bare-ground DEM and the cartographic DTW index (shaded dark to light blue) along and off a 1500 m seismic line scan within the EMEND area, overlaid on aerial photograph. (See color plate section for colored image.)

by way of multispectral and hyperspectral image analyses (Ghiyamat and Shafri, 2010). The maps could also be used to assess biological diversity across the landscape, as this diversity can be expected to increase with topographic complexity and related variations in soil moisture regimes and other vegetation determining conditions referring to local changes in precipitation, soil nutrient and light availability, acidity, and salinity. Finally, addressing other VI-influencing factors such as variations in soil permeability, occurrences of footslope seepage, and elevation changes in climate conditions would allow for further model applications and generalizations. Altogether, this approach shows significant promise in facilitating site-specific restoration activities intended to reestablish desired vegetation communities on disturbed areas across the boreal forest and elsewhere.

Note that these previously discussed methods assigned a particular soil moisture regime preference class to each species (Table 4.2). The next step would reassign these values according to species-specific soil moisture tolerances, so that those species with wide tolerances would carry less weight in the plot-based VI assignments than those species with rather narrow tolerances.

SUMMARY AND CONCLUSIONS

This chapter has described a new method for modeling and mapping vegetation type according to species-specific soil moisture preferences from hydric to xeric across the landscape at 1-m resolution. This method relates a plot-assigned hydric to xeric VI to the cartographically determined and LiDAR-derived DTW, and uses the resulting relationship for vegetation type mapping across two study areas: the Willmore Wilderness Park within the Alberta Rocky Mountains and Foothills, and the EMEND study area within the boreal plain near Peace River, Alberta. The VI maps thus generated conform fairly closely to the plot-based VI assignments, with r^2 up to 75% following local slope and aspect corrections. The maps thus obtained, or modified versions thereof, present essential base layers for vegetation management in general, and will likely be of operational benefit to reclaiming and restoring uplands and wetlands from the planning to the monitoring and evaluation stages.

Through plot-based indexing of vegetation type by soil wetness (VI), and correlating this to the LiDAR- and cartographically derived DTW, it was possible to model and map moisture-based VI variations across the Willmore Wilderness Park and the EMEND forest area at 1-m resolution, with up to about 75% capture of the plot-by-plot VI variations. This constitutes a considerable improvement over previous moisture-based VI indexing techniques either associated with image-based spectral analyses, or other topographically derived wetness indices, notably TWI. Hence, the maps for the two study areas in particular could be useful in developing detailed response measures to disturbance scenarios (actual or anticipated) that are intended, for example, to: (1) conserve and protect the Willmore Wilderness Park from physical and biological intrusions as much as possible; (2) follow up on soil-mitigated vegetation responses to various forest management actions within the EMEND area; and (3) serve as examples of how VI mapping results could be applied to other locations with specific land reclamation and restoration interests and needs.

ACKNOWLEDGMENTS

This work was financially supported through research grants and in-field assistance received from the Alberta Sustainable Resources Department, supplemented by Parks Division, Alberta Tourism, Parks and Recreation.

Special thanks go to Joshua Noseworthy, David Campbell, Sheena Briggs, Karen Anderson, and Marge Meijer for field assistance.

REFERENCES

Anderson, R. P. A., Peterson, T., Egbert, S. L. (2006). Vegetation-index models predict areas vulnerable to purple loosestrife (*Lythrum salicaria*) invasion in Kansas. *The Southwestern Naturalist*, **51**, 471–480.

Austin, M. P. (1980). Searching for a model for use in vegetation analysis. *Plant Ecology*, **42**, 11–21.

Beckingham, J. D. and Archibald, J. H. (1996). *Field guide to ecosites of Northern Alberta*. Alberta: Natural Resources Canada, Canadian Forest Service, Northwest Region, Northern Forestry Centre. ISBN 0-660-16369-1.

EMEND. (2006). Ecosystem Management Emulating Natural Disturbance (EMEND) Project. Address: <http://www.emend.rr.ualberta.ca/>.

Farrar J. L. (1995). *Trees in Canada*. Marham, ON: Fitzhenry and Whiteside Limited. Canadian Forest Service, pp. 1–502.

Franklin, J. (1995). Predictive vegetation mapping: geographical modeling of biospatial patterns in relation to environmental gradients. *Progress in Physical Geography*, **19**, 474–499.

Garbrecht, J., Ogden, F. L., DeBarry, P. A., Maidment, D. R. (2001). GIS and distributed watershed models I: data coverages and sources. *Journal of Hydrological Engineering*, **6**, 506–514.

Gerling, H. S., Willoughby, M. G., Schoepf, A., Tannas, K. E., Tannas, C. A. (1996). *A Guide to Using Native Plants on Disturbed Lands*. Edmonton, AB: Alberta Agriculture, Food and Rural Development and Alberta Environmental Protection, pp. 174–233.

Ghiyamat, A. and Shafri, H. Z. M. (2010). A review on hyperspectral remote sensing for homogeneous and heterogeneous forest biodiversity assessment. *International Journal of Remote Sensing*, **31**, 1837–1856.

Goward, S. N., Xue, Y., Czajkowski, K. P. (2002). Evaluating land surface moisture conditions from the remotely sensed temperature/vegetation index measurements: an exploration with the simplified simple biosphere model. *Remote Sensing of Environment*, **79**, 225–242.

Halounová, L. (2008). Reclamation areas and their development studied by vegetation indices. *International Journal Digital Earth*, **1**, 155–164.

Hornberger, G. M. and Boyer, E. W. (1995). Recent advances in watershed modeling. *Reviews of Geophysics*, **33**, 949–957.

Humbert, L., Gagnon, D., Kneeshaw, D., Messier, C. (2007). A shade tolerance index for common understory species of northeastern North America. *Ecological Indicators*, **7**, 195–207.

Jaeger, K. L., Montgomery, D. R., Bolton, S. M. (2007). Channel and perennial flow initiation in headwater streams: management implications of variability in source-area size. *Journal of Environmental Management*, **40**, 775–786.

Kershaw, L. J., MacKinnon A., Pojar, J. (1998). *Plants of the Rocky Mountains*. Edmonton, AB: Lone Pine Publishing, pp. 1–384.

Kopecký, M. and Čížková, Š. (2010). Using topographic wetness index in vegetation ecology: does the algorithm matter? *Applied Vegetation Science*, **13**, 450–459.

Latifovic, R., Fytas, K., Chen, J., Paraszczak, J. (2005). Assessing land cover change resulting from large surface mining development. *International Journal of Applied Earth Observation Geoinformation*, **7**, 29–48.

Moss, E. H. and Packer, J. G. (1983). *Flora of Alberta*, 2nd edn. Toronto, ON: University of Toronto Press, pp. 1–687.

Murphy, P. N. C., Ogilvie, J., Arp, P. A. (2009). Topographic modeling of soil moisture conditions: a comparison and verification of two models. *European Journal of Soil Science*, **60**, 94–109.

Murphy, P. N. C., Ogilvie, J., Connor, K., Arp, P. A. (2007). Mapping wetlands: a comparison of two different approaches for New Brunswick, Canada. *Wetlands*, **27**, 846–854.

Murphy, P. N. C., Ogilvie, J., Meng, F.-R., et al. (2011). Modeling and mapping topographic variations in forest soils at high resolution: a case study. *Ecological Modeling*, **222**, 2314–2322.

Naeth M. A., Chanasyk, D. S., Burgers, T. D. (2011). Vegetation and soil water interactions on a tailings sand storage facility in the Athabasca oil sands region of Alberta, Canada. *Physics and Chemistry of the Earth*, **36**, 19–30.

Nash, J. C. (2010). Lineal inventory of the little smoky caribou. Foothills Landscape Management Forum (FLMF). Address: <http://foothillsresearchinstitute.ca/Content_Files/Files/FLMF/FLMF_2010_10_report_LinealInventory_Final.pdf>.

O'Callaghan, J. F. and Mark, D. M. (1984). The extraction of drainage networks from digital elevation data. *Computer Vision, Graphics and Image Processing*, **28**, 323–344.

Rowe, J. S. (1956). Uses of undergrowth plant species in forestry. *Ecology*, **37**, 461–473.

Schmidtlein, S. (2005). Imaging spectroscopy as a tool for mapping Ellenberg indicator values. *Journal of Applied Ecology*, **42**, 966–974.

Sitters, J., Holmgren, M., Stoorvogel, J. J., López, B. C. (2012). Rainfall-tuned management facilitates dry forest recovery. *Restoration Ecology*, **20**, 33–42.

Tappeiner, U., Tasser, E., Tappeiner, G. (1998). Modeling vegetation patterns using natural and anthropogenic influence factors: preliminary experience with a GIS based model applied to an alpine area. *Ecological Modeling*, **113**, 225–237.

Tarboton, D. G. (1997). A new method for the determination of flow directions and upslope areas in grid digital elevation models. *Water Resources Research*, **33**, 309–319.

Tarboton, D. G., Bras, R. L., Rodriguez-Itube, I. (1991). On the extraction of channel networks from digital elevation data. *Hydrological Processes*, **5**, 81–100.

University of British Columbia. (2009). *E-flora BC: Electronic Atlas of the Plants of British Columbia*. Address: <http://www.geog.ubc.ca/biodiversity/eflora/>.

Venterink, H. O. and Wassen, M. J. (1997). A comparison of six models predicting vegetation response to hydrological habitat change. *Ecological Modeling*, **101**, 347–361.

Woodward, F. I. (1987). *Climate and Plant Distribution*. Cambridge, UK: Cambridge University Press.

Yilmaz, M. T., Hunt, Jr., E. R., Goins, L. D., et al. (2008). Vegetation water content during SMEX04 from ground data and LANDSAT 5 thematic mapper imagery. *Remote Sensing of Environment*, **112**, 350–362.

SARA KOROPCHAK, DALE H. VITT, ROSEMARY BLOISE,
AND R. KELMAN WIEDER

5

Fundamental paradigms, foundation species selection, and early plant responses to peatland initiation on mineral soils

INTRODUCTION

Exploration and development of oil sands began in northern Alberta in the early twentieth century. Since the 1960s, the industry has grown exponentially. The oil sands deposits cover approximately one-quarter of Alberta's land area, which is a mosaic of peatland and upland ecosystems. Because of its locally destructive nature, surface (open-pit) mines have become the poster child of the Alberta oil sands' mining, even though this method constitutes only about 10%–20% of all mining activity. The remaining 80%–90% of mining is performed *in situ* (drilling) because oil sands deposits are too deep to surface mine. A common method of *in situ* mining is steam-assisted gravity drainage (SAGD). In peatlands, SAGD begins with clearing of trees and installation of a 2-m mineral soil pad to support drilling equipment. Two parallel pipes are then installed; one injects steam to liquefy the oil sands deposits, and a second transports liquefied bitumen out of the deposit. When the oil sands deposits are exhausted after a few decades, the pads are seeded with exotic grasses and legumes, and then abandoned. Currently, there are no regulations or protocols for reclaiming these mining pads to peatlands.

Restoration of disturbed or destroyed ecosystems must be informed by an understanding of the processes responsible for the assembly and structuring of plant, microbial, and animal communities. Reassembly of these communities follows a set of community assembly rules first developed by Diamond (1975). These rules include the size and structure of the local species pool, the abiotic environment, and interspecific

Restoration and Reclamation of Boreal Ecosystems, ed. Dale Vitt and Jagtar Bhatti. Published by Cambridge University Press. © Cambridge University Press 2012.

interactions. When areas have been disturbed to the point that none of the original soil structure, plant, or microbial communities remain, then ecological restoration must begin by locally establishing proper abiotic features and then introducing local species selected from the regional species pool; however, the fundamental issues here are how to identify critical states for the abiotic features and which of the species should be chosen. Once these initial decisions are made, the critical next step is whether these foundational species will establish, prosper, and develop an organic soil base. This young community may or may not resemble any historical community in the local area.

Novel ecosystems are ones in which species, structure, and/or functions are not similar to those present in historic ecosystems (Hobbs et al., 2006). Species composing these novel ecosystems may not be native to the area and may have functional properties different from historical ecosystems. Hobbs et al. (2009) also reviewed the concept of a "hybrid ecosystem," defined as "one that retains characteristics of the historic system but whose composition or function now lies outside of the historic ranges of variability." Unfortunately, the historic range of variability for ecosystems and their characteristics are rarely known (Landes et al., 1999). There is, however, one major exception to these important unknowns, and that is peatlands. Peatlands are ecosystems that accumulate organic material (peat) in which the records (proxies) of past species, past climate, and past environmental conditions are all preserved in the order in which they occurred. These deposits provide evidence of both the historic variability of the local ecosystem as well as its initiation and early formation. Thus, we have a detailed record of the species and the abiotic factors that occurred at the time of initiation that we can use to develop current restoration strategies for disturbed peatland ecosystems.

DEVELOPMENT OF THE WESTERN CANADIAN BOREAL LANDSCAPE

About 10,000–15,000 y (cal) BP, glaciers on the western Canadian landscape receded, leaving a landscape of young mineral soils that at first were largely devoid of vegetation, but were quickly revegetated by plants tolerating mineral soils. During the early Holocene, proglacial lakes, hummocky moraines, bedrock from the Canadian Shield, and deposits of till formed a complex matrix across the landscape. Vegetation cover included *Betula glandulosa*, *Populus*, *Salix*, *Juniperus*, herbs, and graminoids (MacDonald 1987a,b; Vance, 1986). Between about 9000 and 11,000 y (cal) BP, spruce forests began to dominate as far north as the MacKenzie Basin

(MacDonald, 1987b). Summer solar radiation reached its maximum about 11,000 y (cal) BP, and July temperatures remained about 1° C warmer than current temperatures until about 7500 y (cal) BP (MacDonald et al., 2006; Pisaric et al., 2003). Pollen-based reconstructions show drier-than-modern conditions in central Canada (Viau and Gajewski, 2009), and the diatom record at Otasan Lake in northeastern Alberta suggests low lake levels from 9200–8100 y (cal) BP (Prather and Hickman, 2000). Thus, the general early Holocene climate appears to have been somewhat warmer and drier than at present. Peatlands were rare, only developing through terrestrialization around infilling lakes. Between 8000 and 6000 y (cal) BP, modern upland vegetation established in northern Alberta (MacDonald, 1987a; Vance, 1986).

At the beginning of early Holocene warming at 11,500 y (cal) BP, peatland initiation increased dramatically across much of the global boreal region (MacDonald et al., 2006); however, a dry regional climate in western Canada limited peatland establishment to terrestrialization events surrounding lakes (Nicholson and Vitt, 1990). A sustained period of peatland initiation persisted worldwide until around 8000 y (cal) BP. However, peatland initiation in western Canada was delayed compared to other regions of the boreal forest, beginning only after 8000 y (cal) BP, despite the fact that the landscape was available for peat formation since deglaciation at around 15,000 y (cal) BP (Campbell et al., 2000). After 8000 y (cal) BP, the highest rates of peatland initiation were cyclic across the western Canadian boreal region, with paludified peatlands initiating during coeval warm periods in the North Atlantic (Yu et al., 2003). Thus, across the western boreal landscape of Canada, a region sensitive to drought (Hogg, 1997), extensive peatland development followed three periods of initiation events that followed a 1450-year interval of regional increases in moisture and temperature (Yu et al., 2003). In regions of the boreal landscape that are less sensitive to drought, these millennial scale oscillations and initiation responses are less evident, and since 8000 yr (cal) BP, overall peatland initiation events have decreased worldwide.

Across the western Canadian region (provinces of Alberta, Saskatchewan, and Manitoba) peatlands presently occupy 23% of the land base. These peatlands have largely initiated over the past 8000 years in response to climate oscillations that provided conditions suitable for swamping of upland, mineral soil areas, or localized sites occupying former shallow lakes. Macrofossil evidence from a number of sites (Bauer et al., 2003; Kubiw et al., 1989; Kuhry, 1997; Kuhry, et al., 1992; Nicholson and Vitt, 1990) shows three structural types of vegetation; however, these data are not sufficient to outline the exact

species that comprised the initial plant communities. The three structural types are: an emergent to aquatic environment identified by rem-
nants of *Chara*, snail shells, and emergent vascular plants such as *Typha*;
bryophytes are absent. Abundant herbaceous fragments characterize the
second structural type, especially Cyperaceae, with few or no bryophytes.
The third features abundant wood fragments, some rich fen bryophyte
species, occasional mesotrophic species of *Sphagnum*, and woody roots.
The first of these structural types represents terrestrialization or infilling of a shallow water body; the second represents a *Carex*-dominated
plant community on moist mineral soil, and the third represents a moist
wooded environment that is paludifying. None of these macrofossil data
sets provides sufficient information for us to determine the exact species
composition of these initializing early wetland communities.

Our challenges in boreal peatland restoration are to: (1) understand the environmental conditions necessary for peatland initiation; (2)
choose a suite of foundation species necessary for organic soil development; and (3) implement the sequence of events necessary for peatland
community development. Here we provide data that help address these
central challenges. Specifically, we discuss peatland initiation in northern Alberta and responses of a foundational species to substrate variability. We highlight results of a field experiment in its third year that is
investigating methods for establishing peatland plants on wet mineral
soils. These results underscore the importance of utilizing the historical
record in future reclamation procedures associated with anthropogenic
disturbances.

THE HISTORICAL PARADIGM AND PEATLAND INITIATION

Methods

We began a detailed study of peatland initiation by selecting 32 peatland sites in northeastern Alberta, Canada, between 54° and 57°N latitude and 116° and 111°W longitude. Sites consisted of seven bogs, 10
poor fens, six rich fens, four marshes, and five peatland sites on active
oil sands mines that could not be characterized with certainty. Sites
were classified using the vegetation criteria from the Alberta Wetland
Inventory Standards, Version 2.0 (Halsey et al., 2002). At each site, two
0.5-m long cores were taken at the peat/mineral soil interface using a
Macaulay peat corer, with an inner diameter of 4 cm. Cores were taken
to a depth 10 cm below the peat/mineral interface at randomly chosen positions within each site, and the two cores were spaced about

0.5 m apart. From each core, mineral soil and peat appearances were recorded before cutting. The core was then cut along the peat/mineral soil interface, which was identified by visual inspection; the division between organic peat soil and inorganic mineral soil in cores was clearly observable by sight. This interface was later confirmed by determining organic matter content of each sample. Both the mineral soil and the peat soil portions were sliced into 1-cm contiguous samples using a band saw. In general, 10 samples were mineral soil and 35–40 samples were organic soil. Mineral soil samples from one core from each of the 32 sites were combined in order to determine soil texture using the Bouyoucos hydrometer method (Dane and Topp, 2002; Gibson, 1980). Botanical content of the cores was determined by macrofossil components on cores from 27 sites using methods described by Bauer et al. (2003). For each peat sample, a 1-cm^3 plug was placed in a Plexiglas S-shaped channel template, and wetted with distilled water. Observations were made at 20–25X magnification without chemical treatment or sieving. Peat botanical composition, charcoal presence, and debris percentages were estimated. Charcoal, identified as black, shiny, and friable particles, was separated into two categories: large charcoal, 0.75–>2.00 mm, and fine charcoal, particles <0.75 mm. Debris was defined as fine organic particles, too small to identify as plant material, and obviously not sand or mineral soil. Debris varied in appearance with the particles both dark and light colored, dull-surfaced, and irregularly shaped. Debris content was then used to indicate levels of peat decomposition and/or changes in peat type within the peat column. When available, bryophyte and vascular plant fragments and seeds were identified to genus, and when possible, fragments, leaves, and seeds were identified to species. Vascular plant fragments and seeds were identified as described in Lévesque et al. (1988), and bryophytes were identified as described in Crum and Anderson (1981) for true mosses, and Crum and Anderson (1981), Daniels and Eddy (1985), and Vitt and Slack (1975) for *Sphagnum* mosses. To organize the core segments into groups, the macrofossil data were compared by cluster analysis performed with PC-ORD software, using a flexible beta method and Sørenson (Bray-Curtis) distance measure (McCune and Grace, 2002; McCune and Mefford, 1999).

Results and discussion

Underlying mineral soils were six soil texture types: loam, sandy clay, clay loam, silty loam, silty clay, and silt. Of the 32 sites, 38% had silty loam texture; 34% had medium loam texture; 13% had sandy clay texture; 9%

had clay loam texture; 3% had silty clay texture; and 3% had silt texture. Underlying soil textures did not differ between present day fens and bogs (P < 0.1057, χ^2 = 22.08, df = 15); however, bogs tended to have a higher percentage of sites with sandy clay loam (50% compared to 6% for fens), while fens had a higher number of sites with silty loam soils (31% versus 0% for bogs). Although there are peatlands that have formed on past proglacial lakebeds that dried during the early Holocene, none of our sites initiated on these clay substrates and no substrates contained more than 50% clay. Upland soils in northern Alberta are silty loam and sandy loam textures (Szwaluk and Strong, 2003; Tan et al. 2005) and are generally somewhat more coarse-textured than most of our wetland substrates. In summary, none of our 32 wetlands formed on clay substrates and soil textures, although in general, those finer than upland soils were highly variable.

Clustering of the 1-cm core segments yielded six macrofossil groups, each identified here by 1–2 indicators: (1) *Sphagnum*/debris, (2) *Sphagnum*, (3) charcoal, (4) *Carex*, (5) wood/woody shrub, and (6) debris/charcoal. Group 1 consists of samples that contained 30%–60% *Sphagnum*, and 20%–40% debris. Group 2 consists of samples that contained 40%–80% *Sphagnum* and <20% of any other individual macrofossil type. Group 3 consists of samples made up of 40%–80% charcoal and <15% of any individual macrofossil type. Group 4 consists of samples containing 40%–50% of the "plant bits" macrofossil type and particles that were not bryophyte, wood, or charcoal in origin. Group 5 consists of samples that contained 30%–60% woody parts, 20%–40% debris, and <15% of any other individual macrofossil type. Group 6 consists of samples that contained 20%–40% debris and 20%–40% charcoal, but <10% of any other individual category. In addition, Group 6 samples have less charcoal than Group 3, and more debris than any other macrofossil component.

All 27 cores exhibited a clear, sharp transition from mineral to organic soil, with the first 3 cm of organic soil above the mineral horizon having a mean percent organic matter content of 80%. Seventy percent of the sites began with the presence of charcoal or charcoal and debris, while 22% contained vascular plant remains; none had evidence of *Typha* or emergent plants. At 6 cm above the mineral/organic interface, only 48% of the sites had a charcoal presence, whereas 28% were vascular plant dominated and 24% *Sphagnum* dominated. At the 17/18 cm level, 50% of the sites were *Sphagnum* dominated, 45% vascular plant dominated and only one site (5%) had charcoal. There were no apparent differences between initiation of bogs, poor fens, and rich fens. Nearly all of the bog and fen sites had bryophyte dominance at 25 cm. Evidence of aquatic vegetation in the basal peat was present only at a single site and gyttja, an indication of the peatland having initiated in a pond or lake, was not observed in any of the 32 cores. Gyttja presence has been found in basal sediments from a few peatland sites that currently are associated with lakes (Bauer et al. 2003; Kubiw et al., 1989; Nicholson and Vitt, 1994); however, they rarely underlie large peatland expanses. The lack of gyttja and absence of aquatic vegetation at the peat–mineral interface suggest that terrestrialization was not involved in the initiation of these mid-boreal peatlands.

Charcoal is resistant to decay and almost certainly was concentrated in the lower portions of the cores; however, the very sharp transition from mineral to organic soil, and the early presence of terrestrial vascular plants (either sedges or shrubs/trees) strongly suggest a paludification scenario for the initiation of these peatlands. Although it is certainly possible that differential decay may have influenced the initial organic soil components, the lack of *Sphagnum* (and all bryophytes) at the 1-cm core level, followed by increases in bryophyte dominance in many of the cores in core segments at 2–6 cm, suggests that bryophytes are not common early colonizers of these sites. Here we demonstrate that paludification of mineral soils is a major mechanism of peatland initiation in northern Alberta. Bogs and fens have similar origins and succession to *Sphagnum* dominance is variable in core position in both fens and bogs.

HABITAT PARAMETERS OF A KEY FOUNDATION SPECIES

In order to initiate a successful reclamation, there should be a solid understanding of the mechanism of community assembly for the final ecosystem. Based on peat records from northern Alberta, paludification is the dominant mechanism of peatland initiation and owing to particular site hydrology and chemistry, a number of plant species could be involved. Macrofossil analysis of peat cores has found that one of the three types of early peatland communities comprised herbaceous plants, particularly Cyperaceae, with few or no bryophytes, growing on mineral soils. As the goal of reclamation has now become to initiate reclamation onto a mineral soil oil/gas pad, this early peatland type may be a viable option on which to base our community assembly. It is unknown which sedge species were present in these early peatland communities; thus current ecological knowledge of local sedges must be used to develop a community assemblage that could create a successional pathway toward a mature peatland. To date, one sedge has shown promise for this purpose because of its wide distribution and apparent broad range of ecological tolerances.

Water sedge (*Carex aquatilis* Wahlenb. var. *aquatilis*) has a circumboreal distribution and is a common sedge species in boreal peatlands (Ament, 1995; Bliss, 1988; Gignac et al., 2004; Hultén, 1968; McKendrick, 1987; Titus et al., 1999). *C. aquatilis* has adventitious roots that spread in a mat from the main plant, and exhibits a clumped stoloniferous growth form (Damman, 1963; Johnson et al., 1995). Plants vary in height from 15 to 150 cm tall (Johnson et al., 1995; USDA, 2009a,b). Mature plants have three to six fertile spikes on the main stem with male spikes always terminally located (Johnson et al., 1995). *C. aquatilis* is biannual and produces new rhizomatous shoots twice a year, in late summer and from winter to early spring (Bernard and Gorham, 1978; Gorham and Somers, 1973). Shoots have life spans ranging from 12 months to about 18 months. Mature shoots begin flowering around May to June, fruiting for the remainder of the summer, and are dead by early fall.

Because there are few data describing abiotic or biotic limitations to the distribution of *C. aquatilis*, environmental limitations to its local distribution are not well understood. From the available global environmental data, *C. aquatilis* has a wide range of tolerances for pH (3.0–8.5), conductivity (0–1522 μS) and Ca^{2+} concentration (0.2–146.6 mg L^{-1}), which would be consistent with a distribution in extreme rich fens, moderate rich fens, poor fens, bogs, and many disturbed sites (DuReitz, 1949; Gignac et al. 2004; Jeglum, 1971; Sjörs, 1952, 1961, 1963; Vitt and Slack, 1975; Vitt et al., 1975). In addition, *C. aquatilis* has been known to occur in a wide range of soil types, from sandy to clay soils, as well as peat as deep as 5 m (Chapin, 1981; Hansen et al., 1988; Lewis and Dowding, 1926; Pearce and Cordes, 1987). Although *C. aquatilis* is common in northern Alberta, there is only one known study that examined its range of tolerances in this region (Gignac et al., 2004).

Overall, much of the data available are inconsistent. Most studies describe patterns of *C. aquatilis* distribution in European peatlands, which differ from continental Canadian peatlands in their chemistry and both the type and magnitude of disturbance. Because *C. aquatilis* seems to have such a wide range of tolerances, it could be a good candidate for reclamation. Two studies were simultaneously conducted to assess the value of *C. aquatilis* as a pioneer species in boreal peatland reclamation in northern Alberta: one that quantified the range of *C. aquatilis* occurrence across several ecological variables, and a second that assessed *C. aquatilis* performance in a controlled reclamation experiment.

QUANTIFYING THE DISTRIBUTION OF THE FOUNDATIONAL
SPECIES *CAREX AQUATILIS*

Methods

A survey of a variety of wetland types was conducted throughout northern Alberta, Canada. Over two summers in 2008 and 2009, 64 sites were surveyed, including extreme rich fens, moderate rich fens, poor fens, disturbed sites, and marshes/wet meadows in order to represent wide ranges of ecological factors experienced by *C. aquatilis*. Sites were assigned to a priori groups using indicator species and other site characteristics (Sjörs, 1951; Slack et al., 1980; Vitt and Chee 1990; Vitt et al., 1975; Zoltai, 1976).

Restricted random plot placement was used to sample specific areas within sites, ensuring that the abundance of *C. aquatilis* was sampled in multiple mesohabitats within sites (Schlup and Wagner, 2008). In each plot, the percentage cover of all species present was estimated (nomenclature followed Moss (1983) for vascular plants and Vitt et al. (1988) for non-vascular plants). In the same plots, abiotic factors were measured including surface water pH, conductivity, water depth, and the percentage of organic matter of the substrate.

Surface water conductivity and pH, standardized to 25 °C, were measured in the field. Conductivity values were reduced for hydrogen ion concentrations (Sjörs, 1952). Water depth was measured from the base of the plant for six plants per plot; water levels below the base of the plant were given negative values, and where *C. aquatilis* was absent, depth was measured from the substrate surface. Substrate samples were collected from around plant roots, dried at 65 °C for three days, and processed via dry-ashing at 500 °C for the percentage of organic matter (OM) content (Harden et al., 2004).

Nonmetric multidimensional scaling (NMDS) was performed with DECODA 3.01 using site averages of community data to visualize site–level associations (Minchin, 2004). Analysis of similarity (ANOSIM) of a priori groups was performed with DECODA to determine whether the assigned groups were distinct. Vector fitting of environmental data was performed to determine which factors were related to community assemblages. Centroid analysis was performed with DECODA to calculate the mean ordination location for all species. Spearman's rank correlation analyses were run comparing the percentage cover of *C. aquatilis* with the environmental variables (SAS 9.1.3 2002). Data were analyzed at the plot level to account for within-site variability.

Table 5.1. *Strength of dissimilarity (r-values) between groups and P-values indicating whether groups were significantly distinct*

	Extreme rich fen	Moderate rich fen	Poor fen	Marsh/wet meadow
Moderate rich fen	0.33			
	($P = 0.0037$)			
Poor fen	0.97	0.42		
	($P < 0.0001$)	($P < 0.0001$)		
Marsh/wet meadow	0.49	0.56	0.97	
	($P = 0.0009$)	($P < 0.0001$)	($P < 0.0001$)	
Disturbed sites	0.08	0.22	0.67	−0.02
	($P = 0.2568$)	($P = 0.0016$)	($P < 0.0001$)	($P = 0.5562$)

Results and discussion

Community data

The extreme rich fen, moderate rich fen, poor fen, and marsh/wet meadow site types were clustered in the ordination, indicating that the community compositions of these groups were distinctive (Figure 5.1A); ANOSIM confirmed the distinction of these groups (Table 5.1). The disturbed sites were the most variable and scattered throughout the ordination, indicating greater variability in community composition than the other site types. Disturbed sites were not a distinct group. Centroid analysis showed that *C. aquatilis* was located at the center of the ordination, indicating a lack of association to any of the site types (Figure 5.1B).

Environmental factors associated with community structure were pH ($P < 0.0001$), conductivity ($P = 0.048$), and the percentage of organic matter of the substrate ($P < 0.0001$). In the ordination, vector analysis showed that pH increased as sites transitioned from poor fens to moderate rich fens, to extreme rich fens, and finally to the more eutrophic marshes and wet meadows (Figure 5.1B). Reduced conductivity increased from the cation-poor peatland sites to the marshes/wet meadows and disturbed sites. The percentage of organic matter increased from marshes/wet meadows and some of the disturbed sites to peatland sites. The *C. aquatilis* vector was not significant ($P = 0.78$).

Carex aquatilis was not associated with any of the defined site types, primarily because *C. aquatilis* was fairly ubiquitous and, in fact, the most abundant species overall. This is likely due to sampling bias for sites

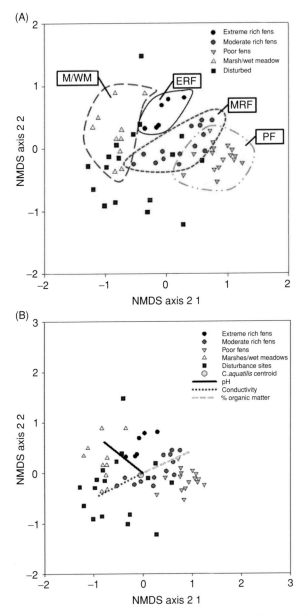

Figure 5.1. (**A**) Nonmetric multidimensional scaling (NMDS) ordination of surveyed sites, stress = 0.182. Outlined clusters are true groups. (**B**) NMDS ordination plotting the ordination centroid for *Carex aquatilis* and significant ecological vectors.

containing *C. aquatilis*. The omnipresence of *C. aquatilis* could be due to its role as a dominant species in disturbed sites, as many sites were affected by some degree of disturbance; however, the four site types that were relatively undisturbed did form separate clusters in the ordination and were found to be distinct site types. Therefore it seems more likely that *C. aquatilis* is actually adapted to a wide variety of habitats and thus has wide ranges of tolerance.

Environmental data

Because absence from plots could occur for a variety of reasons, all plots were graphed, but correlations were only performed with plots where *C. aquatilis* was present. Relationships between percentage cover and both pH (P = 0.0701, r = 0.12) and reduced conductivity (P = 0.1512, r = 0.10) were not significant. Of the plots where *C. aquatilis* was present, the pH range was from 3.1 to 9.2 and the reduced conductivity ranged from 36 μS to 8820 μS, which are also the pH and conductivity ranges of all the surveyed plots. Most absences occurred where pH was between 5.7 and 7.0, but two plots where *C. aquatilis* was absent had pH ≤ 4. Many more plots in both ranges contained an abundance of *C. aquatilis*. The reduced conductivity where *C. aquatilis* was absent ranged from 60 μS to 6380 μS, but most absences occurred in plots with reduced conductivity values below 609 μS. As with pH, many more plots in this range contained *C. aquatilis*.

From the vegetation surveys, *C. aquatilis* has been shown to be a common species in a variety of habitat types. As such, it has a wide range of tolerance for a variety of environmental factors, particularly the percentage of organic carbon content of the substrate, pH, and reduced conductivity. In the plots surveyed, *C. aquatilis* plants were observed growing on sites with pH and reduced conductivity values representative of the full range of peatland types, as well as more eutrophic sites (Chee and Vitt, 1989; Gorham et al, 1987; Sjörs, 1952). *Carex aquatilis* has thus far been documented in sites where pH was as low as 3.0 and as high as 7.9; therefore, this study has increased the upper end of the known pH range (Jeglum, 1971). Prior studies have also documented the upper end of the conductivity range as 1522 μS (DuReitz, 1949; Gignac et al., 2004; Sjörs, 1952, 1952, 1961, 1963; Vitt and Slack, 1975; Vitt et al., 1975); while this study found *C. aquatilis* in sites where conductivity was as high as 8820 μS.

The correlation between water depth and percentage cover was significant (P = 0.0114, r = 0.17; Figure 5.2A). Of all surveyed plots, water table depth ranged from −80 to 80 cm from the base of the plant, and *C. aquatilis* occurred in plots where water table depth ranged from −80 cm

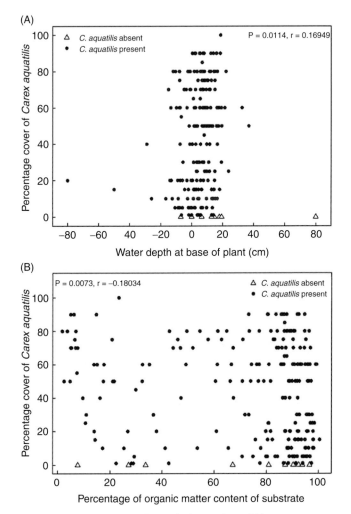

Figure 5.2. Spearman's rank correlation analyses (**A**) between percentage cover of *C. aquatilis* and mean plot water depth (P = 0.0114), and (**B**) between plot percentage cover of *C. aquatilis* and the percentage of organic matter of the substrate (P = 0.0073). Values where *C. aquatilis* was present and where it was absent are plotted separately.

below to 37 cm above the base of the plant. The majority of plots where *C. aquatilis* was present were within the range of −20 to 20 cm. There are no previous data that indicate a range of tolerance for water depth; therefore, these data report the first observed range. Although there was not a significant correlation between water table depth and percentage cover of *C. aquatilis* when all sites were included, other factors could be responsible for the absence of *C. aquatilis*. When sites with no *C. aquatilis* were excluded, a positive correlation was seen between water table depth and percentage cover. *Carex aquatilis* prefers wetter sites, but it was found in much drier sites in which the water level was 80 cm below the base of the plant, and sites where the water was deeper than 37 cm had no *C. aquatilis* present. Most sites in which *C. aquatilis* was present ranged in depth from approximately −20 cm to 20 cm, but the entire range in which *C. aquatilis* was observed growing was from −80 cm to 37 cm. Because this tolerance range has never before been reported, it is unknown whether there was site selection bias for sites that were more accessible or whether this is a true estimate of the water depth tolerance of *C. aquatilis*.

There was a negative correlation between the percentage of OM of the substrate and *C. aquatilis* abundance (P = 0.007, r = −0.18, Figure 5.2B). *Carex aquatilis* was observed growing where the concentration of OM ranged from 1.8% to 100%, or from mineral soil to peat. Most plots where *C. aquatilis* was absent had a concentration of OM higher than 65%.

Carex aquatilis has been documented as being tolerant of a wide range of soil types, including sand, clay, and peat (Chapin, 1981; Hansen et al., 1988; Lewis and Dowding, 1926; Pearce and Cordes, 1987). While this study did not examine soil texture, *C. aquatilis* was found to be established on sites with various levels of OM. In this study, *C. aquatilis* percentage cover was negatively correlated to the concentration of OM of the substrate, indicating that it is less abundant on peat substrates. This correlation is weak (r = −0.13) and probably indicates that *C. aquatilis* is a generalist in terms of soil type.

Implications for reclamation

Oil sands-related disturbances create extreme and novel environmental conditions that must be within the ranges of tolerance for plant species that are expected to establish. Because the reestablishment of a mosaic of upland and peatland ecosystems on the abandoned disturbed sites is ideal, identifying native peatland plants with high tolerances for these conditions will be essential for effective wetland reclamation. *Carex aquatilis* is believed to be an ideal pioneer species of disturbed landscapes because it can establish by seed and spread rhizomatously, it grows on a variety of substrate types, and it has been shown to have a wide range of tolerances for environmental conditions in both European and Canadian peatlands. The lack of association to a particular type of peatland or disturbed site demonstrates the wide range of environmental tolerances of *C. aquatilis*, which was confirmed by the environmental data.

In SAGD mined areas, the primary reclamation constraints are the lack of peat substrate, completely altered hydrology, and water chemistry. This study found that *C. aquatilis* was present on substrates ranging from 1% to 100% OM concentration, indicating that this plant should be able to reestablish onto the mineral soil pads that remain after SAGD mining if water levels and chemistry are suitable. *Carex aquatilis* was present across wide ranges of other environmental variables including pH (3.1–9.2), conductivity (36–8820 µS), and water depth (−80 to 36 cm). These data indicate that *C. aquatilis* should be able to tolerate the conditions present after oil sands mining and exploration.

YEAR THREE PLANT RESPONSES TO PEATLAND RECLAMATION ON MINERAL SOILS

Methods for peatland reclamation on mineral soils

We initiated this study to determine whether selected foundational species, including *C. aquatilis*, could establish on mineral soils and return structure and function to the disturbed landscape. The study area is located 50 km east of Peace River, Alberta (56°23N, 116°46W) near Shell Canada's Carmin Creek *in situ* plant. In the summer of 2007, we selected two 20-year-old mineral soil-filled well sites within a peatland complex, designated pads 12 and 16 by Shell. The pads were decommissioned in 2000 and are approximately 100 m × 100 m with 1–2 m of clay fill on top of bog organic soil. Both pads were planted with *Melilotus alba* and *M. officinalis*.

Our overall design is hierarchical, with planting nested within amendment, within cultivation within water level, within pad. One pad was fertilized (10:10:10) and the other was not, and as there were only two pads available to us, we do not have replication at the pad (fertilization level). For an experiment of this scale though, replication at this treatment level would have been undesirable (Hurlburt, 1994). Amendments were arrayed across pads in a Latin rectangle design to account for spatial differences across pads.

In August 2007, an area of about 30 m × 100 m on each pad was leveled to near natural water table elevation of the bog. Following this rough grading, pads were divided into two 30 m × 50 m areas; one graded to 4–6 cm above seasonal water level (referred to as wet) and the other to about 15 cm above seasonal water level (referred to as dry). Within each water level treatment area, three ditches about 20 cm deep were dug to increase water contact within mineral soils. Soils were saturated and inundated by shallow waters during spring runoff.

The following spring, we installed 192 2 m × 2 m plots on each pad, each separated by a distance of 1 m, and installed boardwalks between all plots. Each water level was divided into a cultivated section and a non-cultivated section (each with 48 plots). The 2 m × 2 m plots were treated with one of six amendments: commercial peat, stockpiled peat, slough hay, woodchips, landscape fabric, or control (no amendments). Each amendment was replicated six times within the water level/cultivation block. On pad 16, 30 g of 10:10:10 fertilizer was added in the spring of 2008, 2009, and again in 2010 and 2011 to each plot. Each 2 m × 2 m plot was divided into four 1 m × 1 m plots that received different planting treatments. One subplot remained an unplanted control; a second was planted with nine C. aquatilis plants; a third was planted with four C. aquatilis plants and five Salix lutea plants; and the fourth was planted with three C. aquatilis, three S. lutea, and three Larix laricina plants (in 2009).

Over the summers of 2008 and 2009, we monitored the health and reproduction of the original C. aquatilis plants that were planted in June of 2008, and found that the original 16 plants had increased to an average of 58 plants per 2 m × 2 m plot. Because C. aquatilis is a biannual plant, by 2010 the original shoots planted had died off, so we quantified health within 1 m × 1 m subplots as percentage cover of C. aquatilis in that area. Relative plot wetness was also quantified using a "wetness index." Plots that were completely dry with cracked soil were given values of −2, plots where water was at the soil surface were given values of 0, and depth was measured for plots with standing water. Larix and Salix plants were also monitored, but these results will not be discussed here. Year one and year two results are presented in Vitt et al. (2011), whereas in the present chapter we focus on the results for year three.

Peatland reclamation on mineral soils: results and discussion

Both 2009 and 2010 were abnormally dry years compared to 2008 and water levels at both pads were lower than those in 2008. Overall, on our wetness scale (see Methods), mean 2008 wetness was −1.35 compared to a mean of −1.18 in 2010 (for all sites over both pads). Despite these dry conditions, C. aquatilis continued to perform well, achieving up to 60%–80% cover in some plots (median cover for all plots was 20%). For 2010, water levels varied on our wetness scale from a dryness of −2.0 to a wetness of +1.6 (median −1.1); however, almost 93% of the plots had wetness values of −1.5 to −1.0; thus water levels during dry conditions became remarkably uniform (Figure 5.3A,B). *Carex aquatilis* cover was quite variable (from 8% to 81%), but plots with greater than 30% cover occurred almost exclusively in plots with intermediate wetness values (from −1.5 to −1.0; Figure 5.4), suggesting that for best growth response neither extremely dry nor extremely wet conditions are favorable.

On pad 16 (fertilized), the mean percentage cover of *C. aquatilis* was highest in control subplots and lowest in the woodchip and hay subplots. In general, wet plots had a slightly higher percentage cover than dry plots (Figure 5.5A). Furthermore, dry plots showed somewhat less variation between amendments than wet plots. In both wet and dry plots, control plots had among the highest percentage cover of all the amendments. The lowest percentage covers were in the dry bagged peat plots and wet woodchip plots. The percentage cover of *C. aquatilis* was lowest on the dry side of pad 16. Pad 16 also exhibited greater variation in percentage cover between the different amendments than did pad 12 (Figure 5.5B).

Moving toward practical application: seeding and germination success in 2009

In 2009, we also initiated a broadcast seeding experiment to determine whether *C. aquatilis* would establish by seed, and whether a peat amendment was required for germination. *Carex aquatilis* seeds were collected in a roadside ditch near pad 16 in mid May 2009. Three blank 4 m² plots were selected on the wet side of pad 16 and two 4 m² plots were selected on the wet side of pad 12. Half of each plot was covered with approximately 4 cm of stockpiled peat left over from the initial reclamation site set up. Each plot half was divided into 2 halves (1 m²): one had 5 ml (approximately 600 seeds) of *Carex aquatilis* seeds scattered across it, and one had no seeds added.

In July 2010, plots were reassessed by counting the number of *Carex aquatilis* shoots that resulted from seeds in each subplot. Shoots that obviously resulted from vegetative propagation from older shoots were not counted. In addition, the weeds present in each subplot were identified and percent cover was estimated.

Seeding experiment results and discussion

The number of *C. aquatilis* plants did not differ between peat and mineral soil subplots (P = 0.58). Subplots with seeds added had more *C. aquatilis*

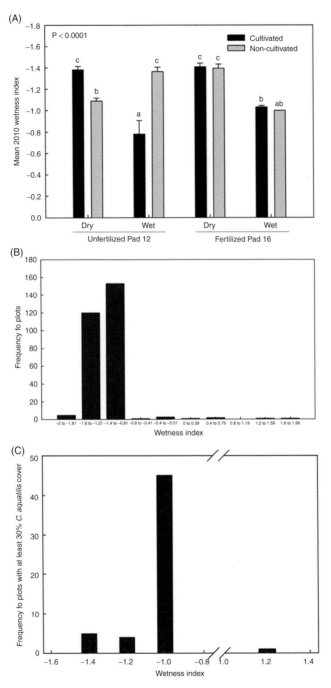

Figure 5.3. (**A**) Mean wetness index values for 2010 across all treatments. Error bars represent standard deviation. (**B**) Frequency histogram of wetness index for all plots. (**C**) Frequency histogram of wetness indices in plots with *C. aquatilis* percentage cover ≥30%.

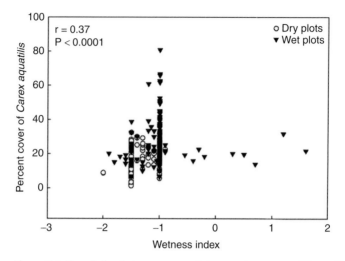

Figure 5.4. Correlation between mean plot percentage cover of *C. aquatilis* and mean plot wetness index with wet and dry plots highlighted.

plants than subplots with no added seeds (P = 0.0002; Figure 5.6A). Subplots with a peat substrate had double the species richness of weeds than subplots with mineral soil (P = 0.0004; Figure 5.6B). The results of this study indicate that broadcast seeding could be used to introduce *C. aquatilis* to mineral soil pads after SAGD mining. Seeds were able to germinate on both the mineral soil and peat substrates. In addition, weed species richness was higher in the subplots with stockpiled peat present. This indicates that stockpiled peat is not necessary for *C. aquatilis* establishment, and instead, primarily serves as a vector of weed propagules.

SUMMARY

In summary, exploration and production of oil and gas in Alberta continues to expand, with more wells drilled each year. Many of these are abandoned without reclamation, especially those located on organic soils. Development of peatland reclamation techniques has lagged behind those of other landscape types. Here we argue that establishment of peat-forming vegetation on mineral soils left from oil/gas activities requires knowledge of basic natural processes–processes that have clues present in Alberta's natural peat deposits. From these clues we propose, first, that local conditions for fen initiation can be established by emulating paludification through providing proper water levels. Second, we argue that it is fundamental to establish the foundation species of fens, which

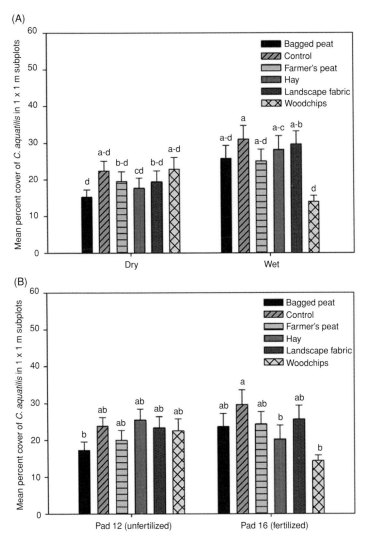

Figure 5.5. (A) Effects of water level and amendment (P = 0.0009), and (B) of pad and amendment (P = 0.0153) on percentage cover of *C. aquatilis* in July 2010. Bars are means of 1 × 1 m subplots, error bars are calculated standard errors, and letters represent significant differences between means calculated by Tukey's HSD.

is accomplished by a thorough knowledge of the natural responses of individual species. Third, as the site develops, the establishment of additional species diversity is of key importance, and the development of a healthy soil microbial flora that is comparable to local benchmarks is

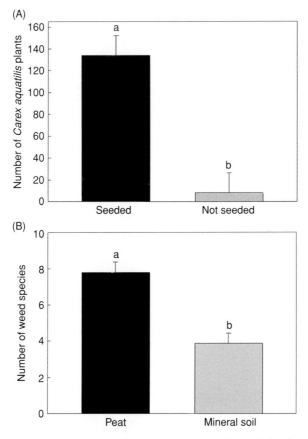

Figure 5.6. (**A**) Number of *C. aquatilis* plants in the seeded and unseeded subplots P = 0.0002). (**B**) Weed species richness in the peat and mineral soil subplots (P = 0.0004).

required. From an application perspective, we have shown here that at least one foundation species can be introduced to the reclamation site through locally collected and dispersed seeds.

REFERENCES

Ament, R. J. (1995). Pioneer plant communities five years after the 1988 Yellowstone fires. Thesis, Montana State University, Bozeman, MT.
Bauer, I. E. Gignac, L. D., Vitt, D. H. (2003). Development of a peatland complex in boreal western Canada: lateral site expansion and local variability in vegetation succession and long-term peat accumulation. *Canadian Journal of Botany*, **81**, 833–847.

Bernard, J. M. and Gorham, E. (1978). Life history aspects of primary production in sedge wetlands. In R. E. Good, D. F. Whigham, R. L. Simpson, eds., *Freshwater Wetlands*. New York, NY: Academic Press, Inc., pp. 39–51.

Bliss, L. C. (1988). Arctic tundra and polar desert biome. In M. G. Barbour and W. D. Billings, eds., *North American Terrestrial Vegetation*. Cambridge, UK: Cambridge University Press, pp. 1–32.

Campbell, I. D., Campbell, C., Yu, Z. C., Vitt, D. H., Apps, M. J. (2000). Millennial-scale rhythms in peatlands in the western interior of Canada and in the global carbon cycle. *Quaternary Research*, **54**, 155–158.

Chapin, F. S. (1981). Field measurements of growth and phosphate absorption in *Carex aquatilis* along a latitudinal gradient. *Arctic and Alpine Research*, **13**, 83–94.

Chee, W. L. and Vitt, D. H. (1989). The vegetation, surface water chemistry and peat chemistry of moderate rich fens in central Alberta, Canada. *Wetlands*, **9**, 227–257.

Crum, H. and Anderson L. (1981). *Mosses of Eastern North America*. New York, NY: Columbia University Press.

Damman, A. W. H. (1963). *Key to the Carex species of Newfoundland by Vegetative Characteristics*. Department of Forestry Publication 1017, Ottawa, ON.

Dane, J. H. and Topp, G. C., eds. (2002). *Methods of Soil Analysis Part 4, Physical Methods*. Series #5 edn. Soil Science Society of America, Inc., Madison, WI.

Daniels, R. E. and Eddy, A. (1985). *Handbook of European Sphagna*. Institute of Terrestrial Ecology, Abbots Ripton, Huntingdon, UK.

Diamond, J. M. (1975). Assembly of species communities. In M. L. Cody and J. M. Diamond, eds., *Ecology and Evolution of Communities*. Cambridge, MA: Harvard University Press.

DuReitz, G. E. (1949). Huvudenheter och huvugranser i svensk myrvegetation. *Svenska Botaniska Tidskrift*, **43**, 274–309.

Gibson, D., ed. (1980). *Soil Analysis Manual*. UCNW, Bangor, Wales.

Gignac, L. D., Gauthier, R., Rochefort, L., Bubler, J. (2004). Distribution and habitat niches of 37 peatland Cyperaceae species across a broad geographic range in Canada. *Canadian Journal of Botany*, **82**, 1292–1313.

Gorham, E., Janssens, J. A., Wheeler, G. A., Glaser, P. H. (1987). The natural and anthropogenic acidification of peatlands. In T. C. Hutchinson and K. M. Meema, eds., *Effects of Atmospheric Pollutants on Forests, Wetlands and Agricultural Ecosystems*, Berlin: Springer-Verlag, pp. 493–510.

Gorham, E. and Somers, M. G. (1973). Seasonal changes in the standing crop of two montane sedges. *Canadian Journal of Botany*, **51**, 1097–1108.

Halsey, L., Vitt, D. H., Beilman, D., et al. (2002). *Alberta Wetlands Inventory Standards*, Version 2.0. National Wetlands Working Group, Edmonton, AB.

Halsey, L. A., Vitt, D. H., Zoltai, S. (1997). Climatic and physiographic controls on wetland type and distribution in Manitoba, Canada. *Wetlands*, **17**, 243–262.

Hansen, P. L., Chadde, S. W., Pfister, R. D. (1988). *Riparian Dominance Types of Montana*. Miscellaneous Publication No. 49. Missoula, MT: University of Montana, School of Forestry, Montana Forest and Conservation Experiment Station.

Harden, J. W., Neff, J. C., Sandberg, D. V., et al. (2004). Chemistry of burning the forest floor during the FROSTFIRE experimental burn, interior Alaska, 1999. *Global Biogeochemical Cycles*, **18**, GB3014.

Hobbs, R. J., Arico, S., Aronson, J., et al. (2006). Novel ecosystems: theoretical and management aspects of the new ecological world order. *Global Ecology and Biogeography*, **15**, 1–7.

Hobbs, R. J., Higgs, E., Harris, J. A. (2009). Novel ecosystems: implications for conservation and restoration. *Trends in Ecology and Evolution*, **24**, 599–605.

Hogg, E. H. (1997). Temporal scaling of moisture and the forest-grassland boundary in western Canada. *Agricultural and Forest Meteorology*, **84**, 115–122.

Hultén, E. (1968). *Flora of Alaska and Neighboring Territories: a Manual of the Vascular Plants*. Stanford, CA: Stanford University Press, pp. 250–251.

Hurlburt, S. H. (1994). Pseudoreplication and the design of ecological field experiments. *Ecological Monographs*, **54**, 187–211.

Jeglum, J. K. (1971). Plant indicators of pH and water level in peatlands at Candle Lake, Saskatchewan. *Canadian Journal of Botany*, **49**, 1661–1676.

Johnson, D., Kershaw, L., MacKinnon, A., et al. (1995). *Plants of the Western Boreal Forest and Aspen Parkland*. Edmonton, AB: Lone Pine Publishing, pp. 227–243.

Kubiw, H., Hickman, M., Vitt, D. H. (1989). The developmental history of peatlands at Muskiki and Marguerite lakes, Alberta. *Canadian Journal of Botany*, **67**, 3534–3544.

Kuhry, P. (1997). The palaeoecology of a treed bog in western boreal Canada: a study based on microfossils, macrofossils and physico-chemical properties. *Review of Paleobotany and Palynology*, **96**, 183–224.

Kuhry, P., Halsey, L. A., Bayley, S. E., Vitt, D. H. (1992). Peatland development in relation to Holocene climate-change in Manitoba and Saskatchewan (Canada). *Canadian Journal of Earth Sciences*, **29**, 1070–1090.

Landres, P. B., Morgan, P., Swanson, F. J. (1999). Overview of the use of natural variability concepts in managing ecological systems. *Ecological Applications*, **9**, 1179–1188.

Lévesque, P., Dinel, H., Larouche, A. (1988). *Guide to the Identification of Plant Macrofossils in Canadian Peatlands*. Ottawa, ON: Canadian Government Publishing Centre.

Lewis, F. J. and Dowding, E. S. (1926). The vegetation and retrogressive changes of peat areas ("muskegs") in central Alberta. *Journal of Ecology*, **14**, 317–341.

MacDonald, G. M. (1987a). Postglacial vegetation history of the Mackenzie River Basin. *Quaternary Research*, **28**, 245–262.

MacDonald, G. M. (1987b). Postglacial development of the subalpine-boreal transition forest of western Canada. *Journal of Ecology*, **75**, 303–320.

MacDonald, G. M., Beilman, D. W., Kremenetski, K. V., et al. (2006). Rapid early development of circumarctic peatlands and atmospheric CH4 and CO2 variations. *Science*, **314**, 285–288.

McCune, B. and Grace, J. (2002). *Analysis of Ecological Communities*. MjM Software Design, Gleneden Beach, OR.

McCune, B. and Mefford, M. (1999). *PCORD*. MjM Software Design, Gleneden Beach, OR.

McKendrick, J. D. (1987). Plant succession on disturbed sites, North Slope, Alaska, USA. *Arctic and Alpine Research*, **19**, 554–565.

Minchin, P. (2004). *DECODA*. ANUTECH Pty. Ltd., Canberra, Australia.

Moss, E. H. (1983). *Flora of Alberta*, 2nd edn. J. G. Packer, ed. Toronto, ON: University of Toronto Press Inc.

Nicholson, B. J. and Vitt, D. H. (1990). The paleoecology of a peatland complex in continental western Canada. *Canadian Journal of Botany*, **68**, 121–138.

Nicholson, B. J. and Vitt, D. H. (1994). Wetland development at Elk Island National Park, Alberta, Canada. *Journal of Paleolimnology*, **12**, 19–34.

Pearce, C. M. and Cordes, L. D. (1987). Plant distribution and vegetation dynamics in northern wetlands: examples from the Mackenzie Delta, N.W.T. In C. D. A. Rudec and R. P. Overend, compilers. Symposium '87: *Wetlands/peatlands Proceedings*, Edmonton, AB, Canada. Ottawa, ON: Canadian National Committee, International Peat Society, pp. 475–482.

Pisaric, M. F. J., Holt, C., Szeicz, J. M., Karst, T., Smol, J. P. (2003). Holocene tree-line dynamics in the mountains of northeastern British Columbia, Canada, inferred from fossil pollen and stomata. *Holocene*, **13**, 161–173.

Prather, C. and Hickman, M. (2000). History of a presently slightly acidic lake in northeastern Alberta, Canada as determined through analysis of the diatom record. *Journal of Paleolimnology*, **24**, 183–198.

Schlup, B. M. and Wagner, H. H. (2008). Effects of study design and analysis on the spatial community structure detected by multiscale ordination. *Journal of Vegetation Science*, **19**, 621–632.

Sjörs, H. (1952). On the relation between vegetation and electrolytes in North Swedish mire waters. *Oikos*, **2**, 241–258.

Sjörs, H. (1961). Surface patterns in boreal peatlands. *Endeavor*, **20**, 217–224.

Sjörs, H. (1963). *Bogs and Fens on the Attawapiskat River, Northern Ontario*. National Museum of Canada Bulletin 186, Contributions to Botany, 1960–1961, Ottawa, ON.

Slack, N. G., Vitt, D. H., Horton, D. G. (1980). Vegetation gradients of minerotrophically rich fens in western Alberta. *Canadian Journal of Botany*, **58**, 330–350.

Statistical Analysis Software (SAS). Version 9.1.3. (2002). SAS Institute Inc., Cary, NC.

Szwaluk, K. S. and Strong, W. L. (2003). Near-surface soil characteristics and understory plants as predictors of *Pinus contorta* site index in southwestern Alberta, Canada. *Forest Ecology and Management*, **176**, 13–24.

Tan, X., Chang, S. X., Kabzems, R. (2005). Effects of soil compaction and forest floor removal on soil microbial properties and N transformations in a boreal forest long-term soil productivity study. *Forest Ecology and Management*, **217**, 158–170.

Titus, J. H., Titus, P. J., del Moral, R. (1999). Wetland development in primary and secondary successional substrates fourteen years after the eruption of Mount St. Helens, Washington, USA. *Northwest Science*, **73**, 186–204.

United States Department of Agriculture (USDA). (2009a). Fire Effects Information System. Address: <http://www.fs.fed.us/database/feis/plants/graminoid/caraqu/all.html> (Accessed Feb 26, 2009).

United States Department of Agriculture (USDA). (2009b). USDA Plant Database. Address: <http://plants.usda.gov/index.html> (Accessed May 15, 2008).

Vance, R. E. (1986). Pollen stratigraphy of Eaglenest Lake, northeastern Alberta. *Canadian Journal of Earth Science*, **23**, 11–20.

Viau, A. E. and Gajewski, K. (2009). Reconstructing millennial-scale, regional paleoclimates of boreal Canada during the Holocene. *Journal of Climate*, **22**, 316–330.

Vitt, D. H., Achuff, P., Andrus, R. E. (1975). The vegetation and chemical properties of patterned fens in the Swan Hills, north central Alberta. *Canadian Journal of Botany*, **53**, 2776–2795.

Vitt, D. H. and Chee, W. L. (1990). The relationships of vegetation to surface-water chemistry and peat chemistry in fens of Alberta, Canada. *Vegetatio*, **89**, 87–106.

Vitt, D. H., Marsh, J. E., Bovey, R. B. (1988). *Mosses, Lichens and Ferns of Northwest North America*. Edmonton, AB: Lone Pine Publishing.

Vitt, D. H. and Slack, N. G. (1975). An analysis of the vegetation of *Sphagnum*-dominated kettle-hole bogs in relation to environmental gradients. *Canadian Journal of Botany*, **53**, 332–359.

Vitt, D. H., Wieder, R. K., Xu, B., Koropchak, S. (2011). Peatland establishment on mineral soils: effects of water level, amendments, and species after two growing seasons. *Ecological Engineering*, **37**, 354–363.

Yu, Z. C., Campbell, I. D., Campbell, C., et al. (2003) Carbon sequestration in western Canadian peat highly sensitive to Holocene wet-dry climate cycles at millennial timescales. *Holocene*, **13**, 801–808.

Zoltai, S. C. (1976). Wetlands classification. Proceedings of the 1st meeting of the Canadian Committee on Ecological (Bio-physical) Land Classification, Petawawa, ON. Petawawa National Forestry Institute, Chalk River, ON, pp. 61–71.

Part II   The challenges of reclamation
          in boreal ecosystems

6

Advances in oil sands tailings handling: building the base for reclamation

INTRODUCTION

On average, about two tons of oil sands are required to produce a barrel of bitumen. The complexity of tailings management is largely due to the difficulties in managing the enormous volumes of material involved. Each barrel of bitumen produced also requires the use of two tons of water in the extraction process (Alberta Chamber of Resources, 2004; Fine Tailings Fundamentals Consortium, 1995; Kasperski, 1992). This represents approximately 12.5 barrels of water per barrel of bitumen. An oil sands operation extracting 250,000 barrels of bitumen per day requires 182 Mm^3 of water and 182 megatons of ore annually. Figures 6.1 and 6.2 illustrate some of these volumes and the associated mineral distributions. It can be seen from Figure 6.1 that, after recovery of the bitumen, there is a bulking factor of about 1.4, which means that the resulting tailings or reject material (the sand and fluid tailings) occupies approximately 1.4 times the volume of the original oil sands and would not fit back into the space left from the mining operation. It can also be seen from Figure 6.1 that most of the water used in the extraction process is recovered and recycled. These volumes do not include the significant volumes of overburden and original soil horizons that are removed and stored for future reclamation. The significant advances that the oil sands industry has made in reclamation of treed landscapes have largely been on overburden deposits, and not on process-affected tailings.

In general, there are three oil sands tailings streams: coarse or sand tailings from the primary bitumen separation step, fine tailings (silts and clays) from the secondary and/or tertiary bitumen recovery step,

Restoration and Reclamation of Boreal Ecosystems, ed. Dale Vitt and Jagtar Bhatti. Published by Cambridge University Press. © Cambridge University Press 2012.

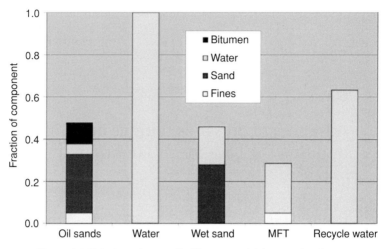

Figure 6.1. Relative volumes of tailings material (wet sand and mature fine tailings [MFT]) for a conventional tailings management scenario.

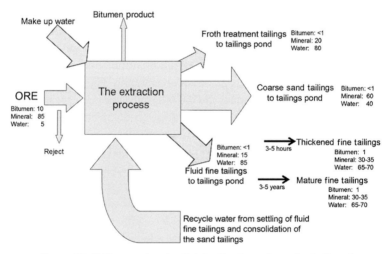

Figure 6.2. Tailings and water distribution in surface-mined oil sands.

and froth treatment tailings. The nature of these tailings streams can be very different depending upon the properties of the ore body being mined and the tailings management options that each operator chooses to use. The oil sands industry uses a convention whereby "sand" is defined as mineral particles larger than 44 μm and "fines" as mineral particles smaller than 44 μm. Coarse tailings from the primary separation step are usually transported hydraulically to the tailings area using the fluid fine tailings from secondary flotation and froth treatment as a carrier fluid. Figure 6.2 shows the properties of these streams schematically. The fluid fine tailings can be handled in two distinct ways, depending upon the tailings management system in place. Figure 6.2 depicts the fluid fine tailings going to either a recycle water pond or tailings pond and reaching 30–50 wt% solids in three to five years. Alternatively, they can be sent to a thickener which, with appropriate chemical intervention, can achieve 25–30 wt% solids in just hours, allowing for the return of hot water to the extraction process. The long-term accumulated volumes of tailings are similar for either scenario, as are the tailings management options.

The froth treatment tailings are a relatively small stream, but are environmentally significant because of the solvent that is used to separate the bitumen from the sand and silt minerals, and the water in the bitumen froth or concentrate (Afara et al., 2010; Kasperski et al., 2010). Some operators keep this tailings stream separate from the bulk of the tailings while others combine all three into a single tailings deposition area or recycle water pond. In this outline of new tailings technologies, it is assumed that the froth treatment tailings are simply a part of the total tailings.

The overburden from the mining operation or sand from the tailings is compacted to form the dikes used to contain the fluid fine tailings and the water for the extraction process. The fluid fine tailings settle over time to provide water that is recycled back to the extraction process, and the resulting settled fine tailings accumulate in the bottom of the recycle water pond. As noted earlier, in most mine plans, it is assumed that in three to five years, the fluid fine tailings will concentrate to about 30% or 35% solids (at which time they are sometimes referred to as mature fine tailings or MFT), but no further. As the volumes of fluid fine tailings have accumulated over the years, an increasing number of tailings ponds have been required to accommodate the increased volume of fluid tailings and the recycle water required for extraction. As can be seen in Figure 6.1, the volume of MFT is approximately 1.5 times that of the bitumen produced (Alberta Chamber of Resources, 2004; Fine Tailings Fundamentals Consortium, 1995; Kasperski, 1992). After more than 40 years of commercial operations, this volume of accumulated MFT is considerable, estimated to be between 750 million and one billion cubic meters (nearly a cubic kilometer).

This discussion will be restricted to the volume management issues and the resulting changes this might produce in the relative volumes of tailings that will be reclaimed as dry landscape, as opposed to wet landscape reclamation involving storage of MFT at the bottom of end-pit lakes. The dry stackable tailings management technologies highlighted here provide a base for reclamation that could be applied to anything from the original boreal forest to various wetlands. In tailings management terms, wet landscape reclamation refers to capping of fluid fine tailings or MFT with water to create a lake environment, while dry stackable tailings would provide a basis for other options. In general, the reclamation scheme for these tailings materials would first require a sand cap, for strength and to isolate the less-than-ideal water chemistry, followed by return of the overburden, with the actual reclamation occurring on the original soil horizon.

In order to minimize the amount of make-up water required to maintain extraction rates, it is desirable to maximize the amount of water recovered from the wet sand tailings and the fluid fine tailings. Water conservation via improved tailings management practices is driven by the desire to minimize impact on the Athabasca River and the realization that unlimited increases in the volume of water (fluid tailings) stored on any given lease are not sustainable. The oil sands industry has a policy of zero discharge of process-affected water, and this has a significant impact on the volume of tailings material stored on a given lease. As a result, the tailings and recycle water ponds continue to increase in number and volume. Recent changes in the regulatory environment around surface-mined oil sands have culminated in the issuance of Directive 74 by the Alberta Energy Resources Conservation Board, which mandates tailings management performance in much the same way that bitumen recovery is regulated. Continued storage of fluid fine tailings will be limited by Directive 74 and, by 2013, 50% of the fines in the ore body must be stored in a dedicated disposal area (DDA) where they will have to have a strength of 10 kPa within five years.

With four commercial bitumen operations in the Athabasca oil sands, there are considerable variations in tailings properties due to ore geology, extraction process water chemistry, tailings process water chemistry, and the choice of tailings management options. The following discussion will outline some examples of tailings technology implementation that are specific to particular oil sands operations and designed to meet the requirements of Directive 74. Four of the tailings management technologies that have been commercialized, or are well along the large-scale demonstration path, will be discussed. These include the consolidated or composite tailings process, thin lift dewatering (Suncor's tailings reduction operation, or TRO), rim ditching, and centrifugation.

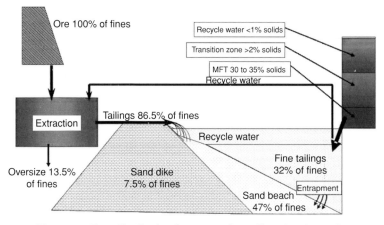

Figure 6.3. Fines distribution for mature fine tailings (MFT) containment and recycle water pond.

Each of these is different in terms of how the water is recovered for reuse, the portion of coarse tailings sand required, and the time frame for strength development. Depending upon the mine plan and associated tailings handling strategy, the requirement for 50% of the fines in the ore to be separated to a DDA may result in no further accumulation of fluid fine tailings in the recycle water ponds. This occurs because, under certain conditions, a significant portion of the fines is already captured in the beached sand tailings. This phenomenon is illustrated in Figure 6.3, which is a schematic of a tailings impoundment. After time, the settled fines (MFT) can develop sufficient strength to become entrapped as the sand beach encroaches on and captures the MFT. As the figure shows, the portion of fines entrapped in the sand beach below water can represent a significant fraction of the total fines from the ore body.

DISCUSSION

Figure 6.1 is a bar graph showing the tailings stream volumes associated with a conventional tailings management strategy, common until the mid-1990s, with the coarse tailings used to contain the fluid fine tailings. For the purposes of this example and those that follow, the froth treatment tailings have simply been added to the coarse and fine tailings volumes. In this example, there is an assumed average coarse sand solids content of about 80 wt%. In reality, the coarse sand is used for dike construction to contain the fluid fine tailings, and contains components with relatively low solids content (beach below the water line) and with relatively high solids content (sand or beach above water). For the present example, this complexity is obscured in the average expressed in Figure 6.1. The fluid fines are assumed to have consolidated to an average solids content of 35 wt% (as MFT). These assumptions are typical of those found in many oil sands planning submissions.

Figure 6.1 shows that, for each volume of bitumen produced, about four volumes of water are lost to the pore spaces in the sand and in the fluid fine tailings (MFT at 35 wt% solids). In fact, this relationship between water lost to tailings and bitumen production is a function of the bitumen and fines in the ore and typically varies from three to five barrels of water per barrel of bitumen produced. The low settling rate of the fluid fine tailings and the accumulation of the resulting MFT makes large containment areas for tailings and recycle water (at 35% solids, MFT) a necessity. Tailings management is essentially a question of water management, and any tailings technology or process that changes the fluid tailings into solid, stackable tailings will also reduce the amount of water lost per unit of bitumen produced. This will, in turn, reduce the amount of make-up water required from the river and other sources, and increase the total dissolved solids in the pore water of the remaining tailings. The reclamation implications of this increased salinity are not known, but there is an expectation that the sand cap and overburden layers will minimize interaction with the soil horizon and the reclamation layers.

Prior to 1989, it was assumed that the best available method of dealing with the accumulated MFT was to transfer it from the recycle water/tailings pond into the mined-out area and cover it with a layer of water. This so-called wet-landscape reclamation proposed to create an artificial lake of over several million cubic meters of accumulated MFT. The Fine Tailings Fundamentals Consortium, established in 1989 to investigate alternatives to wet-landscape reclamation, led to the development of several tailings management options and, in the years since its dissolution, has prompted the industry to develop many other tailings dewatering strategies (Fine Tailings Fundamentals Consortium, 1995; Kasperski and Mikula, 1995b). The most significant of these options is the consolidated tailings treatment process commercialized by Suncor in 1994 (Mikula et al., 1989, 1998), and generally adopted by the industry and regulators until the recent introduction of Directive 74. As noted earlier, there are several other so-called dry stackable tailings technologies undergoing active development, all of which promise to significantly reduce the amount of make-up water required per unit of bitumen production.

Each of these will have different impacts on the relative volumes of fluid and dry stackable tailings stored on the lease at closure, and will therefore influence the reclamation strategy.

Consolidated, composite, or nonsegregating tailings

The basis of this process is to replace the water in the pore spaces of the sand tailings with MFT, making the volume of water previously occupying the sand pore spaces available for reuse in the extraction process. This is achieved by developing enough strength in the mature or fluid fine tailings that the mixture can support a sand content from four to five times the fines content in the consolidated/composite tailings (CT)/nonsegregating tailings (NST) mix (Mikula and Zrobok, 1999; Mikula et al., 1996a, 1998). The presence of the sand helps to consolidate the mixture in a relatively short period of time, with the resulting consolidated mix containing in excess of 80 wt% solids. At this point, the tailings will have enough strength to support a sand cap and, ultimately, can be reclaimed with replacement of the overburden and the original soil horizons.

There are many additives that can be used to achieve the required strength in the mature or fluid fine tailings so that it can support the sand fraction. Suncor has implemented this process using gypsum as the additive to manipulate the fluid fine tailings strength (Mikula and Zrobok, 1999). The Canadian Natural Resources Ltd. Horizon Project is proposing the use of carbon dioxide as the additive in order to achieve the same dry stackable tailings material (Mikula et al., 2010a). Other process aid options include alum, lime, acid-plus-lime, and polymers, as well as various other additives and combinations. The tailings management options known as composite or nonsegregating tailings are simply alternative names for the same basic process, with perhaps some modification to the sand-to-fines ratio, solids content, or chemical additive used. The impact on the recycle water chemistry is a function of the choice of additives.

Figure 6.4 shows the impact of a typical implementation strategy for the CT process on the water recycle volume, following the template in Figure 6.1. This figure shows that, if it were possible to implement the CT process on all of the available fluid fine tailings, the net water lost to tailings per volume of bitumen produced would be reduced significantly from about four to three, with assumptions about the clay or fines contents in the ore similar to those used in generating Figure 6.1.

Because the fluid containment is often constructed from the sand component of the tailings, the sand availability for dike construction and

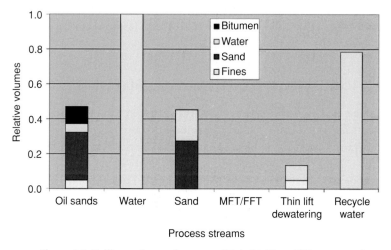

Figure 6.4. Tailings volumes for a consolidated tailings (CT) process using all of the mature fine tailings (MFT). FFT, fluid fine tailings.

the sand requirement for CT production are often at odds, and it is generally not possible to treat all of the fluid fine tailings or MFT using this process. The commercial-scale implementation of the CT process in Suncor's pond 5 suffered to some extent from production of out-of-specification CT, where either the sand, the MFT, or the gypsum additive were not in the proportions defined by the CT "recipe." As a result of the deposition of significant volumes of off-specification CT tailings, a significant effort was required to cap the relatively weak material collected in the pond. In spite of these difficulties, Suncor's pond 5 is on schedule to be capped and the reclamation process is to begin in late 2012.

Mature fine tailings drying/dewatering

It may be possible to simply dry the MFT in order to create a solid substrate for reclamation (Demoz et al. 2010, 2011; Suncor Inc., 2009; Wells and Riley, 2007), as long as sufficient surface area is available on the lease. Mature fine tailings drying processes have been evaluated for decades, usually enhanced with "farming" techniques that blend in sand or overburden to enhance strength development. Until recently, the volume of MFT that could be treated in this manner per unit of available area was quite small. In 2009, Suncor announced the development of the TRO process and, in 2010, Shell announced a similar process called atmospheric fines drying (AFD) (Shell Canada Energy, 2010; Suncor Inc., 2009).

Both of these processes are variations on thin lift MFT drying or dewatering. The basis of thin lift technology is the chemical manipulation of the clay structure in the MFT slurry and the deposition of MFT in thin layers that can rapidly dewater by drainage and drying to create a trafficable surface that meets the strength requirements of Directive 74. These methods require some chemical manipulation of the flocculated clay mineral structure. Recently, there has been a trend toward the use of organic flocculants rather than inorganic reagents in order to minimize impacts on the recycle water chemistry. Small pilot-scale tests of this concept at Suncor were successful and testing from 2005 to 2008 resulted in Suncor's development of the TRO process (Demoz et al., 2011; Suncor Inc., 2009). The test program showed that sufficient strength has to be imparted to the MFT to enable it to maintain a slope. This is to ensure that rainfall will run off and not impede the evaporative dewatering. Further research is required in order to determine the relative proportions of dewatering that can be expected due to drainage versus evaporation, as a function of both clay content in the fluid fine tailings and the addition rate of process aids. Addition of polymer flocculant at a rate of approximately 1000 ppm (on a mass basis, compared to the solids in the MFT) is the basis of the Suncor TRO process, and although inorganic process aid options are available, the current preference is to avoid the recycle water chemistry changes that would result from their use. In its submission to the Energy Resources Conservation Board, Suncor claims a dewatering rate that would allow for the treatment of 4 m^3 of MFT for every square meter of available surface area. Suncor further claims that, for an equivalent 30 wt% solids content MFT, a change to 60 wt% solids is due to drainage, and a change from 60 wt% to 80 wt% solids is due to evaporation (Demoz et al., 2011; Suncor Inc., 2009). Although these claims have yet to be verified, these proportions are important in evaluating the potential changes in recycle water chemistry associated with this process and potential reductions in the make-up water requirement. Figure 6.5 shows the impact of thin lift dewatering on recycle water and tailings volumes, assuming water drainage to reach 60 wt% solids.

Rim ditching

Rim ditching is a tailings management approach that is used in several industries, most notably the Florida phosphate industry. The concept is that, with the appropriate chemical treatment to modify the strength of the tailings, a ditch can be constructed around the perimeter of the deposit. This ditch not only allows for the removal of rainwater, but also

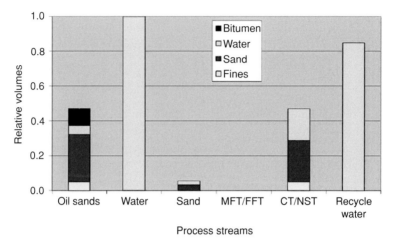

Figure 6.5. Tailings volumes for a thin lift dewatering process dewatering all of the mature fine tailings (MFT) to 60 wt% solids. CT, consolidated tailings; FFT, fluid fine tailings; NST, nonsegregating tailings.

provides a lateral water drainage path, increasing the dewatering rate significantly. In a recent test program at Syncrude Canada, a 50,000-m³ pit test was filled with 80,000 m³ of treated MFT (Mikula et al., 2010b). This performance was made possible by the simultaneous removal of 30,000 m³ of water. The process aid in this case was a polymer flocculant added at a dosage of approximately 800 g ton⁻¹ of MFT solids. The initial rapid dewatering observed in the field trial suggests that this technology will have applicability in treating tailings from surface-mined oil sands. However, like the CT process, rim ditching initially requires fluid containment. In addition, as with CT/NST, at commercial scales, it would take many years to fill a deposit, which would meet the spirit, but not the letter, of Directive 74, which requires a demonstrated strength of 5 kPa in the DDA within one year.

Centrifugation

Centrifugation was first tested as an MFT treatment in the late 1980s but was discounted due to the costs associated with the process (Devenny et al., 1991). The concept was revived in the late 1990s as a result of a successful demonstration on a Utah Asphalt Ridge tar sand (Coleman and Adams, 2004; Mikula et al., 2000, 2006). During a 20-ton hour⁻¹ pilot demonstration of a tar sand extraction process, the sand tailings stream was dewatered in a sand screw, and the fluid fine tailings stream

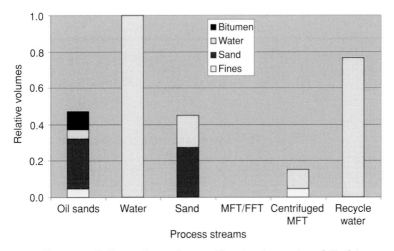

Figure 6.6. Tailings volumes for centrifugation dewatering of all of the mature fine tailings (MFT) to 55 wt% solids. FFT, fluid fine tailings.

was thickened and then centrifuged to produce conveyable, dry-stackable tailings. Although the clay content of the Utah tar sand is less than that typically found in the Athabasca oil sands, subsequent laboratory tests demonstrated that similar thickening, or even direct polymer flocculant addition, could produce an Athabasca MFT stream amenable to centrifugation. This work culminated in large-scale demonstrations at Syncrude in 2008 and 2010, with further testing planned for 2011. The centrifuge tailings treatment can produce a centrate of sufficient quality to join the recycle water stream, and a cake material of 50%–60% solids that can be deposited without fluid containment. This is a significant improvement over tailings management approaches that require fluid containment for a period of years before there is sufficient strength in the deposit for the tailings to be considered stackable. The success of the initial test programs at Syncrude has resulted in an ongoing program directed at determining if this technology would be a viable option to meet Directive 74. Figure 6.6 illustrates the tailings volume change implications of a centrifugation process that produces a cake containing 55 wt% solids.

Directive 74

Directive 74 requires that a certain proportion of the fines in the ore be treated in some fashion in order to create a deposit that will have a strength of 5 kPa after one year and 10 kPa after 5 years (Energy Resources Conservation Board, 2009). Beginning at 20% of the fines in the ore in

2011, the directive extends the requirement to 50% of the fines in the ore by 2013. In order to show compliance, the treated tailings are to be deposited in a DDA in which the volumes, tonnages, and strength can be measured and performance demonstrated. Any material that does not meet the prescribed strength criteria is to be removed for further treatment. Although, superficially, the directive appears to address only a portion of the environmental or operating issues associated with accumulated fluid fine tailings, it is much more proscriptive than it appears. Note that Figure 6.3 suggests that, for an MFT operation, almost 50% of the fines are already trapped in the slumping sand beach that is created during pond construction. For newer ponds, and for some tailings deposition strategies, the proportion of fines contributing to MFT accumulation is significantly higher, but importantly, all of the fines in the ore are not necessarily even available for capture and treatment in a DDA. Given the relatively short time between its conception in November 2008 and implementation in February 2009, the terms of the directive will not be met by all of the operating surface-mined oil sands companies within the prescribed 2013 timeframe. However, all companies will submit plans that will demonstrate compliance at some future date so that the integrated tonnages of fines treated over time will be equivalent to the quantities that would have been treated with directive compliance starting in 2010−2011.

Aside from the directive, there are environmental and economic incentives for reducing the amount of make-up water required for the extraction process. There are limits to the water licenses that control the volumes of fresh water taken from the environment, and there are limits to the volumes of water (in the form of wet or fluid tailings) that can be stored on a lease before tailings storage options are exhausted or tailings containment begins to sterilize the ore in adjacent mineable areas. Figure 6.7 shows the projected linear increase in water storage for the first 15 years of a 280,000 barrels day^{-1} surface-mined oil sands operation. In a shift from this unsustainable trajectory of water storage, implementation of a CT process captures the MFT in dry stackable tailings and significantly reduces the yearly increase in tailings volume to a more sustainable rate.

Figure 6.8 shows the flow of water in the Athabasca River near Fort McMurray, Alberta, with the high and low flows over a ten-year period denoted by the error bars. Also shown in this figure are the average flow and the water license or permitted withdrawals by agriculture and industry on the Athabasca River. Noted on the graph are the levels above which water withdrawals might impact the aquatic ecosystem in the

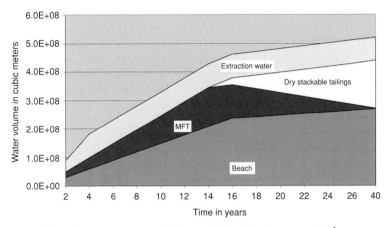

Figure 6.7. Water accumulation model for 280,000 barrels day^{-1} production with consolidated tailings implementation at year 15. MFT, mature fine tailings.

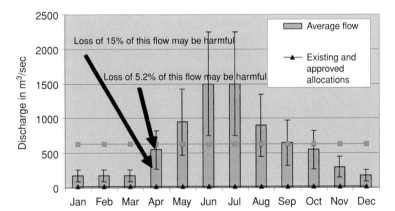

Figure 6.8. Average flow rate of the Athabasca River near Fort McMurray, Alberta, and ten-year averages of extreme highs and lows (represented by the error bars). The existing and approved water license allocations are shown as the triangles along the X-axis. The squares represent the overall long-term average flow.

river. Over the years, some discussion has developed over the withdrawal limit criteria and, in 2007, a joint report by the Federal Department of Fisheries and Oceans and Alberta Environment discussed limits based on 15% exceedances of the average flow or 5.2% of low-flow situations. For the data set shown, these flows are approximately the same and, for reference, Figure 6.9 shows the flow rate as 5.2% of the low flows from

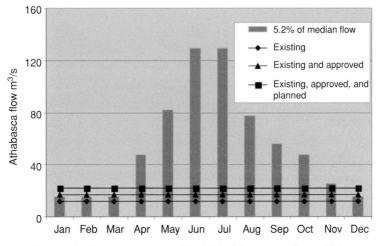

Figure 6.9. Flow rate represented by 5.2% of the average flow, which may represent a water withdrawal that would impact the river ecosystem.

Figure 6.8. Also shown in Figure 6.9 are the licensed water volumes for approved expansions and for future expansions. The approved expansions include permitted water volume withdrawals that might impact the river in the low-flow winter months and that trigger some restrictions according to the in-stream flow needs report referenced earlier. In order to ensure that enough water is available for the extraction process, water could be stockpiled in tailings/recycle water ponds. Space would be available for this contingency water volume if less water were stored in tailings, which would occur with the implementation of the dry stackable tailings technologies discussed earlier. Although the foregoing discussion is a simplification of complex water withdrawal criteria, to a first approximation, Figures 6.8 and 6.9 illustrate the environmental issues driving Directive 74 and the move to dry stackable tailings.

Water chemistry implications of tailings management options

The oil sands extraction process requires an elevated temperature, mechanical energy, and the appropriate water chemistry in order to achieve the high bitumen recoveries mandated by the current regulations. Increasing the proportion of recycled water through the implementation of some of the dry stackable tailings technologies discussed here will proportionately increase the total dissolved salts content in the extraction process water. Table 6.1 gives the relationship

Table 6.1. *Comparison of various tailings treatment options and the resulting bulking factor and impact on recycle water chemistry*

35 wt% solids MFT, 100% of fines form MFT	Bulking factor: volume of tailings compared to volume of ore	Ratio of make-up water to connate water	Relative water chemistry change
Conventional deposition	1.57	8.3	1
CT/NST in theory	1.13	4.3	1.9
CT/NST best in practice	1.35	6.3	1.3
Thin lift dewatering, 60 wt% solids	1.25	5.3	1.6
Centrifugation, 55 wt% solids	1.29	5.7	1.5
35 wt% solids MFT, 50% of fines form MFT	Bulking factor	Make-up/ connate	Relative water chemistry change
Conventional deposition	1.35	6.3	1
CT/NST in theory	1.13	4.3	1.5
CT/NST best in practice	1.24	5.3	1.2
Thin lift dewatering, 60 wt% solids	1.19	4.8	1.3
Centrifugation, 55 wt% solids	1.21	5	1.3
30 wt% solids MFT, 50% of fines form MFT	Bulking factor	Make-up/ connate	Relative water chemistry change
Conventional deposition	1.41	6.9	1
CT/NST in theory	1.13	4.3	1.6
CT/NST best practice	1.27	5.6	1.2
Thin lift dewatering, 60 wt% solids	1.19	4.8	1.4
Centrifugation, 55 wt% solids	1.21	5	1.4

MFT, mature fine tailings; CT/NST, consolidated/nonsegregating tailings.

between the tailings bulking factor and the increase in total dissolved salts for the technologies modeled in Figures 6.1, 6.4, 6.5, and 6.6. This table assumes that organic polymers are used as the process aids and, therefore, that there is no additional impact due to gypsum, lime, acid, alum, or other potential dry stackable tailings process additives. For simplicity, this table assumes the sand component of the tailings reaches 80 wt%, as it also does for the CT/NST tailings. This is only meant to illustrate the potential changes, as there is no accounting of tailings dewatering beyond that for the assumptions in the table. For dewatering due to drying or evaporation, the make-up water requirement would not change, but the deposit would, of course, be much stronger due to the higher solids content achieved. For the CT process, neither of the proposed performance levels has been achieved. It is not possible to treat 100% of the fines from MFT as CT because there would not be enough sand available for dike and fluid containment. Similarly, the theoretical optimum would probably not be achieved due to operational performance factors that would need to be considered in any commercial operation. When one adds the impact of process aids, either for extraction or to support the various dry tailings options, the quantity of total dissolved ions and the associated likelihood of an impact on extraction will go up proportionally (Kasperski and Mikula, 1995a,b; Mikula and Kasperski, 1995; Mikula et al., 1996b). This is one of the main drivers for the use of polymer process aids in tailings. At some point, increased ionic strength has an impact on the recovery of bitumen. With the current policy of zero discharge of water to the environment, the extraction recycle water chemical load will inevitably increase to equal the dissolved ion concentration in the connate water from the ore, diluted by the make-up water. As the implementation of dry stackable tailings technologies progresses, the dissolved ion concentrations will increase, potentially influencing tailings reclamation strategies. More research is required and reclamation strategies should study extraction and tailings chemistry models to understand the water chemistry of the pore water in the stacked tailings that will form the base of the reclaimed landscape.

Implications of tailings management options for tailings pond areas/volumes

Implementation of dry stackable tailings technologies will significantly change the volumes of material that will be available for conventional reclamation (as opposed to wet landscape, end-pit lakes with MFT), but the impact on tailings pond areas in the short-term will be minimal. This is because of the nature of pond construction and the relationship

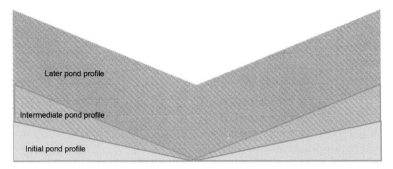

Figure 6.10. Series of pond profiles showing that, at intermediate times, the sand beaching results in a steeper profile that effectively increases the useable volume of the pond. At later times, the beach angle does not change as the pond grows. As a result, the pond volume remains the same, even though the pond wall height has doubled again.

between pond footprint and useable volume. Figure 6.10 presents a series of pond profiles showing the startup, initial infilling and pond construction, and finally the buildup of a mature pond. Although the figure is an oversimplification of the actual pond area, total volume, and useable volume relationships, it is useful for illustrative purposes. In the first profile, a relatively gentle slope defines the pond total volume and the useable volume. In this example, it can be seen that the useable storage is about 50% of the total volume of a cylinder having the dimensions shown. As the pond fills, sand is compacted for the dike wall construction and the remaining sand slumps into the pond at an angle twice as steep as the original pond profile. The resulting pond (shown in the second profile) occupies twice the volume of the first, and with 50% of the volume still useable, double the storage volume. From this point on, however, as seen in the third profile, a further doubling of the pond volume does not increase the storage volume at all. The slumping of the beach sand and intersection of the resulting slopes from opposite sides of the pond in the later stages means that increasing the height of the pond and the total volume does not increase the available volume for fluid fine tailings and/or recycle water. Although this simplification is extreme, it illustrates the reality that, after a certain point in the expansion of the tailings ponds, the useable storage does not increase enough to justify increasing the height of the pond walls.

Implementation of dry stackable tailings is currently managed by utilizing the already somewhat consolidated MFT in the bottom of existing tailings ponds. Removing this volume of material does not significantly impact the area required for containment of tailings and recycle water. It is simply the reverse of the previous discussion, wherein the rate of increase in MFT and water storage is diminished as the ponds get larger. Reducing the pond area by any significant amount would not be possible, even with the use of 100% of the MFT in dry stackable tailings technologies. However, the pond volume aboveground would not have to increase with full implementation of dry stackable tailings technologies, and this would ultimately allow for more flexibility in defining and creating the final reclamation landscape.

SUMMARY

Several significant developments in tailings management and therefore water utilization have occurred in the last few years in surface-mined oil sands. These technologies offer the potential to significantly reduce, if not eliminate, the need for long-term storage or reclamation of MFT in the bottom of end-pit lakes. End-pit lakes will still be required to manage water runoff from the mine site and from the reclaimed dry stackable tailings discussed here; however, without the need for MFT or fluid fine tailings storage, the design, construction, and operation of these lakes will be much more straightforward. With the adaptive management philosophy around tailings management, MFT reclaimed in the base of an end-pit lake may yet be added to the arsenal of tailings management tools available. With Directive 74, the use of dry stackable tailings technologies will continue to expand, bringing with it new challenges in understanding the altered pore water chemistry and its influence on the final reclamation strategy in terms of defining sand cap and overburden thickness, not only for strength development, but also for hydraulic isolation and control of pore water release to the environment. Dry stackable tailings options characterized by a significant amount of water reduction via evaporation (and therefore require larger proportions of make-up water) will result in a more favorable recycle water chemistry. It is unlikely that there is an optimal dry stackable tailings technology for all surface mining operations; tailings management options must be evaluated based on the specific lease topography, nature of the ore, and the connate water chemistry at each site.

ACKNOWLEDGMENTS

The author would like to thank PERD, the Federal Panel on Energy Research and Development, for financial support.

REFERENCES

Afara, M., Munoz, V. A., Mikula, R. J. (2010). Naphtha interaction with bitumen and clays: a preliminary study. *Proceedings of the 2nd International Conference on Oil Sands Tailings*, Edmonton, AB.

Alberta Chamber of Resources. (2004). *Oil Sands Technology Roadmap: Unlocking The Potential*. Edmonton, AB: Alberta Chamber of Resources.

Coleman, P. W. and Adams, R. B. (2004). Study and demonstration of a process to extract bitumen from a Utah tar sand. *Proceedings of the SPE International Thermal Operations and Heavy Oil Symposium*, Bakersfield, CA, paper 86945.

Demoz, A., Munoz, V. A., Mikula, R. J. (2010). Optimizing MFT dewatering by controlling polymer mixing, *Proceedings of the 2nd International Conference on Oil Sands Tailings*, Edmonton, AB.

Demoz, A., Munoz, V. A., Mikula, R. J. (2011). Thin lift dewatering of oil sand tailings: optimizing dewatering of fluid fine tailings by controlling polymer mixing, *Proceedings of the 2011 World Heavy Oil Congress*, Edmonton, AB, paper 586.

Devenny, D. W., Corti, A., Paul, R. (1991). Induced consolidation to solidify oil sand sludge, *Proceedings: 44th Canadian Geotechnical Conference*, Calgary, AB.

Energy Resources Conservation Board. (2009). *Tailings Performance Criteria and Requirements for Oil Sands Mining Schemes*, Directive 074.

Fine Tailings Fundamentals Consortium. (1995). *Advances in Oil Sands Tailings Research*. Vol. 2–12 and Vol. 3–52. Edited by the Fine Tails Fundamentals Consortium.

Kasperski, K. L. (1992). A review of properties and treatment of oil sands tailings. *AOSTRA Journal of Research*, **8**, 11–53.

Kasperski, K. L. and Mikula, R. J. (1995a). *Modeling the Effect of Gypsum Addition on Suncor Plant Water Chemistry: Interim Report*. Division Report WRC 95–13 (CF), CANMET, Natural Resources Canada, Devon, AB.

Kasperski, K. L. and Mikula, R. J. (1995b). *Tailings Release Water Chemistry and Toxicity: Comparison of Tailings Treatments*. Division Report WRC 95–11 (CF), CANMET, Natural Resources Canada, Devon, AB.

Kasperski, K., Munoz, V. A., Mikula, R. J. (2010). Naphtha evaporation from oil sands tailings ponds. *Proceedings of the 2nd International Conference on Oil Sands Tailings*, Edmonton, AB.

Mikula, R. J., Afara, M., Namsechi, B., Demko, B., Wong, P. (2010a). Carbon dioxide sequestration in oil sands tailings streams. *Proceedings of the 2nd International Conference on Oil Sands Tailings*, Edmonton, AB.

Mikula, R. J., Demoz, A., Lahaie, R. (2010b). Laboratory and field experience with rim ditch dewatering of MFT. *Proceedings of the 2nd International Conference on Oil Sands Tailings*, Edmonton, AB.

Mikula, R. J. and Kasperski, K. L. (1995). *Nonsegregating Tailings Release Water Chemistry*. Division Report WRC 95–23 (CF), CANMET, Natural Resources Canada, Devon, AB.

Mikula, R. J., Kasperski, K. L., Burns, R. (1996a). Consolidated tailings release water chemistry. *Proceedings, Tailings, and Mine Waste*, Colorado State University, Fort Collins, CO.

Mikula, R. J., Kasperski, K. L., Burns, R., MacKinnon, M. D. (1989). The nature and fate of oil sands fine tailings In L. L. Schramm, ed., *Suspensions, Fundamentals and Applications in the Petroleum Industry*. Washington D.C.: American Chemical Society, pp. 677–723.

Mikula, R. J., Munoz, V. A., Kasperski, K. L. (1996b). *Comparison Of Tailings Behaviour for Several Bitumen Extraction Methods*. Division Report WRC 96–19 (CF), CANMET, Natural Resources Canada, Devon, AB.

Mikula, R. J., Munoz, V., Kasperski, K. L., Omotoso, O., Sheeran, D. (1998). Commercial implementation of a dry landscape oil sands tailings reclamation option: consolidated tailings. *Proceedings, 7th UNITAR Conference*, No. 1998.096, Beijing, China, pp. 907–921.

Mikula, R. J., Munoz, V. A., Omotoso, O. (2006). Laboratory and pilot experience in the development of a conventional water based extraction process for the Utah Asphalt Ridge tar sands. *Proceedings of the Canadian International Petroleum Society*, Calgary, AB, paper 06–131.

Mikula, R. J., Munoz, V. A., Zrobok, R., Omotoso, O., Kasperski, K. L. (2000). *A Water-Based Extraction Process for Asphalt Ridge Tar Sands*. Division Report CWRC 00–46 (CF) CANMET, Natural Resources Canada, Devon, AB.

Mikula, R. J. and Zrobok, R. (1999). Oil sands tailings reclamation via manipulation of clay behaviour: the role of rheology. *Meeting of the Engineering Foundation*, Hawaii.

Shell Canada Energy (2010). *Muskeg River Mine Atmospheric Fines Drying Phase 1 – 250 ktonne fines capture test*. ERCB directive 074 submission.

Suncor Inc. (2009). *Tailings reduction operations application, project application and environmental support information*. Submission to Alberta Environment and the Energy Resources Conservation Board.

Wells, P. S. and Riley, D. A. (2007). MFT drying – case study in the use of rheological modification and dewatering of fine tailings through thin lift deposition in the oil sands of Alberta. *10th International Seminar on Paste and Thickened Tailings*, Perth, Australia.

ELLEN MACDONALD, SYLVIE QUIDEAU, AND SIMON LANDHÄUSSER

7

Rebuilding boreal forest ecosystems after industrial disturbance

INTRODUCTION

The boreal forest represents almost 25% of the world's closed canopy forest (Atlas of Canada, 2009). Occupying northern latitudes around the globe, this region is characterized by a spatially and temporally dynamic mosaic of vegetation types, most of which are dominated by varying mixtures of broadleaf and conifer trees. The boreal region also hosts rich reserves of nonrenewable natural resources such as coal, conventional and nonconventional oil and gas, and a variety of minerals (Atlas of Canada, 2009). Rapid expansion of activity related to locating and extracting these resources has resulted in dramatic increases in boreal forest land area subjected to industrial disturbance (Schneider et al., 2003). For example, the Alberta Oil Sands Region (AOSR) of northeastern Alberta is the current focus of large-scale intensive and extensive industrial activity. Thus, there is an urgent need to develop a scientific knowledge base for the restoration of boreal ecosystems and to identify practical restoration approaches for these areas.

Vegetation composition in the boreal region is a reflection of the combined influence of site characteristics including local climate, landform, topography, parent material and soils (Bridge and Johnson, 2000). The temporal dynamics of boreal ecosystems are influenced by natural disturbance and post-disturbance successional development (Chen and Popadiouk, 2002). The structure and function of boreal forest ecosystems are thus characterized by complex interactions and feedbacks that are in a continual state of flux: site and soil conditions regulate the establishment of vegetation, the development of which is a function of species

Restoration and Reclamation of Boreal Ecosystems, ed. Dale Vitt and Jagtar Bhatti. Published by Cambridge University Press. © Cambridge University Press 2012.

ecological properties and competitive interactions; vegetation then feeds back into soil characteristics and development. Moreover, when disturbances occur, the physioecological structure is reorganized, creating the template for the next stages of forest development. An understanding of natural processes, relationships, and dynamics in these forest ecosystems is key to informing approaches for their restoration after industrial disturbance.

PATTERN AND PROCESS IN BOREAL FORESTS: LEARNING FROM NATURE

In Canada, the boreal region is distributed across two physiographic regions: the boreal shield in the east and the boreal plain in the west (Atlas of Canada, 2009). The boreal shield is characterized by Precambrian rocks, which have subsequently been reformed by erosion, while the boreal plain is formed on sedimentary rocks. The entire boreal region was glaciated and surficial materials represent a complex mosaic of loosely consolidated glaciolacustrine, glaciofluvial, and till materials. Although the topography is generally flat, erosional and depositional processes have resulted in regional- and local-scale topographic relief that plays an important role in soil and vegetation development (Bridge and Johnson, 2000). Climate is an important limiting factor controlling soil and vegetation development in the boreal. In the boreal forest climatic zone, the winters are long and cold and the summers short. The majority of precipitation falls as rain during the growing season, while winters are relatively dry. Although precipitation is generally low, it varies among regions; for example, from about 400 mm yr^{-1} in western Canada to 800 mm yr^{-1} in the eastern Canadian boreal. However, potential evapotranspiration is generally greater than precipitation; thus, water can be an important limitation for vegetation establishment on upland sites. Deep soils are therefore important for water availability during dry years. The impact of topography is strong in northern latitudes due to the low position of the sun (Bonan and Shugart, 1989). The aspect and degree of the topographic slope affect energy input, soil and air temperature, soil moisture content, and evapotranspiration (Dolgin, 1970; Kumar et al., 1997; Nicolau et al., 2005), which, in turn, influence soil and vegetation development, including rooting depth. The boreal region is characterized by a regime of relatively frequent and severe natural disturbances, largely in the form of wildfire (Johnson, 1992). Blowdown and insect outbreaks also play an increasingly important role in the eastern Canadian boreal, where moisture is higher and wildfire is less frequent (Bergeron and Leduc, 1998). Forest composition in the boreal is therefore the overall product of site factors, natural disturbance, and the ecological proper-ties of species (Bergeron, 2000; Bergeron and Dubuc, 1989; Chen and Popadiouk, 2002; Peters et al., 2005).

Pedogenesis in natural boreal forests

Soil properties vary both horizontally and vertically across the landscape, and evolve with time through the combined influence of a series of pedo-genic processes and pathways. The empirical equation published by Hans Jenny in his 1941 book, *Factors of Soil Formation*, provides an elegant con-ceptual framework linking soil variation to its environment. This uni-versally recognized and used soil model, sometimes referred to as the "clorpt" equation, stipulates that the soil system can be defined by five independent variables or forming factors:

$$S = f(cl, o, r, p, t, \ldots) \qquad [7.1]$$

where S can be any given soil property, f stands for "function of," cl is the climate factor, o represents organisms (the biotic factor, including microorganisms, plants, animals, and man), r is the relief factor (topog-raphy and drainage), p is the parent material, t is time, and the ellipsis represents additional, unspecified factors that may need to be included in the equation (Jenny, 1941).

The relative influence of each soil-forming factor may vary from place to place, although climate is typically the driving factor on the larger, regional to global scale. Boreal climatic conditions impose limita-tions on soil development and are largely responsible for many of their characteristics and their differences when compared to soils from other parts of the world. Low temperatures limit microbial activity and litter decomposition rates, leading to the accumulation of relatively unpro-cessed soil organic matter. Soils from the boreal forest biome represent a huge carbon pool on a global basis. The amount of carbon they store is estimated to be 471 Gt – more than 20% of the global amount of carbon present at the surface of the earth (Watson et al., 2000). In addition, low temperatures limit the rate and type of weathering processes occurring in these soils. Their effect is compounded by the relatively young age of these soils. Many of the characteristic properties of soil profiles take thousands of years to develop, and insufficient time (<10,000 yr) has elapsed since the last glaciation during the Pleistocene epoch to signifi-cantly alter parent materials. As a result, soils are relatively more shallow and less chemically altered than soils from lower latitudes. Alteration of clay minerals in Canadian soils stays minimal in most cases (Komada, 1979).

Podzol is often referred to as the characteristic soil of the boreal forest, which covers a large area of northern Europe and Canada (Chesworth, 2008). In Canada, the vast majority of Podzols are found in areas underlain by the Canadian Shield, but they are also extensive in coastal areas, namely the Appalachian region and the western coastal parts of the Cordilleran region (Clayton et al., 1977). Podzols dominate on coarse-textured, often acidic parent materials, such as stony glacial till or sandy glaciofluvial deposits. They require sufficient water percolating through their sola, hence they require a wet (humid or wetter) climate. Podzols are not present in the AOSR, where the medium- to fine-textured parent materials derived from calcareous glacial deposits instead favor the development of gray Luvisol soils, as is typical of the northern part of the Interior Plains region (Turchenek and Lindsay, 1982). In coarse-textured deposits, moderate amounts of rainfall (<450 mm mean annual precipitation) lead to weakly developed leaching processes that are not extensive enough for profiles to meet the requirements of Podzols, but are more conducive to the presence of Brunisolic soils.

The AOSR is, for the most part, located within the Central Mixedwood Natural Subregion of the Boreal Forest Natural Region (Downing and Pettapiece, 2006). Forest vegetation is characterized by a mosaic of trembling aspen (*Populus tremuloides*), white spruce (*Picea glauca*), and mixedwood stands on finer-textured soils of upland sites; with jack pine (*Pinus banksiana*) stands on coarser soil materials; and peat bogs and sedge fens with black spruce (*Picea mariana*) or tamarack (*Larix laricina*) in low-lying lands. The majority of the region is underlain by Cretaceous sedimentary rocks, mostly marine shales and sandstones (Green, 1972). The surficial materials within the area consist primarily of glacial or post-glacial deposits, including glacial till, glaciolacustrine sediments, and glaciofluvial outwash materials (Turchenek and Lindsay, 1982). More recent deposits of eolian and fluvial origin are found south of Lake Athabasca. Soils in upland areas have developed in glacial till that is derived mostly from local sources. Gray Luvisolic soils are found on medium- to fine-textured parent materials, with Brunisols on sands. Mineral soils, from the Gleysolic order, and organic soils have developed under poorly drained conditions and occupy a significant portion of the low-lying landscape area. Additional soil orders present in the AOSR include: Regosols, with minimal profile development, often associated with Brunisols on recently deposited fluvial materials; Solonetzic soils developed on saline materials, often associated with Luvisols on glaciolacustrine plains; and Cryosols, formed under the influence of permafrost in organic deposits.

The dominant pedogenic process in Luvisolic soils is lessivage (i.e., the physical movement without chemical alteration) of clay-sized mineral particles from the upper to the lower portion of the soil solum (Duchaufour, 1982). This results in the formation of Bt horizons with moderate to strong structure underlying a well-developed, platy Ae horizon (Howitt and Pawluk, 1985). Additional processes in Luvisolic soils include the leaching of soluble salts and calcium carbonates from the solum into the C horizon, and the addition of organic matter to form organic (L, F, H) horizons on the mineral soil surface. Gray Luvisols, the typical mineral soils of the AOSR (Turchenek and Lindsay, 1982), are distinguished from the other great group of the Luvisol order, the gray-brown Luvisols, in that they lack the high biological activity needed to incorporate organic matter into the mineral soil and have thin or absent Ae or Ahe horizons (Clayton et al., 1977).

In Brunisols, there are no strong translocations or transformations of the original parent material like those characterizing some of the other orders, including Luvisols and Podzols. Instead, soils of the Brunisolic order are distinguished by the presence of brownish Bm horizons that have undergone only moderate development. Eutric and Dystric Brunisols both occur in the AOSR and are typically found on sandy deposits (Turchenek and Lindsay, 1982). A combination of factors, including insufficient time available for soil development, moderate rainfall, and very low clay and sesquioxide contents in the parent material, has limited the extent of lessivage and podzolization in these soils. Eutric Brunisols usually occur on calcareous parent materials, while Dystric Brunisols develop in more acidic parent materials with low base saturation (Clayton et al., 1977). Many of the Brunisolic soils of the AOSR exhibit evidence of incipient podzolization, including subsoil Bm horizons, which show enrichment in extractable Fe and Al, higher chromas, and redder hues than the underlying parent material (Lanoue, 2003).

Forest canopy composition and dynamics

The dominant tree species in the Canadian boreal include three broadleaf species: trembling aspen, balsam poplar (*Populus balsamifera*), and paper birch (*Betula papyrifera*); and six conifers: jack pine, lodgepole pine (*Pinus contorta ssp. latifolia*), white spruce, balsam fir (*Abies balsamea*), tamarack, and black spruce (Rowe, 1972). Aspen, poplar, and birch are early successional species that have prolific seed production as well as vegetative reproduction. Of these, birch and poplar tend to have higher moisture requirements (Burns and Honkala, 1990). While aspen and balsam poplar are very shade intolerant, birch can tolerate some level of shade (Landhäusser and Lieffers, 2001). The two pine species dominate on drier sites and have serotinous cones, allowing for rapid regeneration after fire (Burns and Honkala, 1990). White spruce is a shade tolerant, masting species that can regenerate immediately following fire or after a lag period (Peters et al., 2005, 2006). Black spruce, a moderately shade tolerant conifer with semi-serotinous cones, and tamarack, a relatively shade intolerant deciduous conifer, form the dominant forest cover on subhygric to hydric sites.

Naturally, many boreal forest stands are made up of mixtures of tree species, the compositions of which are determined by site conditions as well as temporal variation following disturbances (i.e., wildfires); this results in a shifting mosaic of early, mid-, and late successional communities across boreal landscapes. Post-disturbance successional dynamics are initially a function of the regeneration processes of the different tree species, while subsequent structural and compositional dynamics of the canopy are driven by differences in growth rates, competitive ability, and mortality (Chen and Popadiouk, 2002). Regeneration depends upon the availability of reproductive propagules, suitable microsites for establishment, and favorable site and environmental conditions. The pre-disturbance composition of the forest is influenced by landform, parent material, and soils, and defines the pool of species from which viable propagules might remain on-site after the disturbance, or which could potentially disperse in from adjacent areas (Fyles, 1989; Johnstone and Chapin, 2006b; Pennanen et al., 2004). The severity, spatial pattern, and seasonal timing of the disturbance filters this pool down to those species for which reproductive propagules were able to survive the disturbance, and/or those which have adequate dispersal capability (Lee, 2004; Rydgren et al., 2004; Wang, 2003). Disturbance severity also affects forest floor quality, soil properties, and nutrient cycling through removal of organic matter and effects on soil chemical properties (Brais et al., 2000; Grenon et al., 2004; Norris et al., 2009; Thiffault et al., 2008). Landform, parent material and soils affect the post-disturbance environmental conditions, which serves as a third filter for the pool of potentially regenerating species (Bridge and Johnson, 2000; La Roi, 1992). Finally, the availability of suitable microsites for germination or vegetative reproduction acts as a fourth and last filter for the regeneration of species (Greene et al., 2005; Johnstone and Chapin, 2006a; Peters et al., 2005).

Following the initial period of establishment, ecological properties of species (e.g., growth rate) and their interactions (e.g., competition)
begin to play an increasingly important role in boreal forest dynamics
(Bergeron, 2000; Chen and Popadiouk, 2002). The abundance and composition of the initially establishing herbaceous layer, for example, can
have a strong influence on growth and survival of establishing trees
(Lieffers et al., 1993). In general, post-disturbance boreal forests are initially dominated by rapidly regenerating, shade-intolerant species such as
aspen, poplar, or pine. As time since disturbance increases, shade-tolerant
conifers become more prominent (Bergeron, 2000; Chen and Popadiouk,
2002). In the southern portions of the boreal forest across Canada, mesic
sites are dominated by forests composed of varying mixtures of aspen
and white spruce (i.e., the mixedwood boreal forest). Following natural disturbance, mixedwood forests regenerate quickly to an overstory
of aspen, while the slower-growing and longer-lived white spruce establishes under the aspen (Brais et al., 2004; Lieffers et al., 1996; Peterson and
Peterson, 1992). Because post-disturbance regeneration and dynamics of
boreal forests are driven by such a complex series of factors and processes,
there are many different possibilities for post-disturbance forest composition outcomes (Chen and Popadiouk, 2002; Elliot et al., 1993; Haeussler
and Bergeron, 2004; Lieffers et al., 2003).

Understory plant communities

There is much greater diversity of understory plant species (including
all non-tree vascular plant species) than of canopy plant species in the
boreal landscape (Hart and Chen, 2006). Similar to the forest canopy, the
development, diversity, and composition of forest understory plant communities are regulated by site conditions, post-disturbance regeneration
processes, competition, and other biotic interactions (e.g., competition,
herbivory) (Grime, 2001; Grubb, 1977; Tilman, 1985). Interspecies variation in ecological tolerances regulates abundance of understory plant
species along gradients of moisture and nutrients; this explains observed
patterns of variation in understory community richness and composition in relation to hillslope position and surficial geology (Chipman and
Johnson, 2002; Légaré et al., 2001; Qian et al., 2003; Szwaluk and Strong,
2003; Wang, 2000).

The vast majority of herbaceous species in the boreal understory are
perennials with extensive ability to regenerate vegetatively and exploit
available above- and belowground resource pools (Rowe, 1956). However,
there is a suite of disturbance-adapted species with long-lived seedbanks

or high dispersal capability; these are adapted to quickly dominate sites following disturbance (Archibold, 1979; Lee, 2004). Understory community redevelopment following natural disturbance is strongly influenced by severity, as this regulates survival of vegetative propagules, survival and germination potential from the seed bank, and creation of regeneration microsites (Granstrom and Schimmel, 1993; Purdon et al., 2004; Schimmel and Granstrom, 1996). Following natural disturbance, boreal forest sites are initially dominated by fast-growing, shade-intolerant herbaceous species arising from the budbank or seedbank (Archibold, 1979; DeGrandpré et al., 1993; Granstrom, 1982). This initial vegetation layer can have an important influence on establishment, survival, and growth of the trees (e.g., Landhäusser and Lieffers, 1998).

As the forest canopy develops following natural disturbance, it begins to regulate the availability of resources including light, soil water, and nutrients for the understory; it also affects environmental conditions, such as understory microclimate, forest floor quality, and pH (Macdonald and Fenniak, 2007; Okland et al., 1999; Saetre et al., 1997; van Oijen et al., 2005; van Pelt and Franklin, 2000). These effects, along with the concordant ecological tolerances in tree and understory species, result in close relationships between the forest canopy and the understory plant community (Beatty, 1984; Berger and Puettmann, 2000; Chavez and Macdonald, 2010; Légaré et al., 2001; Macdonald and Fenniak, 2007; Okland et al., 1999; Saetre et al., 1997; Startsev et al., 2008; van Oijen et al., 2005; van pelt and Franklin, 2000). Thus, longer-term, successional development of understory plant communities follows that of canopy development (De Grandpré et al., 2003; Hart and Chen, 2006; Roberts, 2004). However, because a large number of boreal understory species exhibit relatively wide ecological tolerances (Frelich et al., 2003; Qian et al., 1998; Rowe, 1956), successional development of boreal forest understory communities is characterized more by changes in relative abundance than by species turnover (i.e., initial floristics sensu) (Egler, 1954).

Soil–vegetation relationships

Several pedogenic processes operating on different temporal scales typically coexist in soils (Targulian and Krasilnikov, 2007). In boreal forests, alterations of the subsoil and differentiation of the originally uniform parent material through, for example, lessivage and podzolization, are long-term processes that occur over thousands of years. Shorter-term processes, such as litterfall leading to the accumulation of a forest floor, are cyclic (i.e., responsive to natural disturbance events) and are more closely tied to vegetation composition and successional development.

More than 80% of the total carbon stored in boreal forests (excluding peatlands) is located belowground, either in the mineral soils or in the forest floor layers, and the amount stored in the forest floor alone accounts for 10%–35% of the ecosystem total stocks (Dixon et al., 1994; Hannam et al., 2005). In these boreal systems, the forest floor is a storehouse of nutrients and a major determinant of biogeochemical fluxes at the ecosystem level (Prescott et al., 2000). Factors influencing forest floor properties include the type of trees and understory vegetation growing on site, stand age, and mineral parent material, with soil parent material potentially being the most significant factor (Lamarche et al., 2004). Within the fine-textured gray Luvisols found in western Canada, forest floors dominated by trembling aspen stands exhibit more rapid carbon and nitrogen cycling, as well as distinct chemical composition and microbial communities compared to forest floors arising from white spruce-dominated stands (Hannam et al., 2004, 2006; Lindo and Visser, 2003). The presence of white spruce, whether in pure or mixed stands, seems to drive differences in both soil microbial community structure and function (Hannam et al., 2004). Similar differences in forest floor biochemical properties and microbial communities linked to vegetation have been reported for Fennoscandian boreal forests. These differences arose from the interactive effects of plant community composition, soil pH, and nitrogen content of the forest floors (Högberg et al., 2007). Specifically, concurrent changes in vegetation and microbial communities are thought to be related to the role of vegetation as a controller of litter quality and provider of labile carbon sources for soil microbes (Merilä et al., 2010).

In mature boreal forests, forest floor composition, microbes, and plant communities establish an equilibrium whereby internal biogeochemical cycling between plants and soils is tightly regulated. Nitrogen, in particular, is effectively retained and recycled within the system, and losses are small compared to internal fluxes (Bashkin, 2003). Vegetation-induced changes in forest floor microbial communities are fairly resilient to moderate levels of disturbance, including harvesting and changes in abiotic environmental conditions (Hannam et al., 2006; Swallow et al., 2009). On the other hand, changes in forest floor biomass and chemical composition have been observed to occur shortly following harvesting (Hannam et al., 2005). Fire drives temporal fluctuations in forest floor quality, including its carbon composition and ability to retain nutrients (Norris et al., 2009; Thiffault et al., 2008). While the forest floor may at first decrease–either as a direct result of disturbance, or because of increased decomposition losses and lower litter inputs following disturbance–disturbance effects on forest soil carbon stocks are believed to be short-lived and the forest floor rapidly accrues carbon after the initial drop (Johnson and Curtis, 2001); however, several decades are typically required to recover to pre-disturbance conditions under boreal climates (Carrasco et al., 2006; Norris et al., 2009; Trumbore and Harden, 1997).

Over millennia, boreal forest ecosystems have developed in response to the combined influence of parent materials, topography, climate, and natural disturbance to form a diversity of ecosystem types, which can be characterized by their soils, vegetation, successional dynamics, and ecological resilience (Beckingham and Archibald, 1996). These natural ecosystem types, and the processes driving their development, can provide important foundational understanding for reconstruction and restoration of boreal forests.

REBUILDING BOREAL ECOSYSTEMS

The restoration of forest ecosystems is a complex, multistep process that is subject to topographic and climatic factors, and in which the redevelopment of soils, hydrology, and biota on a particular site must be equally and collectively considered. Sites subject to severe industrial disturbance have pedogenetically young soils; thus, the conditions for forest reclamation correspond more closely to the early stages of primary succession than to the more frequently observed process of secondary succession following natural disturbance. In natural primary succession, soils and belowground microbial communities develop slowly on boreal sites as they simultaneously progress from an unvegetated state, through several forb, grass, and shrub stages, to forested ecosystems; this process can easily take hundreds of years (Mann and Plug, 1999; Merilä et al., 2010; Nossov et al., 2011; Svensson and Jeglum, 2003). A priority in the reclamation and certification of lands disturbed by industrial activities is expeditious redevelopment to forested landscapes, including rapid reestablishment of tree cover. There is therefore an urgent need for development of reclamation approaches that can facilitate more rapid development of forest ecosystems.

Reclamation in the AOSR is regulated by the Environmental Protection and Enhancement Act (EPEA) of the Government of Alberta (GOA), which states that industrial operators are responsible for conservation and reclamation of the lands affected by their operations. Requirements and conditions are updated regularly in response to new knowledge and technologies. Under current EPEA regulations, operators are required to create reclaimed soils and landforms that are "capable of supporting a self-sustaining, locally common boreal forest," and then to "revegetate the disturbed land to target the establishment of a self-sustaining, locally common boreal forest, integrated with the surrounding area. . . . " The expectation is that reclaimed sites should be like natural boreal landscapes in appearance and ecological function (Alberta Environment, 2006; Cumulative Environmental Management Association, 2009). A number of recent changes in the EPEA approval conditions are aimed at achieving these objectives. These include a requirement for separate salvage, stockpiling, and placement of different soil materials (e.g., upland surface soil, separately for drier versus moister ecosites) and subsoils of different qualities (good/fair versus poor). Furthermore, there is now a requirement to use upland surface soils, including the litter, fibric, humic layers (LFH), in reclamation. In addition, there have been increases in the required depth for placement of reclamation material (from 20 cm to 50 cm, minimum) and for the depth of a clean cap placed over deleterious materials such as lean oil sands, consolidated tailings, or saline or sodic overburden material (from 80 cm to 100 cm, minimum) (Alberta Environment, 2010).

The targets for reclamation are based on natural boreal forest ecosystems and incorporate an understanding of the important relationships between their biotic and abiotic components. Reclamation activities should control the initial suite of species propagules on the site and result in initial abiotic conditions that will facilitate their development into an early successional forest community. Reclaimed sites, for which site types and ecosite characteristics serve as the model, should be characterized by natural plant communities and successional trends (Alberta Environment, 2010; Beckingham and Archibald, 1996). At the same time, developmental trajectories of reclaimed systems should focus on meeting desired end land use objectives while requiring minimal ongoing inputs. Additionally, reclaimed sites should exhibit resilience against future natural disturbance or stress. The rebuilding of boreal forest ecosystems needs not be directed toward some historical benchmark, and indeed, such narrowly defined directional objectives for restoration may be ill-advised in the context of global climate change (Harris et al., 2006; Higgs, 2003).

Reconstructing functioning boreal forest soils

In Jenny's original clorpt model, man was included in the "organisms" soil-forming factor, alongside microorganisms, vegetation, and other animals (Jenny, 1941). Since then, many soil scientists have suggested that the human factor be recognized as a sixth factor. Human influence on soils and soil formation range from the alteration of a given soil horizon (e.g., an anthropogenically induced organic matter enrichment of the surface horizon resulting from continued manuring) to more drastic effects, including the construction of completely artificial soils. In all cases, whether it is included as part of the biotic factor or separated as an additional variable in the clorpt equation, man has the potential to influence all of the original five soil-forming factors. In the case of surface mining, man becomes the prevalent soil-forming factor. The t factor is reset to zero, and man exerts a controlling influence on both r and p when entire landscapes are reconstructed during land rehabilitation efforts. These reconstructed soils are recognized in the World Reference Base for Soil Resources as the newly established Technosols reference group (Rossiter, 2007).

Surface mining operations in the AOSR involve removal of the overburden materials to gain access to the oil-impregnated sands. Overburden materials may include lean oil sands (<10% oil), Pleistocene glacial deposits, and various Cretaceous silts, shales, and sandstones. Suitable overburden materials, as well as tailing sands, one of the by-products of bitumen extraction, are used to build storage areas and terraced dykes. Surface soils and near-surface geological materials (to a depth of 3 m) salvaged prior to the onset of the mining activities are used as reconstructed soil cover on the new landforms. Mineral soils that are salvaged for reclamation prior to mining onset include a broad range of materials, from lacustrine deposits, with relatively high clay content, to fluvial and till materials, characterized by coarser textures and occasionally significant coarse fragment contents (Turchenek and Lindsay, 1982). Tailings sand, being a suitable rooting medium, also makes up a substantial proportion of the reclaimed soil profile on some landforms (Macyk and Turchenek, 1995). Tailings sand has less than 5% of fine particles (i.e., particles with a diameter <0.05 mm), while overlying soil materials may vary greatly in terms of particle size distribution. Finally, an organic amendment (20–50 cm) is typically used to cap the reconstructed mineral soils, in order to increase their nutrient content and water-holding capacity. In the AOSR, this is predominantly peat, due to its availability in large portions of the mining footprint. When possible, salvage operations strip the forest floor, a rich source of native plant seeds and propagules, from pre-mining upland areas (Mackenzie and Naeth, 2010). These materials can then be used alone or in addition to the peat material as a surface soil amendment, which has been shown to stimulate soil microbial activity, as indicated by increased microbial biomass and nitrification rates when compared to the use of peat alone (McMillan et al., 2007).

The overall objective of land rehabilitation in the AOSR is to produce sustainable ecosystems that will fall within their natural range of variability in terms of productivity. Reconstructing functioning soils must be the first step toward this goal. Soils provide many necessary ecosystem services that need to be restored (Dominati et al., 2010). These include providing physical support to boreal trees and other plants, storing and filtering the water supply, providing a habitat for microbes by serving as a reservoir of biodiversity, and insuring fertility renewal through cycling of carbon and other nutrients. Reestablishing efficient soil biogeochemical processes is at the basis of restoring site productivity (Banning et al., 2008); hence, biochemical variables are probably the most frequently used criteria in determining soil quality (Hobbs, 2007). Soil microbial function, which is sensitive to environmental changes (Pennanen, 2001; Trasar-Cepeda et al., 1998), is often used as an indicator of soil recovery after disturbance and has long been recognized as a crucial target in mine restoration (Harris, 2009; Machulla et al., 2005; Mummey et al., 2002; Visser, 1985). Soil organic matter is also very often used as a proxy for soil quality due to its central role in soil fertility and ecosystem functioning. Many of its chemical and physical characteristics have been shown to be sensitive indicators of changing environmental conditions (Lorenz and Lal, 2007; Rumpel et al., 1999; Turcotte et al., 2009).

Soil characteristics proposed for use as indicators of ecosystem sustainability in reconstructed oil sands soils (i.e., key response variables) were measured and compared to characteristics found in boreal forest soils representative of the AOSR area (Table 7.1), generating the first dataset describing the sustainability of different reclamation prescriptions from the integrative perspective of soil nutrient availability, organic matter quality, and microbial communities. Specifically, key response variables were characterized in a series of reconstructed soils covering different reclamation treatments, vegetation, and age classes, and were compared to the range of natural forest soils found in the region. Overall results indicate that the peat materials used for reclamation, at least initially, are structurally and functionally different from the natural soil organic matter found in non-disturbed forests (Rowland et al., 2009; Turcotte, 2008). In the AOSR, the conditions are different from many other reclamation scenarios (Bendfeldt et al., 2001; Insam and Domsch, 1988), in that there is no paucity of organic matter in the reconstructed soils. However, while the addition of peat may be able to replenish the soil total carbon stocks to levels comparable to natural boreal forest soils of

Table 7.1. *Examples of soil quality criteria used to assess sustainability in reconstructed soils of the Alberta Oil Sands Region (AOSR)*

Soil quality criteria	Key response variables	Methodology

Nutrient supply	*In situ* soil solution supply
	In situ net/gross
	  mineralization rates
	Potential mineralization
	  rates
		(PRS)[TM]-probes[1]
		Field incubations[2]
		Laboratory incubations[1]

Organic matter
  quality
	Carbon pools and forms
	Carbon structural
	  composition
	Molecular biomarkers
		Fractionation techniques[3]
		CPMAS[1,3] CNMR[3]
		GC-FID[4]

Microbial
  communities
	Microbial biomass and
	  activity
	Structural diversity
	Molecular diversity
	Functional diversity
		CFE and respiration[5]
		PLFA[6]
		PCR-DGGE[6]
		Enzyme activities[6]

From: [1]Rowland et al., 2009, [2]Hemstock et al., 2010, [3]Turcotte et al., 2009, [4]Turcotte, 2008, [5]Dimitriu, 2009, [6]Dimitriu et al., 2010.

the region, available evidence suggests that soil organic matter processes are not restored to equivalent levels. Instead, restoring soil functioning similar to that found in natural forests may require the promotion of plant growth and litter production to stimulate *in situ* organic matter accumulation (Vetterlein and Hüttl, 1999). As vegetation continues to develop on the reconstructed soils, biogeochemical processes similar to those of natural soils can be expected to develop, although currently we do not know the rates at which this will occur.

As mentioned by Bradshaw (1997), during restoration of mined lands, longer-term pedological development must be separated from the "biological" soil development that can happen much more rapidly. Biological processes, such as plant-driven surficial accumulation of organic matter and nutrients, and the related immigration of soil microbes and fauna occur, over decadal time scales, while abiotic or physical processes, including mineral weathering and horizon differentiation, may not be observable for several centuries (Bradshaw, 2000). This overall framework and these relationships are fully applicable to the AOSR environment. As opposed to the observed changes in soil biochemical properties presented in Table 7.1, there have been few changes in the physical properties of reconstructed soils within the current time frame (Yarmuch, 2003). Both natural and constructed soils are subject to similar soil forming processes, but these processes may vary between the two groups in terms of their intensity and kinetics. For instance, physical disturbance during soil reconstruction may expose new mineral surfaces and increase weathering rates, as has been observed in lysimeter soils (Quideau et al., 1996). On the other hand, interfaces between reclamation layers act as capillary barriers (Naeth et al., 2011), which could benefit plants by increasing available water. However, these interfaces can also inhibit soil development by limiting the percolation of water through the soil profile. In all cases, it is important to plan for future soil development; to quantify and monitor all pedogenic rates – both short-term and long-term – in reconstructed soils; and to compare these rates to those occurring in a natural setting.

Rebuilding boreal forest vegetation

Planting trees remains one of the most effective strategies in rehabilitating boreal forest areas affected by industrial disturbance to functioning forest ecosystems. The development of a continuous tree canopy on a site helps suppress the establishment of weedy forb and grass species, which can significantly hinder tree survival and growth (Landhäusser and Lieffers, 1998; Maundrell and Hawkins, 2004). The rapid establishment of a closed tree canopy will also encourage buildup of the litter and forest floor layers (LFH layers), facilitating soil redevelopment on reclaimed sites (Klinka et al., 1990).

Establishment of boreal forest tree species through direct seeding on reclamation sites is rare and irregular, as seedling establishment from seed has several key requirements: a seed source, an appropriate growing medium and microclimatic conditions, and relatively low levels of competition. Reclaimed sites may fall short of meeting some or all of these criteria. In large mining areas, good seed sources (seed trees) may be too far away and seeds of boreal tree species are generally not contained in a soil seed bank. Additionally, the substrate available may not be ideal for seedling establishment due to nutritional imbalances or other limitations (Landhäusser et al. 2010; Pinno et al. 2012; Wolken et al. 2010); however, natural seedling establishment has been observed in mining reclamation sites for balsam poplar and aspen (Schott and Landhäusser, unpublished), both of which have efficient long-distance seed dispersal.

To allow for the successful establishment of trees and other vegetation, an appropriate substrate for the rooting zone has to be created using a suitable medium that aids plant development and the redevelopment of soil processes (Burger et al., 2005). To create a suitable medium, the substrates used should not have major confining layers (e.g., physical or chemical in nature) within the natural rooting zone for the selected tree species. As in the natural boreal forest, site conditions including climate, landform, and topography are important factors regulating vegetation development in reclaimed landscapes. The climatic conditions in the boreal regions can pose a substantial challenge for reclamation, as the short growing season leaves little time for species to become established on a site during the first growing season. Topographic factors, such as slope and aspect, affect energy input, microclimate, and other processes, and are therefore significant drivers of vegetation establishment and growth in reclaimed mining landscapes, particularly in northern latitudes. Because slope and aspect play a large role in the design of reconstructed landscapes after mining (Badia et al., 2007), the potential for limitations, including limited moisture, means that deep soils and rapid root expansion are critically important.

Selecting the appropriate tree species and populations for an area and climate are crucial to the successful rehabilitation of a reclamation area. The circumpolar boreal forest region is known to have few native tree species available for use in rehabilitating boreal forest ecosystems, and current government regulations in Canada prohibit the use of non-native tree species in forest reclamation of public lands. The most appropriate species for the harsher boreal reclamation sites are the two broadleaf species, balsam poplar and trembling aspen, and the two pine species, Jack pine and lodgepole pine. Replicating natural forest conditions by planting mixtures of early and late successional species could prove beneficial in reclamation, as it may decrease the risk of failure and increase the resiliency (recovery potential) of a site after natural disturbances such as insects, diseases, and fire. Aspen has a wide natural range, extending from Alaska, across Canada and the USA, to northern Mexico (Fowells, 1965; Little, 1971). The use of aspen, a fast-growing and drought-tolerant native tree species, as forest cover on severely disturbed sites offers significant advantages over the use of other tree species. Aspen is well known for its prolific vegetative regeneration in forest stands disturbed by fire or harvesting. When disturbances such as these kill the aboveground portion of trees or clones, regeneration occurs through root suckers (ramets) that are produced by adventitious buds on lateral roots (Frey et al., 2003; Kemperman, 1978; Maini and Horton, 1966; Steneker, 1976). This adaptation provides the species with a high resiliency to disturbance, which is an important component of successful boreal forest reclamation, as reclaimed sites may be subjected to natural disturbance by fire or insects in the future.

Access to good seedlings with high survival and early growth is essential to achieving reforestation success. Although there is significant experience in growing seedling stock of some commercially important species (particularly pine and spruce), little is known about seedling production techniques for other boreal tree species such as tamarack, aspen, and birch. In addition, we have yet to determine characteristics that can be used to identify good quality seedlings with the potential for success on harsh reclamation sites. Defining seedling quality is difficult, as it is species- and site-specific (Puttonen, 1997). There are several reviews concerning assessment of quality in conifer seedlings (Mattsson, 1996; Stape et al. 2001); however, little is known about the boreal broadleaf species. Defining seedling quality as "fitness for purpose" might be the most useful approach, in terms of reclamation objectives (Mattsson, 1996). Stape et al. (2001) suggest that planting stock of good quality has to have: (1) no sign or symptoms of disease; (2) a sturdy stem and a fibrous root system free of deformities, with an optimal balance between root and shoot mass; (3) sufficient conditioning to withstand cold storage temperatures and a short period without water after planting; and (4) good carbohydrate reserves and mineral nutrient content. Assessments of quality include both material and performance attributes of seedlings. Material attributes (e.g., stem height and diameter, root to shoot ratio, number of buds, stomatal conductance, stem water potential, carbohydrate reserves, and days to bud break) measure the stress tolerance, avoidance, or resistance potential of seedlings (Grossnickle, 2000; Ritchie, 1984). Performance attributes (e.g., root growth potential and photosynthesis) measure the functional integrity and growth potential of seedlings (Grossnickle, 2000; Ritchie, 1984). The most common assessment of seedling quality is, however, root growth potential. It can be argued that nonstructural carbohydrate reserves represent a readily available carbon pool that can be utilized by seedlings for growth. Planting stock with increased carbohydrate reserves should have an advantage, particularly under stressful conditions, as this carbon may be necessary to initiate root growth and to access water and soil nutrients under adverse conditions (Landhäusser et al., unpublished). Indeed, height growth of aspen seedlings planted at a variety of sites was positively correlated with root total nonstructural carbohydrates (Figure 7.1).

Drought is likely a significant driver of seedling establishment success in reconstructed landscapes in the boreal landscape. Under dry conditions, newly planted seedlings must be able to quickly develop a root

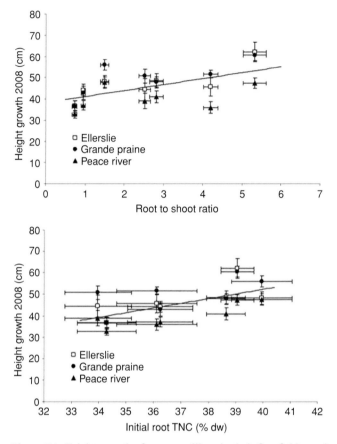

Figure 7.1. Height growth of aspen seedlings in their first field growing season (2008) in relation to initial root-to-shoot ratio ($r^2 = 0.33$; P = 0.007) and root total nonstructural carbohydrate (TNC) reserves ($r^2 = 0.38$; P = 0.003). Data are from seven experimentally grown seedling planting stock types outplanted at Edmonton, Grande Prairie, and Peace River, AB, Canada.

system that is in close contact with the surrounding soil environment in order to allow sufficient water and nutrient uptake (Radoglou and Raftoyannis, 2002; Seifert et al., 2006). Characteristics such as root-to-shoot ratio and carbohydrate reserves might play a significant role in the drought adaptation of seedling stock. Increased root-to-shoot ratio in aspen seedlings has been correlated with improved height growth (Figure 7.1) and increased stress tolerance (Rodriguez et al., unpublished); however, as large initial root volume in red oak did not enhance drought tolerance after outplanting, it remains uncertain whether it is the root to shoot ratio or the increased carbon reserves that is important (Jacobs et al., 2005). Overall, the most effective mechanisms for establishment and avoidance of drought in seedlings appear to be initial root growth and higher growth allocation to roots, relative to shoots, after outplanting (Jacobs et al., 2005, Landhäusser et al., 2012a).

Another important aspect of forest canopy development is the planting density of species, which should be determined according to species and their shade tolerance. In Canada, planting densities in reclamation areas have generally been based on forestry standards ranging from 1500–2500 stems ha^{-1}. In other jurisdictions, densities of >10,000 stems ha^{-1} are not uncommon. Planting density and species mixtures can play a significant role in the development of the new forest canopy, thereby affecting development of the forest floor and soil, as well as the understory plant community.

Understory plant communities

The challenge in reestablishing understory vegetation during boreal forest reclamation lies in provision of reproductive propagules, availability of regeneration microsites, and reestablishment of canopy–understory–soil relationships. Planting of non-tree native forest understory plants on reclaimed sites is extremely limited due to lack of availability. For the vast majority of native forest understory species, seeds are not commercially available (Alberta Native Plant Council, 2010; Johnson, 1987), and frequently, there is little information regarding the conditions necessary for successful germination (Harrington et al., 1999; King, 1980). Furthermore, there has been little investigation into greenhouse propagation techniques for these species and, as previously discussed in terms of tree species, the characteristics of the seedlings produced can be extremely important for post-planting success (see also Burton and Burton, 2003).

In areas impacted by intense industrial disturbance, there is little or no legacy of the previous plant community. For example, in the AOSR, reclamation begins with reconstruction of landforms and placement of soil materials, which typically have no live seedbank or vegetative propagules. The peat materials used to enrich reclaimed soils in organic matter may contain some legacy of plant propagules; however, because these materials are derived from low-lying wet forest ecosystems, the species they carry may not be suited to conditions on reclaimed upland sites and do not represent the natural understory plant communities of mesic forests (Mackenzie and Naeth, 2010). Recently, there has been interest in stripping forest floor materials (the LFH layer), which are a better

Table 7.2. *Number of understory vascular plant species encountered in: sampling of a young aspen-dominated forest site (aboveground); emerging from samples of the forest floor and surface mineral soils in the greenhouse study (belowground); total number of species from both the aboveground and the belowground; and at a coal mine site that was reclaimed by direct transfer of forest floor and surface mineral soil from the aspen forest. Also given is the percentage of species that were shared. (Fair et al., unpublished data)*

	Number of species	% shared with belowground	% shared with reclaimed
Forest–aboveground	31	35.5	64.5
Forest–belowground	42		69.0
Forest–both	62		58.0
Reclaimed	71		

source of native plant seeds and propagules than salvaged peat materials, from pre-mining upland areas and placing them either directly, or from stockpiles, onto the reclamation site (Mackenzie and Naeth, 2010). Application of LFH as a surface soil amendment during reclamation can result in greater plant species richness and higher occurrence of native plant species (Mackenzie and Naeth, 2010); however, there can also be dramatic loss of reproductive propagules during stripping, storage in stockpiles, and subsequent placement of these materials (Koch et al., 1996; Rokich et al., 2000). Direct placement reduces the occurrence of these problems and allows the transfer of seeds or vegetative propagules for a greater diversity of native forest plant species. For example, in a coal mine reclaimed using direct placement of forest floor and surface mineral soils from a young aspen forest, more than 60% of the species from that forest were found growing on the reclaimed site in the first year (Table 7.2). Nevertheless, the forest floor propagule bank can often be quite dissimilar to the established understory plant community (Qi and Scarratt, 1998); only 35.5% of species found in the aboveground vegetation at a young aspen site emerged from samples of the forest floor and mineral soil in a greenhouse study (Table 7.2). Thus, while utilization of LFH can help to provide reproductive propagules for some native forest understory species, the plant community of the recently reclaimed site is still likely to be dominated by shade-intolerant, early successional native and non-native species (Fair et al., unpublished data).

The top soil layer is important as a substrate for plants (mainly trees) deployed via planting, but it is also important as a seedbed for other establishing species (Pinno et al., 2012). Variations in microtopography, substrate type, and distribution lead to a diversity of regeneration microsites. Surface roughness also allows for the capture of moisture and litter (Johnson and Fryer, 1992). This microsite variation is important for natural ingress of plant species. The success of natural ingress of native forest plant species depends upon distance to locally available native populations and the dispersal ability of species; thus, the reliability of natural revegetation in areas undergoing reclamation can be quite poor. A review of unassisted plant establishment in two large sites in the AOSR suggested that only a few native species had established naturally and were able to persist (Geographic Dynamics Corp., 2006). Aspen was the only tree that established naturally, along with a few native shrubs (*Rubus idaeus*, *Amelanchier alnifolia*, and a few species of *Salix* sp.). Naturally establishing forbs were mainly early successional species, while native grasses showed relatively good natural ingress, but poor persistence. It was encouraging, however, that non-native and other weedy species that had rapid, early establishment and high abundance showed substantial decline by 10–20 years after establishment of the reclaimed site (Geographic Dynamics Corp., 2006).

As previously mentioned, canopy composition is known to affect understory plant communities. Coniferous canopies such as white spruce provide year-round shade as the trees have long crowns, resulting in more effective interception of light (Stadt and Lieffers, 2000). On the other hand, a trembling aspen canopy can provide periods of high light transmission during the leaf-off periods in spring and fall (Constabel and Lieffers, 1996). Disturbed sites are likely to be initially monopolized by a semi-stable community of early to mid-successional forb and grass species (Landhäusser and Lieffers, 1998; Maundrell and Hawkins, 2004). In addition to their competitive impacts on establishing trees, some of these undesirable species can persist in the understory of developing forest stands, where they can impede the establishment of species typically found in natural understory communities. Through suppression of shade-intolerant early successional native and non-native plant species, the forest canopy can prolong the availability of regeneration microsites, thereby facilitating development of a more diverse and natural forest plant community over time.

There are a number of other approaches which could be used to facilitate reestablishment of native plant communities on reclaimed boreal sites. It is important, for example, to ensure that native species selected for reclamation are tolerant of conditions on the reclaimed site (Khasa et al., 2002; Purdy et al. 2005; Redfield et al. 2003). Survival and stress tolerance of planted seedlings can be improved by inoculation with nitrogen-fixing bacteria or mycorrhizal fungi (Bois et al., 2006; Kernaghan et al., 2002; Lefrancois et al., 2010; Quoreshi, 2008). Utilization of natural forest sources of organic matter, such as peat or LFH, as reclamation soil amendments can help provide a natural source of innoculum for mutualistic organisms, such as mycorrhizal fungi (Bois et al., 2005).

Soil–vegetation relationships of reclaimed sites

Plantation forestry remains one of the most effective approaches for tree establishment and the development of a closed canopy. The provision of an appropriate rooting zone is key to the redevelopment of forests (Burger et al., 2005) and the associated soil processes (Frouz et al., 2009). To achieve this, a top horizon (capping material) that will not limit the development of natural soil processes and plant root growth (e.g., through unfavorable pH, salts, and/or toxic elements) should be applied. This soil layer must be able to supply and store sufficient water in the short term and nutrients in the longer term. The top soil horizon, however, is not the only soil layer that plays a role in reestablishment. The deeper subsoil horizon is also critical to successful revegetation, as it can facilitate access to stored water and provide structural stability for trees on these sites by allowing for deep root penetration. Consequently, substrates (top and subsoil) must be deposited at the thickness necessary for the short- and long-term moisture supply for trees and other vegetation throughout their lifetime, and should not have major confining layers (e.g., physical or chemical in nature) within the natural rooting zone of the selected tree species (Burger et al., 2005). The importance of a suitable rooting medium, careful planting technique, and establishment of a compatible mix of trees and lower vegetation has been emphasized in forest reclamation initiatives (e.g., Appalachian Regional Reforestation initiative, 2011), as has avoidance of soil compaction. Unfortunately, because open-pit mining in the boreal forest currently uses shovel and truck to extract the resource, significant traffic may occur throughout the building of the reclaimed area. Depending on soil texture and conditions, this exposure to traffic could result in soil compaction, potentially limiting soil aeration, water infiltration, and consequently, the expansion of root systems.

Reestablishment of vegetation–soil relationships is critical to successful boreal forest reclamation. While plants growing on recently reclaimed soils will rely initially on the organic matter and nutrients supplied during the reclamation process for their growing needs, these resources must be replaced by inputs from litterfall and fine root turnover by the appropriate overstory and understory. The rapid establishment of a closed tree canopy will have significant effects on soil development, especially of the litter layers (LFH layers) of reclaimed sites (Klinka et al., 1990). Soils developing under forest canopies on upland sites are strikingly different from soils that develop in open and grass-dominated systems due to differences in the plant species assemblages and their associated microbiological communities (Griffiths et al., 2005; Hart et al., 1993). Both the density and selection of tree species will influence the quantity and quality of organic material inputs to the developing soils through litterfall.

On reclaimed sites of the AOSR, several soil quality indicators have been found to grow more similar over time to conditions observed in natural boreal forest soils. In particular, the surficial organic matter layer reflected a shift from peat to woody plant inputs, as evidenced by the temporal changes in its chemical composition observed by solid-state nuclear magnetic resonance (Turcotte and Quideau, 2012; Turcotte et al., 2009). Results confirm that development of a surface organic layer is enhanced by the presence of shrubs (Rowland et al., 2009) and a deciduous (i.e., aspen) tree cover (Figure 7.2) (Sorenson et al., 2011). Temporal changes in organic matter composition were also accompanied by the onset of observable differences in soil microbial communities under different tree species (Sorenson et al., 2011), a condition similar to those observed in natural boreal forest soils (Hannam et al., 2006; Swallow et al., 2009). In the Czech Republic and Germany, vegetation type and litter quality were similarly found to be of great importance, even more so than the composition of the soil substrate, in the recovery of soil microbial activity in post-mining sites planted to pine and oak (Sourkova et al., 2005). On the other hand, the texture of the substrate used to reconstruct soils in an open-pit mine from Poland was found to be of greater consequence than the planted forest vegetation for recovering microbial properties (Chodak and Niklinska, 2010). It is apparent from these studies that both the original properties of the reclamation substrate and vegetation-induced changes in these properties have the potential to influence the recovery of efficient biogeochemical cycling within the reclaimed ecosystems.

One productive approach to reestablishment of soil-vegetation relationships on reclaimed sites is to utilize natural forest ecosystems as models. An example of such an approach is to use naturally saline ecosystems to inform approaches for reclamation of salinized soils, which can be common in reconstructed landscapes of the AOSR (Kessler et al., 2010). Purdy et al. (2005) documented relationships between soil salinity and the richness and composition of wetland and forest plant communities on naturally saline sites in the boreal region, providing insight into which

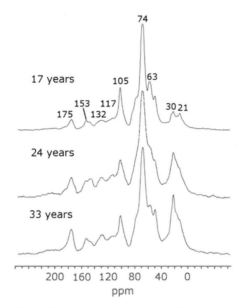

Figure 7.2. Organic matter composition in reconstructed soils planted to aspen as determined using ramped-cross-polarization 13C nuclear magnetic resonance. Changes with time since reclamation include an increase in the alkyl region (0–45 ppm) of the spectra indicative of litter inputs from the tree canopy. (Adapted from Sorenson et al., 2011.)

species may be expected to tolerate which levels of salinity in salt-affected reclaimed soils. These results also provide a knowledge base from which targets for species richness and composition in reclaimed plant communities can be established. Studies of naturally saline sites in the boreal forest revealed that native commercially important tree species, such as white spruce and trembling aspen, are able to exist on sites where soils are highly saline and have extreme pH values, as long as these properties are confined to the deeper soil layers; these sites can support commercially productive growth of aspen and white spruce, as long as moisture and nutrient conditions are not otherwise limiting (Table 7.3) (Lilles et al., 2010, 2012). Naturally saline boreal forest ecosystems also hosted understory plant communities with richness and composition similar to mixedwood boreal forests on non-saline sites (Lilles et al., 2012).

CONCLUSIONS

Boreal forests are complex, spatially and temporally variable systems that develop under the influence of local climate, landform, parent material,

Table 7.3. *Vegetation and soil characteristics at naturally saline boreal forest sites in Alberta dominated by white spruce and aspen*

Site	Plot salinity	Total tree volume (m³ ha⁻¹)	Volumetric water content (m³ m⁻³)	Total nitrogen (kg ha⁻¹)	Electrical conductivity Surface soil	Electrical conductivity upper subsurface	Electrical conductivity lower subsurface	Site index
White spruce								
Benchmark	Low	241	0.42	4719	1.0	2.5	10.1	12.8
	Medium	388	0.46	3979	0.5	1.5	5.2	12.4
	High	303	0.30	3915	0.6	1.7	3.7	12.1
Clearwater	Low	305	0.37	7630	4.1	9.4	18.7	16.3
	Medium	170	0.41	9482	1.7	2.7	4.2	14.3
	High	236	0.33	8111	0.9	1.0	2.2	10.4
Salt Plains	Low	236	0.33	7308	2.7	7.9	22.8	7.0
	Medium	260	0.39	10023	1.0	1.5	5.1	5.7
	High	233	0.35	10478	0.9	0.9	3.2	5.6
Aspen								
Child Lake	Low	61[1]	0.20	12031	1.9	4.5	15.0	22.3
	Medium	363	0.19	4883	1.7	4.6	9.7	19.5
	High	373	0.21	5062	1.1	3.4	7.8	N/A
Salt Pan Lake	Low	260	0.16	5544	0.2	1.5	3.5	16.6
	Medium	182	0.13	5551	0.4	0.3	2.1	15.1
	High	384	0.13	5630	0.3	0.2	1.7	11.5
Zama Marsh	Low	103	0.35	12722	1.5	6.2	8.8	16.3
	Medium	380	0.40	9341	3.0	6.1	8.2	14.4
	High	400	0.46	6621	0.4	1.8	5.4	12.8

For plots of high, medium, and low salinity (representing increasing distance from an adjacent saline wetland), values are given for: total tree volume, volumetric soil water content, total nitrogen (for the forest floor and surface mineral soil), electrical conductivity (dS m⁻¹) at three soil depths: surface (0–20 cm), upper subsurface (20–50 cm), and lower subsurface (50–100 cm), and site index (height at a breast height age of 50) for the dominant tree species. Such information can be used to inform approaches to reclamation of salt-affected soils. (Modified from Lilles et al., 2010, 2012.)

[1] trees were younger than in the other plots (20 versus 60 years).

and disturbance regime. The extensive literature on ecological processes and dynamics following natural or other types of anthropogenic disturbance (e.g., forest harvesting) provides valuable insight into these matters, which can be applied to restoration of boreal forest ecosystems. While we still have much to learn about forest reclamation after industrial disturbance, there is a growing body of literature on this topic. The reclamation and restoration research area has evolved from observational and descriptive research to experimental, pattern- and process-oriented research. A recent review suggests that one-quarter of research papers examining forest reclamation dealt with sites post-mining or following other industrial developments (Burton and Macdonald, 2011). The vast majority of these forest restoration papers focused mainly on reestablishment of tree species, often with associated consideration of non-tree vegetation; studies on reconstruction of soils and restoration of ecological processes are much more scarce (Burton and Macdonald, 2011).

The critical aspects for rebuilding boreal forest ecosystems after industrial disturbance are: (1) construction of a suitable soil; (2) reestablishment of the plant community; and (3) ongoing development of, and interactions between, soils and vegetation (Figure 7.3). Soils of natural boreal forests vary both vertically and horizontally across the landscape as a function of soil-forming factors. Soil development involves longer-term pedogenic processes as well as biological soil development, which occurs on a much shorter time-scale. As we rebuild soils following mining disturbance, we need to be careful to recreate a belowground landscape mosaic that is comparable to the undisturbed landscape. Recreating the pre-disturbance mineral soils may not be a realistic goal; however, it is important to understand how these soils have developed and how they function in a natural setting, so that we can use this knowledge to reconstruct soils and reinitiate their functioning. The addition of organic matter to the soil can come from peat, which is in ample supply, or forest floor material, which offers the advantages of stimulating microbial activity, providing native plant propagules, and facilitating mycorrhizae. A reconstructed soil should be uncompacted and of sufficient depth to allow deep rooting and to ensure that unsuitable conditions (e.g., salinity) are kept below the rooting zone. It should also be able to store and supply moisture and nutrients, provide habitat in support of microbial and faunal diversity, and provide a variety of microsite types for plant establishment.

Once soil reconstruction is complete in the post-mining landscape, recovery of ecosystem functions can be accelerated by encouraging

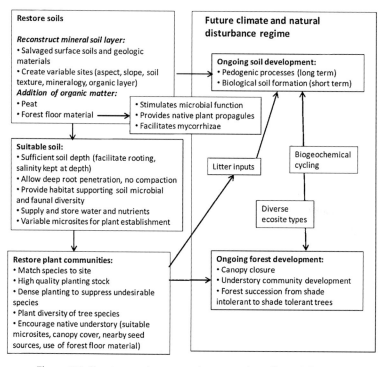

Figure 7.3. Key steps and processes in restoration of boreal forest ecosystems following industrial disturbance.

rapid reestablishment of forest vegetation. Planting tree species plays an important role in this. The key ingredients for success are matching species to sites and selecting good quality planting stock. Planting a diversity of tree species can contribute to ecosystem resilience in the longer term. Additional knowledge and seed sources are needed to support more rapid establishment of native understory species, but use of natural forest floor as a soil amendment may be of at least some help. Establishment of a dense tree canopy will help suppress shade-intolerant, weedy herbaceous species and facilitate development of a more natural forest understory community. Reestablishing biogeochemical cycling between reconstructed soils and plant communities is one of the most critical factors required to ensure long-term sustainability in reclaimed boreal forest landscapes. Indeed, ecological processes such as nutrient cycling and biological interactions between the aboveground and belowground components of the restored ecosystems are crucial to their long-term persistence, and can also provide useful information on their resilience to future disturbance (Hobbs, 2007; Ruiz-Jaen and Aide, 2005). Ongoing successional development of reconstructed forests will continue in the context of future climate change and natural and anthropogenic modifications to natural disturbance regimes. While ecosystem processes are complex, and require long-term monitoring, it is essential to take them into consideration when planning and measuring restoration success.

REFERENCES

Alberta Environment. (2006). *Land Capability Classification for Forest Ecosystems in the Oil Sands*, 3rd edn. Volume 1: Field manual for land capability determination. Edmonton, AB: Alberta Environment, Pub. No. T/875.

Alberta Environment. (2010). *Guidelines for Reclamation to Forest Vegetation in the Athabasca Oil Sands Region*, 2nd edn. Prepared by the Terrestrial Subgroup of the Reclamation Working Group of the Cumulative Environmental Management Association, Fort McMurray, AB.

Alberta Native Plant Council. (2010). Native plant source list. Address: http://www.anpc.ab.ca/content/index.php

Appalachian Regional Reforestation Initiative. (2011). Address: http://arri.osmre.gov./ (Accessed April 2011).

Archibold, O. W. (1979). Buried viable propagules as a factor in postfire regeneration in northern Saskatchewan. *Canadian Journal of Botany*, **57**, 54–58.

Atlas of Canada. (2009). Address: atlas.nrcan.gc.ca/site/english/index.html (Accessed April 2011).

Badia, D., Valero, R., Gracia, A., Marti, C., Molina, F. (2007). Ten-year growth of woody species planted in reclaimed mined banks with different slopes. *Arid Land Research and Management*, **21**, 67–79.

Banning, N. C., Grant, C. D., Jones, D. L., Murphy, D. V. (2008). Recovery of soil organic matter, organic matter turnover, and nitrogen cycling in a post-mining forest rehabilitation chronosequence. *Soil Biology and Biochemistry*, **40**, 2021–2031.

Bashkin, V. N. (2003). *Modern Biogeochemistry*. Dordrecht: Kluwer Academic Press.

Beatty, S. E. (1984). Influence of microtopography and canopy species on spatial patterns of forest understory plants. *Ecology*, **65**, 1406–1419.

Beckingham, J. D. and Archibald, J. H. (1996). Field guide to ecosites of Northern Alberta. Edmonton, AB: Canadian Forest Service, Northwest Region, Northern Forestry Centre. Special Report 5. [ISBN 0-660-16369-1]

Bendfeldt, E. S., Burger, J. A., Daniels, W. L. (2001). Quality of amended mine soils after sixteen years. *Soil Science Society of America Journal*, **65**, 1736–1744.

Berger, A. L. and Puettmann, K. J. (2000). Overstory composition and stand structure influence herbaceous plant diversity in the mixed aspen forest of northern Minnesota. *American Midland Naturalist Journal*, **143**, 111–125.

Bergeron, Y. (2000). Species and stand dynamics in the mixed woods of Québec's southern boreal forest. *Ecology*, **81**, 1500–1516.

Bergeron, Y. and Dubuc, M. (1989). Succession in the southern part of the Canadian boreal forest. *Vegetatio*, **79**, 51–63.

Bergeron, Y. and Leduc, A. (1998). Relationships between change in fire frequency and mortality due to spruce budworm outbreak in the southeastern Canadian boreal forest. *Journal of Vegetation Science*, **9**, 492–500.

Bois, G., Bigras, F. J., Bertrand, A., et al. (2006). Ectomycorrhizal fungi affect the physiological responses of *Picea glauca* and *Pinus banksiana* seedlings exposed to a NaCl gradient. *Tree Physiology*, **26**, 1185–1196.

Bois, G., Piche, Y., Fung, M. Y. P., Khasa, D. P. (2005). Mycorrhizal inoculum potentials of pure reclamation materials and revegetated tailing sands from the Canadian oil sand industry. *Mycorrhiza*, **15**, 149–158.

Bonan, G. B. and Shugart, H. H. (1989). Environmental factors and ecological processes in boreal forests. *Annual Review of Ecology, Evolution, and Systematics*, **20**, 1–28.

Bradshaw, A. (1997). Restoration of mined lands–using natural processes. *Ecological Engineering*, **8**, 255–269.

Bradshaw, A. (2000). The use of natural processes in reclamation–advantages and difficulties. *Landscape and Urban Planning*, **51**, 89–100.

Brais, S., Harvey, B. Bergeron, Y., et al. (2004). Testing forest ecosystem management in boreal mixedwoods of northwestern Quebec: initial response of aspen stands to different levels of harvesting. *Canadian Journal of Forest Research*, **34**, 431–446.

Brais, S., Pare, D., Ouimet, R. (2000). Impacts of wild fire severity and salvage harvesting on the nutrient balance of jack pine and black spruce boreal stands. *Forest Ecology and Management*, **137**, 231–243.

Bridge, S. R. J. and Johnson, E. A. (2000). Geomorphic principles of terrain organization and vegetation gradients. *Journal of Vegetation Science*, **11**, 52–70.

Burger, J., Graves, D., Angel, P., Davis, V., Zipper, C. (2005). The forestry reclamation approach. Forest Reclamation Advisory No. 2. The Appalachian Regional Reforestation Initiative.

Burns, R. M. and Honkala, B. H., eds. (1990). *Silvics of North America: 1. Conifers; 2. Hardwoods*. Agriculture Handbook 654. Washington, DC: U.S. Department of Agriculture, Forest Service.

Burton, C. M. and Burton, P. J. (2003). *A Manual for Growing and Using Seed from Herbaceous Plants Native to the Northern Interior of British Columbia*. Smithers, BC: Symbios Research and Restoration.

Burton, P. J. and Macdonald, S. E. (2011). The restorative imperative: assessing objectives, approaches and challenges to restoring naturalness in forests. *Silvae Fennica*, **45**, 843–863.

Carrasco, J. J., Neff, J. C., Harden, J. W. (2006). Modeling physical and biogeochemical controls over carbon accumulation in a boreal forest soil. *Journal of Geophysical Research*, **111**, G02004.

Chávez, V. and Macdonald, S. E. (2010). The influence of canopy patch mosaics on understory plant community composition in boreal mixedwood forests. *Forest Ecology and Management*, **259**, 1067–1075.

Chen, H. Y. H. and Popadiouk, R. V. (2002). Dynamics of North American boreal mixedwoods. *Environmental Reviews*, **10**, 137–166.

Chesworth, W., ed. (2008). Biomes and their soils. In *Encyclopedia of Soil Science*. Berlin: Springer-Verlag, pp. 61–191.

Chipman, S. J. and Johnson, E. A. (2002). Understory vascular plant species diversity in the mixedwood boreal forest of western Canada. *Ecological Applications*, **12**, 588–601.

Chodak, M. and Niklinska, M. (2010). Effect of texture and tree species on microbial properties of mine soils. *Applied Soil Ecology*, **46**, 268–275.

Clayton, J. S., Ehrlich, W. A., Cann, D. B., Day, J. H., Marshall, I. B. (1977). *Soils of Canada*. Agriculture Canada. Publication 1544.

Constabel, A. J. and Lieffers, V. J. (1996). Seasonal patterns of light transmission through boreal mixedwood canopies. *Canadian Journal of Forest Research*, **26**, 1008–1014.

Cumulative Environmental Management Association. (2009). A framework for reclamation certification criteria and indicators for mineable oil sands. Prepared by the Reclamation Working Group of the Cumulative Environmental Management Association, Fort McMurray, AB.

DeGrandpré, L., Bergeron, Y., Nguyen, T., Boudreault, C., Grondin, P. (2003). Composition and dynamics of the understory vegetation in the boreal forest of Quebec. In F. S. Gilliam and M. R. Roberts, eds., *The Herbaceous Layer in Forests of Eastern North America*. New York, NY: Oxford Unviersity Press, pp. 238–261.

DeGrandpré, L., Gagnon, D., Bergeron, Y. (1993). Changes in the understory of Canadian southern boreal forest after fire. *Journal of Vegetation Science*, **4**, 803–810.

Dimitriu, P. A. (2009). Functional and compositional responses of microorganisms to reclamation of surface-mined boreal forest soils. Ph.D. Diss., Department of Forest Sciences, University of British Columbia, Vancouver, BC.

Dimitriu, P. A., Prescott, C. E., Quideau, S. A., Grayston, S. J. (2010). Impact of reclamation of surface-mined boreal forest soils on microbial community composition and function. *Soil Biology and Biochemistry*, **42**, 2289–2297.

Dixon R. K., Brown, S., Houghton, R. A., et al. (1994). Carbon pools and flux of global forest ecosystems. *Science*, **263**, 185–190.

Dolgin, I. M. (1970). Subarctic meteorology. In *Ecology of the Subarctic Region. Proceedings of the Helsinki Symposium*. UNESCO, Paris, pp. 41–61.

Dominati, E., Patterson, M., Mackay, A. (2010). A framework for classifying and quantifying the natural capital and ecosystem services of soils. *Ecological Economics*, **69**, 1858–1968.

Downing, D. J. and Pettapiece, W. W. (2006). *Natural Regions and Subregions of Alberta*. Natural Regions Committee, Government of Alberta. Publication Number T/852.

Duchaufour, P. (1982). *Pedology: Pedogenesis and Classification*. London, UK: George Allen and Unwin.

Egler, F. E. (1954). Vegetation science concepts. I. Initial floristic composition–a factor in old-field vegetation development. *Vegetatio*, **4**, 412–417.

Elliot, J. A., Morris, D. M., Kantor, J. L. (1993). Studying successional pathways in forest communities: an annotated bibliography. Sault Ste. Marie, ON: Ontario Ministry of Natural Resources, Forest Research Information Paper No. 110.

Fowells, H. A. (1965). *Silvics of Forest trees of the United States*. Agriculture Handbook 271. Washington, DC: United States Department of Agriculture, Forest Service.

Frelich, L. E., Machado, J.-L., Reich, P. B. (2003). Fine scale environmental variation and structure of understorey plant communities in two old-growth pine forests. *Journal of Ecology*, **91**, 283–293.

Frey, B. R., Lieffers, V. J., Landhäusser, S. M., Comeau, P. G., Greenway, K. J. (2003). An analysis of sucker regeneration of trembling aspen. *Canadian Journal of Forest Research*, **33**, 1169–1179.

Frouz, J., Pizl, V., Cienciala, E., Kalcik, J. (2009). Carbon storage in post-mining forest soil, the role of tree biomass and soil bioturbation. *Biogeochemistry*, **94**, 111–121.

Fyles, J. W. (1989). Seed bank populations in upland coniferous forests in central Alberta. *Canadian Journal of Botany*, **67**, 274–278.

Geographic Dynamics Corp. (2006). Investigation of natural ingress of species into reclaimed areas. Prepared for the Cumulative Environmental Management Association–Wood Buffalo Region, Reclamation Working Group,

Soil/Vegetation Subgroup, Fort McMurray, AB. Edmonton, AB: Geographic Dynamics Corp.

Granström, A. (1982). Seed banks in five boreal forest stands originating between 1810 and 1963. *Canadian Journal of Botany*, **60**, 1815–1821.

Granström, A. and Schimmel, J. (1993). Heat effects on seeds and rhizomes of a selection of boreal forest plants and potential reaction to fire. *Oecologia*, **94**, 307–313.

Green, R. (1972). Geological map of Alberta. Edmonton, AB: Research Council of Alberta. Map 35.

Greene, D. F., Macdonald, S. E., Cumming, S., Swift, L. (2005). Seedbed variation from the interior through the edge of a large wildfire in Alberta. *Canadian Journal of Forest Research*, **35**, 1640–1647.

Grenon, F., Bradley, R. L., Titus, B. D. (2004). Temperature sensitivity of mineral N transformation rates, and heterotrophic nitrification: possible factors controlling the post-disturbance mineral N flush in forest floors. *Soil Biology and Biochemistry*, **36**, 1465–1474.

Griffiths, R., Madritch, M., Swanson, A. (2005). Conifer invasion of forest meadows transforms soil characteristics in the Pacific Northwest. *Forest Ecology and Mangement*, **208**, 347–358.

Grime, J. P. (2001). *Plant Strategies, Vegetation Processes and Ecosystem Properties*, 2nd edn. New York, NY: Wiley.

Grossnickle, S. C. (2000). *Ecophysiology of Northern Spruce Species: the Performance of Planted Seedlings*. Ottawa, ON: NRC Research Press.

Grubb, P. J. (1977). The maintenance of species-richness in plant communities: the importance of the regeneration niche. *Biological Reviews*, **52**, 107–145.

Haeussler, S. and Bergeron, Y. (2004). Range of variability in boreal aspen plant communities after wildfire and clear-cutting. *Canadian Journal of Forest Research*, **34**, 274–288.

Hannam, K. D., Quideau, S. A., Kishchuk, B. E. (2006). Forest floor microbial communities in relation to stand composition and timber harvesting in northern Alberta. *Soil Biology and Biochemistry*, **38**, 2565–2575.

Hannam, K. D., Quideau, S. A., Kishchuk, B. E., Oh, S.-W., Wasylishen, R. E. (2005). Forest floor quality declines following clearcutting in trembling aspen- and white spruce-dominated stands of the boreal mixedwood forest. *Canadian Journal of Forest Research*, **35**, 2457–2458.

Hannam, K. D., Quideau, S. A., Oh, S.-W., Kishchuk, B. E., Wasylishen, R. E. (2004). Forest floor composition in aspen- and spruce-dominated stands of the boreal mixedwood forest. *Soil Science Society of America Journal*, **68**, 1735–1743.

Harrington, C. A., McGrath, J. M., Kraft, J. M. (1999). Propagating native species: experience at the Wind River Nursery. *Western Journal of Applied Forestry*, **14**, 61–64.

Harris, J. (2009). Soil microbial communities and restoration ecology: facilitators or followers. *Science*, **325**, 573–574.

Harris, J. A., Hobbs, R. J., Higgs, E., Aronson, J. (2006). Ecological restoration and global climate change. *Restoration Ecology*, **14**, 170–176.

Hart, S. A. and Chen, H. Y. H. (2006). Understory vegetation dynamics of North American boreal forests. *Critical Reviews in Plant Science*, **25**, 381–397.

Hart, S. C., Firestone, M. K. and Paula, E. A. (1993). Flow and fate of soil nitrogen in an annual grassland and a young mixed-conifer forest. *Soil Biology and Biochemistry*, **25**, 431–442.

Hemstock, S., Quideau, S. A., Chanasyk, D. S. (2010). Nitrogen availability from peat amendments used in boreal oil sands reclamation. *Canadian Journal of Soil Science*, **90**, 165–175.

Higgs, E. (2003). *Nature by Design: People, Natural Process, and Ecological Restoration*. Cambridge, MA: MIT Press.

Hobbs, R. J. (2007). Setting effective and realistic restoration goals: key directions for research. *Restoration Ecology*, **15**, 354–357.

Högberg, M. N., Högberg, P., Myrold, D. D. (2007). Is microbial community composition in boreal forest soils determined by pH, C-to-N ratio, the trees, or all three? *Oecologia*, **150**, 590–601.

Howitt, R. W. and Pawluk, S. (1985). The genesis of a Gray Luvisol within the boreal forest region. *Canadian Journal of Soil Science*, **65**, 1–19.

Insam, H. and Domsch, K. H. (1988). Relationship between soil organic carbon and microbial biomass on chronosequences of reclamation sites. *Microbial Ecology*, **15**, 177–188.

Jacobs, D. F., Salifu, K. F., Seifert, J. R. (2005). Growth and nutritional response of hardwood seedlings to controlled-release fertilization at outplanting. *Forest Ecology and Management*, **214**, 28–39.

Jenny, H. (1941). *Factors of Soil Formation. A System of Quantitative Pedology*. New York, NY: McGraw-Hill.

Johnson, D. W. and Curtis, P. S. (2001). Effects of forest management on soil C and N storage: meta analysis. *Forest Ecology and Management*, **140**, 227–238.

Johnson, E. A. (1992). *Fire and Vegetation Dynamics: Studies from the North American Boreal Forest*. New York, NY: Cambridge University Press.

Johnson, E. A. and Fryer, G. I. (1992). Physical characterization of seed microsites movement on the ground. *Journal of Ecology*, **80**, 823–836.

Johnson, L. A. (1987). Management of northern gravel sites for successful reclamation: a review. *Arctic and Alpine Research*, **19**, 530–536.

Johnstone, J. F. and Chapin, F. S. (2006a). Effects of soil burn severity on post-fire tree recruitment in boreal forests. *Ecosystems*, **9**, 14–31.

Johnstone, J. F. and Chapin, F. S. (2006b). Fire interval effects on successional trajectory in boreal forests of Northwst Canada. *Ecosystems*, **9**, 268–277.

Kemperman, J. A. (1978). Sucker root relationships in aspen. Ontario Ministry of Natural Resources, Forest Research Note No. 12.

Kernaghan, G., Hambling, B., Fung, M., Khasa, D. P. (2002). In vitro selection of boreal ectomycorrhizal fungi for use in reclamation of saline–alkaline habitats. *Restoration Ecology*, **10**, 43–51.

Kessler, S., Barbour, S. L., van Rees, K. C. J., Dobchuk, B. S. (2010). Salinization of soil over saline-sodic overburden from the oil sands in Alberta. *Canadian Journal of Soil Science*, **90**, 637–647.

Khasa, P. D., Hambling, B., Kernaghan, G., Fung, M., Ngimbi, E. (2002). Genetic variability in salt tolerance of selected boreal woody seedlings. *Forest Ecology and Management*, **165**, 257–269.

King, P. J. (1980). Review of seed pretreatments required for germination of candidate native tree and shrub species in the eastern slopes of the Rocky Mountains and Foothills of Alberta. Edmonton, AB: Alberta Energy and Natural Resources, Alberta Forest Service. ENR Report Number 154, p. 56.

Klinka, K., Wang, Q., Carter, R. E. (1990). Relationships among humus forms, forest floor nutrient properties, and understory vegetation. *Forest Science*, **36**, 564–581.

Koch, J. M., Ward, S. C., Grant, C. D., Ainsworth, G. L. (1996). Effects of bauxite mine restoration operations on topsoil seed reserves in the jarrah forest of Western Australia. *Restoration Ecology*, **4**, 368–376.

Komada, H. (1979). Clay minerals in Canadian soils: their origin, distribution, and alteration. *Canadian Journal of Soil Science*, **59**, 37–58.

Kumar, L., Skidmore, A. K., Knowles, E. (1997). Modelling topographic variation in solar radiation in a GIS environment. *International Journal of Geographical Information Science*, **11**, 475–497.

Lamarche, J., Bradley, R. L., Paré, D., Légaré, S., Bergeron, Y. (2004). Soil parent material may control forest floor properties more than stand type or stand age in mixedwood boreal forests. *Écoscience*, **11**, 228–237.

Landhäusser, S. M., Deshaies, D., Lieffers, V. J. (2010). Disturbance facilitates rapid range expansion of aspen into higher elevations of the Rocky Mountains under a warming climate. *Jounal of Biogeography*, **37**, 68–76.

Landhäusser, S. M. and Lieffers, V. J. (1998). Growth of *Populus tremuloides* in association with *Calamagrostis canadensis*. *Canadian Journal of Forest Research*, **28**, 396–401.

Landhäusser, S. M. and Lieffers, V. J. (2001). Photosynthesis and carbon allocation of six boreal tree species grown in understory and open conditions. *Tree Physiology*, **21**, 241–248.

Landhäusser, S. M., Pinno, B. D., Lieffers, V. J., Chow, P. S., (2012a). Partitioning of carbon allocation to reserves or growth determines future performance of aspen seedings. *Forest Ecology and Management*, **275**, 43–51.

Landhäusser, S. M., Rodriquez-Alvarez, J., Marenholtz, E. H., Lieffers, V. J., (2012b). Effect of stock type characteristics and time of planting on field performance of aspen (*Populus tremuloides Michx*) seedings on boreal reclamation sites. *New Forests* [in press].

Lanoue, A. (2003). Phosphorus content and accumulation of carbon and nitrogen in boreal forest soils. M.Sc. thesis, Department of Renewable Resources, University of Alberta, Edmonton, AB.

La Roi, G. H. (1992). Classification and ordination of southern boreal forests from the Hondo–Slave Lake area of central Alberta. *Canadian Journal of Botany*, **70**, 614–628.

Lee, P. (2004). The impact of burn intensity from wildfires on seed and vegetative banks, and emergent understory in aspen-dominated boreal forests. *Canadian Journal of Botany*, **82**, 1468–1480.

Lefrancois, E., Quoreshi, A., Khasa, D., et al. (2010). Field performance of alder-Frankia symbionts for the reclamation of oil sands sites. *Applied Soil Ecology*, **46**, 183–191.

Légaré, S., Bergeron, Y., Leduc, A., Paré, D. (2001). Comparison of the understory vegetation in boreal forest types of southwest Quebec. *Canadian Journal of Botany*, **79**, 1019–1027.

Lieffers, V. J., Macdonald, S. E., Hogg, E. H. (1993). Ecology and control strategies for *Calamagrostis canadensis* in boreal forest sites. *Canadian Journal of Forest Research*, **23**, 2070–2077.

Lieffers, V. J., Messier, C., Burton, P. J., Ruel, J.-C., Grover, B. E. (2003). Nature-based silviculture for sustaining a variety of boreal forest values. In P. J. Burton, C. Messier, D. W. Smith, W. L. Adamowicz, eds., *Towards Sustainable Management of the Boreal Forest*. Ottawa, ON: National Research Council of Canada Research Press, pp. 481–530.

Lieffers, V. J., Stadt, K. J., Navratil, S. (1996). Age structure and growth of understory white spruce under aspen. *Canadian Journal of Forest Research*, **26**, 1002–1007.

Lilles, E. B., Purdy, B. G., Chang, S. X., Macdonald, S. E. (2010). Soil and groundwater characteristics of saline sites supporting boreal mixedwood forests in northern Alberta. *Canadian Journal of Soil Science*, **90**, 1–14.

Lilles, E. B., Purdy, B. G., Macdonald, S. E., Chang, S. X. (2012). Growth of aspen and white spruce on naturally saline sites in northern Alberta: implications for development of boreal forest vegetation on reclaimed saline soils. *Canadian Journal of Soil Science*, **92**, 213–227.

Lindo, Z. and Visser, S. (2003). Microbial biomass, nitrogen and phosphorus mineralization, and mesofauna in boreal conifer and deciduous forest floors following partial and clear-cut harvesting. *Canadian Jounal of Forest Reseach*, **33**, 1610–1620.

Little, E. L., Jr. (1971). *Atlas of United States Trees. Vol. 1. Conifers and Important Hardwoods*. Washington, DC: United States Department of Agriculture, Forest Service, Miscellanous Publication 1146.

Lorenz, K. and Lal, R. (2007). Stabilization of organic carbon in chemically separated pools in reclaimed coal mine soils in Ohio. *Geoderma*, **141**, 294–301.

Macdonald, S. E. and Fenniak, T. E. (2007). Understory plant communities of boreal mixedwood forests in western Canada: natural patterns and responses to variable-retention harvesting. *Forest Ecology and Management*, **242**, 34–48.

Machulla, G., Bruns, M. A., Scow, K. M. (2005). Microbial properties of mine spoil materials in the initial stages of soil development. *Soil Science Society of America Journal*, **69**, 1069–1077.

Mackenzie, D. D. and Naeth, M. A. (2010). The role of the forest soil propagule bank in assisted natural recovery after oil sands mining. *Restoration Ecology*, **18**, 418–427.

Macyk, T. M. and Turchenek, L. W. (1995). Tailings sand and natural soil quality at the operations of Syncrude Canada Ltd. Edmonton, AB: Alberta Research Council.

Maini, J. S. and Horton, K. W. (1966). *Reproductive Response of Populus and Associated Pteridium to Cutting, Burning, and Scarification*. Ottawa, ON: Canadian Department of Forest and Rural Development, Forestry Branch. Department Publication 1155.

Mann, D. H. and Plug, L. J. (1999). Vegetation and soil development at an upland taiga site, Alaska. *Ècoscience*, **6**, 272–285.

Martens, L., Landhäusser, S. M., Lieffers, V. J. (2007). First-year growth response of cold-stored, nursery-grown aspen planting stock. *New Forests*, **33**, 281–295.

Mattsson, A. (1996). Predicting field performance using seedling quality assessment. *New Forests*, **13**, 223–248.

Maundrell, C. and Hawkins, C. (2004). Use of an aspen overstory to control understory herbaceous species, bluejoint grass (*Calamagrostis canadensis*), and Fireweed (*Epilobium angustifolium*). *Northern Journal of Applied Forestry*, **21**, 74–79.

McMillan, R., Quideau, S. A., MacKenzie, M. D., Birjukova, O. V. (2007). Nitrogen mineralization and microbial biomass in reclaimed boreal forest soils. *Journal of Environmental Quality*, **36**, 1470–1478.

Merilä, P., Malmivaara-Lamsa, M., Spetz, P., et al. (2010). Soil organic matter quality as a link between microbial community structure and vegetation composition along a successional gradient in a boreal forest. *Applied Soil Ecology*, **46**, 259–267.

Mummey, D. L., Stahl, P. D., Buyer, J. S. (2002). Microbial biomarkers as an indicator of ecosystem recovery following surface mine reclamation. *Applied Soil Ecology*, **21**, 251–259.

Naeth, M. A., Chanasyk, D. S., Burgers, T. D. (2011). Vegetation and soil water interactions on a tailings sand storage facility in the Athabasca oil sands region of Alberta Canada. *Physics and Chemistry of the Earth, Parts A/B/C*, **36**, 19–30.

Nicolau, J. M., Moreno, M., Espigares, T. (2005). Ecohydrology of rilled slopes derived from opencast mining reclamation in a semiarid area. *Geophysical Research Abstracts*, **7**, 85–95.

Norris, C. E., Quideau, S. A., Bhatti, J. S., Wasyslishen, R. E., MacKenzie, M. D. (2009). Influence of fire and harvest on soil organic carbon in jack pine sites. *Canadian Journal of Forest Research*, **39**, 642–654.

Nossov, D. R., Hollingsworth, T. N., Ruess, R. W., Kielland, K. (2011). Development of *Alnus tenuifolia* stands on an Alaskan floodplain: patterns of recruitment, disease and succession. *Journal of Ecology*, **99**, 621–633.

Okland R. H., Rydgren, K., Okland, T. (1999). Single-tree influence on understorey vegetation in a Norwegian boreal spruce forest. *Oikos*, **87**, 488–498.

Pennanen, J., Greene, D. F., Fortin, M.-J., Messier, C. (2004). Spatially explicit simulation of long-term boreal forest landscape dynamics: incorporating quantitative stand attributes. *Ecological Modelling*, **180**, 195–209.

Pennanen, T. (2001). Microbial communities in boreal coniferous forest humus exposed to heavy metals and changes in soil pH–a summary of the use of phospholipid fatty acids, Biolog, and 3H-thymidine incorporation methods in field studies. *Geoderma*, **100**, 91–126.

Peters, V. S., Macdonald, S. E., Dale, M. R. T. (2005). The interaction between masting and fire is key to white spruce regeneration. *Ecology*, **86**, 1744–1750.

Peters, V. S., Macdonald, S. E., Dale, M. R. T. (2006). Patterns of initial versus delayed regeneration of white spruce in boreal mixedwood succession. *Canadian Journal of Forest Research*, **36**, 1597–1609.

Peterson, E. B. and Peterson, N. M. (1992). Ecology, management, and use of aspen and balsam poplar in the prairie provinces, Canada. Forestry Canada, Northwest Regiment, Northern Forestry Centre, Edmonton, AB. Special Report 1.

Pinno, B. D., Landhäusser, S. M., Mackenzie, M. D., Quideau, S. A., Chow, P. S. (2012). Trembling aspen seedling establishment, growth, and response to fertilization on contrasting soils. *Canadian Journal of Soil Science*, **92**, 133–151.

Prescott, C. E., Maynard, D. G., Laiho, R. (2000). Humus in northern forests: friend or foe? *Forest Ecology and Management*, **133**, 23–36.

Purdon, M., Brais, S., Bergeron, Y. (2004). Initial response of understorey vegetation to fire severity and salvage-logging in the southern boreal forest of Quebec. *Applied Vegetation Science*, **7**, 49–60.

Purdy, B. G., Macdonald, S. E., Lieffers, V. J. (2005). Naturally saline boreal communities as models for reclamation of saline oil sand tailings. *Restoration Ecology*, **13**, 667–677.

Puttonen, P. (1997). Looking for the "silver bullet" – can one test do it all? *New Forests*, **13**, 9–27.

Qi, M. Q. and Scarratt, J. B. (1998). Effect of harvesting method on seed bank dynamics in a boreal mixedwood forest in northwestern Ontario. *Canadian Journal of Botany*, **76**, 872–883.

Qian, H., Klinka, K., Kayahara, G. J. (1998). Longitudinal patterns of plant diversity in the North American boreal forest. *Plant Ecology*, **138**, 61–178.

Qian, H., Klinka, K., Okland, R. H., Krestov, P., Kayahara, G. J. (2003). Understorey vegetation in boreal *Picea mariana* and *Populus tremuloides* stands in British Columbia. *Journal of Vegetation Science*, **14**, 173–184.

Quideau, S. A., Chadwick, O. A., Graham, R. C., Wood, H. B. (1996). Base cation biogeochemistry and weathering under oak and pine: a controlled long-term experiment. *Biogeochemistry*, **35**, 377–398.

Quoreshi, A. M. (2008). The use of mycorrhizal biotechnology in restoration of disturbed ecosystems. In Z. A. Siddiqui, M. S. Akhtar, K. Futai, eds., *Mychorrizae: Sustainiable Agriculture and Forestry*. Amsterdam: Springer, pp. 303–320.

Radoglou, K. and Raftoyannis, Y. (2002). The impact of storage, desiccation and planting date on seedling quality and survival of woody plant species. *Forestry*, **75**, 179–190.

Redfield, E., Croser, C., Zwiazek, J. J., MacKinnon, M. D., Qualizza, C. (2003). Responses of Red-Osier Dogwood to oil sands tailings treated with gypsum or alum. *Journal of Environmental Quality*, **32**, 1008–1014.

Ritchie, G. A. (1984). Assessing seedling quality. In M. L. Duryea, T. D. Landis, eds., *Forest Nursery Manual: Production of Bareroot Seedlings*. The Hague, the Netherlands: Martinus Nijhoff/Dr. W. Junk, pp. 243–266.

Roberts, M. R. (2004). Response of the herbaceous layer to natural disturbance in North American forests. *Canadian Journal of Botany*, **82**, 1273–1283.

Rokich, D. P., Dixon, K. W., Sivasithamparam, K., Meney, K. A. (2000). Topsoil handling and storage effects on woodland restoration in Western Australia. *Restoration Ecology*, **8**, 196–208.

Rossiter, D. G. (2007). Classification of urban and industrial soils in the World Reference Base for soil resources. *Journal of Soils and Sediments*, **7**, 96–100.

Rowe, J. S. (1956). Uses of undergrowth plant species in forestry. *Ecology*, **37**, 461–473.

Rowe, J. S. (1972). *Forest Regions of Canada*. Ottawa, ON: Department of Fisheries and the Environment, Canadian Forestry Service, Publication 1300.

Rowland, S. M., Prescott, C. E., Grayston, S. J., Quideau, S. A., Bradfield, G. E. (2009). Recreating a functional forest soil in reclaimed oilsands in northern Alberta: an approach for measuring success in ecological restoration. *Journal of Environmental Quality*, **38**, 1580–1590.

Ruiz-Jaen, M. C. and Aide, T. M. (2005). Restoration success: how is it being measured? *Restoration Ecology*, **13**, 569–577.

Rumpel, C., Kögel-Knabner, I., Hüttl, R. F. (1999). Organic matter composition and degree of humification in lignite-rich mine soils under a chronosequence of pine. *Plant and Soil*, **213**, 161–168.

Rydgren, K., Økland, R. H., Hestmark, G. (2004). Disturbance severity and community resilience in a boreal forest. *Ecology*, **85**, 1906–1915.

Saetre, P., Saetre, L. S., Brandtberg, P.-O., Lundkvist, H., Bengtsson, J. (1997). Ground vegetation composition and heterogeneity in pure Norway spruce and mixed Norway spruce – birch stands. *Canadian Journal of Forest Research*, **27**, 2034–2042.

Schimmel, J. and Granstrom, A. (1996). Fire severity and vegetation response in the boreal Swedish forest. *Ecology*, **77**, 1436–1450.

Schneider, R. R., Stelfox, J. B., Boutin, S., S. Wasel. (2003). Managing the cumulative impacts of land uses in the Western Canadian Sedimentary Basin: a modeling approach. *Conservation Ecology*, **7**, 8.

Seifert, J. R., Jacobs, D. F., Selig, M. F. (2006). Influence of seasonal planting date on field performance of six temperate deciduous forest tree species. *Forest Ecology Management*, **223**, 371–378.

Sorenson P. T., Quideau, S. A., MacKenzie, M. D., Landhäusser, S. M., Oh, S. W. (2011). Forest floor development and biochemical properties in reconstructed boreal forest soils. *Applied Soil Ecology*, **49**, 139–147.

Sourkova, M., Frouz, J., Fettweis, U., et al. (2005). Soil development and properties of microbial biomass succession in reclaimed post mining sites near Sokolov (Czech Republic) and near Cottbus (Germany). *Geoderma*, **129**, 73–80.

Stadt, K. J. and Lieffers, V. J. (2000). MIXLIGHT: a flexible light transmission model for mixed species stands. *Agricultural and Forest Meteorology*, **102**, 235–252.

Stape, J. L., Goncalves, J. L. M., Goncalves, A. N. (2001). Relationships between nursery practices and field performance for Eucalyptus plantations in Brazil– a historical overview and its increasing importance. *New Forests*, **22**, 19–41.

Startsev N., Lieffers, V. J. and Landhäusser, S. M. (2008). Effects of leaf litter on the growth of boreal feathermosses: implication for forest floor development. *Journal of Vegetation Science*, **19**, 253–260.

Steneker, G. A. (1976). Early performance of poplar clones in Manitoba. Edmonton, AB: Environment Canada, Canada Forestry Service, Northern Forestry Research Centre, Information Report NOR-X-156.

Svensson, J. S. and Jeglum, J. K. (2003). Spatio-temporal properties of tree-species belts during primary succession on rising Gulf of Bothnia coastlines. *Annales Botanici Fennici*, **40**, 282.

Swallow, M., Quideau, S. A., MacKenzie, M. D., Kishchuk, B. E. (2009). Microbial community structure and function: the effect of silvicultural burning and topographic variability in northern Alberta. *Soil Biology and Biochemistry*, **41**, 770–777.

Szwaluk, K. S. and Strong, W. L. (2003). Near-surface soil characteristics and understory plants as predictors of *Pinus contorta* site index in southwestern Alberta, Canada. *Forest Ecology and Management*, **176**, 13–24.

Targulian, V. O. and Krasilnikov, P. V. (2007). Soil system and pedogenic processes: self-organization, time scales, and environmental significance. *Catena*, **71**, 373–381.

Thiffault, E., Hannam, K. D., Quideau, S. A., et al. (2008). Chemical composition of forest floor and consequences for nutrient availability after wildfire and harvesting in the boreal forest. *Plant Soil*, **308**, 37–53.

Tilman, D. (1985). The resource-ratio hypothesis of plant succession. *The American Naturalist*, **125**, 827–852.

Trasar-Cepeda, C., Leiros, C., Gil-Sotres, F., Seoane, S. (1998). Towards a biochemical quality index for soils: an expression relating several biological and biochemical properties. *Biology and Fertility of Soils*, **26**, 100–106.

Trumbore, S. E. and Harden, J. W. (1997). Input, accumulation and turnover of carbon in soils of the BOREAS northern study area. *Journal of Geophysical Research*, **102**, 28,816–28,923.

Turchenek, L. W. and Lindsay, J. D. (1982). Soils inventory of the Alberta Oil Sands Environmental Research Program study area. Alberta Research Council Report 122.

Turcotte, I. (2008). Soil organic matter quality in northern Alberta's oil sands reclamation area. M.Sc. thesis, Department of Renewable Resources, University of Alberta, Edmonton, AB.

Turcotte, I. and Quideau, S. A. (2012). Phenolic profiles in natural and reconstructed soils from the oil sands region of Alberta. *Canadian Jounal of Soil Science*, **92**, 153–164.

Turcotte, I., Quideau, S. A., Oh, S.-W. (2009). Organic matter quality in reclaimed boreal forest soils following oilsands mining. *Organic Geochemistry*, **40**, 510–519.

van Oijen, D., Markus, F., Hommel, P., den Ouden, J., de Waal, R. (2005). Effects of tree species composition on within-forest distribution of understory species. *Applied Vegetation Science*, **8**, 155–166.

van Pelt, R. and Franklin, J. F. (2000). Influence of canopy structure on the understory environment in tall, old-growth, conifer forests. *Canadian Journal of Forest Research*, **30**, 1231–1245.

Vetterlein, D. and Hüttl, R .F. (1999). Can applied organic matter fulfill similar functions as soil organic matter? Risk-benefit analysis for organic matter application as a potential strategy for rehabilitation of disturbed ecosystems. *Plant and Soil*, **213**, 1–10.

Visser, S. (1985). Management of microbial processes in surface mined land reclamation in Western Canada. In R. L. Tate and D. A. Klein, eds., *Soil Reclamation Processes: Microbiological Analyses and Applications*. New York, NY: Marcel Dekker, Inc., pp. 203–241.

Wang, G. G. (2000). Use of understory vegetation in classifying soil moisture and nutrient regimes. *Forest Ecology Management*, **129**, 93–100.

Wang, G. G. (2003). Early regeneration and growth dynamics of *Populus tremuloides* suckers in relation to fire severity. *Canadian Journal of Forest Research*, **33**, 1998–2006.

Watson, R. T., Noble, I. R., Bolin, B., et al. (2000). IPCC Special Report: *Land Use, Land-Use Change, and Forestry*. Intergovernmental Panel on Climate Change, Cambridge, UK: Cambridge University Press.

Wolken, J. M., Landhäusser, S. M., Lieffers, V. J., Dyck, M. (2010). Differences in initial root development and soil conditions affect establishment of trembling aspen and balsam poplar seedlings. *Botany*, **88**, 275–285.

Yarmuch, M. (2003). Measurement of soil physical properties to evaluate soil structure quality in reclaimed oil sands soils. M.Sc. thesis, University of Alberta, Edmonton, AB.

CARLA WYTRYKUSH, DALE H. VITT, GORD MCKENNA,
AND ROB VASSOV

8

Designing landscapes to support peatland development on soft tailings deposits

Syncrude Canada Ltd.'s Sandhill Fen Research Watershed initiative

INTRODUCTION

As part of its oil sands mine reclamation in northeastern Alberta, Syncrude Canada Ltd. has constructed numerous wetlands, most as central components of instrumented watersheds. Some "opportunistic" wetlands have formed elsewhere on reclaimed land due to subtle differential settlement of overburden fills. Most of these reclaimed wetlands are open water marshes and ponds, and more than 20 years of research has been carried out on these systems; this research is being summarized in a Wetlands Reclamation Manual to be published in 2012. We have recently turned our attention to learning how to design and construct watersheds that support peat-forming wetlands (fens) on the reclaimed landscape.

Syncrude's closure groundwater modeling has indicated that large areas of the reclaimed landscape will have a phreatic surface (water table) within 50 cm of the ground surface. Depending on the underlying stratigraphy, the water balance, and the water chemistry, most wetlands on the reclaimed landscape will be a system of open-water marshes and fen-like wetlands. Syncrude's watershed research program is designed to provide guidance for planners, designers, and reclamation specialists as to which areas can be reclaimed to which type of wetland, how they are connected with each other and the surrounding natural and reclaimed upland areas, and how we might enhance the development of these new wetlands. This research program is a crucial component in reaching our

Restoration and Reclamation of Boreal Ecosystems, ed. Dale Vitt and Jagtar Bhatti. Published by Cambridge University Press. © Cambridge University Press 2012.

goal of building landscapes to support self-sustaining, locally common boreal forest watersheds that include both wetlands and forests.

In June 2007, Syncrude was issued a new approval under the province of Alberta Environmental Protection and Enhancement Act. This approval contained two new clauses that relate directly to wetlands and their watersheds and provided the impetus for the Sandhill Fen Research Watershed initiative. The clauses state the following:

> The approval holder shall undertake, or participate in, a study on reclamation techniques . . . that examines the viability of bog/fen creation for a portion of the final landscape. . . . The approval holder shall undertake construction of pilot wetlands and their watersheds by December 31, 2012 to provide opportunities for monitoring, model validation . . .

The Sandhill Fen Watershed is designed as an instrumented research watershed in order to develop operational techniques and guide future wetland reclamation at Syncrude. Currently, the fen is nearing the end of its three-year construction period. This chapter summarizes Syncrude's approach to design, location, and components of the watershed, along with a summary of current and proposed research programs.

To meet the 2012 deadline, a site investigation was conducted in 2008, the last of the tailings deposition was completed in 2009, hummocks and watershed berms were constructed in 2010, reclamation material was placed in 2011, and vegetation introduction is scheduled for spring 2012. The fen will operate as a closely monitored instrumented watershed for at least 10 years.

APPROACH

The first step was to determine the overall objective of our watershed design: to design and create appropriate initial conditions to allow the development of a self-sustaining fen wetland and its watershed. Because watersheds are complex, and include a diverse array of components, and constructing a fen of this size had never been attempted previously anywhere, we commissioned an advisory panel to assist our design and research program. We approached a variety of experts, many with experience in the oil sands (and many of whom had been involved in previous instrumented watershed research at Syncrude). These experts were from a variety of disciplines including civil and geological engineering, peatland ecology, upland revegetation, wetland construction, and hydrology and hydrogeology. We asked the advisory panel to focus on two tasks: (1) design a watershed appropriate for current environmental conditions;

Figure 8.1. East-In-Pit, a former mined out pit, filled with tailings and composite tailings, showing the location of the Sandhill Fen Watershed area in the northwest corner. (See color plate section for colored image.)

and (2) maximize the research opportunities so that we can make real recommendations for future reclamation. Syncrude proposed to create an instrumented watershed on sand-capped soft tailings. This watershed would test the viability of practical techniques for soft tailings reclamation and fen development (techniques ranging from construction to vegetation introduction, to monitoring success). This research program would also provide the opportunity to develop soft tailings reclamation technology to implement operationally. Given that Syncrude expects wetlands to be a significant component of the closure landscape, a well-designed, well-constructed and well-monitored, research-oriented prototype wetland within an instrumented watershed is seen as crucial to Syncrude's success.

WATERSHED LOCATION

The Sandhill Fen Watershed is located at the northwestern corner of Syncrude's East-In-Pit (EIP) soft tailings deposit (Figure 8.1) and covers an area of 52 ha; it is 1000 m long by approximately 500 m wide. Engineered dykes and berms define the watershed boundary. The watershed will eventually drain to Mildred Lake Reservoir, just north of the fen.

The EIP was mined between 1977 and 1999. Deposition of tailings sand and composite tailings (CT) into the mined-out pit began in 1999 and is nearing completion. Composite tailings is a nonsegregating tailings slurry produced of tailings sand and fine tailings with gypsum (a coagulant). The tailings deposit under the fen watershed consists of a 10-m tailings sand cap underlain by 35 m of inter-bedded CT and tailings sand layers (Syncrude, 2008). The last of the tailings sand slurry deposition was used to shape the fen watershed in 2008.

A comprehensive site investigation program conducted in 2008 included installation of 54 piezometers, two seepage meters, and four settlement benchmark anchors along with soil and water testing. The following sections summarize the results from these investigations that were undertaken to inform the design process.

Site hydrology

Wetlands in the region persist in a water deficit (precipitation less than evaporation) for most of the year. At the Syncrude site, the climate is sub-humid, with mean annual potential evapotranspiration (PET) of 607 mm (Syncrude, 2008), whereas the long-term mean of annual precipitation is only 438 mm (ranging from 242 mm to 676 mm). About half of the annual precipitation occurs as rainfall from June through September, and the remainder falls as snow. Mean monthly temperature ranges from $-20°C$ in January to $17°C$ in July.

A shallow swale at a 0.3% slope was created at the fen watershed using tailings sand slurry discharges from the berms at the northern, western, and eastern limits of the watershed (a 3-m drop over a 1000-m long swale). The distal (east) end of the watershed was constructed nearly flat (0.1% slope) and was the area chosen to construct the wetland (Syncrude, 2008).

The hydraulic conductivity of the tailings sand cap is several orders of magnitude greater than that of the surrounding units. The tailings sand is typically well-graded, fine-grained ($d_{50} \sim 200$ μm) with a fines content (<44 μm) of less than 15%. The data suggest that the tailings deposit is behaving like a "bath tub," with recharge from precipitation occurring throughout slightly higher areas of the EIP and discharge in the wetland area. The discharge water either runs off to the east or evaporates (Syncrude, 2008).

Groundwater monitoring indicated average depth of water throughout the watershed of less than one meter. Horizontal ground-water gradients follow topography, and vertical gradients are slightly downward on the watershed perimeter and slightly upward in the center of the watershed. The small gradients (and lack of measurable settle-ment) suggest that consolidation of the soft tailings at depth is essen-tially complete, and the upward moving fluxes of consolidation water from soft tailings are negligible (but the measured upward flux of water from the tailings sand cap into the fen is large [156 mm/yr]) (Syncrude, 2008).

Seepage water quality

Seepage water within the fen wetland is dominated by flow through the 10-m tailings sand cap. As flushing of the tailings water by percolating precipitation has just begun, seepage water into the fen has its original tailings water signature. Standpipe piezometers within the sand cap show seepage water is dominated by sodium (Na^+) and chloride (Cl^-), (reflecting the marine origin of the sediments), although sulfate (SO_4^{-2}) is significant (CONRAD, 1999; Syncrude, 2008). The groundwater is subalkaline and basic (pH ~8.3), moderately saline (EC 4100 μS/cm), and has elevated naphthenic acids (Syncrude, 2008). Net percolation into bare tailings sand has been estimated at 110–140 mm/yr, 50–100 mm/yr for tailings sand with a 0.5 m-thick vegetated reclamation material cap.

Based on research and expert opinion, Syncrude's advisory panel recommended establishing control of the salinity to less than 1000 μS/cm in the wetland early in the design phase. More recent research has indi-cated several native fen plants that are able to tolerate EC >1000 μS/cm (Koropchak, 2010). Given the high electrical conductivity of the tailings water seeping into the fen, it was decided that a fresh water source would be required for the first years of the fen establishment.

DESIGN COMPONENTS

The main design components of the Sandhill Fen Watershed include con-structed upland hills (termed hummocks in the design), vegetated swales, a fresh water storage pond, a fen wetland, a fen underdrain system, and two perched fens (Figure 8.2). The two perched fens (each 1.2 ha in area) are experimental sites designed to test whether perched fen-like wetlands can be successful where water inputs are only from precipitation. There is evidence of these peatland types in natural areas in the region (Devito and

(A)

(B)

Figure 8.2. Sandhill Fen Watershed. (**A**) Photograph of fen area in the summer of 2011 during the construction phase. (**B**) Satellite photograph of the watershed on July 30, 2011, showing the status of construction activities including peat placement in perched and main fens and reclamation soils on all but the two eastern hummocks. (See color plate section for colored image.)

Mendoza, personal communication). Other infrastructure was included in the design for specific research purposes: paths and boardwalks, instrumentation (piezometers, flow meters, weather stations, and eddy covariance instrumentation), a research trailer, pole-mounted time-lapse camera system, access roads, and a heated weir at the downstream end of the

Figure 8.3. Aerial photograph of 28 test cells (10 m × 20 m) constructed to investigate the vegetation response to peat source, placement depth, degree of compaction, timing of placement, and water source. Note the white pick-up truck at the top of the picture, to scale. (Photograph from BGC Engineering.) (See color plate section for colored image.)

fen/watershed. More instrumentation and infrastructure may be added as research programs are implemented. The following sections summarize the general approach used in designing the components of the watershed.

The area to perimeter ratio for the Sandhill Fen wetland was compared to the average ratios of wetland perimeter and area observed in over 6000 natural fen wetlands (Bloise, unpublished data) to ensure that the dimensions of the designed fen were within the range of natural fen wetlands in the region.

Hummocks and topography

The as-built tailings sand surface in the watershed had very low gradients (0.1%–0.5%). To create distinct upland recharge areas that provide a sustainable groundwater supply to the fen and to add topographic diversity, uplands in the form of seven hills (hummocks) of varying size and configuration were built, with mechanically placed tailings sand around the fen perimeter (Figure 8.2). The largest hummock is approximately 350 m long and 100 m wide and about 8 m above the surrounding topography. A majority of the hummocks are 180 × 60 m and 3–4 m high. The volume of all the hummocks together is 825,000 m^3. The hummock long axis is oriented parallel to the fen to maximize the seepage face contacting the fen (Syncrude, 2008). The geometry of the hummocks also allows for flushing of the salts over the long term, and lowers the water table so that growth of upland tree species can be supported.

Numerical modeling suggested the phreatic surface within these hummocks would be about 0.5 m above the fen elevation. Flushing estimates (Syncrude, 2008) suggest that the upland hummocks will take approximately 20 years to flush tailings pore water. Salinity levels in the fen wetland area are expected to decrease on completion of flushing.

Water supply

Groundwater modeling results show the water levels in the fen are sustainable from the contributing uplands, but that EC will rise above 1000 μS/cm unless freshwater is imported to the watershed. Salinity above this threshold was indicated as a significant risk to establishing a self-sustaining wetland in the region during early design discussions. An unknown period of time (estimated from 5 to 10 years) is required before the watershed will begin supplying sufficient non-saline groundwater for the fen to become self-sustaining. In the interim, freshwater from the Mildred Lake Reservoir (derived from the Athabasca River) will be piped in to saturate reclamation soils and assist in plant species survival. Fresh water from Mildred Lake Reservoir has an EC of approximately 500 μS/cm, compared to 4000 μS/cm in the tailings deposit. The water will be discharged into a clay-lined pond and diffused to the fen through a narrow gravel dam. The two perched fens will also be supplied with piped water until the areas are vegetated (Syncrude, 2008).

Salinity control

Control of the water table in the tailings sand cap is considered a critical means of limiting salinization of the fen. To facilitate sand cap dewatering, an underdrain system (perforated 8-in high density polyethylene (HDPE) covered with a fine-screen geotextile cloth) was ploughed in beneath the fen area in the winter of 2008 prior to placement of reclamation soils. The water collects in the underdrains and flows to a sump at the watershed outlet, where it is pumped out of the watershed. Surface water will exit the fen through a spillbox and weir structure in the same location as the sump.

Cover soils

For the fen area, a 0.5-m thickness of fine-grained material (clay-till) was placed directly over tailings sand to provide a mineral soil base to the fen and a confining layer to limit diffusion of tailings pore water into the fen. A 0.5-m layer of recently salvaged peatland material was placed over the clay till providing an organic soil. Five of the upland hummocks will receive a soil prescription consisting of clay-till or fluvial sand subsoil (0.3–0.4 m) and harvested litter, fibric, humic (LFH) material from the forest floor (0.1–0.2 m) of a predominantly jack pine ecotype. Two of the upland hummocks and surrounding swales will receive a clay-till subsoil (0.3–0.4 m) and harvested LFH material from the forest floor (0.1–0.2 m) from a moist aspen/white spruce ecotype. One of the perched fens will have 1.0-m layer of recently salvaged peatland material over 0.5 m of clay-till, and the second perched fen will have 0.5 m of the peatland material over 0.5 m of tailings sand over the clay-till (Syncrude 2008).

Initial water

In the summer of 2012, following peat and reclamation material place-ment, fresh water from Mildred Lake Reservoir was pumped into the fen area to help saturate the peat and maintain downward seepage gradients to the underdrains to control salinity until the permanent water system is constructed.

Vegetation introduction

Planting prescriptions for the fen and upland areas were developed with consideration for the targeted ecotype and the prescribed reclamation soils. A variety of fen species will be planted from seed in the fen. Seed collections are currently under way, with full seeding of the fen wetland scheduled for the winter of 2011. Among the species that have been col-lected are: bog birch (*Betula glandulosa*), a variety of sedges (including *Carex aquatilis*, *C. diandra*, *C. paupercula*, *C. utriculata*), arrow grasses (*Triglochin mar-itima* and *T. palustre*), rushes (*Scirpus lacustris* and *S. cyperinus*), and slough grass (*Beckmannia syzigachne*). A variety of upland tree species and shrubs are proposed for the hummocks. The hummocks will be dominated with either trembling aspen (*Populus tremuloides*) or jack pine (*Pinus banksiana*), interspersed with white spruce (*Picea glauca*). Hummocks planted and dominated by aspen will also be planted with a variety of shrubs includ-ing: low-bush cranberry (*Viburnum edule*), dogwood (*Cornus stolonifera*), and buffaloberry (*Sheperdia canadensis*). Those hummocks dominated by jack pine will be planted with green alder (*Alnus crispa*), blueberry (*Vaccinium myrtilloides*), and bearberry (*Arctostaphylos uva-ursi*) as shrub understory. All of these trees and shrubs are components of the planned research activities (see research section for more details).

ONGOING AND FUTURE RESEARCH

Syncrude is constructing the Sandhill Fen Watershed to support a multi-year, multidisciplinary, multi-university research initiative to understand how our watershed functions and whether our initial conditions are appropriate to allow the development of a self-sustaining fen wetland in the long-term, and to provide operational recommendations for future wetland reclamation. There are a variety of programs planned and under way, and a portion of these are summarized as follows.

Responses to peat placement and process water (trials: 2008–2011)

A parallel research program was undertaken to help understand operational methods for placement and performance of a variety of types of organic matter as a base for the fen wetland. Twenty-eight test cells, each 10 m × 20 m, were constructed on a CT deposit 7 km north of the Sandhill Fen site (Figure 8.3) in order to evaluate the vegetation response to different operational treatments including: peat source, peat placement depth (15, 50, and 100 cm), degree of peat compaction, summer versus winter peat salvage and placement, and water source (fresh water versus mine process water). Cells were filled with either live plant material transplanted from a bog wetland or stockpiled peat during summer and winter peat placement trials that were conducted in September 2008 and January 2009, respectively. During the trials, operational techniques were developed to salvage, transport, and place live *in situ* peat material for potential use in wetland reclamation (Figure 8.4).

Seedlings of a variety of species were planted in each cell and their growth and survival were monitored over three seasons. At the same time, a number of species were examined in the greenhouse for their salinity tolerances. These experimental cells and greenhouse experiments provided critical results that have been instrumental in the vegetation design of Sandhill Fen. Some early results from these test cells include plant responses to peat depth and water chemistry. Using peat stockpiled on the Syncrude lease, peat was placed at 15, 50, and 100 cm depth (each depth with four cells, each of these with five replicated plots with six species of plants). These 12 cells were watered with fresh water and, in 2010, had [Na^+] varying from 16 to 86 mg L^{-1} and conductivity ranging from 388 to 1360 uS cm^{-1}. Although responses were highly variable among the six species, no differences among the three peat depths were present for any of the species (Figure 8.5A). Plant responses to fresh versus

Figure 8.4. Selected photographs from the live peat salvage and placement operation. (**A**) Excavator with a modified bucket approaches the salvage area. (**B**) Excavator makes a first cut through the peat to the mineral layer. (**C**) Operator lifts out the peat slab using the modified bucket.

Figure 8.4 (*cont.*) (**D**) Excavator places the slab on a metal plate, which is then loaded onto a semi-transport truck. (**E**) Salvaged peat slabs being transported to the placement area on a semi-transport truck. (**F**) Field monitor directs placement of the peat slab (Syncrude, 2008).

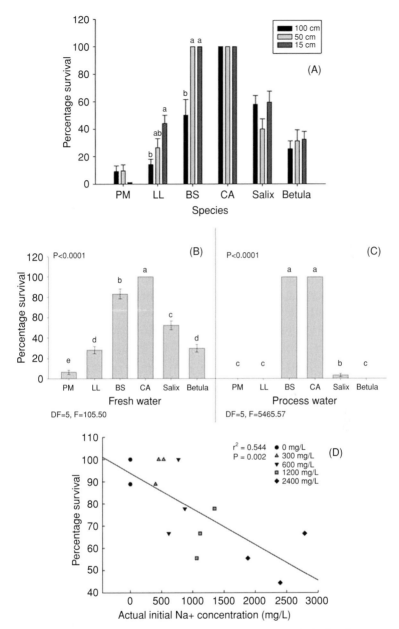

Figure 8.5. Plant responses to peat/water trials. (**A**) Survival after three years for six wetland species when grown in three stockpile peat depths (15, 50, and 100 cm). (**B**) Survival after three years for six wetland species when watered with fresh water (all three peat depths combined). (**C**) Survival after three years for six wetland species when watered with process water (see text – all three peat depths combined). (**D**) *Typha latifolia* survival across a sodium gradient; lines represent standard error and letters represent Tukey's significant groups. PM, *Picea mariana*; LL, *Larix laricina*; BS, *Beckmannia syzigachne*; CA, *Carex aquatilis*; Salix, *Salix* sp., Betula, *Betula glandulosa*.

process water were also evaluated for six species. Process water chemistry (for 2010) included [Na$^+$] values ranging from 219 to 484 mg L^{-1} and conductivity ranging from 1040 to 4070 µS cm^{-1}. The pH values did not differ between process water and fresh water, ranging from 6.0 to 8.3. After three years, two of the six species tested have continued to respond well in both fresh and process waters (Figures 8.5B,C). We conclude that there are native species available (*Carex aquatilis* [see Chapter 5] and *Beckmania syzigachne*) that tolerate the saline conditions of the water that may be present in early stages after reclamation.

Initiation of any boreal wetland is vulnerable to invasion by aggressive marsh species, especially *Typha latifolia*. To assess the potential of *T. latifolia* invasion into the Sandhill Fen reclamation, we grew *T. latifolia* in the greenhouse in a dilution series of sodium (0, 300, 600, 1200, and 2400 mg L^{-1}), using NaCl to prepare the gradient. After six weeks, plant survival was tallied. *Typha latifolia*, like many plants, is adversely affected by sodium. At levels exceeding 300 mg L^{-1}, survival was decreased; however, decreases were not significant until concentrations reached 2400 mg L^{-1} (Figure 8.5D). These data indicate that *Typha latifolia* is negatively affected by sodium; however, it is still unknown how these responses will manifest when combined with overall community interactions from the desirable native wetland plants. For this reason, it is difficult to assess what the cumulative effects will be on the Sandhill Fen reclamation. The decreased performance of *T. latifolia* across the sodium gradient does indicate that the site chemistry potentially could keep *T. latifolia* invasion somewhat in check.

Islands composed of a variety of peat sources (stockpiled peat, fresh peat, live peat), as well as sand and clay islands may be replicated in the Sandhill Fen wetland and perched fens. Performance of these islands and any plant egress from them will be monitored. The results from this program will be used to develop cover soil prescriptions for future wetland reclamation.

VEGETATION RESEARCH AT SANDHILL FEN

Upland forests

The vegetation research program on the upland hummocks comprises tree and shrub research, and addresses a number of questions critically related to the underlying hydrology and the development of sustainable specific ecotypes. Two ecotypes; namely, a dry, jack pine-dominated ecosite and a moist, aspen-dominated ecotype of varying tree densities and initial conditions are targeted. The research will focus on a variety of topics including but not limited to effects of tree density on hummock hydrology and early stage responses, initial floristics versus relay floristics, relation between initial leaf area index and leaf area development to water balance; effect of slope and aspect on tree performance, and the potential for natural vegetation and tree regeneration on sites with and without coarse woody debris. In addition, underground rhizotrons will be installed to examine tree root morphology and behavior in relation to soil hydrologic site conditions and other factors that may affect root growth.

The objective of shrub research is to develop methods for the collection, vegetative propagation, and deployment of a variety of boreal forest shrub species that are important components of the target ecotypes. These shrubs will be planted on the hummocks of Sandhill Fen and their success monitored. This work is tightly linked to the upland tree research and may provide insight into modeling tree and shrub spatial and temporal dynamics. Syncrude recognizes that an understanding of shrub and tree performance will allow the development of sound operational practices that lead to the development of sustainable ecosystems on the reclaimed landscape.

Wetlands

A variety of research programs are under way and planned to aid in the understanding of operational methods for wetland vegetation introduction and performance of those plants, as well as to understand the basic ecosystem processes associated with early plant establishment. A portion of this research focuses on achieving a better understanding of the establishment and growth responses of key plant species to water and soil (peat) qualities found in the Sandhill Fen Watershed, as well as amendments that are proposed for peatland construction. The establishment tolerances of foundational rich fen plant species for early reclamation will be determined. The research is designed to isolate specific variables that are key to understanding plant responses to environmental conditions present at the northern portion of the EIP and then using these results to establish protocols for plant cultivation and vegetation establishment for the full-scale Sandhill Fen Watershed. The research comprises: (1) growth responses to Sandhill Fen conditions and to amendments for the dominant plant species; (2) establishment responses for additional fen species that could be utilized to increase diversity, including small sedge species, mosses, and dicots; (3) ecosystem processing of nitrogen and an understanding of how the chemical regimes of the water and peat columns change over the first years of plant introduction; and (4) development of the soil microbial flora.

We also will investigate community-scale vegetation responses. The objective of this work is to understand natural successional processes in Sandhill Fen. We will track natural vegetation egress, monitor its success, and compare outcomes to those from conventional vegetation methods. This work will help us to understand the rate at which plant communities develop naturally and through planting on a variety of reclamation materials (sand, clay, stockpiled peat, fresh peat, live peat), and water quality conditions.

Carbon and water balance research

Syncrude plans to undertake research to elucidate the carbon and water balance in the wetlands. The objectives of this research are to determine the ecosystem-scale annual water/energy and carbon balance and compare this to other northern wetlands. This work will help to assess the success of our design as reflected in the performance of reclaimed fen function.

Hydrology and hydrogeology research

This work is planned to help identify optimal methods for design of fen wetlands and their watersheds to maintain appropriate hydrology and water balances to support fen vegetation in the long term. The studies comprise several focus areas.

One component addresses the controls of hummock size and orientation on groundwater interactions. A second component of this research investigates the controls of riparian–upland configuration on peatland water balance, and a third component will elucidate the succession of fen groundwater and fen biogeochemistry. Finally, natural analogues will be investigated to provide reference variability in natural fen hydrologic responses to longer-term climatic changes in comparison with the constructed fen. This information will be required to assess the relative role of climatic variability versus watershed settling and fen succession on the long-term maintenance of the constructed fen.

Interactive Sandhill Fen Research/monitoring data system

In support of the Sandhill Fen Research Project, Syncrude will support the development of a spatially explicit metadata catalogue system. This will incorporate an online survey and an integrated system that includes a metadata catalogue and guidelines for data collection, creation, and importation. The results of this work will allow Syncrude to surmount major communication problems involving large datasets collected in the Sandhill Fen Watershed Research program for a variety of purposes by diverse methodologies and by different researchers. We will also be able to refine our monitoring of spatial and temporal changes in the fen to operational requirements.

CONCLUSIONS

The Sandhill Fen Watershed represents Syncrude's and the oil sands industry's first attempt to establish an instrumented fen wetland and surrounding watershed on a soft tailings sand deposit. As planned, the site will be a pioneering watershed for oil sands reclamation research, and form the basis for creating viable, self-sustaining fen wetlands in the oil sands region. The conservative landform design, with controls over surface water and groundwater/seepage inputs, was guided by a detailed hydrological site investigation, groundwater modeling, and a parallel reclamation research program. A critical element of the fen design is control of salinity in the fen. It is hoped that by piping freshwater into the fen and under-draining the fen that salinity can be controlled until the wetland is self-sustaining. Wetland construction is expected be completed during the summer of 2012, and the integrated, multidisciplinary, long-term research program will begin in earnest. Syncrude's watershed approach is fundamental to understanding how landforms function, and will provide us with the best techniques for the reclamation of self-sustaining boreal landscapes.

ACKNOWLEDGMENTS

Results from the Syncrude experimental cells were provided by Melissa House (Southern Illinois University) and for the greenhouse experiment by Sara Koropchak (Southern Illinois University). Our appreciation is expressed to members of the Sandhill Fen Technical Advisory Panel (Lee Barbour, Jan Ciborowski, Kevin Devito, Lee Foote, Simon Landhäusser, Carl Mendoza). Dale Vitt and Gord McKenna are also members of the panel. Lynne Barlow of Syncrude Canada Ltd. was crucial in steering the watershed construction. BGC Engineering provided fundamental design guidance and engineering expertise. Clara Qualizza provided the vision and inspiration for this project.

REFERENCES

CONRAD (Canadian Oil Sands Network for Research and Development). (1999). *Reclamation Research and Development Strategy Development Sessions*. Canadian Oil Sands Network for Research and Development Environmental Technical Planning Group, Alberta Research Council, Calgary, AB.

Koropchak, S. C. (2010). *Carex aquatilis as a Pioneer Species for Boreal Wetland Reclamation in Northern Alberta*. M.Sc. thesis, Southern Illinois University, Carbondale, IL.

Syncrude Canada Ltd. (2008). *EIP Instrumented Watershed Sandhill Fen-Permit Level Design*.

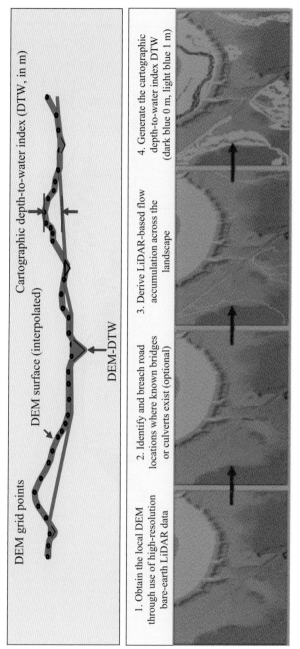

DEM grid points

Cartographic depth-to-water index (DTW, in m)

DEM surface (interpolated)

DEM-DTW

1. Obtain the local DEM through use of high-resolution bare-earth LiDAR data

2. Identify and breach road locations where known bridges or culverts exist (optional)

3. Derive LiDAR-based flow accumulation across the landscape

4. Generate the cartographic depth-to-water index DTW (dark blue 0 m, light blue 1 m)

Figure 4.2. Overview and principles of the GIS-based flow channel and cartographic depth-to-water modeling and mapping processes.

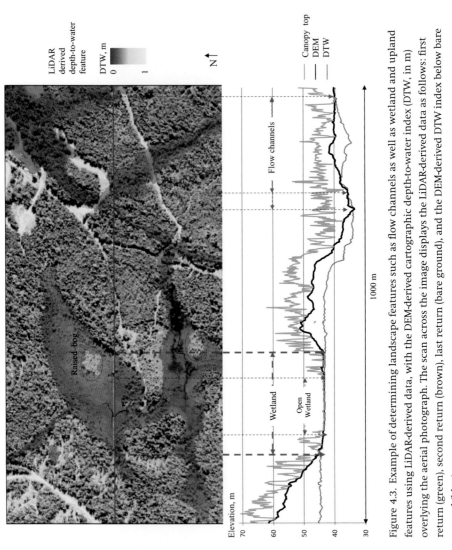

Figure 4.3. Example of determining landscape features such as flow channels as well as wetland and upland features using LiDAR-derived data, with the DEM-derived cartographic depth-to-water index (DTW, in m) overlying the aerial photograph. The scan across the image displays the LiDAR-derived data as follows: first return (green), second return (brown), last return (bare ground), and the DEM-derived DTW index below bare ground (blue).

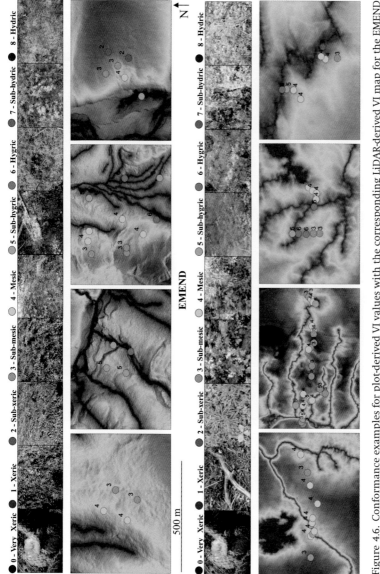

Figure 4.6. Conformance examples for plot-derived VI values with the corresponding LiDAR-derived VI map for the EMEND area (lower images), and the Willmore Wilderness Park (upper images), also showing xeric to hydric ground vegetation images.

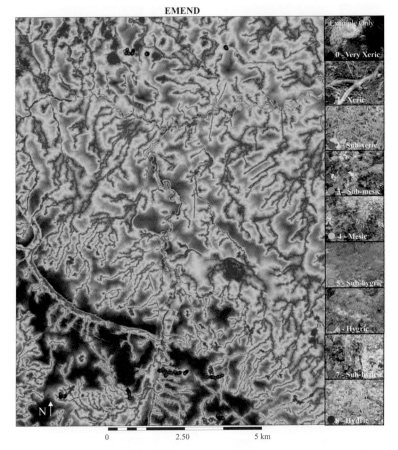

Figure 4.7. Vegetation index for the EMEND area.

Willmore Wilderness Park

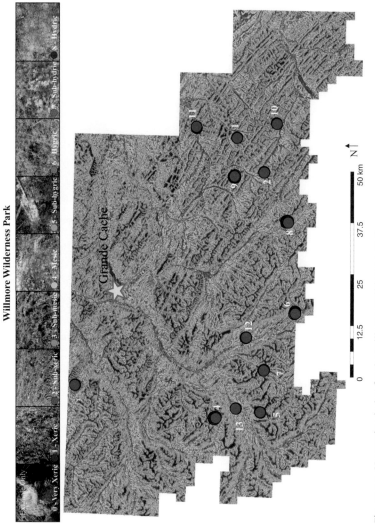

Figure 4.8. Vegetation index for the Willmore Wilderness Park.

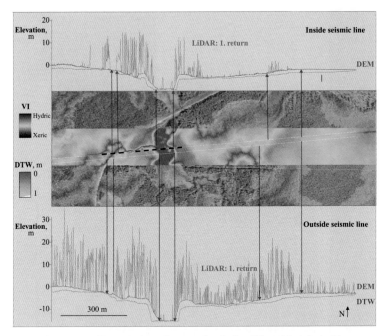

Figure 4.9. LiDAR-generated vegetation index (VI) and height (m) in relation to bare-ground DEM and the cartographic DTW index (shaded dark to light blue) along and off a 1500 m seismic line scan within the EMEND area, overlaid on aerial photograph.

Figure 8.1. East-In-pit, a former mined out pit, filled with tailings and composite tailings, showing the location of the Sandhill Fen Watershed area in the northwest corner.

(A)

(B)

Figure 8.2. Sandhill Fen Watershed. (**A**) Photograph of fen area in the summer of 2011 during the construction phase. (**B**) Satellite photograph of the watershed on July 30, 2011, showing the status of construction activities including peat placement in perched and main fens and reclamation soils on all but the two eastern hummocks.

Figure 8.3. Aerial photograph of 28 test cells (10 m × 20 m) constructed to investigate the vegetation response to peat source, placement depth, degree of compaction, timing of placement, and water source. Note the white pick-up truck at the top of the picture, to scale. (Photograph from BGC Engineering.)

Figure 9.1. Looking north at the Suncor Fen site known as the TLC, pre-construction, on Suncor's lease in Fort McMurray, AB. The site approximates 675 m at its widest extent near the south end. (Photo credit: Gord McKenna.)

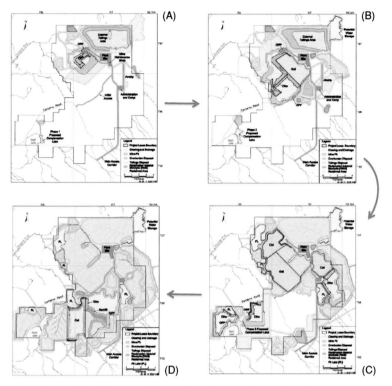

Figure 15.1. Schematic illustration of progressive reclamation (green areas) on the Kearl Lake mine footprint for the periods 2012–2016 (**A**), 2022–2026 (**B**), 2032–2041 (**C**), and 2052–2060 (**D**).

CHRISTINE DALY, JONATHAN PRICE, FEREIDOUN REZANEZHAD,
RÉMY POULIOT, LINE ROCHEFORT, AND MARTHA D. GRAF

9

Initiatives in oil sand reclamation

Considerations for building a fen peatland in a post-mined oil sands landscape

INTRODUCTION

Originally, wetlands comprised over 50% of the land base in northeastern Alberta; over 90% of these were peatlands (Vitt et al., 1996). In the Athabasca oil sands region, the landscape is disturbed by either *in situ* or open-pit mining activities to recover bitumen below the surface. Open-pit mining removes entire landscapes, which oil companies are entrusted to reconstruct to the best of their abilities. By law, mining disturbances must be reclaimed to a state of "equivalent land capability" (OSWWG, 2000). As all wetland types and aquatic systems fall within the same land use capability class (Class 5) (CEMA, 2006), there is some latitude on reclamation target landscapes. However, provincial directives, developed in collaboration with industry and other stakeholders, aim to reclaim some of these areas to peatlands.

Although peatlands are the dominant wetland type in the Athabasca region, marshes have been the focus of reclamation projects, because they are hydrologically simpler than peatlands and may develop spontaneously in poorly drained sections of disturbed landscapes (Harris, 2007). Moreover, many marsh species are resistant to salt contamination present in post-mined oil sands landscapes (Daly and Ciborowksi, 2008; Hornung and Foote, 2007). Peatland vegetation, especially mosses, is not believed to be tolerant of saline conditions (Boerner and Forman, 1975); however, fen peatlands can be dominated by sedge and shrub vegetation, accumulate carbon (peat), and still fulfill several other ecological functions characteristic of marshes (Trites and Bayley, 2009).

Restoration and Reclamation of Boreal Ecosystems, ed. Dale Vitt and Jagtar Bhatti. Published by Cambridge University Press. © Cambridge University Press 2012.

As fens were the dominant ecosystem in the pre-mined landscape, recent efforts have focused on fen reclamation. Fens have a peat layer of 40 cm or more and support brown mosses and graminoid vegetation (i.e., sedges, grasses) (National Wetlands Working Group, 1997). If fens were systematically replaced by marshes in the post-mined landscape, there would be a loss of habitat for diverse biota, such as amphibians (Mazerolle, 1999), birds (Lachance et al., 2005), moose, caribou (Berg, 1992), unique plants (*Sarracenia purpurea*) (Johnson et al., 1995), and rare plants (*Liparis loeselii, Cardamine dentata*) (Griffiths, 2007).

Peatlands are complex ecosystems that are difficult to construct as they take thousands of years to develop naturally (Clymo, 1983). Studies by Price et al. (2007; 2010) challenged this concept and present a conceptual model. This model (referred to as the fen model throughout this chapter) aims to create fen peatlands using peat from newly expanded oil sands mine operations and to support created fens with groundwater inflow from a constructed watershed.

The fen model was later adapted into Alberta Environmental Protection and Enhancement Act (AEPEA) approvals, which recommended testing this concept in the field. Hence, some oil sands mining companies are now mandated to attempt peatland reclamation. The goal of this chapter is to describe the peatland reclamation initiatives that are taking place in the Alberta oil sands, with a focus on the Suncor pilot fen watershed being constructed at Suncor Energy Inc. (Suncor).

SUNCOR PILOT FEN WATERSHED PROGRAM

The Suncor pilot fen (Suncor Fen) program commenced in 2008 in order to validate the fen model recommendations and to meet the terms and conditions of the AEPEA. The goal of the Suncor Fen program is to establish the hydrology necessary to maintain fen plant communities in a constructed fen. The objectives of the program are to construct a fen that: (1) is a self-sustaining ecosystem; (2) is capable of accumulating carbon; (3) is capable of supporting a variety of habitats and typical fen species; and (4) enables techniques for future fen creation to be tested and refined.

Several challenges were inherent to this project. First, fen watershed reclamation had not yet been attempted in boreal Canada when the program was initiated. Thus, there was a limited knowledge base upon which to build. Second, elevated concentration of sodium (Na) and naphthenic acids (NAs)[1] are present in tailings materials used to construct the

---

[1] Strictly speaking, naphthenic acids are deprotonated naphthenate anions that are naturally present in bitumen, but become concentrated during oil sands extraction.

fen watershed. Both Na and NAs negatively affect the growth of typical fen plants, such as sedges and bryophytes, as both can be toxic to wetland plants (Apostol et al., 2004; Trites and Bayley, 2008). Elevated salinity causes toxic accumulation of ions in plants, which inhibits plant growth (Jacobs and Timmer, 2005; Timmer and Teng, 2004).

The design of a fen system in the post-mined landscape requires a broad range of understanding of the flows and stores of water to and within the system, the transport and fate of contaminants and their impact on the germination, growth, and survival of plants, and how these contribute to developing a self-sustaining, carbon accumulating system. This chapter outlines the theoretical, empirical, and procedural considerations undertaken in the design of the Suncor fen.

RESTORATION AND RECLAMATION HYDROLOGY

Wetlands are essentially a hydrological landscape. Although once commonly regarded as a nuisance, we now recognize the importance of wetland functions, and consequently, wetland restoration and reclamation have become important and often required activities. It is essential to distinguish between restoration and reclamation. Restoration takes advantage of the residual function of a degraded system situated in a landscape and aims to restore a site to its previous community structure or ecosystem functions (SER 2002). There have been many failures, which often arise from the inability to replicate the hydrological functions that drive the ecology (Mitsch and Wilson, 1996). Restoration of site hydrology may fail due to poor understanding of site-specific factors, which ultimately can compromise the local water budget, or when broader landscape changes have occurred, wetland restoration sites may no longer be suitable for supplying water at the same rate or volume as in the original system. In contrast to restoration, reclamation is the process of making land fit for a designated function. In the case of wetlands, this function can range from recreational wetlands (i.e., duck hunting, angling), to detention basins for hydrological and water quality control (Bishay et al., 1993), to more-or-less functional ecosystems (US EPA, 1993). In any of these, the design specifically accounts for the hydrology to achieve the desired function. However, to reclaim a fully functional wetland ecosystem, the hydrological design must foster the appropriate biogeochemical and ecological functions, which requires a detailed understanding of the abiotic and biotic processes. While great advances have been made in this regard (Mitsch and Wilson, 1996), each reclaimed wetland is unique, and there remains considerable uncertainty as to how the interdependent mechanisms of hydrology, biogeochemistry, and ecology will manifest in any particular instance. Because the oil sands open-pit mining process completely removes the original ecosystem, wetland reclamation rather than restoration has become a focus.

The climate of the Western Boreal Plain (WBP) near Fort Mc-Murray, Alberta, is cool and dry, with average annual total precipitation (P) of 456 mm, with 34% as snow (Environment Canada, 2011; www.climate.weatheroffice.ec.gc.ca). Potential evapotranspiration (PET) in the WBP is approximately 517 mm (Bothe and Abraham, 1993), although actual evaporation (ET) is far less than PET. Carey (2008) reported average annual evapotranspiration as 251 mm/y (2003–2005) from reclaimed oil sands overburden materials. However, ET from open wetland areas where water is not generally limited will approach the potential rate (Lafleur, 1990; Price, 1994). The point is that evapotranspiration demand is high in this region and wetlands will only develop where surface and groundwater inflows are present, which may occur only sporadically during wet years.

Devito et al. (2005) noted that water availability coincides with the period of maximum evapotranspiration demand, and thus there is limited opportunity for overland flow and runoff to feed these systems. Given that fens comprise about half of the landscape in the oil sands region (Vitt and Chee, 1989), the upland area that could contribute to water fluxes is relatively small, of the order of 1:1. Furthermore, the connections between upland and fen are often transient. Significant recharge to fens of the WBP may therefore take place only during infrequent wet years that occur in a 10–15-year cycle (Ferone and Devito, 2004). In fact, flow reversal (peatland water supplies mineral upland) occurs because the water table of upland areas often drops sufficiently during dry periods due to the high water demand of poplars (Ferone and Devito, 2004; Smerdon et al. 2008). From a reclamation design point of view, however, there is sufficient uncertainty regarding the mechanisms of surface and groundwater inputs, as well as their frequency and magnitude of input, that a conservative approach is essential. The design must include appropriate consideration of hydrological processes beyond the wetland/upland boundary.

Many of the principles of peatland reclamation can be derived from peatland restoration research in Canada. This has focused mainly on bogs, for which a successful method has been developed (Rochefort et al., 2003). This approach uses a "moss transfer" method (see Chapter 14), whereby shredded material including Sphagnum mosses and rhizomes of vascular plants are milled from an undisturbed "donor" site, spread thinly onto prepared cutover peat surfaces of a rewetted bog (i.e., ditches blocked), and covered with a straw mulch to reduce ET losses (Price et al., 1998). A similar approach has been used for fen restoration in Quebec (Cobbaert et al., 2004; Graf and Rochefort, 2008), and direct plantings and seeding have also been used in small alpine fens in Colorado (Cooper and MacDonald, 2000). However, no critical moisture thresholds have been established for fen species reestablishment, as was done for bogs (Price and Whitehead, 2004). While vascular plants can extract moisture with considerable suction, *Sphagnum* mosses rely on capillary rise (Price et al., 2009) generated by the relatively weak tension in the large pores that form between the stems and leaves of individual plants clustered tightly together in a community (Price and Whittington, 2010).

The aforementioned hydrological research on mosses has been restricted to *Sphagnum* species and no similar work has been done on the brown mosses that occur in fens. However, Cobbaert et al. (2004) reported successful reestablishment of fen plants, excluding brown mosses, in a previously mined peatland where soil-water pressures temporarily dropped as low as -200 mb. However, given that fens typically have a higher water table than bogs (Ingram, 1983), it seems probable that non-vascular species (especially brown mosses) are poorly adapted to dry conditions. Indeed, Graf et al. (2008) found that on abandoned harvested fens in eastern Canada, Cyperaceae and Gramineae species were especially successful, but bryophytes did relatively poorly.

To date, fen reclamation over oil sands overburden and tailings sand structures is an untested concept. While fen peatlands are under construction at Suncor and Syncrude Canada Ltd. (Syncrude), we are far from being able to assess their long-term persistence in the landscape. These reclaimed fens aim to provide a peat substrate (imported from land clearance elsewhere on their leases) that can support fen vegetation, but they manipulate the hydrology in very different ways to achieve the target substrate conditions. The Syncrude fen relies on a managed water supply, whereas the Suncor fen incorporates an integral upland system intended to provide an adequate water supply, but is subject to the vagaries of weather. The fundamental problem for fen reclamation is to design a groundwater system that can provide the inflows required to sustain the hydrological, biogeochemical, and ecological processes and functions.

OIL SANDS PROCESS WATER, SODIUM AND NAPHTHENIC ACIDS TRANSPORT THROUGH PEAT, AND THE IMPACT ON FEN VEGETATION

It is not known whether fen plants can survive long-term exposure to oil sands process water (OSPW) containing sodium (Na) and naphthenic acids (NAs), naturally occurring substances in the oil sand deposit, or how these substances move through peat and interact with plant roots. A research program was initiated to address these challenges to reclaiming fens. In this program, laboratory and greenhouse mesocosm experiments were run to determine how OSPW is transported through peat driven by evapotranspiration from a moss and/or vascular plant cover, and how these plants and microbial communities react to OSPW contamination. The main objectives were to characterize: (1) the movement of process-affected water in peat substrate, and (2) survival and growth of common fen species native to the oil sands region.

Adsorption and dispersion of oil sands process-affected water in peat

Flow and transport in peat soils are dependent upon the chemical characteristics of the solute (Hill and Siegel, 1991), microbiological processes (Todorova et al., 2005), and the physical characteristics of the peat porous matrix (Ours et al., 1997; Price and Woo, 1988). Oil sands-derived aqueous mixtures of Na and NAs are readily transported through porous geological media (Gervais and Barker, 2005), but very little information is available in the literature on their transport through peat. Peat has a complex cell structure that results in a dual porosity comprising open, dead-end, and closed or partially closed pores that can delay the passage of nonreactive solutes (Hoag and Price, 1997). However, both Na and NAs are strongly adsorbed by organic matter (Ho and McKay, 2000; Janfada et al., 2006). Thus, an understanding of the migration and persistence of Na and NAs in the rooting zone of peat is needed, because these factors will control the critical toxicity levels in the reclaimed fen, where OSPW is expected to be present within the boundaries of the peatland as a result of the use of tailings sand as one of the construction materials.

To characterize the fate and transport of OSPW in peat, Rezanezhad et al. (2010) ran a series of experiments to determine the amount of adsorption and how the solute behaves in a solution flowing through the dual-porosity porous medium. Sorption of Na and NAs in OSPW on fen peat from Alberta was tested by mixing it at different concentrations with dried peat and measuring the concentration of the eluent. They found that approximately 94% of the 43.5 mg L^{-1} of NAs in OSPW was adsorbed by 1 kg of peat. For Na, ~84% sorption occurred with 382 mg L^{-1} kg^{-1} of peat. The adsorption of NAs and Na on peat fit Freundlich linear isotherms with distribution coefficients of 6.53 and 5.74 L kg^{-1}, respectively. This relationship is important to describe how much solute is removed from a flowing solution; for example, during transport modeling. This was done for Na through the fen peat by administering a step input of known concentration into a peat column and measuring the time for solute to break through to the outflow. Rezanezhad et al. (2010) showed the retardation of Na was R = 1.92 (i.e., 1.92 times slower than the average velocity of water molecules) using a two-region (mobile and immobile) non-equilibrium transport model to represent the dual porosity soil. The model confirmed that part of retardation is attributed to solute exchange between the mobile and immobile phases. Breakthrough tests were not performed on NAs due to poor analytical precision at low concentrations.

Rezanezhad et al. (2011) also examined OSPW migration in peat monoliths in the greenhouse, which were covered with either moss or vascular plants (see next section). Oil sands process water with concentrations representing field values ($\sim$40 mg L^{-1} NAs and 385 mg L^{-1} Na) was introduced to the base of the 76-cm thick mesocosms and drawn upward by evaporation from the mosses (0.5 to 1.6 mm d^{-1}) and evapotranspiration from the vascular plants (2.7 to 4.7 mm d^{-1}).

In the moss mesocosm, the increase in mass of Na and NAs in the liquid phase was sequentially delayed at higher elevations in the profile over 310 days of evapotranspiration. At a depth of -5 cm, the adsorption rate was 17.5% for Na and $\sim$8% for NAs, respectively. In the vascular plant mesocosms, Na concentration of the -5-cm and -10-cm layer exceeded that of the -15- and -25-cm layer because of evapoconcentration. At a depth of -5 cm, the adsorption rate was 25% for Na and $\sim$5% for NAs, respectively. In both mesocosms the amount of solute in the solid phase, due to sorption, was approximately one order of magnitude larger than in the liquid phase. These high concentrations, although considerably delayed, were detrimental to the moss health, but not the vascular plants (see next section).

Response of moss and vascular plants to oil sands process water

The effects of OSPW on fen vascular plants and mosses needs to be established to determine the target species for reclamation. Bryophytes are either absent or not prominent in saline conditions (Adam, 1976; Shacklette, 1961; Vitt, 1976) and salinity might be a driving factor in peatland distribution in the boreal plains (Vitt et al., 1996). Naturally, saline wetlands supporting salt tolerant plant communities are uncommon in the boreal region (Trites and Bayley, 2009) and only a few moss species appear in these saline fens (*Bryum pseudotriquetrum*, *Campylium stellatum*, and *Drepanocladus aduncus* [Vitt et al., 1993]). Salinity in OSPW may limit the development of peat mosses in oil sand post-mined areas due to low tolerances to salinity. Understanding the salinity thresholds of key peatland species is thus essential to peatland reclamation in a post-mined landscape. The type of salt is an important factor influencing plant growth (Franklin and Zwiazek, 2004) and NaCl seems to be the most harmful for boreal species (Nguyen et al., 2006). However, little research on salinity effects has been carried out on peatland mosses (Bloise and Vitt, 2011). Here, we summarize research funded by Suncor that addresses the tolerance of fen species to OSPW on two scales: (1) bryophytes in microcosms (Petri dishes); and (2) mesocosms experiment related to those described in the previous section.

Microscale experiments (Pouliot et al, unpublished) determined the effect of OSPW salts on the growth of mosses by immersing selected species in solutions of NaCl and Na_2SO_4. This includes *B. pseudotriquetrum* and *C. stellatum*, which are found in saline Alberta fens (Vitt et al., 1993); and *Sphagnum warnstorfii* and *Tomenthypnum nitens*, which are common in non-saline fens in the Athabasca region (Chee and Vitt, 1989). Differences between the number of innovations (i.e., new shoots emerging from a moss fragment) counted on ten moss fragments at the beginning and at the end of each experiment, or the number of capitula (for *S. warnstorfii*), used to compare treatments.

First, *C. stellatum*, *S. warnstorfii*, and *T. nitens* were immersed in a saline solution (0, 100, 300, or 500 mg L^{-1} of NaCl) for $\frac{1}{4}$, 1, 3, or 7 days before being placed in Petri dishes and watered with rainwater for 65 (*C. stellatum* and *S. warnstorfii*) or 100 days (*T. nitens*). Moss species tolerated their immersion in saline conditions and, in some cases, showed an increase in the number of innovations or capitula. For *S. warnstorfii*, the situation was different; a longer immersion time increased the number of capitula when salt concentrations were equal to 0 or 100 mg L^{-1} (higher for 0 mg L^{-1}), but peaks were observed around three days (300 mg L^{-1}) and one day (500 mg L^{-1}).

In a second experiment, *B. pseudotriquetrum*, *C. stellatum*, and *T. nitens* were watered with different saline solutions (NaCl, Na_2SO_4, and a combination of both) for approximately 100 days, at concentrations of 0, 30, 50, or 70% of the concentrations found in OSPW, which contains around 500 mg L^{-1} of NaCl and 600 mg L^{-1} of Na_2SO_4 (in OSPW samples taken by Suncor in 2009). Bryophyte growth was not stimulated when they were watered with saline solutions. Salt type had no effect; an increase of salt concentration of either solution inhibited the development of new innovations for two of the three species (*B. pseudotriquetrum* and *T. nitens*).

These data show that the tested moss species common to northeastern Alberta may be tolerant to salt concentrations typical of post-mined oil sands landscapes (Trites and Bailey, 2008). Furthermore, salt concentrations in OSPW were probably not high enough to disrupt photosynthesis (Wilcox, 1984). Contrary to the findings of Nguyen et al. (2006), sodium chloride (NaCl) did not have a stronger effect than Na_2SO_4 on mosses. Thus, all tested species would likely survive periodic inundations in OSPW as may occur during spring snowmelt or after heavy rains. Furthermore, as immersion time had a positive effect on the number of initiations, punctual saline stress perhaps prompted mosses to be more productive. However, constant growth in salt concentration, even at only 30% of concentration in OSPW, was sufficient to reduce the number of new innovations and would be detrimental for mosses. Hence, persistent inundation with OSPW should be avoided if the restoration of a moss carpet is an objective. Our experiment showed that threshold levels for salt tolerance of the species tested were possibly not reached. However, evapoconcentration of Na (and other salts) has been shown to reach 1.2 to 23.5 g L^{-1}, in moss and vascular plant experiments, respectively (Rezanezhad et al. 2011). Therefore, under field conditions the stress on mosses (and many vascular species) will be high. We conclude that B. pseudotriquetrum and C. stellatum already found in saline fens (Vitt et al., 1993) seem to be the best choice in fen creation following oil sands exploitation. The sensitivity to NAs was not tested.

In fen reclamation, it is necessary to understand the ability of candidate plant species to survive and grow on a peat substrate receiving OSPW. A greenhouse experiment with five replicates was conducted to test the response of whole plant transplants of five vascular plants (Calamagrostis stricta, Carex atherodes, C. utriculata, Trichophorum cespitosum, and Triglochin maritima) growing in peat and receiving varying concentrations of OSPW (Pouliot et al., in press). The OSPW effect was tested at different concentrations: (a) nondiluted OSPW (approximately 54 mg L^{-1} of naphthenic acid and 569 mg L^{-1} of Na); (b) diluted OSPW (approximately 40 mg L^{-1} NAs and 400 mg L^{-1} Na); and (c) rain water (control treatment). All these species are common in rich fens of the oil sands region (Chee and Vitt, 1989). The experiment was run over two growing seasons, where the first was wetter than the second. A plant health index was noted for all species, ranging from 7 (100% healthy) to 1 (100% dead). Over both growing seasons there was no significant decrease between the OSPW treatments for plant health for vascular plants (health index averaged 5.3), although at the end of each season there were signs of senescence (health index averaged 4.1). Similar results were observed in another experiment where only one OSPW concentration was tested for *C. aquatilis* and *C. stricta* (approximately 54 mg L^{-1} of naphthenic acid and 569 mg L^{-1} of Na) (Rezanezhad et al., 2011). The increase in Na and NAs in the rooting zone (see previous section), especially during the relatively dry second growing season, had little apparent effect on vascular plant health.

It appears that peat has a high buffering capacity which adsorbs many substances found in OSPW, and the transport of Na and NAs in peat substrates is highly retarded (see the previous section). In addition, peat affected the concentration of potentially toxic compounds in the rooting zone. Vascular plants that received OSPW did not show signs of stress. This is consistent with the results of Trites and Bayley (2008), which showed that whole plant transplants of vascular wetland species were able to grow in oil sands wetlands. Here, the concentrations are low enough that Gramineae and Cyperaceae, for example, do not require adaptations such as maintaining high potassium concentrations in their tissue to block the entry of sodium (Albert and Popp, 1977; Cooper, 1982; Gorham et al., 1980). Peat thicknesses in the Suncor pilot fen currently under construction will be much greater (~2 m) than in the tested experimental units. This suggests that several years may pass before any effect of OSPW on plants is detectable, potentially allowing a healthy cover of graminoid vegetation to establish. Moreover, normal precipitation in the oil sands district is higher than was simulated in the greenhouse, and potentials for leaching, horizontal transport, and surface runoff losses are present in the field. Some plants regenerated better and began reproducing more quickly than others. These plants also produced much more biomass, indicating that they might be better peat-accumulating species. *Carex aquatilis*, *C. atherodes*, *C. utriculata*, and *T. maritima* produced more aboveground biomass than *C. stricta* or *T. cespitosum*, making them more useful species for restoring a vegetative cover quickly and, potentially, creating a peat-accumulating system.

In the greenhouse experiment described in the previous section, mosses were not affected during the first growing season when watering was more similar to the amount of precipitation that historically falls each summer in the oil sands region (plant health index of 6.6), but they rapidly declined in the second growing season (dropping to a plant health index of 1.5). We interpret that decline in moss health in the OSPW-affected mesocosms to toxicity coupled with water stress (in the drier second season). Contrary to the Petri dish experiment, where mosses grew in the presence of OSPW in a closed environment with high humidity, OSPW treatments in the greenhouse were detrimental for mosses in situations of water stress, indicating that water control should be a crucial step in fen creation following oil sands exploitation.

SUNCOR FEN SITE INVESTIGATION, DESIGN, CONSTRUCTION, REVEGETATION, AND MONITORING

The Suncor fen design uses an upland linked to fen peat placed at the base of a slope designed to provide the requisite amount of water to keep peat sufficiently wet to support fen vegetation. The simulations of Price et al. (2007; 2010) tested a range of material types (by varying hydraulic properties) and geometric arrangements (slope, upland contributing area, layer thickness, etc.), under: (1) severe drought, and (2) climatic conditions characteristic of the Fort McMurray area. The simulations were examined to determine the ability of the system to sustain a critical threshold pressure in the peat during drought conditions. Price et al. (2007; 2010) caution, however, that the threshold condition (soil water pressure at 10 cm depth ≥ 100 mb) was set for *Sphagnum* mosses in drained cutover bogs (Price and Whitehead, 2004), and as previously noted, has not been tested for fen species.

The final design for the Suncor fen (unpublished) was based on the fen model recommendations using materials meeting the hydraulic requirements they specified. However, the final design was modified in consultation with geotechnical engineers to accommodate the specific morphological and hydrogeological conditions of the site. It will rely on a thick peat layer (~ 2 m) to delay and disperse transport of contaminants to the rooting zone.

Moving from concept to design began by establishing the goals and objectives of the program, as previously outlined. The program was then divided into five parts: (1) site investigation, (2) watershed design, (3) vegetation strategies, (4) construction, and (5) research and monitoring.

Site investigation

First, an appropriate location for the constructed fen watershed was required. Site selection was based on the following criteria: (1) Suncor had no future plans to disturb the location; (2) the sediments were geotechnically stable and capable of supporting a wet environment; (3) the location's topography contained gentle slopes, which facilitated the fen model recommendations outlined by Price et al. (2010); (4) the region was large enough to enable all fen dimensions to be a minimum of 100 m to minimize edge effects; (5) close proximity to natural areas that may

Figure 9.1. Looking north at the Suncor Fen site known as the TLC, pre-construction, on Suncor's lease in Fort McMurray, AB. The site approximates 675 m at its widest extent near the south end. (Photo credit: Gord McKenna.) (See color plate section for colored image.)

act as natural seed banks and wildlife corridors; (6) materials planned for use in construction were nearby, so as to minimize haul route costs; and (7) the area was in an easily accessible, low mine traffic area, safe for researchers and tours. Suncor reclamation staff compiled a list of all available areas on Suncor's open-pit mining leases and compared each potential site to the site selection criteria. An area known as the tailings line corridor (TLC) met all of these criteria and was selected as the optimal site for fen reclamation. The TLC is located on Suncor's Millennium lease in the southwest corner of the active Millennium mine and east of the wildlife corridor, a parcel of natural forest over 100 m wide along the Athabasca River (Figure 9.1). The TLC was a pit previously mined for bitumen and later filled in with overburden. Part of an intact natural ravine with wildlife habitat (i.e., birds and small mammals) at the south end of the construction site was incorporated into the design.

Fen watershed design

After site selection was complete, an investigation of the construction site was initiated to provide an understanding of the site-specific hydrogeological setting and how the fen model recommendations could be incorporated. Specifically, the site investigation examined the stratigraphic profile, geotechnical stability, groundwater hydrology, and water quality.

The geologic formations present include Devonian limestone below a thin layer (~5 m) of fluvial sands. The Middle and Lower McMurray formations overlay the fluvial sands and were capped with overburden material containing a mixture of lean oil sand, glacial material, clay, shale, and loamy sand (Kessler et al., 2010). In general, the overburden materials varied from uniform sand, consisting of approximately 85% sand and 15% silt and clay-sized particles to a well-graded material consisting of 40% sand and 60% silt and clay-sized particles, based on the Unified Soil Classification System (Kessler et al., 2010).

Once the site investigation was complete, the fen watershed design phase commenced. Both the site investigation and fen watershed designs were completed by BGC Engineering Inc. and O'Kane Consultants Inc. The Suncor pilot fen designs were modified from the Price et al. (2007; 2010) fen watershed design recommendations to meet site-specific conditions, and were as follows (Figure 9.2):

1. Construct the base of the fen watershed with a liner that has a relatively uniform hydraulic conductivity (K) less than or equal to 1×10^{-10} m s^{-1}. For the site-specific conditions, a synthetic liner is suggested because it more than meets the minimum hydraulic requirements and minimizes cut and fill volumes, thus cost.
2. Use a liner slope of 3%, which provides a sufficient hydraulic gradient to move water downslope (i.e., without excessive seepage or ET loss).
3. Construct the upland aquifer of tailings sand with $K = 1 \times 10^{-4}$ m s^{-1}, which enables groundwater to flow relatively rapidly toward the fen. The recommended thickness of the sandy aquifer is 3 m near the fen to 2 m at the upland end of the system. This is intended to keep the water table a relatively constant 2 m below the surface, given a wedge-shaped saturated zone expected to develop over the liner. Otherwise a shallow water table in the upland near the fen boundary would be susceptible to salinization.
4. Construct the system with an upland:fen area ratio of ~3:1.
5. Strategically place a series of gentle swales and hummocks on the upland to intercept and recharge surface water (i.e., snowmelt) from adjacent slopes.
6. Use a relatively thin (20 cm depth) LFH (boreal forest) soil acquired from newly cleared lease areas over the upland aquifer to promote

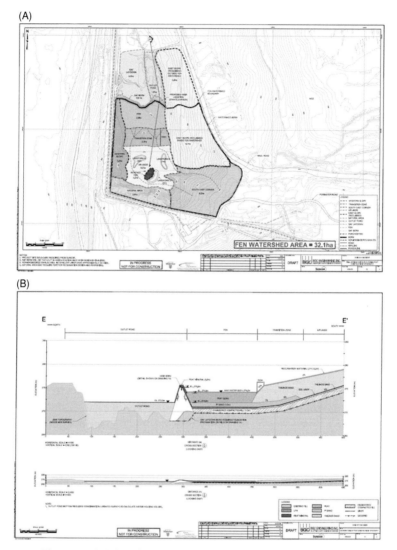

Figure 9.2. (**A**) Plan view and (**B**) cross-section of the Suncor Fen watershed conceptual-level designs.

infiltration while maintaining an adequate moisture content to support plant growth.

7.   Peat should be placed 2 m deep in the fen, overlying a 50 cm layer of glaciofluvial sand that extends part-way upslope, with the intent of precluding a discharge zone at the upland–fen interface, and instead, distributing the water (and salts) more uniformly beneath the fen.

The Suncor fen watershed designs covered 32.1 hectares (Figure 9.2). Fen peat (2 m deep) from a new lease being opened for development is to be placed at the base of the upland aquifer system. This system is designed to supply groundwater and surface runoff. The benefit of using a relatively thick peat layer is that: (1) it can dampen water table drawdown (Price, 2003; Whittington and Price, 2006); and (2) it will increase dispersion of contaminants and delay their passage to the rooting zone (Rezanezhad et al., 2010). The upland:fen ratio will be 2.7:1 for the constructed system; however, the ratio increases to 10.1:1 when the surrounding slopes (western slope, east slope, southeast corner, and natural area) are included.

Some settlement of basal sediments is anticipated within the site as it was previously mined out (2001–2004) and later in-filled with overburden (2005–2006). Consequently, geogrid and 1 m-thick engineered compacted clay underlay were placed under a thin layer of tailings sand (0.3-m deep) beneath a geosynthetic clay liner, to protect against localized, uneven settlement that could challenge the integrity of the liner. A geosynthetic clay liner was selected because it went beyond the optimal requirement of 1×10^{-10} m s^{-1} to sustain a perched water table. A berm has been constructed around the entire watershed to ensure that surface water flows, spills, etc. from nearby operations cannot enter the system. Excess water in the fen will discharge over an adjustable weir into an outlet pond that is directed northward via an engineered stream channel to a containment pond designed to contain OSPW water within Suncor's lease. The adjustable weir allows for fine-tuning of the water level in the fen following construction–it is not intended to be used (adjusted frequently) for long-term management but only to allow flexibility as the system comes to equilibrium and until we determine the optimal weir setting. A small (0.2 ha) perched fen with 0.3-m deep fen peat will be placed above tailings sand in the upland area adjacent to a hummock at a 1:1 hummock to fen ratio. This will be a small scale study within the Suncor pilot fen program to investigate whether perched fens can develop over sand within a small watershed in a similar manner to the natural perched fens present within the regional landscape (Devito et al., 2011).

Fen watershed construction

Construction of the fen watershed commenced in 2010 and is planned to continue through 2012. Construction is managed by Suncor Reclamation Operations, carried out by local contractors, and monitored by a third party contractor and surveyor.

Revegetating the Suncor fen watershed

The Suncor fen watershed fell within the boreal mixedwood ecological area (Beckingham and Archibald, 1996). Plants characteristic of this region were selected for planting within the watershed. Planting strategies were divided between fen and upland regions.

Fen planting strategies

Based on the significant volume of peat (2-m depth) within the constructed fen, the nutrient rich coversoils (forest soils and mixed organic and mineral soils) overlaying the surrounding upland watershed and the underlying tailings sand, the Suncor pilot fen is expected to receive alkaline nutrient-rich water, which is characteristic of a moderate-to-extreme rich fen. Trees will not be planted in the fen itself, although they will be planted on upland slopes. Target plant communities for the fen include shrub, forb, grass, sedge, and moss species. Therefore, the Suncor fen is expected to develop into either a shrubby or, if the shrubs do not adapt well, a graminoid moderate rich to rich fen. Target species were selected using the following criteria: (1) rich fen plant; (2) shrub, sedge, grass, forb, or moss species; (3) shows some sign of saline tolerance; (4) good peat accumulator; and (5) present in local fens. The target species are: sage-leaved willow (*Salix candida*), diamondleaf willow (*S. planifolia*), dwarf birch (*Betula pumila*), water sedge (*C. aquatilis*), beaked sedge (*C. utriculata*), slender sedge (*C. lasiocarpa*), two-stamened sedge (*C. diandra*), marsh reed grass (*Calamogrostis canadensis*), seaside arrow grass (*T. maritima*), northern reedgrass (*C. stricta*), golden moss (*T. nitens*), drepanocladus moss (*Drepanocladus aduncus*), scorpidium moss (*Scorpidium scorpioides*), tufted moss (*Aulacomnium palustre*), and Warnstorf's peat moss (*S. warnstorfii*). The selected species met most if not all of the criteria. There were a few exceptions. A few species were added to the target species list for their ecological or cultural significance to local aboriginal peoples, even though they only met a few of the target species criteria. Such species included: cloudberry (*Rubus chamaemorus*), round-leafed sundew (*Drosera rotundifolia*), pitcher plant (*Sarracenia purpurea*), and small bog cranberry (*Oxycoccus microcarpus*).

Although poor water quality may occur shortly after fen watershed construction due to the presence of salt ions and some organics (i.e., NAs), water quality is expected to improve over time as rainwater flushes the sand aquifer with fresh water. Consequently, many salt tolerant species were selected for revegetating the constructed fen. However, it will likely evolve into a freshwater system over the long-term.

Four vegetation strategies will be tested in the Suncor pilot fen to determine the optimal strategy for vegetating oil sands constructed fens. The strategies are as follows: (1) moss transfer; (2) seedlings plantation; (3) direct seeding; and (4) the control or spontaneous revegetation (i.e., seedbank within the fen peat; aerial seed rain).

The "moss transfer" method was a technique developed to restore harvested peatlands in Canada, mainly bogs (Rochefort et al., 2003). This approach has been used for fen restoration in Quebec (Cobbaert et al., 2004; Graf and Rochefort, 2008). Direct plantings and seeding have been used successfully in small alpine fens in Colorado (Cooper and MacDonald, 2000). Shrub, sedge, grass, and forb seed was collected from natural fens and marshes on Suncor's lease starting in July 2010 and is ongoing. Seed will be used to produce seedlings in a local greenhouse for the seedling planting method and to sow directly into the fen as per the seed planting method. Both methods focus only on vascular plant introduction and exclude bryophytes. However, in some cases bryophytes have been known to colonize restored fens spontaneously. For example, bryophytes colonized sloping fen restoration sites in Colorado, as early as seven years after restoration, where only vascular plants had been introduced (D. Cooper, personal communication). Revegetation of the fen is planned for 2012.

Upland planting prescriptions

The planting prescriptions for the upland regions in the system were developed using the *Revegetation Manual* (CEMA, 2010), which categorizes planting prescriptions according to soil characteristics and the position of the site on the reclaimed landscape. Aspect, slope, and soil type and texture were derived from the fen watershed designs and used to predict moisture and nutrient regimes. The upland, southeast corner and western slopes, referred to in Figure 9.1, were prescribed the following site types: moist poor site, dry site, and moist rich site, respectively. The dominant vegetation in the moist poor site type is jack pine (*Pinus banksiana*), black spruce (*Picea mariana*), labrador tea (*Ledum groenlandicum*), and an assortment of other shrubs. The dominant vegetation in the dry site type is jack pine (*P. banksiana*), white spruce (*P. glauca*), blueberry (*Vaccinium myrtilloides*), and an assortment of other shrubs. The dominant vegetation in the moist rich site type is white spruce (*P. glauca*), aspen (*Populus tremuloides*), and an assortment of shrubs. Because the *Revegetation Manual* only focuses on developing planting prescription for upland forests, the *Field Guide to Ecosites of Northern Alberta* (Beckingham and Archibald,

1996) was used to develop planting prescriptions for the wetter transition zone. Moisture and nutrient regimes were predicted from the watershed designs. The transition zone, referred to in Figure 9.1, will be planted to a tree-rich fen (k1) ecosite as it represents the lagg zone (periphery of a peatland). The dominant vegetation will be tamarack (*Larix laricina*), black spruce (*P. mariana*), willow (*Salix spp.*), dwarf birch (*Betula pumula*), and an assortment of other shrubs, grasses, sedges, and forbs.

Research and monitoring in the Suncor fen watershed

Research and monitoring of the Suncor pilot fen is viewed as an important step in the reclamation process because it will determine success with the program's goals of creating a self-sustaining ecosystem that is carbon-accumulating, capable of supporting a representative assemblage of species, and resilient to normal periodic stresses. Furthermore, it is essential to understanding design implications and to the development of more optimal designs and cost-effective protocols.

A five-year integrated hydrological, biogeochemical, and ecological research program was developed by Dr. Jonathan Price (University of Waterloo), in collaboration with Drs. David Cooper (Colorado State University), Rich Petrone (Wilfrid Laurier University), and Maria Strack (University of Calgary). Research funded by the Environmental Reclamation Research Group (ERRG) of the Canadian Oil Sands Network for Research and Development (CONRAD ERRG) focuses on hydrology, water quality, revegetation, carbon dynamics, plant establishment success, and microbial communities in the constructed fen and in nearby reference fens. Reference fens in the region will be analyzed to determine natural vegetation composition, above- and belowground production by species where possible, microbial processes, and other factors relevant to judging the success of fen reclamation in the oil sands region. Finally, wildlife monitoring cameras will be established in the watershed to determine whether wildlife is returning to the region after the construction and revegetation of the program is completed.

LOOKING FORWARD

Although marshes have been a major focus of oil sands research and reclamation, considerable effort has been put into constructing fen peatlands as they are the dominant wetland type in the Athabasca oil sands region. To date, some uncertainty exists with regard to whether the hydrogeological, biogeochemical, and ecological attributes of a natural fen peatland can be engineered. Detailed research and monitoring will provide answers to optimize future reclaimed peatlands and provide best management practices, such as habitat design and revegetation strategies.

To date, laboratory and greenhouse fen mesocosm experiments have revealed that fen graminoid plants native to the Athabasca oil sands region are capable of tolerating a realistic contamination scenario (~385 mg L^{-1} of Na salts and ~40 mg L^{-1} of NAs) and probably do not need particular management actions to counteract OSPW additions. However, mosses appeared to have a lower tolerance threshold to OSPW, especially under drier conditions when they acquire water by capillarity from OSPW. Further experiments are needed to clearly identify those thresholds and to test the resistance of mosses to OSPW or salts, because they are an important part of fen vegetation and should be included in reclamation of the oil sands region.

Program results also indicate that transport of Na and NAs in peat substrates becomes delayed due to adsorption onto peat and dispersion in the dual porosity medium, thereby affecting the concentration of potentially toxic compounds in the plant rooting zone. This is expected to reduce the stress on plants growing on peat containing OSPW. This lag time before reaching full contamination potential may provide sufficient time for the reintroduced plant communities to form a good litter layer that could further isolate it from the belowground contaminants.

The lessons from the Suncor pilot fen program and similar fen reclamation programs in the region are expected to shape the future of wetland reclamation in the Athabasca oil sands region. Success will be measured in the ability to understand the implications of design choices in a way that guides future restoration efforts. The process of designing, building, and studying the system challenges our theoretical understanding of fen peatlands.

ACKNOWLEDGMENTS

Research funding was provided by Suncor Energy Inc. and the Environmental Reclamation Research Group of the Canadian Oil Sands Network for Research and Development (CONRAD ERRG), in particular Shell Canada Energy, Suncor Energy Inc. and Imperial Oil Resources Limited members. Special thanks to June Atkinson and Gord McKenna of BGC Engineering Inc. and Tyler Birkham, Denise Chapman, and Mike O'Kane of O'Kane Consultants Inc. for producing the Suncor pilot fen watershed designs. Gratitude is expressed to Jon Hornung and Francis Salifu for reviewing this chapter.

REFERENCES

Adam, P. (1976). The occurrence of bryophytes on British saltmarshes. *Journal of Bryology*, **9**, 265–274.

Albert, R. and Popp, M. (1977). Chemical composition of halophytes from the Neusiedler Lake region in Austria. *Oecologia*, **27**, 157–170.

Apostol, K. G., Zwiazek, J. J., MacKinnon, M. D. (2004). Naphthenic acids affect plant water conductance but do not alter shoot Na+ and Cl− concentrations in jack pine (*Pinus banksiana*) seedlings. *Plant and Soil*, **263**, 183–190.

Beckingham, J. D. and Archibald, J. H. (1996). *Field Guide to Ecosites of Northern Alberta*. Vancouver, BC: UBC Press.

Berg, W. E. (1992). Large Mammals. In H. E. Wright Jr., B. A. Coffin, N. E. Aaseng, eds., *The patterned peatlands of Minnesota*. Minnesota, MN: University of Minnesota Press.

Bishay, F. B., Gulley, J. R., Hamilton, S. H. (1993). Constructed wetlands as a treatment system for waste water from an oil sands mining and extraction operation. ASLO/SWS, USA.

Bloise, R. and Vitt, D. (2011). The Creation of Sandhill Fen: Growth Season 2 of the U-Shaped Cell Study. Canadian Oil Sands Network for Research and Development (CONRAD) Environmental Reclamation Research Group (ERRG) Annual Symposium, Edmonton, AB.

Boerner, R. E. and Forman, R. T. T. (1975). Salt spray and coastal dune mosses. *Bryologist*, **78**, 57–63.

Bothe, R. A. and Abraham, C. (1993). Evaporation and evapotranspiration in Alberta, 1986–1992. Addendum. Water Resources Services, Alberta Environmental Protection Service, Edmonton, AB.

Carey, S. K. (2008). Growing season energy and water exchange from an oil sands overburden reclamation soil cover, Fort McMurray, Alberta, Canada. *Hydrological Processes*, **22**, 2847–2857.

Chee, W. L. and Vitt, D. H. (1989). The vegetation, surface water chemistry and peat chemistry of moderate-rich fens in central Alberta, Canada. *Wetlands*, **9**, 227–261.

Clymo, R. S. (1983). Peat. In A. J. P. Gore, ed., *Mires, Swamp, Bog, Fen and Moor*. General Studies (Ecosystem of the World 4A). Amsterdam: Elsevier, pp. 159–224.

Cobbaert, D., Rochefort, L., Price, J. S. (2004). Experimental restoration of a fen plant community after peat mining. *Applied Vegetation Science*, **7**, 209–220.

Cooper, A. (1982). The effects of salinity and waterlogging on the growth and cation uptake of salt marsh plants. *New Phytologist*, **90**, 263–275.

Cooper, D. and MacDonald, L. (2000). Restoring the vegetation of mined peatlands in the southern Rocky Mountains of Colorado, USA. *Restoration Ecology*, **8**, 103–111.

Cumulative Environmental Management Association (CEMA). (2006). *Land Capability Classification System for Forest Ecosystems in the Oil Sands*, 3rd edn. Prepared for Alberta Environment by CEMA.

Cumulative Environmental Management Association (CEMA). (2010). *Guidelines for Reclamation to Forest Vegetation in the Athabasca Oil Sands Region*, 2nd edn., "Revegetation Manual". Prepared by the Terrestrial Subgroup of CEMA.

Daly, C. and Ciborowski, J. J. H. (2008). A review of wetland research at Suncor: re-establishing wetland ecosystems in an oil-sands affected landscape. *1st International Oil Sands Tailings Conference*, Edmonton, AB, pp. 241–252.

Devito, K. J., Creed, I. F., Fraser, C. J. D. (2005). Controls on runoff from a partially harvested aspen-forested headwater catchment, Boreal Plain, Canada. *Hydrological Processes*, **19**, 3–25.

Devito, K. J., Medoza, C., Petrone, R., et al. (2011). Conceptualizing the surface hydrology of reclaimed landscapes using natural analogues: interaction of aspen forest and harvesting with climate and geology on sink-source dynamics in complex terrain. Canadian Oil Sands Network for Research and Development (CONRAD) Environmental Reclamation Research Group (ERRG) Annual Symposium, Edmonton, AB.

Ferone, M. and Devito, K. J. (2004). Variation in groundwater-surface water interactions of pond peatland complexes along a Boreal Plain landscape gradient. *Journal of Hydrology*, **292**, 75–95.

Franklin, J. A. and Zwiazek, J. J. (2004). Ion uptake in *Pinus banksiana* treated with sodium chloride and sodium sulphate. *Physiologia Plantarum*, **120**, 482–490.

Gervais, F. and Barker, J. (2005). Fate and transport of naphthenic acids in groundwater. Bringing groundwater quality to the watershed scale. *Proceedings GQ 2004, 4th International Groundwater Quality Conference*, IAHS Publ. **297**, 305–310.

Gorham, J., Hughes, L. L., Wyn Jones, R. G. (1980). Chemical composition of salt-marsh plants from Ynys Môn (Anglesey): the concept of physiotypes. *Plant, Cell and Environment*, **3**, 309–318.

Graf, M. D. and Rochefort, L. (2008). Techniques for restoring fen vegetation on cut-away peatlands in North America. *Applied Vegetation Science*, **11**, 521–528.

Graf, M. D., Rochefort, L., Poulin, M. (2008). Spontaneous revegetation of cutaway peatlands of North America. *Wetlands*, **28**, 28–39.

Griffiths, G. C. D. (2007). *Cardamine dentata* recently discovered in Alberta. *Iris*, pp. 6–8.

Harris, M. L. (2007). *Guideline for Wetland Establishment on Reclaimed Oil Sands Leases*, revised 2nd edn. Prepared by Lorax Environmental for CEMA Wetlands and Aquatics Subgroup of the Reclamation Working Group, Fort McMurray, AB.

Hill, B. M. and Siegel, D. I. (1991). Groundwater flow and the metal content of peat. *Journal of Hydrology*, **123**, 211–224.

Ho, Y. S. and McKay, G. (2000). The kinetics of sorption of divalent metal ions onto Sphagnum moss peat. *Water Research*, **34**, 735–742.

Hoag, R. S. and Price, J. S. (1997). The effects of matrix diffusion on solute transport and retardation in undisturbed peat in laboratory columns. *Journal of Contaminant Hydrology*, **28**, 193–205.

Hornung, J. and Foote, L. (2007). Oil sands as primary succession substrates and the importance of early carbon production on site. The 34th Annual Aquatic Toxicology Workshop, Halifax, NS.

Ingram, H. A. P. (1983). Hydrology. In Gore, A. J. P., ed., *Mires, Swamp, Bog, Fen and Moor*, General Studies (Ecosystem of the World 4A). Amsterdam: Elsevier, pp. 67–224.

Jacobs, D. F. and Timmer, V. R. (2005). Fertilizer-induced changes in rhizosphere electrical conductivity: relation to forest tree seedling root system growth and function. *New Forests*, **30**, 147–166.

Janfada A., Headley, J. V., Peru, K. M., Barbour, S. L. (2006). A laboratory evaluation of the sorption of oil sands naphthenic acids on organic rich soils. *Journal of Environmental Science and Health Part A*, **41**, 985–997.

Johnson, D., Kershaw, L., MacKinnon, A., Pojar, J. (1995). *Plants of the Western Boreal Forest and Aspen Parkland*. Lone Pine Publishing and the Canadian Forest Service, pp. 92–94 and 210.

Kessler, S., Chapman, D., Birkham, T., et al. (2010). Report from O'Kane Consultants and BGC Engineering Ltd. submitted to Suncor Energy Inc.

Lachance, D. Lavoie, C., Desrochers, A. (2005). The impact of peatland afforestation on plant and bird diversity in southeastern Quebec. *Ecoscience*, **12**, 161–171.

Lafleur, P. M. (1990). Evapotranspiration from sedge-dominated wetland surfaces. *Aquatic Botany*, **37**, 341–353.

Mazerolle, M. J. (1999). Amphibians in Fragmented Peat Bogs: Abundance, Activity, Movements and Size. M.Sc. thesis, Dalhousie University, Halifax, NS.

Mitsch, W. J. and Wilson R. E. (1996). Improving the success of wetland creation and restoration with know-how, time and self design. *Ecological Applications*, **6**, 77–83.

National Wetlands Working Group. (1997). *The Canadian Wetland Classification System*, 2nd edn. Lands Conservation Branch, Canadian Wildlife Service, Environment Canada.

Nguyen, H., Calvo Polanco M., Zwiazek, J. J. (2006). Gas exchange and growth responses of ectomycorrhizal *Picea mariana*, *Picea glauca*, and *Pinus banksiana* seedlings to NaCl and Na2SO4. *Plant Biology*, **8**, 646–652.

Oil Sands Wetlands Working Group (OSWWG). (2000). *Guidelines for Wetland Establishment on Reclaimed Oil Sands Leases*. N. Chymko, ed. Rep. ESD/LM/00–1, Alberta Environment, Environmental Services Publication No. T/517.

Ours, D. P., Siegel, D. I., Glaser, P. H. (1997). Chemical dilation and the dual porosity of humified bog peat. *Journal of Hydrology*, **196**, 348–360.

Pouliot, R., Rochefort, L., Graf, M. D. (2012). Impacts of oil sands process water on fen plants: implications for plant selection in required reclamation projects, ENPO_6567. *Environmental Pollution*. [In Press.]

Price, J. S. (1994). Evapotranspiration from a lakeshore *Typha* marsh and adjacent open water systems. *Aquatic Botany*, **48**, 261–272.

Price, J. S. (2003). The role and character of seasonal peat soil deformation on the hydrology of undisturbed and cutover peatlands. *Water Resources Research*, **39**, 1241.

Price, J. S., Edwards, T. W. D., Yi, Y., Whittington, P. N. (2009). Physical and isotopic characterization of evaporation from Sphagnum moss. *Journal of Hydrology*, **369**, 175–182.

Price, J. S., McLaren, R. G., Rudolph, D. L. (2007). *Creating a Fen Peatland on a Post-Mined Oilsands Landscape: a feasibility modeling study (Phase 2)*. Prepared for the Cumulative Environmental Management Association, CEMA Contract 2006–0012.

Price, J. S., McLaren, R. G., Rudolph, D. L. (2010). Landscape restoration after oil sands mining: conceptual design and hydrological modelling for fen reconstruction. *International Journal of Mining, Reclamation and Environment*, **24**, 109–123.

Price, J. S., Rochefort, L., Quinty, F. (1998). Energy and moisture considerations on cutover peatlands: surface microtopography, mulch cover, and Sphagnum regeneration. *Ecological Engineering*, **10**, 293–312.

Price J. S. and Whitehead, G. S. (2004). The influence of past and present hydrological conditions on *Sphagnum* recolonization and succession in a block-cut bog, Québec. *Hydrological Processes*, **18**, 315–328.

Price, J. S. and Whittington, P. N. (2010). Water flow in Sphagnum hummocks: mesocosm measurements and modeling. *Journal of Hydrology*, **381**, 333–340.

Price, J. S. and Woo, M. K. (1988). Wetlands as waste repositories? Solute transport in peat. Proceedings Of the National Student Conference on Northern Studies, 1986. Association of Canadian Universities for Northern Studies, Ottawa, ON, pp. 392–395.

Rezanezhad, F., Andersen, R., Pouliot, R., et al. (2011). Fen vegetation structure affects the transport of oil sands process-affected waters and microbial functional diversity in a greenhouse mesocosm study. *Wetlands*. [Epub ahead of print.]

Rezanezhad, F., Price, J. S., Rochefort, L., et al. (2010). Oil sands process affected water contamination transport through peat soils: laboratory and greenhouse study. Conference proceedings, 2nd IOSTC. D. Sego and N. Beier, eds. Geotechnical center and Oil Sands Tailing Research Facility, University of Alberta, AB, pp. 177–184.

Rochefort, L., Quinty, F., Campeau, S., Johnson, K., Malterer, T. (2003). North American approach to the restoration of Sphagnum dominated peatlands. *Wetlands Ecology and Management*, **11**, 3–20.

Shacklette, H. T. (1961). Substrate relationship of some bryophyte communities on Latouche Island, AK. *Bryologist*, **64**, 1–16.

Smerdon, B. D., Mendoza, C. A., Devito, K. J. (2008). The influence of subhumid climate and water table depth on groundwater recharge in shallow outwash aquifers. *Water Resources Research*, **44**, W08427.

Society for Ecological Restoration Science and Policy Working Group. (2002). *The SER Primer on Ecological Restoration*. Address: www.ser.org/.

Timmer, V. R. and Teng, Y. (2004). Pretransplant fertilization of containerized *Picea marian* seedlings: calibration and bioassay growth response. *Canadian Journal of Forest Research*, **34**, 2089–2098.

Todorova, S. G., Siegeland, D. I., Costello, A. M. (2005). Microbial Fe(III) reduction in a minerotrophic wetland–geochemical controls and involvement in organic matter decomposition. *Applied Geochemistry*, **20**, 1120–1130.

Trites, M. and Bayley, S. E. (2008). Effects of salinity on vegetation and organic matter accumulation in natural and oil sands wetlands. Final Report CEMA Reclamation Working Group Grant 2005–0018.

Trites, M. and Bayley, S. E. (2009). Organic matter accumulation in western boreal saline wetlands: a comparison of undisturbed and oil sands wetlands. *Ecological Engineering*, **12**, 1734–1742.

United States Environmental Protection Agency (US EPA). (1993). Wetland treatment systems: a case history. The Orlando Easterly Wetlands Reclamation Project. EPA832-R-93–0051.

Vitt, D. H. (1976). A monograph of the genus *Muelleriella Dusen*. *Journal of the Hattori Botanical Laboratory*, **40**, 91–113.

Vitt, D. H. and Chee, W. L. (1989). The vegetation, surface water chemistry and peat chemistry of moderate-rich fens in central Alberta, Canada. *Wetlands*, **9**, 227–261.

Vitt, D. H., Halsey, L. A., Thormann, M. N., Martin, T. (1996). *Peatland Inventory of Alberta*. Prepared for the Alberta Peat Task Force, National Center of Excellence in Sustainable Forest Management, University of Alberta, Edmonton, AB.

Vitt, D. H., Wirdum, G. V., Halsey, L., Zoltai, S. (1993). The effects of water chemistry on the growth of *Scorpidium scorpioides* in the Netherlands. *Bryologist*, **96**, 106–111.

Whittington, P. N. and Price, J. S. (2006). The effects of water table draw-down (as a surrogate for climate change) on the hydrology of a patterned fen peatland near Quebec City, Quebec. *Hydrological Processes*, **20**, 3589–3600.

Wilcox, D. A. (1984). The effects of NaCl deicing salts on *Sphagnum recurvum* P. beauv. *Environmental and Experimental Botany*, **24**, 295–301.

MELISSA HOUSE, DALE H. VITT, AND R. KELMAN WIEDER

10

Plant community recovery on "minimum disturbance" petroleum sites compared to burned sites in bogs of northern Alberta

INTRODUCTION

Disturbance is a major factor in determining vegetation patterns in the boreal forest of Canada. Of particular importance is wildfire (Turetsky et al., 2002). In bogs, wildfire has several significant effects. The tree layer is killed and the aboveground portions of the shrub and herb layers are removed while the underground portions remain viable. The ground layer is partially removed, but much of the topography remains with viable hummocks of *Sphagnum fuscum*. Hollows are largely bare, charred remains of burned peat. Succession after fire has been studied by Benscoter and Vitt (2008), Benscoter et al. (2005), and Wieder et al. (2009). These studies indicate that *Picea mariana* (a semi-serotinous species) establishes within the first one to five years, shrub and herb layers return quickly from living roots, and hummocks have vegetative cover of *S. fuscum* earlier than hollows. Hollows are revegetated by true mosses and facilitate recovery of *Sphagnum* species. These early successional changes take place relatively quickly, and by 20 years post-fire, a nearly complete ground layer is reestablished and the system functions as a carbon sink (Wieder et al., 2009). These naturally disturbed bogs are highly resilient to fire and the succession after fire normally follows a well-defined trajectory, following the "facilitation" model of succession (Connell and Slatyer, 1977).

Bogs are the endpoint in peatland succession, forming a grade of plant communities that over time have undergone a series of developmental changes, including dominance by *S. fuscum*, ombrotrophy, acidic pore waters, low nutrients, and species-poor flora (Vitt, 2006). After

Restoration and Reclamation of Boreal Ecosystems, ed. Dale Vitt and Jagtar Bhatti. Published by Cambridge University Press. © Cambridge University Press 2012.

wildfire, many of these attributes persist, especially ombrotrophy, and bogs rarely lose the *Sphagnum*-dominated ground layer and regress to true moss-dominated rich fens.

Disturbances from man-made causes are also frequent in bogs of the boreal forest and include damming for reservoir creation, harvesting for commercial peat, and exploration and production of oil and gas. In Alberta, the area of land leased to oil sands for *in situ* development was 3.6 million ha as of 2005, and if all leases are developed, 296,000 ha of forest will be cleared (Schneider and Dyer, 2006). Traditionally, conventional oil and gas extraction and exploration entails clearing cut lines, building access roads, and establishing mineral pads that serve as a stable base for heavy equipment. More recently, the petroleum industry has implemented the use of "minimum disturbance" sites that do not require the input of mineral soil. These sites have the aboveground portions of the tree and shrub layers removed (and, in some cases, chipped and left on site). The sites are graded to uniform elevation in winter when the peat is frozen (with hummocks removed), then flooded with water obtained from a local water source, and heavy equipment is moved to the site through neighboring upland and/or wetland communities. In some cases, a well is drilled with drilling mud exposed on site.

In this chapter, we compare a 21-year chronosequence of bogs disturbed by wildfire (i.e., burned) to a chronosequence (of similar ages) of minimum disturbance sites constructed and used for oil and gas activity in order to determine if successional pathways of minimally disturbed sites reflect those of sites disturbed by wildfire. We also relate these successional endpoints to a series of undisturbed bogs. Minimum disturbance sites differ from wildfire-disturbed sites in: (1) complete removal of the tree layer (versus standing dead trees left by wildfire); (2) minimal topography, often graded to an elevation lower than the natural hollow elevation (versus strong hummock–hollow relief of burned sites); (3) introduction of water derived from a source external to the site (versus no allogenous water at burned sites); and (4) possible addition of mineral substrate from drilling activities (versus no mineral additions at burned sites). Due to floristic homogeneity and similar pore water chemistry of bogs in northern Alberta, the chronosequence approach has previously been used to examine short-term patterns of plant succession (Benscoter and Vitt, 2008; Wieder et al.; 2009) and we adopt this approach here. We designed our research to examine three broad questions:

1. What is the revegetation pathway of minimum disturbance sites over a 21-year period?

2. What is the revegetation pathway of the burned bogs over this same 21-year disturbance span?

3. Are there similarities in successional pathways of the minimum disturbance sites compared to those of bogs disturbed by wildfire?

METHODS

Site selection

In 2008–2009, we identified 33 sites in northern Alberta, mostly concentrated near the Wabasca and Slave Lake regions. Selection criteria for minimum disturbance sites were: (1) location completely within a bog landform; (2) known dates of construction; and (3) no history of reclamation efforts, such as seeding. Sites were selected to complete a chronosequence from 1987 to 2008. Aerial photography was used to determine whether sites were located in bogs, and site histories (provided by Alberta Sustainable Resource Development) were referenced to ensure that sites were revegetating naturally without additional reclamation effort. The natural, undisturbed bogs adjacent to the 19 minimum disturbance sites were surveyed at the same time as the disturbed site. The adjacent bog provided a reference for what the disturbed site would have resembled had it not been disturbed. Fourteen recently burned sites were selected with wildfire disturbance having occurred between 1982 and 2002.

Experimental design

A 10 m × 10 m plot was laid out in an area that was representative of the stand. Within this plot, two 4 m × 4 m subplots were placed at the corners. Four 1 m × 1 m subplots were set within the boundary of the 10 m × 10 m plot. The same design was used at minimum disturbance stands, burned stands, and undisturbed bog stands. In two cases, a minimum disturbance site was divided into two or three discrete stands in order to evaluate fully the variation of species richness and plant community differences.

Vegetation and floristic surveys

Within the 10 m × 10 m plot, we identified trees and tallied the number of *P. mariana* individuals. Within the two 4 m × 4 m subplots, vascular plants were identified. In the four 1 m × 1 m subplots, bryophytes and lichens were identified. The canopy cover of each species was visually estimated to the nearest 10% and modified to five cover classes (1 = 0% −1%,

2 = 2%–4%, 3 = 5%–9%, 4 = 10%–19%, and 5 = 20%–100%). A species/stand association table was developed using TWINSPAN (Hill 1979, McCune and Mefford 1999).

Environmental variables

At each stand, we collected a 125 mL water sample to analyze base cation concentrations of the pore water. If water was not present at the surface, a pit was dug and allowed to fill with water for approximately 30 minutes. Distance to the water table was measured prior to collecting the water sample. These samples were analyzed using atomic absorption spectrophotometry. Electrical conductivity and pH were measured in the field from surface water. The pH and electrical conductivity were standardized to 25 °C, and the electrical conductivity was reduced to eliminate the effects of hydrogen ion concentrations, following Sjörs (1950). Shade was measured at the four corners of the 10 m × 10 m plot using a concave, spherical densitometer held at waist height.

Statistical analysis

Nonmetric multidimensional scaling (NMDS) was performed on the species abundance data for the sites using DECODA (Minchen, 1991). The NMDS was used to produce an ordination of all the sites together, then separate ordinations were produced for burned bog stands and minimum disturbance stands to determine if stands of the same age have more similar vegetation than sites of different ages. Significant environmental vectors (P < 0.05) were fitted to the ordinations. Species abundances were plotted against age for burned bogs, poor fen minimum disturbance sites, and rich fen minimum disturbance sites. Curves were fitted to the scatter plots using SigmaPlot (ver. 11.0) for trends that were significant (P < 0.10). Additional primary data are available from House (2011).

RESULTS

An ordination of all 33 stands using plant abundance data (2D minimum stress = 0.20; Figure 10.1) placed natural bog groups together. Burned bogs also form a tight group that partially overlaps the natural bog group, indicating a high degree of vegetative similarity between burned bogs and natural bogs. The minimum disturbance stands scatter throughout the ordination, indicating that these stands have high floristic variability and that some differ considerably from the burned bogs and natural bogs. A

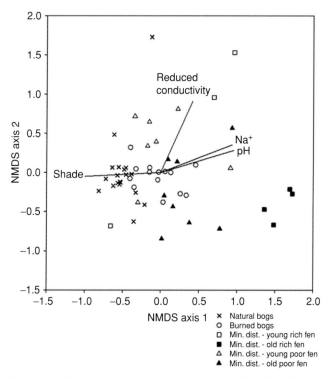

Figure 10.1. Nonmetric multidimensional scaling (NMDS) ordination of all sites based on species abundance data (2D minimum stress = 0.20).

few of the minimum disturbance stands occur within the burned bog and natural bog groups. Four significant environmental vectors were fitted to the ordination: shade (n = 55, max r = 0.46, P = 0.002), reduced electrical conductivity (n = 50, max r = 0.42, P = 0.01), Na^+ concentration in pore water (n = 48, max r = 0.38, P = 0.04), and pH (n = 51, max r = 0.38, P = 0.03). Natural bog stands have the lowest electrical conductivity (reduced 41.4±28.6 µS), lowest pH (3.9±0.2), and lowest Na^+ concentration (1.6±0.3 mg/L), as indicated by the environmental vectors fitted to the ordination. The natural bog stands also have the highest shade (28.0±4.6%), due to the presence of mature *P. mariana*. Burned stands have less shade (11.0±1.7%) due to burnt, but still standing snags of *P. mariana*. Reduced conductivity (59.2±23.2 µS) is slightly higher, but Na^+ concentration (1.7±0.3 mg/L) and pH 3.7±0.1 are quite similar to that of natural bogs. Minimum disturbance stands have the least shade (1.9±0.8%), highest reduced conductivity (62.8±18.5 µS), highest Na^+ concentration (2.7±0.4 mg/L), and highest pH (4.1±0.2). Minimum disturbance stands have no mature trees and thus little or no shade. The pore water chemistry is highly variable, but in general pH, reduced conductivity, and base cations are higher in these sites than in either natural or burned bogs, and they are less similar to natural bogs than are the burned bogs.

Natural bogs

Of the 19 natural bogs, 18 stands form a tight group (Figure 10.1). Only one natural bog stand lies outside of this main group and has vegetation that is not typical of bogs, including the presence of *Equisetum arvense*. In general, natural bogs are species-poor and similar in composition, with high abundances of *Cladina mitis*, *Dicranum undulatum*, *Ledum groenlandicum*, *P. mariana*, *Pleurozium schreberi*, *Rubus chamaemorus*, and *Vaccinium vitis-idaea*. *S. fuscum* dominates the ground layer (Table 10.1).

Burned bogs

Recently burned bogs group closely in the overall stand ordination space and, similar to natural bogs, have relatively little variation (Figure 10.1). After wildfire, burned bog stands have many species in common with mature bogs. Abundant species include *L. groenlandicum*, *Polytrichum strictum*, *R. chamaemorus*, and *S. fuscum*, all of which are species found in unburned bogs (Table 10.1).

An ordination of the 14 burned bog stands was used to examine differences between these stands (2D minimum stress = 0.11; Figure 10.2A). Time is the only significant vector ($n = 14$, max $r = 0.66$, $P = 0.046$). Burned stands form two groups (Complete Linkage Cluster Analysis, not shown), one group of four older stands (1982–1995) on the left side of the ordination, with high vegetation cover, and ten younger stands on the right, with less vegetative cover. The return of *S. fuscum* abundance (35%–40%), high density of *P. mariana*, and low *P. strictum* abundance (1%–20%) is characteristic of the old stands. Younger stands are characterized by more abundant *R. chamaemorus*, while *P. strictum* is more abundant than *S. fuscum*. Fewer lichens are present and *Eriophorum vaginatum* is more frequent. *Pinus banksiana* is also found at some younger burned stands, but is absent at the older burned stands. *S. magellanicum* is more abundant at some young burned stands. Aside from these differences in abundances that appear to be due to the rate of return of some species to the disturbed stands, the vegetative differences among burned stands are few. When burned bogs are compared to natural bogs, *E. vaginatum* and *Chamaedaphne calyculata* are more abundant in post-fire disturbance than in natural bogs.

Table 10.1. *Summary of species abundances in natural bogs, burned sites, and minimum disturbance sites (poor fens and rich fens)*

Species (75)	Natural bog (19)	Burned site (14)	Poor fen (15)	Rich fen (7)
Salix planifolia	1	0	1	2
Pleurozium schreberi	4	2	1	1
Ptilium crista-castrensis	2	0	1	0
Cladina rangiferina	2	1	1	0
Dicranum scoparium	1	0	1	0
Hylocomium splendens	2	0	1	1
Hypogymnia physodes	1	0	1	1
Marchantia polymorpha	0	1	0	1
Dicranum undulatum	3	2	2	1
Cladina mitis	5	2	3	1
Cladonia cornuta	2	1	1	1
Cladonia deformis	1	1	1	1
Cladonia gracilis	2	1	1	1
Peltigera aphthosa	1	1	0	0
Leiomylia anomala	2	1	1	0
Equisetum sylvaticum	1	1	0	1
Cladina stellaris	1	0	1	0
Cladonia chlorophaea	1	0	1	0
Cladonia fimbriata	2	2	1	1
Cladonia pyxidata	2	1	1	0
Icmadophila ericetorum	1	1	1	0
Vaccinium caespitosum	1	1	2	0
Sphagnum capillifolium	2	2	2	1
Picea mariana	6	3	3	1
Vaccinium vitis-idaea	5	3	3	2
Oxycoccos microcarpus	2	2	2	1
Ledum groenlandicum	6	6	5	2
Rubus chamaemorus	4	5	4	2
Cladonia cenotea	1	1	1	0
Cladonia coccifera	1	1	1	0
Peltigera neopolydactyla	1	1	0	0
Warnstorfia fluitans	0	1	1	0
Cladonia coniocraea	1	0	1	0
Smilacina trifolia	2	3	3	1
Ceratodon purpureus	1	2	1	0
Andromeda polifolia	1	2	1	0
Chamaedaphne calyculata	1	2	2	2
Pohlia nutans	2	2	2	2

Species (75)	Natural bog (19)	Burned site (14)	Poor fen (15)	Rich fen (7)
Sphagnum fuscum	6	5	4	3
Sphagnum magellanicum	2	3	2	2
Eriophorum vaginatum	2	3	3	2
Betula papyrifera	0	1	2	1
Polytrichum strictum	2	5	5	3
Phleum pratense	0	0	1	1
Pinus banksiana	0	2	1	0
Equisetum arvense	1	1	1	2
Pedicularis laboradorica	1	0	0	1
Sphagnum russowii	1	0	1	2
Larix laricina	1	0	2	2
Cornus canadensis	0	0	1	1
Tomenthypnum nitens	1	0	0	2
Carex canescens	1	1	1	3
Betula glandulosa	0	0	1	1
Sphagnum squarrosum	0	0	1	2
Betula glandulifera	1	1	1	2
Carex aquatilis	0	0	1	4
Epilobium palustre	1	0	1	1
Carex interior	0	0	0	2
Glyceria grandis	0	0	0	2
Carex limosa	1	0	1	2
Glyceria borealis	1	1	2	4
Salix monticola	0	1	1	5
Trifolium hybridum	0	0	1	1
Betula occidentalis	0	1	0	1
Aulacomnium palustre	2	3	2	4
Sphagnum riparium	1	0	1	2
Sphagnum angustifolium	2	3	2	1
Populus tremuloides	0	2	2	2
Vaccinium myrtilloides	1	1	2	1
Epilobium angustifolium	0	0	2	1

Values are means of TWINSPAN pseudospecies stand values plus one. Rare species (n = 23; those found in fewer the four stands) are not shown. Number of species and stands are given in parentheses.

Species return after wildfire in burned stands

After wildfire disturbance, bog stands undergo a series of gradual species changes over time, with no older stands being more similar to one

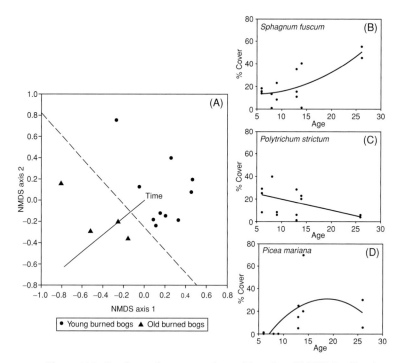

Figure 10.2. Species performance at burned bog sites. (**A**) NMDS ordination of burned bog stands using species abundance data (2D minimum stress $=$ 0.11). The broken line drawn is to separate old stands from young stands. Time is a significant environmental vector ($n = 14$, max. $r = 0.66$, $P =$ 0.046). (**B**) Relationship of *Sphagnum fuscum* abundance and stand age for the burned bog stands ($r^2 = 0.59$, $F = 13.97 + (-0.66^*\chi) + 0.079^*\chi^2$, $P =$ 0.008). (**C**) Relationship of *Polytrichum strictum* abundance and stand age for the burned bog stands ($r^2 = 0.21$, $F = 29.07 + (-0.97)^*\chi$, $P = 0.096$). (**D**) Relationship of *Picea mariana* abundance and stand age of the burned bog stands ($r^2 = 0.392$, $F = -48.95 + 8.55^*\chi + (0.2282)^*\chi^2$, $P = 0.065$).

another than to younger ones (Figure 10.2A). In particular, *S. fuscum* returns to recently burned bogs quickly, and as time since disturbance passes, *S. fuscum* increases in abundance (Figure 10.2B). *Polytrichum strictum* establishes early in recently disturbed stands and is initially more abundant than *S. fuscum*, but decreases in abundance over time (Figure 10.2C). *Rubus chamaemorus* also returns to burned stands quickly, but has a subsequent variable occurrence pattern after disturbance (varying between 0% and 40% at 5–10 years post-disturbance; data not shown). *Picea mariana* is variably present by 15 years post-fire and can achieve high abundances (Figure 10.2D).

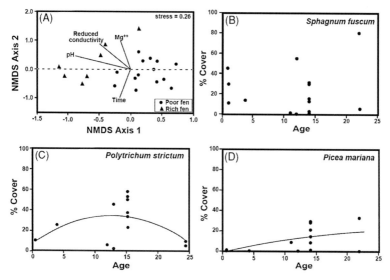

Figure 10.3. Species performance at minimum disturbance sites. (A) NMDS ordination of minimum disturbance sites using species abundance data (2D minimum stress = 0.11). Significant environmental vectors are Mg^{+2} ($n = 19$, max. $r = 0.70$, $P = 0.009$), reduced conductivity ($n = 20$, max. $r = 0.65$, $P = 0.008$), pH ($n = 21$, max. $r = 0.76$, $P = 0.001$), and time since disturbance ($n = 22$, max $r = 0.55$, $P = 0.023$). (B) Relationship of *Sphagnum fuscum* abundance and stand age of poor fen minimum disturbance stands. (C) Relationship of *Polytrichum strictum* abundance and stand age of poor fen minimum disturbance stands ($r^2 = 0.38$, $F = 4.47 + 5.16^*\chi + (-0.22)^*\chi^2$, $P = 0.045$). (D) Relationship of *Picea mariana* abundance and stand age of poor fen minimum disturbance sites ($r^2 = 0.34$, $F = -2.33 + 1.78^*\chi + (-0.03)^*\chi^2$, $P = 0.081$).

Minimum disturbance

The minimum disturbance stands are highly variable (NMDS ordination, 2D minimum stress = 0.20; Figure 10.3A). Using plant species abundance data, minimum disturbance sites can be divided into two groups (Complete Linkage Cluster Analysis; data not shown). When plotted on the NMDS ordination (Figure 10.3A), 14 stands on the right side are stands dominated by common bog and poor fen species, including *L. groenlandicum*, *P. strictum*, *R. chamaemorus*, and *S. fuscum* (Table 10.1). The seven stands on the left side of the ordination are dominated by fen species not found or infrequent in bogs (*Aulacomnium palustre*, *Carex aquatilis*, *Glyceria borealis*, and *Salix monticola*; see Table 10.1 for additional species occurrences and Belland and Vitt (1995) and Vitt and Chee (1990) for species comparisons). Four environmental vectors are significant: Mg^{+2} (n = 19, max r = 0.70, P = 0.009), reduced conductivity (n = 20, max r = 0.65, P = 0.008), pH (n = 21, max r = 0.76, P = 0.001), and time since disturbance (n = 22, max r = 0.55, P = 0.023). Thus, young poor fens appear on the NMDS ordination to the upper right, young rich fens to the upper left, old poor fens to the lower right, and old rich fens to the lower left–young stands are disturbed after 1998, old stands are those disturbed between 1987 and 1997 (Figure 10.3A).

Species return after disturbance in minimum disturbance stands: poor fens

Although vegetation return in poor fens was variable, some important trends are evident. Perhaps most important is that 47% of the poor fens cluster with burned stands (Figure 10.1). *Picea mariana* returns at about the same rate in poor fens as in the burned stands and, at 14 years, can provide up to 35% cover; however, as in a few of the burned stands, some minimum disturbance stands also have limited cover at 20 years (Figures 10.2D, 10.3D). *Sphagnum fuscum* often returns quickly to poor fen stands (Figure 10.3B). At one site, *S. fuscum* cover of over 40% was observed in the growing season following the disturbance; however, abundances of *S. fuscum* were variable and not predictable over the 21-year time frame. *Polytrichum strictum* dominated the ground layer at some stands between 10–15 years post-disturbance–somewhat later than occurred in burned stands (Figures 10.2C, 10.3C)–but, similar to burned stands, most minimum disturbance stands have a decrease in *P. strictum* as *S. fuscum* increases in abundance over time. *Ledum groenlandicum* returned to poor fen sites immediately, often occurring in the range of 10%–20% cover. At 15 years post-disturbance, some sites have *L. groenlandicum* cover of 30%–50%, while other stands continue to have low cover for this species. Likewise, *R. chamaemorus* was found at young sites with varying abundances up to 20%. Between 10 and 15 years post-disturbance, the abundance of *R. chamaemorus* ranges from 0%–25% in poor fen stands while it persists in large abundance in other poor fen stands. Thus, both *R. chamaemorus* and *P. strictum* establish and increase in abundance later in minimum disturbance poor fens compared to their establishment in burned sites.

Species return after disturbance in minimum disturbance stands: rich fens

Species characteristic of rich fens are not present in the natural bog comparison stands (Table 10.1). When compared to burned bog stands in

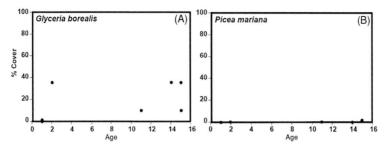

Figure 10.4. Species performance at minimum disturbance sites. (**A**) Relationship of *Glyceria borealis* abundance and stand age of rich fen minimum disturbance stands. (**B**) Relationship of *Picea mariana* abundance and stand age of rich fen minimum disturbance stands.

the NMDS ordination space (Figure 10.1), none of the rich fens are found within the burned stand cluster. Even more important is that the old rich fens are the most dissimilar (Figure 10.1) and have pore waters with the highest pH and conductivity (Figure 10.3A). There are no indicators of these sites succeeding to poor fen/bog communities. This is apparent in the species abundances as well. These stands are dominated by sedges, grasses, willows, and true mosses, and have either very low abundance or complete lack of *P. mariana*, *L. groenlandicum*, and *S. fuscum* (Table 10.1). No patterns of species change are evident over time (*G. borealis* [Figure 10.4A], *P. mariana* [Figure 10.4B]).

DISCUSSION

According to Alberta regulations, all mining disturbances must be reclaimed to equivalent land capability (OSWWG, 2000). All wetland site types and aquatic systems are within the same land use capability system (Class 5: CEMA, 2006). This being so, we believe that some additional exploration of ecological theory might add to the future directions of legislation. Capability (Syn: capacity) is defined in the Webster College Edition dictionary as "capacity of being used or developed." The key phrase could be "capacity to develop." In other words, given that all wetlands are in the same capability class, then how can we proceed to better understand this in an ecological context? One way is to review some aspects of ecological theory; namely, mechanisms of succession.

In 1977, Connell and Slayter proposed the "facilitation model" of succession in which species replacement is orderly and predictable and provides directionality for succession. This ordered, hierarchical system of change in a community was earlier termed "relay floristics" by Egler

(1954). It appears that, at least in part, successional changes occurring after wildfire in boreal bogs follow this model. Burned bogs follow a successional pathway characterized by the establishment of true mosses soon after fire, followed by *Sphagnum* mosses. *Picea mariana* also returns and increases in abundance across the 20-year span studied. These trends in species changes are consistent and predictable across burned sites.

To a lesser extent, poor fen minimum disturbance sites also follow a predictable successional pathway, but abundance of some species is more varied. In a similar fashion to burned sites, *P. strictum* increases in abundance (but more slowly) and then decreases with time. Abundance of *S. fuscum* shows no significant trends over time, suggesting that its presence is not facilitated by *P. strictum*. *Picea mariana* also returns and increases in abundance across the 20-year time span and the rate of return does not differ much from that of *P. mariana* in burned bogs. Both *L. groenlandicum* and *R. chamaemorus* are variably present from the beginning and have no predictable trends over time. Although the dominant species in the minimum disturbance poor fens are species that also dominate the burned bogs, the abundances and return of these species are less predictable. This suggests that a second model of succession may be in control at these sites. This second model, termed the "tolerance model" by Connell and Slatyer (1977), suggests that the presence of early successional species is not essential and that any species can begin the succession after disturbance. Succession procedes by the invasion of later species (e.g., *P. mariana*) or by a thinning of the initial occupants (*R. chamaemorus* and *P. strictum*), depending on the initial conditions.

A third model, the "initial floristic composition" model (Egler 1954) or "inhibition" model by Connell and Slatyer (1977) proposes that succession is very heterogeneous because the development at any one site depends on which species arrive first. Species replacement is not necessarily orderly as each species suppresses new arrivals, and thus succession proceeds either by invasion of later species or a thinning of initial colonists, depending on the initial conditions. This appears to be the case for the minimum disturbance rich fen stands. Resulting communities do not always converge on the climax (in this case, a bog).

In summary, at burned bog sites it appears that succession of many important species follows a facilitation model, with an ordered change in species that results in succession back to a bog. In minimum disturbance sites, two separate mechanistic models of succession possibly explain the situations. First, at sites with pore water chemistry that is unaltered, succession follows the tolerance model where early successional species may not always be present and succession begins with the species that survived the disturbance; species replacement is not affected by the current species. Second, when pore water chemistry is affected by disturbance, the current residents (rich fen species) inhibit replacement species, thus rich fens are perpetuated for the length of this study and show no signs of returning to a bog. Perhaps an understanding of these models of succession may add to our abilities to develop successful return to pre-disturbance conditions and to better define equivalent capabilities.

Disturbance largely controls the set of beginning species. Sites with pore water chemistry similar to that pre-disturbance are currently poor fens that appear to have a suite of species somewhat similar to those of mature bogs. Although not as predictable as burned sites in their successional return, these sites clearly have been affected by minimum disturbance. Unfortunately, a set of seven sites with rich fen vegetation following a model of succession that does not appear to be moving these sites back to a bog condition is also evident from minimum disturbance. The lack of pre-disturbance documentation and detailed operational protocols leaves us without sufficient knowledge to better understand why these sites have developed as they have.

CONCLUSIONS AND RECOMMENDATIONS

We conclude that minimum disturbance of the sites that we surveyed resulted in two different recovery scenarios. Both appear to have somewhat different successional mechanisms that yield different successional endpoints. Burned sites recover without strong chemical changes and with predictable succession proceeding through facilitation. Minimum disturbance sites without strong chemical changes begin recovery with individualized species presences and lag behind recovery of burned sites. These sites have largely nonpredictable species return and succession follows a tolerance model. Finally, minimum disturbance sites with altered pore water chemistry begin recovery with a much different suite of species. Recovery at these sites is unpredictable and has not, in the 21 years of our chronosequence, proceeded toward a bog climax–rather, the species, combined with site conditions, appear to be inhibiting further successional development. In order to better understand why 33% of our minimum disturbance sites strongly deviate from recovery patterns found in burned bogs, we suggest that a more precise set of operational protocols be implemented, as follows:

1.   Each minimum disturbance site should have a clearly documented pre-disturbance history. This includes site pore water chemistry

(pH, conductivity), a simplified vegetation description of the key species abundances (especially ground layer species), and documentation of any connectivity to surrounding water tracks and fens.

2.   Each minimum disturbance site should have operational protocols documented. In particular, (a) source, pH, and reduced conductivity of all water brought to the site; (b) map of wells that were drilled and placement of all drilling mud; (c) elevation of leveled pad relative to water table of the site before water is added; and (d) documented access roads to and from the site.

3.   Five years post-disturbance, the site should be monitored for key species return. Development of a set of benchmark species for bog, poor fen, and rich fen might easily be developed from the available literature.

We conclude that minimum disturbance sites are far superior to sites developed with mineral fill. Do these minimum disturbance sites meet our expectations of "equivalent capacity?"–"yes", wetland structure and function are maintained. Do they fill our expectation to return to pre-disturbance communities, and do they exhibit similar successional mechanisms as do sites recovering from natural disturbance?–no, not in all cases. A better understanding of pre-disturbance history and on-site protocols may be critical to future development.

ACKNOWLEDGMENTS

This chapter is a part of the M.S. thesis (Southern Illinois University Carbondale) of Melissa House. We are grateful to Sara Baer, Juan Benavides, Jeremy Hartsock, Sara Koropchak, Sandi Vitt, and Bin Xu for advice and/or assistance in the field and laboratory. Funding for this research was provided by Shell Canada, Ltd. and Province of Alberta Sustainable Resource Development; Trevor Hindmarch and John Begg, respectively, were instrumental in providing funding resources for which we are thankful.

REFERENCES

Belland, R. J. and Vitt, D. H. (1995). Bryophyte vegetation patterns along environmental gradients in continental bogs. *Ecoscience*, **2**, 395–407.

Benscoter, B. W. and Vitt, D. H. (2008). Spatial patterns and temporal trajectories of the bog ground layer along a post-fire chronosequence. *Ecosystems*, **11**, 1054–1064.

Benscoter, B. W., Wieder, R. K., Vitt, D. H. (2005). Linking microtopography with post-fire succession in bogs. *Journal of Vegetation Science*, **16**, 453–460.

CEMA (Cumulative Environmental Management Association). (2006). *Land Capability Classification System for Forest Ecosystems in the Oil Sands*, 3rd edn. Prepared for Alberta Environment, Edmonton, AB.

Connell, J. H. and Slatyer, R. O. (1977). Mechanisms of succession in natural communities and their role in community stability and organization. *American Naturalist*, **111**, 1119–1144.

Egler, F. E. (1954). Vegetation science concepts. I. Initial floristic composition – a factor in old-field vegetation development. *Vegetatio*, **4**, 412–417.

Hill, M. O. (1979). *TWINSPAN – A FORTRAN Program for Arranging Multivariate Data in an Ordered Two-Way Table by Classification of the Individuals and Attributes*. Ecology and Systematics, Cornell University, Ithaca, NY.

House, M. (2011). *A Comparative Study of Minimum Disturbance Oil Industry Sites and Burned Sites in Bogs in Northern Alberta*. M.S. thesis, Southern Illinois University, Carbondale, IL.

McCune, B. and Mefford, M. J. (1999). *PC-ORD. Multivariate analysis of ecological data*. Version 4.34 MjM Software, Gleneden Beach, OR.

Minchin, P. M. (1991). *DECODA User's manual*. Research School of Pacific Studies, ANU, Canberra.

OSWWG (Oil Sands Wetlands Working Group). (2000). *Guidelines for Wetland Establishment on Reclaimed Oil Sands Leases*. N. Chymko, ed., Report ESD/LM00-I, Alberta Environment, Envronmental Services Publication No. T/517, Edmonton, AB.

Schneider, R. and Dyer, S. (2006). *Death by a Thousand Cuts: Impacts of In Situ Oil Sands Development on Alberta's Boreal Forest*. Edmonton, AB: The Pembina Institute Publications.

Sjörs, H. (1950). On the relation between vegetation and electrolytes in North Swedish mire waters. *Oikos*, **2**, 241–258.

Turetsky, M., Wieder, R. K., Halsey, L. A., Vitt, D. H. (2002). Current disturbance and the diminishing peatland carbon sink. *Geophysical Research Letters*, **29**, 10.1029/2001GL014000.

Vitt, D. H. (2006). Functional characteristics and indicators of boreal peatlands. In R. K. Wieder and D. H. Vitt, eds., *Boreal Peatland Ecosystems, Ecological Studies*. Vol. 188. Springer-Verlag: Berlin, pp. 9–22.

Vitt, D. H. and Chee, W.-L. (1990). The relationships of vegetation to surface water chemistry and peat chemistry in fens of Alberta, Canada. *Vegetatio*, **89**, 87–106.

Wieder, R. K., Scott, K. D., Kamminga, K., et al. (2009). Postfire carbon balance in boreal bogs of Alberta, Canada. *Global Change Biology*, **15**, 63–81.

CLIVE WELHAM, JUAN BLANCO, BRAD SEELY,
AND CAROLINE BAMPFYLDE

11

Oil sands reclamation and the projected development of wildlife habitat attributes

INTRODUCTION

Over the next 10 years, oil sands production in the boreal mixedwood region of Alberta is expected to more than double. As a consequence, the projected disturbance footprint from all mining activities combined may be in the hundreds of thousands of hectares. Eventually, the entire disturbed area must be reclaimed to a capability equivalent to that which existed prior to the onset of mining. Hence, the goal of reclamation is to achieve self-sustaining ecosystems with ecological capabilities equivalent to the pre-disturbance conditions, but which require no ongoing human maintenance (Alberta Environment, 2010).

Large volumes of upland overburden and tailings sand are generated from the mining process. These materials have a low water storage capacity, nutrient status, and organic carbon (C) content. They are therefore capped with a mixture of organic peat and mineral soil (typically 50% each by volume) (Alberta Environment, 2010). This mix constitutes the rooting matrix for the terrestrial reclaimed plant community and is assumed to provide conditions sufficient to support the growth and development of a boreal mixedwood forest. Considerable empirical information is being acquired on the biogeochemistry of capping materials and its potential as a medium for plant growth (Hemstock et al., 2010; MacKenzie and Quideau, 2010; Turcotte et al., 2009). This empirical work is necessary to verify that ecosystem patterns and processes are consistent with anticipated outcomes. Unfortunately, empirical studies alone are not sufficient to guide reclamation planning; reclamation needs to include model-based projections of future performance.

Restoration and Reclamation of Boreal Ecosystems, ed. Dale Vitt and Jagtar Bhatti. Published by Cambridge University Press. © Cambridge University Press 2012.

To date, much of the modeling work conducted within the context of oil sands reclamation has been focused on simulating vegetation productivity (Welham, 2005a,b), with little emphasis on development of other attributes, such as wildlife habitat. For models to be useful as tools for assessing the efficacy of different reclamation plans in achieving target objectives for wildlife, they need to be capable of representing the stand features that determine the suitability of different habitats. A variety of tools have been developed to assist biodiversity planning in forest management. Among these are statistical models that utilize correlations between forest attributes and the presence of a particular wildlife species or guild to determine habitat suitability (Edenius and Mikusinski, 2006). These models have gained popularity because habitat descriptors can be derived from variables commonly available in forestry databases or through modeling (e.g., timber volume, forest age, dominant tree height, and species composition) (Allen, 1983a,b; Eccles et al., 1986; Jalkotsky et al., 1990). When properly applied, they can also be used to predict the response of selected species to forest reclamation and to evaluate the efficacy of alternative practices (Kliskey et al., 1999).

Habitat suitability indices (HSIs) were calculated for ten boreal forest wildlife species common to the forests of the region. The HSIs from the natural forest were compared against HSIs simulated from the Kearl Lake mine reclamation plans. The objective was to compare the temporal trend in a given HSI on the natural landscape (i.e., what would have been present had mining not occurred) versus the temporal trend in HSIs modeled from the projected pattern of progressive reclamation.

METHODS

Study area

The Kearl Lake mine is operated by the Imperial Oil Company Ltd. and is located approximately 70 km north of Ft. McMurray (56°44′N, 111°23′W), AB, Canada. Details of mine development and associated reclamation plans are described within the Kearl Lake Environmental Impact Assessment (EIA) documents. The EIA documents are made available for public scrutiny by the Canadian Environmental Assessment Agency (www.ceaa-acee.gc.ca). The Kearl Lake development consists of four open pits that are to be mined over a 50-year period (2010–2060).

Large volumes of overburden will accumulate when this material is removed to access the underlying oil sand and piled elsewhere. An external tailings area will also be created to store the sandy material that remains following bitumen extraction. These materials have a low water storage capacity, nutrient status, and organic C content. They are therefore capped with a cover soil mixture of organic peat and mineral soil (typically 50% each by volume) (Alberta Environment, 2010). This peat:mineral mix constitutes the rooting matrix for the terrestrial reclaimed plant community. Related infrastructure includes a water intake and water pipeline (to allow water to be withdrawn from the Athabasca River), water storage, an operations camp, roads, and an airstrip. Progressive reclamation is projected to begin in 2016 and continue until 2065, five years after mining operations have ceased. The Kearl project will eventually occupy about 200 km^2 of land, although with progressive reclamation, the actual active footprint may be much smaller at any one time.

THE FORECAST MODEL

Input values for each of ten habitat suitability models were derived from output generated from the ecosystem simulation model, FORECAST. FORECAST is a management-oriented, stand-level forest growth and ecosystem dynamics simulator. The model was designed to accommodate a wide variety of harvesting and silvicultural systems and natural disturbance events (e.g., fire, wind, insect epidemics) in order to compare and contrast their effect on forest productivity, stand dynamics, and a series of biophysical indicators of non-timber values. Projection of stand growth and ecosystem dynamics is based on a representation of the rates of key ecological processes regulating the availability of, and competition for, light and nutrient resources, particularly nitrogen. A complete description of the growth equations and simulation algorithms employed in FORECAST, as well as a detailed description of data requirements, can be found in Kimmins et al. (1999). Details on model application to forest management issues are provided in Kimmins et al. (2010).

FORECAST has been applied to oil sands mine reclamation for more than a decade. In this regard, model output has been used to derive multipliers and nutrient regime classes for a landscape capability classification system (Welham, 2004), and to explore issues associated with peat decomposition rates (Welham, 2005a,b, 2006), including: the depth (Welham, 2005a,b) and type (Welham, 2005b, 2006) of the capping material, nitrogen deposition (Welham, unpublished), subsoil organic matter content (Welham, 2006), species mixes (Welham, 2005a), planting densities (Welham, 2005a, 2006), understory dynamics (Welham, 2005a,b, 2006),

Table 11.1. *Wildlife species selected for habitat suitability modeling*

Species	Spatial component	Reference
Moose (*Alces alces*)	Interspersion and ZOI disturbances	Eccles et al. (1986) Jalkotsky et al. (1990)
Fisher (*Martes pennanti*)	Interspersion	Allen (1983b) Jalkotsky et al. (1990)
Lynx (*Lynx canadensis*)	ZOI disturbances	Imperial Oil (2006)
Snowshoe hare (*Lepus americanus*)	No	Jalkotsky et al. (1990)
Red-backed vole (*Myodes rutilus*)	No	Eccles et al. (1986) Jalkotsky et al. (1990)
Black bear (*Ursus americanus*)	Interspersion and ZOI disturbances	Jalkotsky et al. (1990)
Ruffed grouse (*Bonasa umbellus*)	Interspersion	Jalkotsky et al. (1990)
Pileated woodpecker (*Dryocopus pileatus*)	Nesting habitat units per area	Bonar (2001)
Cape May warbler (*Dendroica tigrina*)	No	Skinner (1996)
Northern goshawk (*Accipiter gentilis*)	Nesting habitat units per area	Schaffer et al. 1999).

ZOI, zone of influence.

and dead organic matter dynamics (specifically snags; Welham, 2005b), all within the context of growth and yield.

SELECTION OF WILDLIFE SPECIES

Ten wildlife species included in the Kearl Lake EIA were used for habitat suitability modeling, as listed in Table 11.1. The models used to calculate the HSIs for a given species are described in Appendix 11.1. For seven of the ten species, the HSI model included a spatial component. In the present study, it was not possible to include spatial metrics, for the following reasons:

1. **Distance to disturbance:** three wildlife species (moose, black bear, and lynx) are sensitive to the presence of humans and human-related disturbances. As a consequence, these species tend to avoid human contact even if habitat conditions are suitable. The HSI for these species includes a correction factor related to the area under the zone of influence (ZOI) of the disturbance, applied after

all other environmental factors have been analyzed. Determining the actual ZOI for a given species will not be possible until after reclamation has been completed (in 2065, or later) and the location of permanent landscape features (e.g., roads) is known;

2. **Habitat fragmentation:** two wildlife species (ruffed grouse and fisher) use different areas for cover versus foraging. Suitable habitat for these species therefore depends on having a mosaic of plant communities interspersed within a given area. Interspersion is included as a modifying factor that accounts for the proportions of cover and forage habitat. Habitat fragmentation is not practical to estimate because reclamation prescriptions are applied at only a coarse resolution;

3. **Neighbouring nests:** two bird species (pileated woodpecker and northern goshawk) are sensitive to intraspecific competition for nesting sites. In this case, habitat suitability depends, in part, on the extent to which available habitat is already occupied and thus limiting to reproductive success. These population parameters are beyond the scope of this analysis.

In these cases, HSIs were calculated by assuming a maximal value for the spatial component. Because the inclusion of spatial metrics could potentially reduce habitat suitability, the HSI values for these species should thus be considered as a best-case outcome.

VARIABLES COMMON TO MOST OF THE HABITAT SUITABILITY MODELS

A description of the key variables common to many of the HSI models and their calculation with respect to FORECAST output is as follows.

- **Canopy closure in year t (CC_t):** all of the wildlife species depend on forests; canopy closure is thus a component in all the models. The CC is the percentage of open sky obscured by tree foliage in the forest canopy, and its inverse is thus the fraction of light passing through the canopy (Alaback, 1982; Martens et al., 2000). Light levels at the bottom of the canopy (a FORECAST output variable) is used to calculate CC as follows:

$$CC_t = \frac{(1 - Light\ canopy\ bottom_t)}{MAX\ (Light\ canopy\ bottom)} \qquad [11.1]$$

- **Structural stage:** tree height (a FORECAST output variable) is used as the proxy for forest structural stage (Table 11.2).

Table 11.2. *Vegetation structural stages as related to vegetation type and height*

Structural stage	Dominant vegetation
Non-vegetated	None–bare soil
Herbaceous	Herbs, grass
Low shrub	Shrubs <1 m height
Medium shrub	Shrub 1–3 m height
Tall shrub	Shrub 3–6 m height
Pole sapling	Trees 7–12 m height, single canopy
Young forest	Trees 7–12 m height with a diverse canopy structure, or 13–18 m height with a single canopy
Mature forest	Trees 13–18 m height with a diverse canopy, or >18 m height with a single canopy
Old-growth forest	Trees >18 m height, stands older than 100 years

Table 11.3. *Coefficients used to calculate shrub cover from foliage biomass*[1]

Coefficient	Low shrub	Medium shrub	Tall shrub
a	103.08237	77.74815	88.113605
b	1.8468465	1.4241986	1.424595
c	0.002010307	0.0017395	0.001640197
d	0.49666059	0.3857529	0.38583571

[1] Data derived from Alaback, 1982, 1986; Gholz et al. 1979; Muukkonen et al., 2006; Nyberg, 1985.

- **Shrub cover in year t (SC_t):** many wildlife species depend on the presence of a shrub layer to produce berries for food and provide cover. The SC is the proportion of ground covered by shrubs, and is calculated using a sigmoidal function that converts foliage biomass (a FORECAST output variable) to percentage cover. The coefficients a, b, c, and d are specific for each understory functional group (Table 11.3).

$$SC_t = \frac{a}{\left(1 + e^{(b-c(Species_a\ foliage\ biomass_t))}\right)^{1/d}} \qquad [11.2]$$

Species common to each shrub functional group and included within a given habitat suitability index (Appendix 11.1) are listed in Table 11.4.

Table 11.4. *Shrub species functional group as defined by height class (low, ≤1 m; medium, 1–<3 m; tall, ≥3 m)*

Low shrub	Medium shrub	Tall shrub
Blue berry	Prickly rose	Alder
Vaccinium angustifolium	*Rosa acicularis*	*Alnus spp.*
Bear berry	Wild raspberry	Paper birch
Arctostaphylos uva-ursi	*Rubus idaeus*	*Betula papyrifera*
Bog cranberry	Low-bush cranberry	Swamp birch
Vaccinium oxycoccus	*Viburnum edule*	*Betula glandulifera*
Crow berry	Currant	Saskatoon
Empetrum nigrum	*Ribes spp.*	*Amelanchier alnifolia*
	Red-osier dogwood	Beaked hazelnut
	Cornus alba	*Corylus cornuta*
		Willow
		Salix spp.
		Buffalo berry
		Sheperdia canadensis
		Choke cherry
		Prunus virginiana
		Pin cherry
		Prunus pennsylvanica

- **Species-specific canopy closure of tree type, a, in year t (S_aCC_t):** many wildlife species prefer a single species or tree type (either conifer or deciduous). Because of a direct link between foliar biomass and canopy closure, S_aCC can be calculated as the total CC (see discussion of "canopy closure") modified by the fraction of total stand foliage biomass represented by a given species or tree type (as outputted from FORECAST):

$$S_aCC_t = CC_t \times \frac{Species_a\ Foliage\ Biomass_t}{Total\ Foliage\ Biomass_t} \qquad [11.3]$$

- **Canopy/shrub height:** some species are directly affected by the height of trees and shrubs, as it affects their movement when seeking cover or food. This variable is determined directly from the FORECAST output.

MODEL APPLICATION

To evaluate the temporal trends in the HSIs for the ten species, two scenarios were simulated: (1) a no-development (natural) scenario, and (2) active mining with progressive reclamation (a reclamation scenario). Each scenario analysis consisted of a set of stand-level runs with the FORECAST model (as described previously), the output of which was used in conjunction with a given HSI model to populate the landscape based either on simulated trends in HSI development, using the pre-mining landscape as the starting condition (in the case of the natural scenario), or on the projected pattern of progressive reclamation proposed for Kearl Lake, as described in the EIA documents (the reclamation scenario). Ecosystem development in each scenario was projected forward for a period of 145 years, beginning in 2016, when reclamation was assumed to start. Habitat suitability indices were subsequently evaluated by species and used to compare each scenario. The specific methods employed in the scenario analysis are described in the following section.

Development of stand attribute tables

The characteristics of the pre-mining landscape were determined from spatial data obtained from the Kearl Lake EIA reports. These data included maps of the proposed mine area describing its ecosites, ecosite phases (*a1*, *b1-b4*, *c1*, *d1-d3*, *e1-e3*)[1], structural stages (Table 11.2), and their total areas (Table 11.5).

To project the long-term development of a given ecosite phase, a series of analysis units were created to reflect the community composition characteristic of each phase and its average productivity (represented as a site index) (Beckingham and Archibald, 1996). Specific assumptions concerning regeneration, species composition, and productivity for each analysis unit are provided in Table 11.6. The same analysis units were used for both the natural and reclamation scenarios.

FORECAST was applied to simulate the growth and development of each analysis unit up to a maximum stand age of 145 years. There was an important distinction in the soil conditions between the two scenarios. In the natural scenario, FORECAST was calibrated with soil data

---

[1] Ecosites are ecological units that develop under similar environmental influences (climate, moisture, and nutrient regime). They consist of groups of one or more ecosite phases, where a given ecosite phase is defined by the dominant tree species in the canopy (Beckingham and Archibald, 1996, for details).

Table 11.5. *Initial conditions for the natural scenario showing total ecosite area, area of each ecosite phase, and structural stage on the pre-mining landscape. Each row is considered to represent a subanalysis unit for the landscape-scale projections*

Ecosite	Total ecosite area (ha)	Ecosite phase	Ecosite phase area (ha)	Stage	Stage year
a	651.2	a1	117.6	Shrub	15
		a1	27.4	Sapling	45
		a1	96.9	Young forest	70
		a1	233.3	Mature forest	90
		a1	176.0	Old-growth	100
b	1317.5	b1	237.9	Shrub	15
		b1	55.5	Sapling	45
		b1	196.1	Young forest	70
		b1	472.0	Mature forest	90
		b1	356.1	Old-growth	100
b	1978	b2	357.1	Shrub	15
		b2	83.3	Sapling	45
		b2	294.4	Young forest	70
		b2	708.6	Mature forest	90
		b2	534.6	Old-growth	100
b	527.9	b3	95.3	Shrub	15
		b3	22.2	Sapling	45
		b3	78.6	Young forest	70
		b3	189.1	Mature forest	90
		b3	142.7	Old-growth	100
b	127.3	b4	23.0	Shrub	15
		b4	5.4	Sapling	45
		b4	18.9	Young forest	70
		b4	45.6	Mature forest	90
		b4	34.4	Old-growth	100
c	509.6	c1	92.0	Shrub	15
		c1	21.5	Sapling	45
		c1	75.8	Young forest	70
		c1	182.6	Mature forest	90
		c1	137.7	Old-growth	100
d	5221.8	d1	942.7	Shrub	15
		d1	220.0	Sapling	45
		d1	777.2	Young forest	70
		d1	1870.6	Mature forest	90
		d1	1411.3	Old-growth	100

Ecosite	Total ecosite area (ha)	Ecosite phase	Ecosite phase area (ha)	Stage	Stage year
d	2532.6	d2	457.2	Shrub	15
		d2	106.7	Sapling	45
		d2	377.0	Young forest	70
		d2	907.3	Mature forest	90
		d2	684.5	Old-growth	100
d	244.7	d3	44.2	Shrub	15
		d3	10.3	Sapling	45
		d3	36.4	Young forest	70
		d3	87.7	Mature forest	90
		d3	66.1	Old-growth	100
e	781.9	e1	141.2	Shrub	15
		e1	32.9	Sapling	45
		e1	116.4	Young forest	70
		e1	280.1	Mature forest	90
		e1	211.3	Old-growth	100
e	1384.0	e2	249.9	Shrub	15
		e2	58.3	Sapling	45
		e2	206.0	Young forest	70
		e2	495.8	Mature forest	90
		e2	374.0	Old-growth	100
e	137.0	e3	24.7	Shrub	15
		e3	5.8	Sapling	45
		e3	20.4	Young forest	70
		e3	49.1	Mature forest	90
		e3	37.0	Old-growth	100

files designed to reflect the moisture and nutrient regimes characteristic of each ecosite, as defined by the approximate centroid of its position on the edatopic grid (Beckingham and Archibald, 1996). In the reclamation scenario, the soil data file was modified to simulate the application of a 50-cm peat:mineral mix, and a medium peat decomposition rate (Welham 2005a,b; see Chapter 15). Output from the model simulations for each scenario was used to generate stand attribute tables with detailed information on the temporal pattern of structural development and species composition for each analysis unit. Lastly, HSI values for the ten wildlife species were calculated for each analysis unit on an annual timestep over the 145-year simulation period, using the stand attribute tables as input to the species-specific HSI models.

Table 11.6. *Analysis units used to represent the different ecosite phases of the Kearl Lake boreal mixedwood upland region for simulations using the FORECAST model*

Ecosite phase	Tree species	Starting site index	Planting density	Understory functional group	Understory starting percentage cover
a1	Jack pine	14	2000	Tall shrub	0.1
				Medium shrub	0.15
b1	Jack pine	16	1500	Tall shrub	0.15
	Aspen		1000	Medium shrub	0.2
b2	Aspen	16	2000	Tall shrub	0.15
				Medium shrub	0.2
b3	Aspen	16	1600	Tall shrub	0.15
	White spruce		400	Medium shrub	0.2
				Low shrub, grass	0.001
b4	White spruce	16	800	Tall shrub	0.15
	Jack pine		1200	Medium shrub	0.2
c	White spruce	14	500	Tall shrub	0.15
	Jack pine		1500	Medium shrub	0.2
d1	Aspen	18	2500	Tall shrub	0.3
				Medium shrub	0.5
				Low shrub, grass	0.1
d2	Aspen	18	1500	Tall shrub	0.3
	White spruce		1000	Medium shrub	0.5
				Low shrub, grass	0.1
d3	White spruce	18	2500	Tall shrub	0.3
				Medium shrub	0.3
				Low shrub, grass	0.5
e1	Aspen	20	2500	Tall shrub	0.1
				Medium shrub	0.3
				Grass	0.1
e2	White spruce	20	1500	Tall shrub	0.1
	Aspen		1000	Medium shrub	0.3
				Grass	0.1
e3	White spruce	20	2500	Tall shrub	0.1
				Medium shrub	0.3
				Grass	0.1

Landscape scale analysis

To facilitate a realistic projection of forest condition for the natural scenario, a given analysis unit (i.e., ecosite phase) on the pre-mining landscape was subdivided into its constituent structural stages (Table 11.5; see Table 11.2 for definitions). The landscape was then "populated" with HSI values for each analysis unit, corrected for structural stage, and these HSI values projected forward in time for a total period of 145 years. To represent the impact of natural disturbance, it was assumed that a stand reaching its maximum age during the simulation period was then immediately burned in a stand-replacing wildfire, after which it regenerated to the same analysis unit as existed previously. Subsequent development of the HSI then occurred until the 145-year total simulation period was reached.

In the case of the mining scenario, mining was assumed to be initiated in year 2010 after all forest stands had been removed from the proposed mine footprint, with reclamation beginning shortly thereafter (year 2016; Table 11.7). The reclaimed landscape was then "populated" with HSI values for each ecosite phase in accordance with the projected pattern of progressive reclamation, as described in the EIA documents (Table 11.7). As with the natural scenario, development of reclaimed stands on the mined landscape was projected forward for a total simulation period of 145 years from the year that reclamation was first initiated.

A weighted HSI was calculated for each species in each simulation year by multiplying the HSI value for a given ecosite by its associated area (the weighting component). A weighted HSI thus represents the number of habitat units (HU; ha) created for a given species in a given year. The total number of HUs for a given species in a given year is then derived from the sum of HUs across all ecosites. For the natural scenario, the age-class distribution and its associated area on the landscape (Table 11.5) were used to initiate the simulations and the weighting procedure. In the case of the mining scenario, the HSI value corresponding to a given ecosite phase that was projected to be reclaimed in a given year was multiplied by its corresponding area (Table 11.7). For some of the time periods when reclamation was scheduled to occur, the EIA documents grouped the *a* and *b* ecosites into a single *a-b* complex because of difficulties in discriminating among their edaphic features (Beckingham and Archibald, 1996) on the reclamation landscape. In this case, the anticipated reclaimed area for this complex was assigned evenly among the ecosite phases that comprise the *a* and *b* ecosites (*a1*, *b1*, *b2*, *b3*, and *b4*). For purposes of

Table 11.7. *Area reclaimed (ha) by ecosite phase and reclamation year for the Kearl Lake mine footprint*

Ecosite	Ecosite phase	Reclamation event (year)									TOTAL[1]
		2016	2026	2031	2036	2041	2046	2051	2056	2061	
a	a1	647.4	–	41.3	547.8	328.3	883.2	279.1	141.5	736.6	3605.1
b	b1-b4	29.4	–	41.3	502.6	82.4	580.7	271.9	141.5	610.3	9040.8
c	c	–	–	2.9	–	–	–	–	–	–	2.9
d	d1-d3	105.2	469.9	214.1	–	91.7	–	1.5	–	102.4	2846.4
e	e1-e3	–	–	0.3	–	–	310.7	103.9	264.7	578.2	3773.4
	TOTAL	1080.7	1409.7	852.8	2558.2	933.1	4138.1	1683.0	1501.4	5219.3	19376.4

[1] Areas apply to each individual phase. Totals are, therefore, the sum for each phase within a given ecosite.

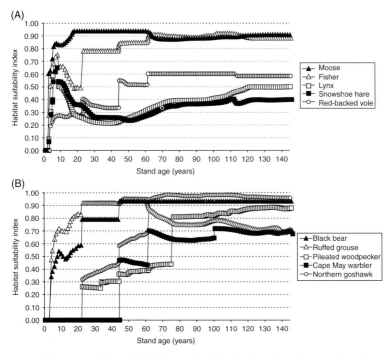

Figure 11.1. (**A**) and (**B**) Habitat suitability index values from ecosite phase *d2* (see Table 11.6) for stands in the natural landscape.

comparative analysis, all *a* and *b* ecosites were grouped into a single *a-b* complex. Finally, while *c* ecosites were reasonably well represented in the pre-mining landscape (~510 ha; Table 11.5), very little reclamation was planned to create them on the mine site (<3 ha; Table 11.7). Hence, this was deemed an insufficient area for a meaningful comparison of the two scenarios and thus was not included in the analysis.

RESULTS AND DISCUSSION

Habitat suitability indices by ecosite phase

There were considerable differences among species in their HSIs for a given ecosite phase. Figure 11.1 illustrates these differences using the *d2* phase as an example. Many of the HSI equations are comprised of step functions (see Methods), and this is often reflected in the trends in the HSI values (Figure 11.1). For most species, their HSIs typically increased with stand age in conjunction with the habitat attributes from which they were derived. For snowshoe hare, their dependence on understory plants as a food source resulted in an initial increase in the HSI, followed by a decline through the middle stand ages and then an increase again at the oldest ages (Figure 11.1A). This trend is consistent with the fact that during stand initiation, light levels at the soil surface are high, then decline during canopy closure as light become increasingly limited (Comeau, 2001), and finally increase thereafter as dominant trees begin to senesce (Hart and Chen, 2008). Snowshoe hares are an important food source for lynx and the HSI for the latter thus incorporates the HSI value for hares (Appendix 11.1). Consequently, there is a consistent and close correlation between the HSI values for these species (Figure 11.1A). Finally, for species such as pileated woodpecker that are dependent on mature and old-growth structural stages (Appendix 11.1), habitat attributes begin to develop only after a protracted period of stand development (Figure 11.1B).

Habitat units by ecosite and reclamation period

The number of habitat units (HUs) for each species is calculated by determining its HSI value corresponding to a given ecosite phase, multiplied by the corresponding reclaimed area within a given simulation year (see Methods). The total HUs created for a particular species therefore depends on: (a) the pattern in available habitat that develops from reclaiming to a given ecosite (or ecosite phase); (b) how much of that ecosite is reclaimed over time; and (c) the relative amount and pattern of development in all other ecosites (as per Table 11.7). With moose, for example, the total number of HUs increased consistently on all except d ecosites, the latter of which levelled off (Figure 11.2A). For lynx, in contrast, the total number of HUs was much less than for moose (about 33% of the maximum for moose) (Figure 11.2B), although the overall pattern of development was similar (Figure 11.2A,B).

Development of the anticipated reclamation landscape on the Kearl Lake mine during the period of active reclamation appears to provide adequate habitat for species such as moose, largely because suitable habitat can be created for a range of ecosite phases. For species in which habitat is relatively more difficult to create, such as snowshoe hare (Figure 11.1A) and, consequently, lynx (Figure 11.2B), the total amount of HUs could be enhanced by increasing the area reclaimed to those ecosite phases that are relatively more favorable. For species like pileated woodpecker, ensuring that stands survive long enough to exhibit attributes typical of mature and old-growth stages is a necessity (Figure 11.1B). There may be a

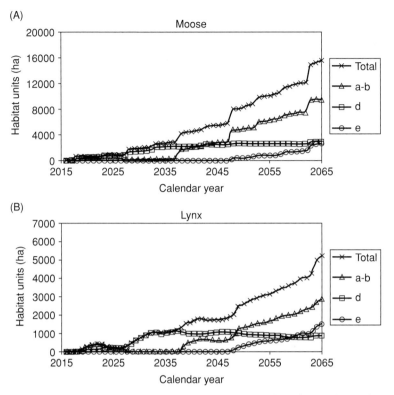

Figure 11.2. Habitat units (ha) created through reclamation on the Kearl Lake mine for moose (**A**) and lynx (**B**) by ecosite, through the years 2016 to 2065.

trade-off with this approach, however, since a range of habitat is required to promote a full suite of biodiversity on the reclaimed landscape.

Comparing habitat units between the natural and mining scenarios

Typically, the initiation of mining activities on a given lease begins with the removal of essentially all ecosystems within the mine footprint, in preparation for bitumen extraction. In the case of Kearl Lake, this is an area of more than 20,000 ha which, at least temporarily, contains no habitat capable of supporting healthy wildlife populations. A well-executed reclamation program has the potential to restore suitable habitat on the mine footprint, but this occurs only progressively. A key question then is to what extent is progressive reclamation, as specified within the Kearl

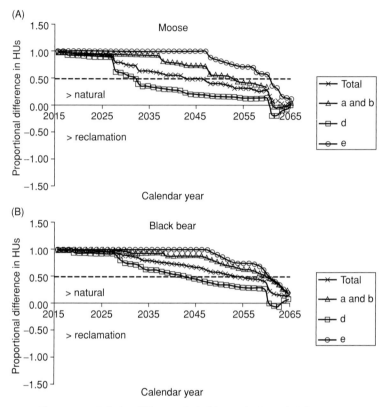

Figure 11.3. Relative difference in habitat units (HUs; ha) for moose
(**A**) and black bear (**B**) between the natural landscape and the Kearl Lake
mine footprint for ecosites a–b, and d–e, from the beginning of mine
reclamation (2016) to mine closure (2065). HUs greater than zero indicate
more habitat in the natural landscape; values less than zero indicate more
habitat on the reclaimed mine area. The horizontal broken line denotes a
50% recovery in the reclaimed versus the natural landscape.

Lake EIA, effective in restoring habitat relative to the natural landscape,
and over what time period?

This question is addressed first by comparing the pattern in habitat development for each species on the reclaimed mine footprint (the
reclamation scenario) relative to what would have occurred on the natural landscape over the same time period had it not been disturbed by
mining (the natural scenario). Results for each species are presented in
Figures 11.3–11.7. With the exception of lynx (Figure 11.4B), snowshoe
hare (Figure 11.5A), and pileated woodpecker (Figure 11.7A), the number

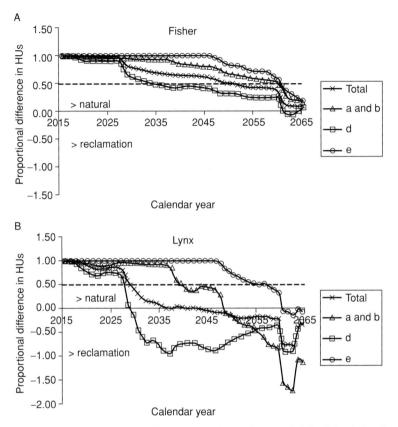

Figure 11.4. Relative difference in habitat units (HUs; ha) for fisher (**A**) and lynx (**B**) between the natural landscape and the Kearl Lake mine footprint for ecosites a–b, and d–e, from the beginning of mine reclamation (2016) to mine closure (2065). HUs greater than zero indicate more habitat in the natural landscape; values less than zero indicate more habitat on the reclaimed mine area. The horizontal broken line denotes a 50% recovery in the reclaimed versus the natural landscape.

of HUs created through reclamation increased steadily and consistently across ecosites. The total number of HUs, however, was consistently less than the natural scenario until very close to the mine closure date (in year 2065). In the case of pileated woodpecker, its habitat requirements were very poorly represented on the reclaimed landscape during this period (Figure 11.7A). This species is heavily reliant on mature and old forests, and an insufficient time had elapsed on any reclaimed site to develop this age class or its associated structural attributes, relative to what was simulated under the natural scenario.

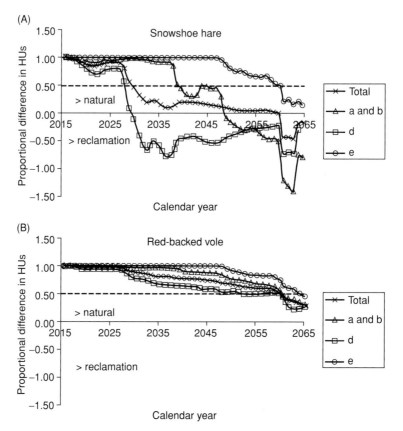

Figure 11.5. Relative difference in habitat units (HUs; ha) for snowshoe hare (**A**) and red-backed vole (**B**) between the natural landscape and the Kearl Lake mine footprint for ecosites a–b, and d–e, from the beginning of mine reclamation (2016) to mine closure (2065). HUs greater than zero indicate more habitat in the natural landscape; values less than zero indicate more habitat on the reclaimed mine area. The horizontal broken line denotes a 50% recovery in the reclaimed versus the natural landscape.

For lynx and snowshoe hare, the number of HUs created in a–b and d ecosites developed relatively rapidly and often exceeded that which would have been present on the natural landscape had mining not occurred (Figures 11.4B; 11.5A). In the case of hare, this species is heavily dependent on an understory plant community for browse (Appendix 11.1). Understory species tend to be abundant immediately after stand-replacing disturbance, but then decline thereafter as forests age and light levels reach critically low levels (Comeau, 2001). In the natural landscape, disturbance events would likely have been much less frequent and of a

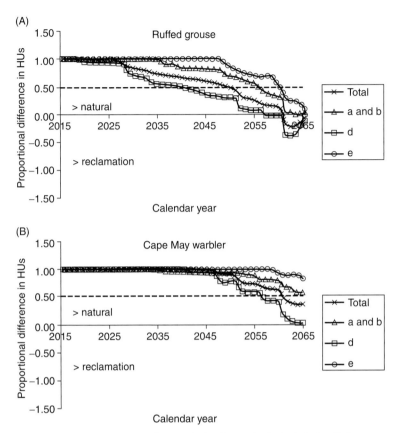

Figure 11.6. Relative difference in habitat units (HUs; ha) of ruffed grouse (**A**) and Cape May warbler (**B**) between the natural landscape and the Kearl Lake mine footprint for ecosites a–b, and d–e, from the beginning of mine reclamation (2016) to mine closure (2065). HUs greater than zero indicate more habitat in the natural landscape; values less than zero indicate more habitat on the reclaimed mine area. The horizontal broken line denotes a 50% recovery in the reclaimed versus the natural landscape.

lesser extent than occurred on the mine site, the latter of which is completely cleared of vegetation in preparation for mining activities. With progressive reclamation, the mine footprint will thus be populated by stands of relatively younger age, thereby favoring understory growth and thus, hare habitat suitability and an abundance of habitat units. Snowshoe hares are a staple food item for lynx (Appendix 11.1). As a result, lynx habitat was strongly correlated with the trends observed for snowshoe hare. These latter species illustrate the point that, over the short-term at

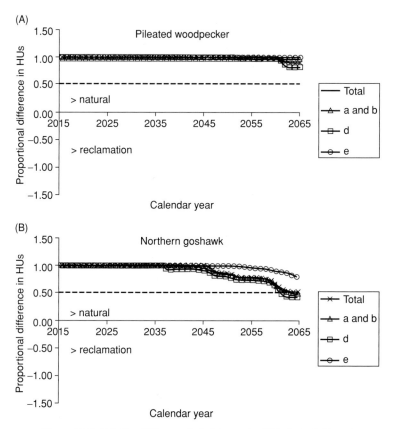

Figure 11.7. Relative difference in habitat units (HUs; ha) of pileated woodpecker (**A**) and northern goshawk (**B**) between the natural landscape and the Kearl Lake mine footprint for ecosites a–b, and d–e, from the beginning of mine reclamation (2016) to mine closure (2065). HUs greater than zero indicate more habitat in the natural landscape; values less than zero indicate more habitat on the reclaimed mine area. The horizontal broken line denotes a 50% recovery in the reclaimed versus the natural landscape.

least, reclamation practices could be creating conditions that generate habitat for species at levels beyond that typical of a natural landscape.

Under the reclamation plan described in the Kearl Lake EIA (and as reflected in the simulation protocol), an average of 35.5±14.1 (SD) years are required following initial reclamation before the number of HUs reaches 50% of the level that would have been present had the mine not been developed (Table 11.8). The variation in recovery rate among species is also considerable. Lynx and snowshoe hare HUs, for

Table 11.8. *Development of total habitat units for ten wildlife species to levels of 50% and 100% of the natural scenario from progressive reclamation beginning in year 2016 and continuing until year 2065*

Species	Years to 50% recovery	Years to 100% recovery
Moose	27	44
Black bear	37	55
Fisher	35	55
Lynx	14	27
Snowshoe hare	14	35
Red-backed vole	45	55
Ruffed grouse	33	45
Cape May warbler	45	55
Pileated woodpecker	55	65
Northern goshawk	50	55
Mean (±SD)	35.5±14.1	49.1±11.3

example, reach 50% recovery in the shortest time, only 14 years; at the other extreme, 50 and 55 years are required for northern goshawk and pileated woodpecker, respectively (Table 11.8). Following the relatively protracted period required to realize a 50% recovery, the number of HUs is projected to increase rapidly thereafter. After an average of 15 additional years (49.3±12.0 yr after initial reclamation) a 100% recovery in HUs is projected (Table 11.8). Despite the fact that for a majority of the 10 species, progressive reclamation can provide for development of a reasonable number of HUs at the point of mine closure, when recovery rates are considered in conjunction with the scale of oil sands mining, the negative impact is not trivial. In the case of Kearl Lake, a majority of reclamation is anticipated to occur during the mid and later phases of mining (Table 11.7), which could be reflected in the general increase in the number of HUs during this period. From the perspective of habitat restoration, however, the greatest benefit would be derived from development plans that allowed for reclamation to be initiated as quickly as possible after mining begins and to the maximum extent thereafter. In addition, our calculations focused on the temporal pattern in HU development from when reclamation was first initiated (in 2016). Given that mining was assumed to begin in 2010, there was thus an additional six years when the mine footprint had essentially no habitat development.

This simulation exercise constitutes a "best-case" assessment of habitat availability because many of the spatial parameters associated with anthropogenic disturbance that comprise a given HSI were not considered explicitly in its calculation. Including a spatial component could improve habitat projections. For practical purposes, however, the nature of the information required as input to the EIA process is only very general and qualitative. It may thus prove difficult to include spatial metrics without any means of constraining and verifying potential options. In addition, inputs into the HSI calculations from projections of forest development made with the FORECAST model were derived without explicit consideration of any potential impacts associated with future climate change (Cerezke, 2008). This protocol thus represents a set of "base-case" scenarios against which scenarios taking climate change into account should be compared. Finally, to properly evaluate the relative impact of the Kearl Lake operation on habitat availability, this project must be evaluated within the context of all existing and proposed mine leases, other types of industrial activity, as well as areas not subject to anthropogenic disturbance.

SUMMARY

Open-pit mining used in the process of oil sands extraction results in the temporary but complete removal of essentially all functioning ecosystems on the mine footprint. Typically, reclamation activities begin early in the life of a mine, although for practical purposes, the majority of reclamation is deferred to just before and immediately after mine closure. Much of the modeling work conducted on reclamation in upland areas has been focused around simulating plant productivity (particularly trees), with little emphasis on development of other attributes, such as wildlife habitat. Habitat suitability indices therefore were calculated for ten boreal forest wildlife species (moose, black bear, snowshoe hare, lynx, red-backed vole, fisher, Cape May warbler, ruffed grouse, pileated woodpecker, and northern goshawk) for ecosystems characteristic of the pre-mining landscape, and for the planned reclamation of the Kearl Lake mine, an area that encompasses more than 20,000 ha. Input values for each HSI were derived from output generated by the ecosystem simulation model, FORECAST.

When considered in the context of the overall mine footprint and the relative optimism of our analysis for recovery for some species, results suggest that habitat loss during active mining is significant, as new habitat develops only relatively slowly. There was roughly a 41-year window following the initiation of mining activities (or, a 35-year window after reclamation was first initiated) when upland habitat suitability on the mine footprint was classed as poor ($\leq$50% of what would have been present had mining not occurred). Habitat suitability was projected to recover relatively quickly thereafter; however, 61 years after mining began (55 years after the beginning of reclamation), nine out of ten species had a suitability index equivalent to what might have been present on the pre-mining landscape.

Recovery of suitable habitat depends on the timing of reclamation events, the type of upland ecosystems reclaimed, and how progressive reclamation impacts the age-class distribution relative to what would have been present had the landscape not been mined. Reclamation practices could be targeted toward the habitat requirements of particular wildlife species by preferentially reclaiming more favorable ecosite phases. Conversely, a broad range of ecosite phases is necessary to promote suitable habitats for a diverse range of species on the reclaimed landscape.

ACKNOWLEDGMENTS

Funding for a component of this work was provided by the Oil Sands and Clean Energy Policy Branch, Alberta Environment (AE), and administered through the Oil Sands Research and Information Network (OSRIN), University of Alberta (Grant NO. 09-GROF02). We are grateful to Stephen Moran (former Director of OSRIN), Chris Powter (current OSRIN Director), Brett Purdy (AE), Robert Magai (AE), and Lori Neufeld (Imperial Oil Ltd.) for support and constructive criticism.

APPENDIX 11.1. SPECIES-SPECIFIC HABITAT SUITABILITY MODELS

Moose (*Alces alces*)

The habitat suitability model for moose takes into account food and cover components, as well as the interspersion of habitat suitable for any of those purposes and the ZOI of disturbances. The model is formulated as:

$$HSI_{food} = SI_{Preferred\ Browse} \qquad\qquad [11A1.1]$$

$$HSI_{cover} = \sqrt[3]{SI_{SconiferCC} \times SI_{CH} \times SI_{CC}} \qquad\qquad [11A1.2]$$

$$HSI_{MOOSE} = \sqrt{(Max(HSI_{food}\ HSI_{cover}) \times SI_{HI})} \qquad\qquad [11A1.3]$$

(no disturbance effect included).

To account for the effect of disturbances, the final HSI is $HSI_{MOOSE} \times SI_{ZOI\ Disturbance\ Coeff}$. Note that the latter is assigned a value of 1 (see Methods). The variables for the model are calculated as follows:

Preferred browse canopy cover ($S_{browse}CC$). These include birch, poplar, and aspen. Additional species are willow, red osier dogwood, saskatoon, low-bush cranberry, buffaloberry chokecherry, and pincherry. The relationship with SI is:

$$\text{If } S_{browse}CC \leq 50\% \ SI_{preferred\ browse} = 3.1791\ S_{browse}CC - 2.5793\ (S_{browse}CC)^2$$

$$[11A1.4]$$

$$\text{If } S_{browse}CC > 50\% \ SI_{preferred\ browse} = 1 \qquad [11A1.5]$$

Conifer canopy closure ($S_{conifer}CC$). The relationship with SI is:

$$\text{If } S_{conifer}CC \leq 60\% \ SI_{SconiferCC} = 0.2 + 1.4263\ S_{conifer}CC$$
$$-0.2512\ (S_{conifer}CC)^2 \qquad [11A1.6]$$

$$\text{If } S_{conifer}CC > 60\% \ SI_{SconiferCC} = 1 \qquad [11A1.7]$$

Canopy height (CH in meters). The relationship with SI is:

$$\text{If } CH \leq 15m \ SI_{CH} = 0.1038\ CH - 0.0027\ CH^2 \qquad [11A1.8]$$

$$\text{If } CH > 15m \ SI_{CH} = 1 \qquad [11A1.9]$$

Tree canopy closure (CC). The relationship with SI is:

$$\text{If } CC \leq 70\% \ SI_{CC} = 0.2 + 0.887\ CC + 0.2891 CC^2 \qquad [11A1.10]$$

$$\text{If } CC > 70\% \ SI_{CC} = 1 \qquad [11A1.11]$$

Habitat interspersion (HI). This variable takes into account how much of the habitat in the area can be considered as habitat for food and how much can be considered as habitat for cover. The proportions of each type of habitat (P_{food} and $P_{cover,}$) are values from 0 to 1 that, when added, equal 1. The ideal proportion is 30% habitat for cover and 70% habitat for food. For other combinations, their relationship with SI is:

$$SI_{HI} = 0.8696e^{-0.5 \cdot \left(\left(\frac{P_{food} - 0.7279}{0.4773} \right)^2 + \left(\frac{P_{cover} - 0.3102}{0.3904} \right)^2 \right)}$$

[11A1.12]

In order to simplify the analysis, the calculations presented in this report assume that the habitat interspersion is in its ideal proportion. In addition, no ZOIs were taken into account, which is equivalent to assuming that there was not reduction of habitat by human structures. As a result, the HSI for moose can be considered as calculated under "optimal" conditions, and actual values will be slightly lower than the one presented.

Black bear (*Ursus americanus*)

The habitat suitability model for black bear takes into account the food and cover components, as well as the interspersion of habitat suitable for any of those purposes and the ZOI of disturbances. The model is formulated as:

$$HSI_{food} = SI_{Berries}$$

[11A1.13]

$$HSI_{cover} = Max \left[SI_{SC}, \left(\sqrt{SI_{CC} \times S_{ST}} \right) \right]$$

[11A1.14]

$$HSI_{BLACK\ BEAR} = \sqrt{(Max(HSI_{food}, HSI_{cover}) \times SI_{HI})}$$

[11A1.15]

(no disturbance effect included).

To account for the effect of disturbances, the final HSI is $HSI_{overall} \times SI_{ZOI\ Disturbance\ Coeff.}$ The disturbance coefficients for black bear are 0.75 for any site less than 500 m from any active road, railway, airstrip, and urban, residential, and industrial sites.

The variables for the model are calculated as follows:

Berry producers ($S_{berries}CC$). Species considered important berry producers include buffaloberry, blueberry, saskatoon, low-bush cranberry, rose, currant, raspberry, bearberry, bog cranberry, and crowberry. The relationship with SI is:

If $S_{berries}CC \leq 50\%$ $SI_{berries} = 0.2 + 1.5985\ S_{berries}CC$

[11A1.16]

If $S_{berries}CC > 50\%$ $SI_{berries} = 1$

[11A1.17]

Table 11A.1. *Suitability index multipliers for black bear in relationships to tree maturity and structural stage*

Structural stage	SI_{ST}
Non-vegetated	0.0
Herbaceous	0.0
Low shrub	0.1
Tall shrub	0.2
Pole sapling	0.5
Young forest	1.0
Mature forest	1.0
Old-growth forest	1.0

Shrub canopy closure (SC). The relationship with SI is:

$$SI_{SC} = 1.9193\,SC - 1.0634\,SC^2 \tag{11A1.18}$$

Tree canopy closure (CC). The relationship with SI is:

$$\text{If } CC \leq 70\% \;\; SI_{CC} = 0.2 + 0.6089\,CC + 0.7172\,CC^2 \tag{11A1.19}$$

$$\text{If } CC > 70\% \;\; SI_{CC} = 1 \tag{11A1.20}$$

Structural stage (ST). The relationship with SI is given in Table 11A.1.

Habitat interspersion (HI). This variable takes into account how much of the habitat in the area can be considered as habitat for food and how much can be considered as habitat for cover. The proportions of each type of habitat (P_{food} and $P_{cover,}$) are values from 0 to 1 that together equal 1. The ideal proportion is 30% habitat for cover and 70% habitat for food. For other combinations, their relationship with SI is:

$$SI_{HI} = 0.8696\,e^{-0.5 \cdot \left(\left(\frac{P_{food} - 0.7279}{0.4773} \right)^2 + \left(\frac{P_{cover} - 0.3102}{0.3904} \right)^2 \right)} \tag{11A1.21}$$

In order to simplify the analysis, the calculations presented in this report assume that the habitat interspersion is in its ideal proportion. In addition, no ZOIs were taken into account, which is equivalent to assuming that there was not reduction of habitat by human structures. As a result, the HSI for black bear can be considered as calculated under "optimal" conditions, and actual values will be slightly lower.

Snowshoe hare (*Lepus americanus*)

The habitat suitability model for snowshoe hare takes into account the food and cover components, and also the interspersion of habitat suitable for any of those purposes and the ZOI of disturbances. The model is formulated as:

$$HSI_{food} = \sqrt[3]{SI_{SC} \times SI_{Preferred\ Browse} \times SI_{SH}} \qquad [11A1.22]$$

$$HSI_{cover} = Max\left[SI_{SC}, \left(\sqrt{SI_{CC} \times SI_{spruce/fir}}\right)\right] \qquad [11A1.23]$$

$$HSI_{SNOWSHOE\ HARE} = \frac{HSI_{food} + HSI_{cover}}{2} \qquad [11A1.24]$$

The variables for the model are calculated as follows:

Preferred browse canopy cover ($S_{browse}CC$). These include alder, paper birch and swamp birch, larch and jackpine, and also saskatoon hazelnut, rose, raspberry, willows, and buffaloberry. The relationship with SI is:

$$\text{If } S_{browse}CC \leq 50\% \ SI_{preferred\ browse} = 0.4 + 1.2376 S_{browse}CC \quad [11A1.25]$$

$$\text{If } S_{browse}CC > 50\% \ SI_{preferred\ browse} = 1 \qquad [11A1.26]$$

Shrub cover (SC). The relationship with SI is:

$$\text{If } SC \leq 90\% \ SI_{SC} = 1.0918 \ SC \qquad [11A1.27]$$

$$\text{If } SC > 90\% \ SI_{SC} = 1 \qquad [11A1.28]$$

Shrub height (SH in meters). The relationship with SI is:

$$\text{If } SH \leq 1.5m \ SI_{SH} = 0.5 + 1.7084 \ SH - 1.3148 \ SH^2 \qquad [11A1.29]$$

$$\text{If } SH > 1.5m \ SI_{SH} = 0 \qquad [11A1.30]$$

Tree canopy closure (CC). The relationship with SI is:

If CC $\leq 50\%$ $SI_{CC} = 0.4 + 0.2735\,CC + 1.7823\,CC^2$ [11A1.31]

If CC $> 50\%$ $SI_{CC} = 1$ [11A1.32]

Spruce of fir canopy closure ($S_{spruce\,fir}$ CC). The relationship with SI is:

If $S_{spruce\,fir}CC \leq 50\%$ $SI_{Spruce\,fir} = 0.733\,S_{spruce\,fir}CC$
$$+ 2.4576(S_{spruce\,fir}CC)^2 \quad [11A1.33]$$

If $S_{spruce\,fir}CC > 50\%$ $SI_{Spruce\,fir} = 1$ [11A1.34]

Lynx (*Lynx canadensis*)

The habitat suitability model for lynx takes into account the food and cover components, as well as the interspersion of habitat suitable for any of those purposes and the ZOI of disturbances. The model for lynx is formulated as:

$$HSI_{food} = HSI_{Snowshoe\,hare} \qquad [11A1.35]$$

$$HSI_{cover} = \sqrt{SI_{CC} \times SI_{SC}} \qquad [11A1.36]$$

$$HSI_{LYNX} = 0.8 \times HSI_{food} + 0.2$$
$$\times HSI_{cover}\ (\text{no disturbance effect included}). \qquad [11A1.37]$$

To account for the effect of disturbances, the final HSI is $HSI_{LYN12} \times SI_{ZOI\,Disturbance\,Coeff.}$ Note that the latter is assigned a value of 1 (see Methods). The variables for the model are calculated as follows:

Tree canopy closure (CC). The relationship with SI is:

If CC $\leq 70\%$ $SI_{CC} = 0.1 + 0.5311\,CC + 1.1181\,CC^2$ [11A1.38]

If CC $> 70\%$ $SI_{CC} = 1$ [11A1.39]

Shrub cover (SC). The relationship with SI is:

If SC $\leq 70\%$ $SI_{SC} = 2.9573\,SC - 2.3116\,SC^2$ [11A1.40]

If SC $> 70\%$ $SI_{SC} = 1$ [11A1.41]

Table 11A.2. *Suitability index multipliers for red-backed vole in relationships to tree maturity and structural stage*

Structural stage	SI_{ST}
Non-vegetated	0.00
Herbaceous	0.05
Low shrub	0.05
Tall shrub	0.05
Pole sapling	0.15
Young forest	0.65
Mature forest	1.00
Old-growth forest	1.00

In order to simplify the analysis, no ZOIs were taken into account, which is equivalent to assuming that there was not reduction of habitat by human structures. As a result, the HSI for lynx can be considered as calculated under "optimal" conditions, and actual values will be slightly lower.

Red-backed vole (*Myodes rutilus*)

The habitat suitability model for red-backed vole is simple and only takes into account a combined measure of both food and cover components. The model is formulated as:

$$HSI_{RED-BACKED\,VOLE} = \sqrt[3]{SI_{ST} \times SI_{CC} \times SI_{SC}}$$
[11A1.42]

The variables for the model are calculated as follows:

Structural stage (ST). The relationship with SI is given in Table 11A.2.

Tree canopy closure (CC). The relationship with SI is:

If $CC \leq 70\%$ $SI_{CC} = 1.8168\,CC$
[11A1.43]

If $CC > 70\%$ $SI_{CC} = 1$
[11A1.44]

Shrub cover (SC). The relationship with SI is:

If SC $\leq$ 70% $SI_{SC} = 0.2 + 1.1572\,SC$ [11A1.45]

If SC $>$ 70% $SI_{SC} = 1$ [11A1.46]

Fisher (*Martes pennanti*)

The habitat suitability model for fisher takes into account the food and cover components, as well as the interspersion of habitat suitable for any of those purposes and the ZOI of disturbances. Given the strong dependence of fisher on small mammals such as snowshoe hares or red-backed voles as main food sources, the models for snowshoe hare and red-backed vole must be calculated first. The model for fisher is formulated as:

$$HSI_{food} = Max\left(HSI_{Snowshoe\,hare}, HSI_{red-backed\,vole}\right) \qquad [11A1.47]$$

$$HSI_{cover} = \sqrt[3]{SI_{CC} \times SI_{conifer} \times SI_{ST}} \qquad [11A1.48]$$

$$HSI_{FISHER} = \sqrt{Max\left(HSI_{food}, HSI_{cover}\right) \times SI_{interspersion}} \qquad [11A1.49]$$

The variables for the model are calculated as follows:

Tree canopy closure (CC). The relationship with SI is:

If CC $\leq$ 70% $SI_{CC} = 0.7075\,CC + 0.9923\,CC^2$ [11A1.50]

If CC $>$ 70% $SI_{CC} = 1$ [11A1.51]

Conifer canopy closure ($S_{conifer}CC$). The relationship with SI is:

If $S_{conifer}CC \leq$ 70% $SI_{conifer} = 0.1 + 3.4435\,S_{conifer}CC$
$$- 3.3647(S_{conifer}CC)^2 \qquad [11A1.52]$$

If $S_{conifer}CC >$ 70% $SI_{conifer} = 0.8$ [11A1.53]

Structural stage (ST). The relationship with SI is given in Table 11.A3

Habitat interspersion (HI). This variable takes into account how much of the habitat in the area can be considered as habitat

Table 11A.3. *Suitability index multipliers for fisher in relationships to tree maturity and structural stage*

Structural stage	SI_{ST}
Non-vegetated	0.0
Herbaceous	0.0
Low shrub	0.2
Tall shrub	0.3
Pole sapling	0.4
Young forest	0.6
Mature forest	0.9
Old-growth forest	1.0

for food and how much can be considered as habitat for cover. The proportions of each type of habitat (P_{food} and $P_{cover,}$) are values from 0 to 1 that together equal 1. The ideal proportion is 60% habitat for cover and 40% habitat for food. For other combinations, their relationship with SI is:

$$SI_{HI} = 0.8612\, e^{-0.5 \cdot \left(\left(\frac{P_{food} - 0.4025}{0.4082} \right)^2 + \left(\frac{P_{cover} - 0.6087}{0.4548} \right)^2 \right)}$$

[11A1.54]

In order to simplify the analysis, the calculations presented in this report assume that the habitat interspersion is in its ideal proportion. As a result, the HSI for fisher can be considered as calculated under "optimal" conditions, and actual values will be slightly lower.

Cape May warbler (*Dendroica tigrina*)

The habitat suitability model for Cape May warbler is simple and only takes into account a combined measure of both food and cover components. The model is formulated as:

$$HSI_{CAP\,MAY\,WARBLER} = \sqrt{\sqrt[4]{SI_{ST} \times SI_{CC} \times SI_{conifer} \times SI_{CH} \times SI_{do\,\min\,ant\,species}}}$$

[11A1.55]

The variables for the model are calculated as follows:

Structural stage (ST). The relationship with SI is given in Table 11A.4.

Table 11A.4. *Suitability index multipliers for Cape May warbler in relationships to tree maturity and structural stage*

Structural stage	SI_{ST}
Non-vegetated	0.0
Herbaceous	0.0
Low shrub	0.0
Tall shrub	0.0
Pole sapling	0.1
Young forest	0.5
Mature forest	0.9
Old-growth forest	1.0

Tree canopy closure (CC). The relationship with SI is:

$$\text{If CC} \leq 70\% \; SI_{CC} = 4.447 \, CC - 5.1009 \, CC^2 \qquad [11A1.56]$$

$$\text{If CC} > 70\% \; SI_{CC} = 0.6$$

Conifer canopy closure ($S_{conifer}CC$). The relationship with SI is:

$$\text{If } S_{conifer}CC \leq 70\% \; SI_{conifer} = 0.1 - 0.1385 \, S_{conifer}CC$$
$$+ 2.0227 \, (S_{conifer}CC)^2 \qquad [11A1.57]$$

$$\text{If } S_{conifer}CC > 70\% \; SI_{conifer} = 1 \qquad [11A1.58]$$

Canopy height (CH). The relationship with SI is:

$$\text{If CH} < 10 \, \text{m} \; SI_{CH} = 0.2 \qquad [11A1.59]$$

$$\text{If CH} \geq 10 \, \text{m and CH} \leq 15 \, \text{m} \; SI_{CH} = 0.8 \qquad [11A1.60]$$

$$\text{If CH} > 15 \, \text{m} \; SI_{CH} = 1 \qquad [11A1.61]$$

Dominant overstory species: The relationship with SI is provided in Table 11A.5.

Table 11A.5. *Suitability index multipliers for Cape May warbler in relationships to dominant overstory species*

Dominant species	$SI_{\text{dominant species}}$
Deciduous	0.3
Other conifer	0.5
Balsam fir	0.7
White spruce	1.0

Ruffed grouse (*Bonasa umbellus*)

The habitat suitability model for ruffed grouse takes into account the food and cover components, and also the interspersion of habitat suitable for any of those purposes. The model is formulated as:

$$HSI_{food} = \sqrt{Max\left(SI_{SC}, \sqrt{SI_{deciduous} \times SI_{STfood}}\right) \times SI_{preferred\,food}} \qquad [11A1.62]$$

$$HSI_{cover} = \sqrt{SI_{CC} \times SI_{ST\,cover}} \qquad [11A1.63]$$

$$HSI_{RUFFED\,GROUSE} = \sqrt{(Max(HSI_{food}, HSI_{cover}) \times SI_{HI})} \qquad [11A1.64]$$

The variables for the model are calculated as follows:

Shrub cover (SC). The relationship with SI is:

$$\text{If } SC \leq 90\% \; SI_{SC} = 3.1191\,SC - 2.5633\,SC^2 \qquad [11A1.65]$$

$$\text{If } SC > 90\% \; SI_{SC} = 0.7 \qquad [11A1.66]$$

Structural stage food (ST$_{food}$). The relationship with SI is given in Table 11A.6.

Deciduous canopy closure (S$_{deciduous}$CC). The relationship with SI is:

$$\text{If } S_{deciduous}CC \leq 80\% \; SI_{deciduous} = 1.2098 S_{deciduous}CC \qquad [11A1.67]$$

$$\text{If } S_{deciduous}CC > 80\% \; SI_{deciduous} = 1 \qquad [11A1.68]$$

Table 11A.6. *Suitability index multipliers for ruffed grouse food availability in relationships to tree maturity and structural stage*

Structural stage	SI_{STfood}
Non-vegetated	0.0
Herbaceous	0.0
Low shrub	0.0
Tall shrub	0.0
Pole sapling	0.4
Young forest	0.8
Mature forest	1.0
Old-growth forest	1.0

Preferred food cover ($S_{preferred\ food}$ CC). Cover of aspen, willow, or berry producers. The relationship with SI is:

If $S_{preferred\ food} CC \leq 50\%$ $SI_{preferred\ food} = 1.8064 S_{preferred\ food} CC$ [11A1.69]

If $S_{preferred\ food} CC > 50\%$ $SI_{preferred\ food} = 1$ [11A1.70]

Tree canopy closure (CC). The relationship with SI is:

If $CC \leq 70\%$ $SI_{CC} = 1.5058 CC$ [11A1.71]

If $CC > 70\%$ $SI_{CC} = 1$ [11A1.72]

Structural stage cover (ST_{cover}). The relationship with SI is given in Table 11A.7.

Habitat interspersion (HI). This variable takes into account how much of the habitat in the area can be considered as habitat for food and how much can be considered as habitat for cover. The proportions of each type of habitat (P_{food} and $P_{cover,}$) are values from 0 to 1 that together equal 1. The ideal proportion is 50% habitat for cover and 50% habitat for food. For other combinations, their relationship with SI is:

$$SI_{HI} = e^{-0.5 \cdot \left(\left(\frac{P_{food} - 0.6009}{0.3115} \right)^2 + \left(\frac{P_{cover} - 0.6009}{0.3115} \right)^2 \right)}$$ [11A1.73]

Table 11A.7. *Suitability index multipliers*
for ruffed grouse cover availability in
relationships to tree maturity and structural
stage

Structural stage	$SI_{STcover}$
Non-vegetated	0.0
Herbaceous	0.0
Low shrub	0.0
Tall shrub	0.0
Pole sapling	0.9
Young forest	1.0
Mature forest	0.4
Old-growth forest	0.0

In order to simplify the analysis, the calculations presented in this
report assume that the habitat interspersion is in its ideal proportion. As
a result, the HSI for ruffed grouse can be considered as calculated under
"optimal" conditions, and actual values will be slightly lower.

Pileated woodpecker (*Dryocopus pileatus*)

The habitat suitability model for pileated woodpecker takes into account
the availability of nesting sites and winter food components. The model
is formulated as:

$$HSI_{food} = \sqrt{SI_{CC} \times SI_{ST}} \qquad\qquad [11A1.74]$$

$$HSI_{nesting} = \sqrt{SI_{deciduous} \times SI_{ST}} \qquad\qquad [11A1.75]$$

$$HSI_{PILEATED\ WOODPECKER} = Min\left(HSI_{food}, HSI_{nesting\ in\ 200\ Ha}\right) \qquad [11A1.76]$$

Deciduous canopy closure ($S_{deciduous}CC$). The relationship with SI
is:

$$\text{If } S_{deciduous}CC \le 80\% \ SI_{deciduous} = 0.4 - 0.0428S_{deciduous}CC$$
$$+ 0.934S_{deciduous}CC^2 \qquad [11A1.77]$$

$$\text{If } S_{deciduous}CC > 80\% \ SI_{deciduous} = 1 \qquad\qquad [11A1.78]$$

Table 11A.8. *Suitability index multipliers for pileated woodpecker in relationships to tree maturity and structural stage*

Structural stage	SI_{ST}
Non-vegetated	0.0
Herbaceous	0.0
Low shrub	0.0
Tall shrub	0.0
Pole sapling	0.0
Young forest	0.3
Mature forest	0.8
Old-growth forest	1.0

Tree canopy closure (CC). The relationship with SI is:

If $CC \leq 5\%$ $SI_{CC} = 0$ \hfill [11A1.79]

If $CC > 5\%$ and $CC \leq 70\%$ $SI_{CC} = 1$ \hfill [11A1.80]

If $CC > 70\%$ $SI_{CC} = 0.8$ \hfill [11A1.81]

Structural stage (ST). The relationship with SI is given in Table 11A.8.

Nesting habitat units per 200 ha ($HSI_{nesting}$). This is a spatial-related variable that accounts for the availability of nesting sites in an area of 200 ha surrounding the site, for which the HSI for pileated woodpecker is being calculated. This variable can be ignored, accepting an implicit value of 1, which is equal to assuming any given prescription for which the HSI is being calculated always has at least one HU for nesting. If it is not ignored, the relationship with SI is:

$$If\ HSI_{nesting} \leq 1\ SI_{nesting\ 200\ ha} = 0.455\ HSI_{nesting} + 0.56(HSI_{nesting})^2 \quad [11A1.82]$$

If $HSI_{nesting} > 1$ $SI_{nesting\ 200\ ha} = 1$ \hfill [11A1.83]

In order to simplify the analysis, the calculations presented in this report assume that the number of nesting habitat units per 200 ha is at least 1. As a result, the HSI for pileated woodpecker can be considered as calculated under "optimal" conditions, and actual values will be slightly lower.

Northern goshawk (*Accipiter gentilis*)

The habitat suitability model for northern goshawk takes into account the availability of nesting sites, quality of the area for breeding, and the ZOI of disturbances. The model is formulated as:

$$HSI_{breeding} = \sqrt[4]{SI_{CH} \times SI_{CC} \times SI_{deciduous} \times SI_{ST}} \qquad [11A1.84]$$

$$HSI_{NORTHERN\ GOSHAWK} = Min\left(HSI_{breeding},\ SI_{nesting\ 500\ ha}\right)$$
$$\text{(no disturbance effect included).} \qquad [11A1.85]$$

To account for the effect of disturbances, the final HSI is $HSI_{NORTHERN\ GOSHAWK} \times SI_{ZOI\ Disturbance\ Coeff.}$ The disturbance coefficients for northern goshawk are described in Table 11A.3.

The variables for the model are calculated as follows:

Canopy height (CH). The relationship with SI is:

$$\text{If CH} \leq 20\,\text{m } SI_{CH} = -0.0014CH + 0.0025CH^2 \qquad [11A1.86]$$

$$\text{If CH} > 20\,\text{m } SI_{CH} = 1 \qquad [11A1.87]$$

Tree canopy closure (CC). The relationship with SI is:

$$\text{If CC} \leq 70\% \ SI_{CC} = 1.9669\,CC - 0.8017\,CC^2 \qquad [11A1.88]$$

$$\text{If CC} > 70\% \ SI_{CC} = 1 \qquad [11A1.89]$$

Deciduous canopy closure (S$_{deciduous}$CC). The relationship with SI is:

$$SI_{deciduous} = 0.4 + 2.1682 S_{deciduous}CC - 2.1293\ S_{deciduous}CC^2$$
$$[11A1.90]$$

Structural stage (ST). The relationship with SI is given in Table 11A.9.

Nesting habitat units per 500 ha (HSI$_{nesting}$). This is a spatial-related variable that accounts for the availability of nesting sites in an area of 500 ha surrounding the site for which the HSI for northern goshawk is being calculated. This variable can be ignored, accepting an implicit value of 1, which is equal to

Table 11A.9. *Suitability index multipliers for northern goshawk in relationships to tree maturity and structural stage*

Structural stage	SI_{ST}
Non-vegetated	0.0
Herbaceous	0.0
Low shrub	0.05
Tall shrub	0.05
Pole sapling	0.1
Young forest	0.3
Mature forest	1.0
Old-growth forest	1.0

assuming any given prescription for which the HSI is being calculated always has at least one HU for nesting. If it is not ignored, the relationship with SI is:

$$\text{If } HSI_{nesting} \leq 5SI_{nesting\,500\,ha} = 0.09\,HSI_{nesting}$$
$$+ 0.022\,(HSI_{nesting})^2 \qquad [11A1.91]$$

$$\text{If } HSI_{nesting} > 5SI_{nesting\,500\,ha} = 1 \qquad [11A1.92]$$

In order to simplify the analysis, the calculations presented in this report assume that the number of nesting habitat units per 500 ha are at least 5. As a result, the HSI for northern goshawk can be considered as calculated under "optimal" conditions, and that actual values will be somewhat lower.

REFERENCES

Alaback, P. (1982). Dynamics of understory biomass in Sitka spruce–Western hemlock forests of Southeast Alaska. *Ecology*, **63**, 1932–1948.

Alaback, P. (1986). Biomass regression equations for understory plants in coastal Alaska: effects of species and sampling design on estimates. *Northwest Science*, **60**, 90–103.

Alberta Environment. (2010). *Guidelines for Reclamation to Forest Vegetation in the Athabasca Oil Sands Region*, 2nd edn. Prepared by the Terrestrial Subgroup of the Reclamation Working Group of the Cumulative Environmental Management Association, Fort McMurray, AB.

Allen, A. W. (1983a). *Habitat Suitability Index Models: Beaver*. Washington, DC: U.S. Fish and Wildlife Service, Department of the Interior Biological Report FWS/OBS-82/10.30, revised.

Allen, A. W. (1983b). *Habitat Suitability Models: Fisher*. Washington, DC: U.S. Fish and Wildlife Service, Department of the Interior Biological Report FWS/OBS-82/10.45.

Beckingham, J. D. and Archibald, J. H. (1996). *Field Guide to Ecosites of Northern Alberta*. Edmonton, AB: Canadian Forest Service, Northern Forestry Centre. Special Report 5.

Bonar, R. L. (2001). *Pileated Woodpecker Habitat Ecology in the Alberta Foothills*. Ph.D. thesis, University of Alberta. Edmonton, AB.

Cerezke, H. F. (2008). Climate change and Alberta's forests: an information and discussion paper of predicted implications. Forest Health Section, Forestry Division, Alberta Sustainable Resource Development, Government of Alberta, Edmonton, AB.

Comeau, P. (2001). Relationships between stand parameters and understorey light in boreal aspen stands. *BC Journal of Ecosystems and Management*, **1**, 1–8.

Eccles, T. R., Green, J. E., Thompson, C., Searing, G. F. (1986). *Slave River Hydro Project Mammal Studies – Volume 1*. Final Report. Prepared for the Slave River Hydro Project Study Group by LGL Ltd., Calgary, AB.

Edenius, L. and Mikusinski, G. (2006). Utility of habitat suitability models as biodiversity assessment tools in forest management. *Scandinavian Journal of Forest Research*, **21**, 62–72.

Gholz, H. L., Grier, C., Campbell, A., Brown, A. (1979). Equations for estimating biomass and leaf area of plants in the Pacific Northwest. Research Paper No. 41. Forest Research Lab., School of Forestry, Oregon State University, Corvallis, OR.

Hart, S. A. and Chen, H. Y. H. (2008). Fire, logging, and overstory affect understory abundance, diversity, and composition in boreal forest. *Ecological Monographs*, **78**, 123–140.

Hemstock, S., Quideau, S. A., Chanasyk, D. S. (2010). Nitrogen availability from peat amendments used in boreal oil sands reclamation. *Canadian Journal of Soil Science*, **90**, 165–175.

Jalkotsky, P., Van Egmond, T. D., Eccles, T. R., Berger, R. (1990). *Wildlife Habitat Evaluation, Assessment and Mapping for the OSLO Wildlife Study Area*. Prepared for the OSLO Project by The Delta Environmental Management Group Ltd., Calgary, AB.

Kimmins, J. P., Blanco, J. A., Seely, B., Welham, C., Scoullar, K. (2010). *Forecasting Forest Futures: a Hybrid Modelling Approach to the Assessment of Sustainability of Forest Ecosystems and their Values*. Earthscan UK.

Kimmins J. P., Mailly, D., Seely, B. (1999). Modeling forest ecosystem net primary production: the hybrid simulation approach used in FORECAST. *Ecological Modeling*, **122**, 195–224.

Kliskey, A. D., Lofroth, E. C., Thompson, W. A., Brown, S., Schreier, H. (1999). Simulating and evaluating alternative resource-use strategies using GIS-based habitat suitability indices. *Landscape and Urban Planning*, **45**, 163–175.

MacKenzie, D. M. and Quideau, S. A. (2010). Microbial community structure and nutrient availability in oil sands reclaimed boreal soils. *Applied Soil Ecology*, **44**, 32–41.

Martens, S. N., Breshears, D. D., Meyer, C. W. (2000). Spatial distributions of understory light along the grassland/forest continuum: effects of cover, height, and spatial pattern of tree canopies. *Ecological Modeling*, **126**, 79–93.

Muukkonen, P., Makipaa, R., Laiho, R., et al. (2006). Relationship between biomass and percentage cover in understorey vegetation of boreal coniferous forests. *Silva Fennica*, **40**, 231–245.

Nyberg, J. (1985). *Predicting Red Huckleberry Biomass from Plant Dimensions and Percent Cover*. Research Branch, Ministry of Forests, Victoria, BC. Publication No. WHR-18.

Schaffer, W., Beck, B., Beck, J., Bonar, R., Hunt, L. (1999). *Northern Goshawk Reproductive Habitat: Habitat Suitability Index Model, Version 3*. Foothills Model Forest, Hinton, AB.

Skinner, D. L. (1996). *Habitat Suitability Models for the Suncor Study Area*. Report by Westworth, Brusnyk and Associates for Suncor Energy Ltd., Ft. McMurray, AB.

Turcotte, I., Quideau, S. A., Oh, S. W. (2009). Organic matter quality in reclaimed boreal forest soils following oilsands mining. *Organic Geochemistry*, **40**, 510–519.

Welham, C. (2004). *Deriving Multipliers and Nutrient Regime Classes for the Land Capability Classification System using the Ecosystem Simulation Model, FORECAST*. Final report in partial fulfillment of CEMA Contract No. 2003–0007.

Welham, C. (2005a). *Evaluating a Prescriptive Approach to Creating Target Ecosites using D-Ecosites as a Test Case*. Final report in partial fulfillment of CEMA Contract No. 2004–0014.

Welham, C. (2005b). *Evaluating Existing Prescriptions for Creating Target Ecosites using the Ecosystem Simulation Model, FORECAST: Implications for Ecosystem Productivity and Community Composition*. Final report in partial fulfillment of CEMA Contract No. 2005–0025.

Welham, C. (2006). *Evaluating Existing Prescriptions for Creating Target Ecosites using the Ecosystem Simulation Model, FORECAST: Implications for ecosystem productivity and Community Composition in Reclaimed Overburden*. Final report in partial fulfillment of CEMA Contract No. 2006–0030.

12

Restoration of peatlands after peat extraction
Impacts, restoration goals, and techniques

INTRODUCTION

In North America peat is extracted mainly for horticultural purposes. Weakly decomposed *Sphagnum* peat is the best horticultural peat; therefore, in the order of 25,000 ha (past and present combined) of *Sphagnum*-dominant peatlands (primarily bogs) are affected by this industry (Environment Canada, 2010). To promote long-term extraction, a minimal peat depth of 2 m and area of 50 ha is encouraged, although not obligatory. Peatlands close to infrastructures, like roads and electricity, are more economical to develop. Additionally, most exploited peatlands are close to human settlements so that labor needs can be met. Peat extraction is an important economic activity in non-urban areas (Keys, 1992; Daigle and Gautreau-Daigle, 2001; Rochefort 2001). This has created a disequilibrium where most disturbed peatlands are located in southern Canada and the northern peatlands remain mostly untouched by industry (Rochefort, 2001). However, new developments in mining, forestry, and the oil and gas industry have begun to disturb northern peatlands (Schneider and Dyer, 2006; Turetsky and St. Louis, 2006).

The most significant areas of peat extraction in North America are in the provinces of Quebec, New Brunswick, and Alberta. An impact assessment of horticultural peat industries on peatlands showed a total of 24,000 ha have been used for peat extraction since the settlement of Canada (Environment Canada, 2010). The last data provided by the Canadian Sphagnum Peat Moss Association showed that 14,000 ha of peatlands were still in production in 2006. Consequently, production

Restoration and Reclamation of Boreal Ecosystems, ed. Dale Vitt and Jagtar Bhatti. Published by Cambridge University Press. © Cambridge University Press 2012.

has ceased on a total of 3900 ha. As of 2006, 1800 ha were restored or were being restored or reclaimed. Finally, from 2007 to 2011, the industry is projecting restoration or reclamation of 3100 ha of peatlands affected (Canadian Sphagnum Peat Moss Association, personal communication). Peatland restoration attempts to resolve the conflict between the economic value and the environmental value of peatlands by allowing the return of ecological functions after peat extraction to restore a wetland habitat in the landscape (Rochefort and Lode, 2006).

SCOPE AND TOPICS OF THIS CHAPTER

The restoration of boreal peatlands affected by peat extraction has already been thoroughly reviewed by other authors (Price et al., 2003; Rochefort et al., 2003; Rochefort and Lode, 2006). This chapter will give a brief overview of the topics already discussed in these previous works. Our aim is to report this information in such a way that is easily accessible to practitioners. We will focus on fen restoration research, as it is extremely pertinent to the recent expansion of the oil and gas industry in northern Alberta. Lastly, we will review how applicable these restoration techniques are to restoration of peatlands affected by other land uses, such as the oil and gas industry and forestry.

Abandoned peatlands with deep layers of residual organic matter are referred to as "cutover" peatlands. "Cutaway" peatlands are where most peat has been removed by industrial means and will often show part of the exposed mineral soil. This terminology will be used throughout this chapter to distinguish the two types of abandoned peatlands.

PEAT EXTRACTION

Modern, large-scale peat extraction is carried out using large vacuums pulled by tractors, which remove thin layers of dry peat at every passage (Figure 12.1A). Peat extraction is carried out in six steps. First, a drainage system is installed by digging deep drainage canals around the area to be extracted and drainage ditches every 30 m. Second, the vegetation layer (acrotelm) including trees, shrubs and *Sphagnum* moss is removed to expose the peat below. Then, each peat field is profiled into a dome-shape to improve drainage (Figure 12.1B). The extraction and pilling of the peat, including the packing, transformation, and delivery are the next steps. Finally, when the upper peat layers have been extracted and mineral ground is exposed or a more decomposed, sedge–peat layer (hereafter referred to as fen peat) is reached, the extraction activities are abandoned because of the low horticultural quality of this peat. Ecosystem

Figure 12.1. Photographs illustrating the extent of the disturbance to a peatland when vacuum-milled. (**A**) shows the vacuum machines being pulled by tractors. (**B**) shows the dome-shaped contour of the peat field (arrow), which facilitates the drying and drainage of the peat. (Photographs by M. Poulin of Peatland Ecology Research Group.)

restoration or rehabilitation is then planned (Keys, 1992; Daigle and Gautreau-Daigle, 2001; Rochefort, 2001).

Drainage and removal of acrotelm

Peatlands are composed of a two-layered (diplotelmic) soil structure; the upper layer is the acrotelm and the lower layer is the catotelm

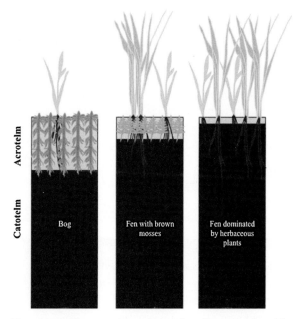

Figure 12.2. The acrotelm and catotelm of bogs and fens. The acrotelm layer is thickest in bogs and thinner in fens. It is virtually nonexistent in fens dominated by herbaceous plants. It is not known how important the acrotelm layer is in the hydroregulation and the carbon-accumulating capacity of fens.

(Figure 12.2). The acrotelm is the uppermost layer of the peat deposit and is composed of live and slightly decomposed vegetation. It is characterized as having a variable water content, high hydraulic conductivity, periodic aeration, and intense biological activity (Ingram, 1978; Ivanov, 1981). The acrotelm contains a propagule bank and has the capacity to regenerate within a few years if a thin part of the top layer is burned by fire (Wieder et al., 2009) or removed mechanically (Rochefort and Campeau, 2002; Rochefort et al., 2003). The catotelm, the lower level of more decomposed peat, is characterized by constant water content, very low hydraulic conductivity, and anaerobic conditions. Natural peatlands rely on this structure to regulate water storage and discharge, thus creating constantly saturated conditions that are ideal for carbon storage (Price et al., 2003). Carbon is sequestered by the submergence of organic matter at the base of the acrotelm, or as seen from the opposite perspective, by the thickening of the catotelm (Clymo, 1984).

The removal of the acrotelm strongly affects the water storage capacity, the magnitude of evaporation losses, as well as soil processes, including carbon storage (Price et al., 2003). Drained peat undergoes subsidence in the unsaturated zone and compression in the saturated zone, which changes the soil pore structure. The peat is further compacted by the numerous passages of machinery. The change in pore structure decreases the water storage capacity and hydraulic conductivity, which exacerbates the fluctuation of the water table (Price et al., 2003). Compression and oxidation can decrease hydraulic conductivity by 75% (Price et al., 2003). The dark color of exposed peat from the catotelm increases surface temperatures and, indirectly, evaporation. All of these factors create conditions that are unfavorable to the establishment of typical peatland plant communities, especially bryophytes (Sagot and Rochefort, 1996).

Increase in pH and peat contamination from mineral soil

In some cases, peat companies remove the entire *Sphagnum* peat layer, leaving either more decomposed fen peat, or in some extreme situations, the part of mineral soil. This residual peat is richer in minerals and higher in pH than the preexisting bog (Wind-Mulder et al., 1996; Wind-Mulder and Vitt, 2000; Graf et al., 2008). Therefore, returning the site back to its previous state is nearly impossible and restoration toward a fen or marsh ecosystem is encouraged. The richer residual peat or the mineral soil allows for the establishment of spontaneous vegetation. These sites are mainly revegetated by wetland species, but peatland species, especially bryophytes and sedges, usually do not reestablish (Graf et al., 2008). They are also more susceptible to be colonized by invasive species (Zedler and Kercher, 2004). The species and cover of the spontaneous vegetation will impact the restoration approach.

Surface instability

Soil erosion caused by water and wind is a common problem in unvegetated areas (Tallis 1987; Quinty and Rochefort 2000). Snowmelt, heavy rains, and periodic flooding can form gullies and move soil sediments away, burying plants and blocking drainage ditches. Peat oxidation on exposed peat areas affects plants by slowly exposing their roots (Waddington and McNeil, 2002).

Rewetted sites are often plagued by surface instability in the form of needle-ice formation. This phenomenon, known as frost heaving, has been recognized as a major factor limiting plant reestablishment on bare peat. Frost heaving not only damages plants, but also destroys the structure of surface peat and contributes to the process of deflation (Groeneveld and Rochefort, 2002). Frost heaving is most destructive to seedlings and bryophytes because they lose contact with the soil surface and become prone to desiccation. If a plant survives its frost heaving period, it has a much better chance of surviving to a productive age. Surface instability is best combated by the use of straw mulch or a nurse plant, as discussed later.

RESTORATION GOALS

In North America, the central goal of peatland restoration after peat extraction is the return of a peat-accumulating system (Rochefort, 2000; Gorham and Rochefort, 2003). Modelization of restored sites showed that this goal could be reached within 20 years (Lucchesse et al., 2010). In order to achieve this long-term goal, the short-term aims are the reestablish-ment of: (1) a plant cover dominated by bryophytes and specifically for bog restoration; and (2) diplothelmic hydrological layers, which ensure the return of important peatland functions. The return of other ecosystem functions, like biodiversity (flora and fauna composition and ecosystem structure) biogeochemical cycling, and resistance to invasive plants are also important (Gorham and Rochefort, 2003; Rochefort, 2000).

A bryophyte-dominated plant cover is important to the peatland's ecosystem functioning (Vitt, 2000). *Sphagnum* is especially important to acrotelm hydroregulation because the loosely woven, expansible surface creates the capacity to store a large amount of water (Clymo and Hayward, 1982). It is not known to what extent brown mosses are important to fen hydrology. Mosses, both *Sphagnum* and brown mosses, are a major contributor to peat accumulation (Vitt, 2000). *Sphagnum* mosses and some species of brown mosses possess properties that create an acidic, nutrient-poor, heat-insulating, and slowly permeable environment ideal for peat accumulation (Andrus, 1986; van Breemen, 1995).

RESTORATION TECHNIQUES

Bog restoration

As peat extraction has mainly affected bogs, these peatlands have been the focus of restoration research. Over 20 years of restoration experi-ments in North America have shown that three active restoration mea-sures are essential to successful bog restoration: (1) plant reintroduction, (2) the application of a protective mulch cover, and (3) the rewet-ting of the site by blocking drainage ditches and surface preparation

(Rochefort et al., 2003; Rochefort and Lode, 2006). The essential steps of the moss layer transfer method will be discussed in more detail in the following sections.

Vegetation introduction

Reintroducing plant fragments in the form of diaspores is an essential step to restoring *Sphagnum*-dominated peatlands. Natural regeneration on cutover peatlands occurs very slowly and is not sufficient to restore the ecological functions of a peatland (Salonen, 1987; Bérubé and Lavoie, 2000; Campbell et al., 2003; Lavoie et al., 2003; Poulin et al., 2005). Many peatlands are void of vegetation after as much as 30 years of abandonment (Poulin et al., 2005), even though spores of mosses and the seeds of various ericaceous shrubs and trees are often abundant in residual peat (Campbell et al., 2000). As moss spores germinate only under specific and constant conditions (Clymo and Duckett, 1986), the reintroduction of fragments has proven to be the only viable alternative for restoring a *Sphagnum* carpet on a short-term basis. Once a *Sphagnum* carpet has been established, it is not necessary to reintroduce other peatland plants, as many will establish from the diaspore bank or will immigrate from residual peatlands in the proximity (Rochefort and Lode, 2006). Important features of successful reintroduction of bog vegetation are outlined as follows:

- *Sphagnum* should occupy a large percentage of the ground cover (>50%) at the donor site (Rochefort et al., 2003). Species such as *S. fuscum*, *S. rubellum*, and *S. angustifolium* should be target species, as they show excellent regeneration capacities (Campeau and Rochefort, 1996; Rochefort et al., 2003).
- Fragments from the top 10 cm of the vegetation surface are recommended as donor material because regeneration potential drops with increasing depth (Campeau and Rochefort, 1996; Rochefort and Lode, 2006).
- A donor site: restoration site ratio of 1:10 to 1:15 (depending on the original moss cover) is recommended to optimize establishment while minimizing donor site damage (Rochefort et al., 2003).
- Restoration should be kept in mind when planning extraction, as the acrotelm of new extraction sites can be used as donor material.
- These techniques can be carried out mechanically using locally available tractors and manure spreaders (see Figure 12.3) in order to restore large areas of cutover peatlands.

Figure 12.3. The six main mechanical steps: (**A**) site preparation, (**B**) diaspora collection, (**C**) spreading donor vegetation, (**D**) mulch application, (**E**) optional fertilization, and (**F**) blocking drainage ditches for the Sphagnum moss layer transfer approach to restore milled peatlands. (Photographs taken by the Peatland Ecology Research Group.)

- Material collection should be carried out in late autumn or early spring when the ground is frozen to minimize damage to the donor sites. If the material is collected at this time, the donor sites regenerate quickly (Rochefort and Campeau, 2002; Rochefort et al., 2003).

Application of mulch and nurse plants

Once the diaspore fragments have been introduced, a protective mulch cover should be applied as quickly as possible to protect fragments from desiccation (Sagot and Rochefort, 1996; Price et al., 1998). Although many forms of mulch have been tested (clear plastic cover, shading screens, snow fences, commercial mulchs), straw proved to be the most economic and effective mulch. The density of the mulch layer should be such that light can pass through it to reach the plant fragments, but thick enough to create an air layer.

Including nurse plants in restoration plans has been shown to improve the microclimate and increase the establishment of *Sphagnum* (Boudreau and Rochefort, 1999; Groeneveld et al., 2007). A common nurse plant for bog restoration is *Polytrichum strictum*, a pioneer moss species that can establish in the harsh conditions of a bare peat surface. Hence, here the restoration works in three successional steps: first, straw mulch improves the microclimate, aiding the establishment of

Polytrichum mosses, and is also an effective measure against frost heaving during the first two years post-restoration; second, a live mulch, such as *P. strictum*, grows thicker and protects the ground as the mulch decomposes and becomes less effective (Groeneveld et al., 2007). Eventually, *P. strictum* will be outcompeted by *Sphagnum* moss, starting plant autogenic succession.

In order to increase *P. strictum* establishment, fertilization with low doses (15 g m^{-2}) of phosphate rock may be carried out (Figure 12.3), although it is not mandatory. The use of fertilization remains a site-specific decision, dependent on the exposure to frost heaving, the probability of invasion by non-peatland invasive plants, and the inherent properties of a specific site (Sottocornola et al., 2007).

Rewetting

Restoring the hydrological regime is necessary for the establishment of target vegetation, nutrient cycling, and increasing energy capture rates of wetlands (Mitsch and Gosselink, 2000). However, simply rewetting a peatland is not an adequate measure to restore the hydrology, as fundamental soil properties are altered during peat extraction (Price et al., 2003). A restoration site should be seen as a new environment with new physical properties, especially in the upper peat layers (Rochefort and Lode, 2006). A number of techniques used to restore peatland hydrology are outlined as follows:

- Blocking drainage ditches is an important step in restoring wetland hydrology (Cooper et al., 1998; Price et al., 2003). This simple step will retain surface water and elevate the ground water level.
- Creating depressions and altering the basin morphology is common for the construction of wastewater wetlands and has also been suggested for peatland restoration (Wheeler and Shaw, 1995; LaRose et al. 1997).
- Shallow retention basins (<20 cm) increase soil moisture and the water table, thereby improving the establishment and growth of *Sphagnum* mosses in bog restoration projects (Price et al., 2002; Campeau et al. 2004).
- Berms, bunds, terracing and polders hold surface water and precipitation on site and are important in retaining snowmelt water in the spring on cutover peatlands with uneven topography (Price et al., 2003).
- The use of mulch or nurse plants increases the moisture level of the microclimate on the peat surface by increasing the relative

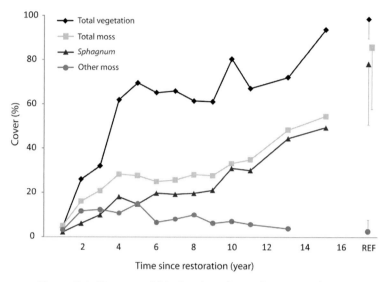

Figure 12.4. Plant cover (%) in function of years since restoration at nine restored sites over 15 years of monitoring. The restored sites are located at Rivière-du-Loup peatland (47°45′N; 69°31′W) where 3.8 ha were restored in year 1995 and monitored with 120 quadrats of 25 cm × 25 cm, 3.0 ha in 1997 with 120 quadrats, 1.2 ha in 1999 with 40 quadrats, 1.6 ha in 2000 with 80 quadrats, 2.4 ha in 2001 with 60 quadrats, 3.6 ha in 2002 with 60 quadrats, 12 ha in 2003 with 80 quadrats, 8 ha in 2005 with 120 quadrats, and 7 ha in 2006 with 80 quadrats, which were last surveyed in 2010.

humidity near the surface and decreasing the evaporation loss compared to a bare peat site (Groeneveld and Rochefort, 2002; Price et al., 2003).

- Border and pipe irrigation can be used to maintain water levels (Rochefort, 2001; Richert et al., 2000). However, such measures, as they are costly, are best used in a *Sphagnum* culture system. Additionally, moving water and sedimentation will impair the establishment of mosses (Quinty and Rochefort, 2000).
- Trees that established spontaneously on the site increase the evapotranspiration of the site (Fay and Lavoie, 2009). In times of critically low water levels, trees may be cut to maintain water levels.

Monitoring

Monitoring is an important part of the restoration process to evaluate if restoration goals have been met or to find adaptive strategies if the restoration trajectory needs to be corrected. The plant recovery of nine restored bog sites is presented in Figure 12.4 as an example of monitoring for the flora. The nine sites were restored by the same peat company within a 15 km² peatland, following the method illustrated in figure 12.3 and sites were not necessarily adjacent. The mean of the nine recovery curves are shown as compared to the mean of seven reference ecosystems of the regions.

FEN RESTORATION

Research on restoring a fen plant community after peat extraction in North America is relatively new (Cooper and MacDonald 2000; Cobbaert et al., 2004; Graf and Rochefort 2008a). Restoring fens is a great challenge because of the complexity of the hydrology and the wide variety of fen plant communities. The approaches are believed to be similar to bog restoration, although the techniques used to apply them may differ. In the next section, we explore some techniques that can be used to restore residual fen peat.

Vegetation introduction

Unlike bog residual peat, cutover peatlands are spontaneously colonized by wetland plants (Famous et al., 1991; Graf et al., 2008); however, typical fen species, such as Cyperaceae and brown moss species, remain virtually absent even in rewetted sites (Graf et al., 2008). Active reintroduction is necessary for these species to reestablish.

Cobbaert et al., (2004) and Graf and Rochefort (2008a) reintroduced fen vegetation using the moss layer transfer method. The fen surface layer is the first 10–15 cm of the soil and includes the seed bank, rhizomes, and diaspores if mosses are present. This method is similar to the vegetation reintroduction used for bog restoration described in the previous section. This method proved to be successful in establishing a *Sphagnum* carpet for the restoration of poor and moderate-rich fens (Graf and Rochefort, 2008a). In a greenhouse experiment, nine poor and moderate fen bryophyte species regenerated better under shade (50% shade) and when the water level was just below the surface (Graf and Rochefort, 2008b). Mälson and Rydin (2007) tested regeneration capacities of brown mosses found in rich fens; these mosses also reproduce vegetatively when diaspores are introduced and covered with protective layers.

Extensive research on restoring of fen plant communities on former agricultural lands has been carried out in Europe (Wheeler and Shaw, 1995; Pfadenhauer and Grootjans, 1999; Kratz and Pfadenhauer, 2001; Lamers et al., 2002). This research is not entirely transferable to milled peatlands, as the desired state is often one of extensive agricultural use or semi-natural, and damage to the European peatlands is often more severe (Graf and Rochefort, 2008a). However, some fen restoration techniques have been tested on cutaway peatlands.

The hay transfer method is often used for restoring fen communities of former agricultural lands (Pfadenhauer and Grootjans, 1999). This technique is ideal for the restoration of large sites, as it is mechanized and relatively inexpensive. Additionally, it has been shown to be effective for reintroducing both vascular plants and bryophytes (Jeschke and Kiehl, 2006). The hay transfer method involves mowing a donor site, when the desired seeds are ripe yet still attached to the stalks, and then transferring the fen "hay" directly onto the restoration site. On European experimental plots, 50%–71% of the fen species were transferred using this method (Patzelt, 1998). In order to ensure success using this technique, a donor:recipient ratio should be 1:1, meaning 1 ha should be mown for the restoration of 1 ha of wetland. The number of species transferred can be augmented if the donor site is diverse, several donor sites are used, and mowing and introduction is done at different times during the vegetation season.

When the moss layer transfer and hay transfer methods were compared directly, the former showed a higher reestablishment of peatland plants (Graf and Rochefort, 2008a). After three vegetation seasons, the percentage cover for *Sphagnum centrale* was ~ 20% on plots where moss layer transfer had been applied and <1% for the hay transfer and control plots (Graf and Rochefort, 2008a). Similarly, the percentage cover for *Carex* species was 10% on the moss layer transfer plots and <1% for the hay transfer and control plots. The moss layer transfer was more effective because it includes fresh seeds, the seed bank, rhizomes, and moss fragments.

For moss layer and hay transfer methods, the availability of donor sites is a limitation. When brown moss species are dominant, a fen has a shallow acrotelm, and the removal of the first 10 cm can expose the peat. Care must be taken when using machinery to take off the diaspore material. However, when the site is undrained and the deeper rhizomes remain untouched, the regeneration of former vegetation occurs quickly. Another option is to search for peatlands that have been highly disturbed or destroyed by new anthropogenic developments, in order to cultivate the material for future restoration projects. For donor sites that are very sensitive or have a high conservation status, the hay transfer method is more appropriate, as it is much less intrusive than the moss layer transfer method. Unlike North American fens, mowing European fens is possible because many have been partially drained for extensive agriculture. The choice of a donor site and the use of light machinery must be done carefully to guarantee the success of this method.

If vascular plants are the focus of revegetation efforts, seeding is another option for reintroducing fen species. Seeding plants is an easy and relatively inexpensive option; however, this technique often produces poor results for wetland plants (Patzelt, 1998; Cooper and MacDonald, 2000; Cronk and Fennessy, 2001). Field germination trials and survival of eight common fen species described in Cooper and MacDonald (2000) only succeeded with *Triglochin maritima*, with a germination rate of 59%. Plugs from seedlings, rhizomes, and stem cuttings were a more effective method, with higher survival rate. Seeds can be collected by hand from nearby sources or purchased from specialty nurseries. Ideally, seeds should be regional to ensure that they are genetically adapted to the local conditions (Falk et al., 2006; Cooper et al., 2008). The timing of collection is vital, as seeds should be collected as they mature, but before they fall to the ground. After collection, close attention must be paid to species-specific requirements for storage and germination. The methods for storing seeds can greatly affect their viability (van der Valk et al., 1999). Baskin and Baskin (1996), Middleton (1999), and Cooper et al. (2008), provide detailed information on the storage and germination requirements of wetland species. Among factors that influence germination and survival rate, there are the seedbed preparation (vegetation cover, microtopography, soil stability), water table depth and variation during the growth season, soil physicochemistry, and the presence of mycorrhizae.

Transplantation is often used for plants that do not establish well from seeds, as is the case for many wetland species (Cronk and Fennessy, 2001). Mature plants tend to be more tolerant of the extreme environmental conditions (Middleton, 1999) found in peat extracted peatlands. Rhizomatous species propagate quickly and extensively. Transplanting of rhizomes or plugs of plants has been an effective technique for establishing a wide assortment of wetland species (van der Valk et al., 1999; Cooper and MacDonald, 2000; Kratz and Pfadenhauer, 2001). In Cooper and MacDonald (2000), seedlings and rhizome transplants of *Carex aquatilis* and *C. utriculata* showed over 50% of survival after three growth seasons. Many of these plants had ten or more shoots from clonal growth. It indicates that one or two plugs per meter square are enough to colonize in a reasonable time frame. A major limitation to this approach is the cost and the labor required. It should be avoided when a large area is to be restored or the budget is limited. Overall, seeding and transplantation can be seen as complementary to the moss layer transfer technique. Seeding and transplantation can be used in places where machinery cannot go or when the peat must be stabilized quickly to avoid erosion.

Using fertilizer for restoration projects can have both positive and negative effects on the development of the restored site. Fertilization may aid the establishment of aggressive, fast-growing plants that can persist for a long time after invasion (D'Antonio and Chambers, 2006), or it may help the reintroduced plants to establish in a harsh environment to stabilize peat soil. Fertilizer should play an important role in fen restoration, as vascular plants are a dominant component of fen vegetation communities. However, little research has been carried out on which fertilizer and what doses are ideal for poor, moderate-rich, and rich fens. The prolific research on European fen meadow restoration does not cover the topic of fertilization as these sites are usually "too rich" to allow fen vegetation to compete. Graf and Rochefort (2008a) showed a higher establishment of *Carex* species on plots that were lightly fertilized with phosphate rock. The dose used in this study, 15 g m^{-2}, is the same amount used for bog restoration and is most certainly not the optimal dose for fen vascular plants. More research is needed on this topic.

Application of mulch

As mentioned previously, if the peatland is not readily restored after abandonment of activities, spontaneous vegetation grows quickly. Depending on the technique used for restoration, mulch application may be an option. If moss layer or hay transfer methods are employed, the peat surface must be refreshed to remove the biological crust. This step also removes the spontaneous vegetation. As discussed previously, straw mulch application is then mandatory. On the other hand, if a site has a high cover of spontaneous vegetation, mulch application is not essential to protect the introduced mosses. In fact, these herbaceous plants can act as a nurse plant, improving moss establishment by improving the microclimatic conditions. It is essential for the mosses to be introduced by hand and put under the canopy of herbaceous plants. A large herbaceous plant, *Scirpus cyperinus*, was shown to be associated with a significantly higher establishment of bryophytes than under straw mulch (Graf et al., 2008). However, prolonged monitoring is necessary to determine if, over time, tall, tussock-forming species can compete with moss cover due to light competition.

Nurse plants should increase fen restoration success, as cutaway peat surface also undergoes instability. Current research is still preliminary and identifying an effective nurse plant species is not obvious. While paleoecological analysis of bogs showed that *P. strictum* is a pioneer species after disturbances like fire events (Lavoie et al., 2001; Benscoter et al. 2005), answering this question is harder in fen systems as fires are rare and most paleological work did not focus on fens.

Rewetting

Fen hydrology is more complicated than bog hydrology because it is connected and dependent on its surrounding environment (Mitsch and Gosselink, 2000). Water levels should be less variable in fen systems than bog systems as there is a constant water input. In order to achieve true fen hydrology on a restored site, it is necessary for the site to be hydraulically connected to the immediate landscape. Additionally, minimal water quality requirements must be respected for the long-term development of fen plant communities. The hydrology of a restoration site and the surrounding areas must therefore be understood before restoration measures can be planned. In this respect, restoring a bog's hydrology is more straightforward.

In the case of cutaway peatlands, we have found that the water level is often so close to the surface that drainage canals are no longer effective. Cutaway peatlands that were no longer being drained were always quickly revegetated with predominantly wetland species (Graf et al., 2008). Therefore, often no active steps must be taken to restore the local hydrology, as the sites are wet enough to support wetland and fen plants. This does not mean that the regional hydrology (i.e., groundwater flow through the site) has been restored; returning a site back to a true fen requires hydrological connectivity with the adjacent landscape. The presence of drainage ditches is often a major obstacle because it stops the water flow. However, filling all the ditches is not a good solution. The peat inside the ditches does not have the same physical properties and will still block underground water flow, although it could improve the surface water flow. The topography is also an important aspect to consider. A slight slope in the right direction can improve surface and groundwater movement; alternatively, it can also create erosion problems. Introducing vegetation can moderate erosion.

In establishing a sustainable fen system, hydrology is the principal concern. Restoring fen hydrology is the greatest challenge of the whole restoration project. Each restoration site is unique, one method will likely not fit most situations, although it is theoretically possible. More research on rewetting techniques must be done and long-term monitoring continued in order to determine the best approaches to restoring fen hydrology.

Can these techniques be transferred to other disturbances?

Forestry, oil, gas, and *in situ* oil sands development have impacted northern Alberta's wetlands through the construction of roads, pipelines, seismic lines, power transmission lines, and well pads (Turchenek, 1990; Forest, 2001). These disturbances lead to the removal or disturbance of the acrotelm, compaction of the catotelm due to drainage and equipment passage, and possible contamination from pipeline or well pad leaks.

Techniques developed to restore cutover and cutaway peatlands are highly pertinent to the restoration of peatlands affected by forestry and energy sector disturbances. The environmental conditions of cutover peatlands are in many ways harsher than the environmental conditions of wetlands affected by forestry and *in situ* disturbances (see Table 12.1). Peat extraction leaves large flat expanses (up to 300 ha) of drained, compacted peat with no plant propagules (Poulin et al., 2005). While forestry and *in situ* disturbances also create areas that are drained, compacted, and void of vegetation, the surrounding peatlands are left intact. Therefore, perhaps restoring the hydrology will be enough as a seed bank and local seed sources are often present.

Open-pit oil sand mining creates a greater disturbance because the entire landscape is removed to access the oil sands layers beneath (e.g., a deep hole up to 350 feet). When peatlands are recreated in the post-mined landscape, the same revegetation stategies can be used as have been for cutover peatlands. The success of revegetation schemes will rely mainly on the ability to create a true fen hydrology in the post-mined landscape.

The following points from research on restoring cutover peatlands could decrease the impact on peatlands affected by other land uses:

- When disturbing these areas (road or pipeline construction), remove the acrotelm for later restoration use or for immediate restoration of decommissioned installations.
- Work in the winter when the peat is frozen.
- The return to a functional ecosystem (which accumulates peat) is possible when all restoration activities (vegetation reintroduction, rewetting, mulching) have been completed. However, restoration and/or creation is a long-term project; therefore, monitoring is

Table 12.1. *A comparison of two types of disturbance affecting boreal wetlands. Can the techniques developed to restore cutover peatlands be used to restore peatland affected by energy sector disturbances?*

Disturbance	Peat extraction	Construction of seismic lines, pipelines, roads, and well pads
Problems	Extensively drained	Locally drained
	Drainage ditches are placed every 30 m across the peatland	Surface and subsurface water flow is impeded (by roads and pipelines)
	Compaction	Local compaction
	Tractors are continually driven across the peatland	No seed bank (roads and well pads)
	No seed bank	Possible soil and water contaminated by hydrocarbons or mineral soil (pipelines, roads, and well pads)
Size of disturbance	Large (up to 300 ha)	Small
		• Well pads: circa 1 ha • Linear disturbances: 6–30 m wide and several km long
Duration of disturbance	20–40 years	40–50 years
Short-term restoration/ remediation goals	Vegetation layer dominated by bryophytes Diplotelmic hydrology	Equivalent land capability. Can be restored as: • wetland • agricultural land • forested land
Long-term goal of restoration/ remediation	Return of the ecosystem's peat accumulating function	Return of an ecosystem functionally and structurally similar to the previous ecosystem.

very important to understanding the processes and to follow the succession trajectory.

- Restoration of the hydrology is key to the return of ecosystem function as typical peatland species or communities cannot establish and survive long term without it. Minimal disturbance of the hydrological system should be targeted.
- Linear disturbances should be parallel to the water flow of the landscape to avoid decreasing the hydraulic connectivity of a fen.
- Peatland archives can give clues about community establishment after disturbance (Lavoie et al., 2001). A closer look at peatland history can help in selecting the best plant communities with which to work.
- Importance of pioneer species for persistence of plant communities over time and to restart plant community autogenic processes.

CONCLUSIONS

Research on restoring ecosystems is a relatively new field in ecology. It is a good opportunity to learn about the ecosystem, as an understanding of the components and their processes is necessary for successful restoration. Restoration of cutover and cutaway peatlands is a challenge because of the extreme impacts of peat extraction activities. After the abandonment of extraction, the damage is permanent. Depending on the conditions of the peat (peat type, depth, physicochemistry), bog or fen restoration can be targeted. Studies have shown us that in both types of peatlands, active intervention is required to return an extracted peatland back to a functioning, peat-accumulating system. Vegetation must be reintroduced and mulch protected, and the site must be rewetted. Unlike open pit oil sand mining or other mining industries, peat extraction leaves a peat body to work with. The creation of peatland systems therefore requires a good understanding of its ecology. Continuing research on peatland restoration gives managers tools with which to face the challenges involved in restoration.

ACKNOWLEDGMENTS

Studies on the ecological restoration of peatlands in North America have been supported throughout the years by the Natural Sciences and Engineering Research Council (NSERC) of Canada in partnerships with the horticultural peat industry and grants from the provincial governments of Québec and New Brunswick.

REFERENCES

Andrus, R. (1986). Some aspects of *Sphagnum* ecology. *Canadian Journal of Botany*, **64**, 416–426.

Baskin, C. C. and Baskin, J. M. (1996). *Seeds – Ecology, Biogeography, and Evolution of Dormancy and Germination*. Toronto, ON: Academic Press.

Benscoter, B. W., Wieder, R. K., Vitt, D. H. (2005). Linking microtopography with post-fire succession in bogs. *Journal of Vegetation Science*, **16**, 453–460.

Bérubé, M. È. and Lavoie, C. (2000). The natural revegetation of a vacuum-mined peatland: eight years of monitoring. *Canadian Field-Naturalist*, **114**, 279–286.

Boudreau, S. and Rochefort, L. (1999). Établissement de sphaignes réintroduites sous diverses communautés végétales recolonisant les tourbières après l'exploitation. *Écologie*, **30**, 53–62.

Campbell, C., Vitt, D. H., Halsey, L. A., et al. (2000). Net primary production and standing biomass in northern continental wetlands. Northern Forestry Centre, Edmonton, AB, Information report No. NOR-X-369.

Campbell, D. R., Rochefort, L., Lavoie, C. (2003). Determining the immigration potential of plants colonizing disturbed environments: the case of milled peatlands in Québec. *Journal of Applied Ecology*, **40**, 78–91.

Campeau, S. and Rochefort, L. (1996). *Sphagnum* regeneration on bare peat surfaces: field and greenhouse results. *Journal of Applied Ecology*, **33**, 599–608.

Campeau, S., Rochefort, L., Price, J. S. (2004). On the use of shallow basins to restore cutover peatlands: plant establishment. *Restoration Ecology*, **12**, 471–482.

Clymo, R. S. (1984). The limits to peat bog growth. *Philosophical Transactions of the Royal Society of London B*, **303**, 605–654.

Clymo R. S. and Duckett, J. G. (1986). Regeneration of *Sphagnum*. *New Phytology*, **102**, 589–614.

Clymo, R. S. and Hayward, P. M. (1982). The ecology of *Sphagnum*. In A. J. E. Smith, ed., *Bryophyte Ecology*. London, UK: Chapman and Hall, pp. 229–289.

Cobbaert, D., Rochefort, L., Price, J. (2004). Experimental restoration of a fen plant community after peat mining. *Applied Vegetation Science*, **7**, 209–220.

Cooper, D. J. and MacDonald, L. H. (2000). Restoring the vegetation of mined peatlands in the southern Rocky Mountains of Colorado, USA. *Restoration Ecology*, **8**, 103–111.

Cooper, D. J., MacDonald, L. H., Wenger, S. K., Woods, S. W. (1998). Hydrologic restoration of a fen in Rocky Mountain National Park, CO, USA. *Wetlands*, **18**, 335–345.

Cooper, D., Wolf, E., Gage, E. (2008). Appendix D. Plant establishment for wetland reclamation: a review of plant establishment techniques and species tolerances for water level and salinity. In M.L. Harris, ed., *Guideline for Wetland Establishment of Reclaimed Oil Sands Leases*. (2nd edn. Fort McMurray, AB, Alberta Envirionment, Canada.

Cronk, J. K. and Fennessy, M. S. (2001). *Wetland Plants: Biology and Ecology*. Lewis, New York, NY.

Daigle, J.-Y. and Gautreau-Daigle, H. (2001). *Canadian Peat Harvesting and the Environment*, 2nd edn. Secretariat to the North American Wetlands Conservation Council Committee, Ottawa, Canada.

D'Antonio, C. and Chambers, J. (2006). Using ecological theory to manage or restore ecosystems affected by invasive plant species. In D. A. Falk, M. A. Palmer, J. B. Zedler, eds., *Foundations of restoration ecology*. Washington, DC, USA: Island Press, pp. 260–279.

Environment Canada. (2010). National Inventory Report 1990–2008: Greenhouse gas sources and sinks in Canada. Address: http://www.ec.gc.ca/ges-ghg.

Falk, D. A., Richards, C. M., Montalvo, A. M., Knapp, E. E. (2006). Population and ecological genetics in restoration ecology. In D. A. Falk, M. A. Palmer, J. B. Zedler, eds., *Foundations of restoration ecology*. Washington, DC, USA: Island Press, pp. 14–41.

Famous, N. C., Spencer, M., Nilsson, H. (1991). Revegetation patterns in harvested peatlands in central and eastern North America. In *Peat and Peatlands: The Resource and its Utilization. Proceedings of the International Peat Symposium*, Duluth, MN, pp. 48–66.

Fay, E. and Lavoie, C. (2009). The impact of birch seedlings on evapotranspiration from a mined peatland: an experimental study in southern Quebec, Canada. *Mires and Peat*, **5**, 1–7.

Forest, S. F. (2001). Peatland management and conservation in boreal Alberta, Canada. M.Sc. , University of Alberta, Edmonton, AB.

Gorham, E. and Rochefort, L. (2003). Peatland restoration: a brief assessment with special reference to Sphagnum bogs. *Wetlands Ecology and Management*, **11**, 109–119.

Graf, M. D. and Rochefort, L. (2008a). Techniques for restoring fen vegetation on cut-away peatlands in North America. *Applied Vegetation Science*, **11**, 521–528.

Graf, M. D. and Rochefort, L. (2008b). Moss regeneration for fen restoration: field and greenhouse experiments. *Restoration Ecology*, **18**, 121–130.

Graf, M. D., Rochefort, L., Poulin, M. (2008). Spontaneous revegetation of harvested peatlands of Canada and Minnesota, USA. *Wetlands*, **28**, 28–39.

Groeneveld, E. V. G., Massé, A., Rochefort, L. (2007). *Polytrichum strictum* as a nurse-plant to facilitate Sphagnum and boreal vascular plant establishment. *Restoration Ecology*, **15**, 709–719.

Groeneveld, E. V. G. and Rochefort, L. (2002). Nursing plants in peatland restoration: on their potential use to alleviate frost heaving problems. *Suo*, **53**, 73–85.

Ingram, H. A. P. (1978). Soil layers in mires: function and terminology. *Journal of Soil Science*, **29**, 224–227.

Ivanov, K. E. (1981). Water movement in Mirelands. Translated from Russian by A. Thomson and H. A. P. Ingram. London, UK: Academic Press, p. 276.

Jeschke, M. and Kiehl, K. (2006). Auswirking von Renaturierungs- und Pflegemaßnahmen auf die Artenzusammensetzung und Artdiversität von Gefäßpflanzen und Kryptogramen in neu angelegten Kalkmagerrasen. *Tuexenia*, **26**, 223–242.

Keys, D. (1992). Canadian Peat Moss and the Environment. Issues Paper, No. 1992–3. North American Wetlands Conservation Council, Canada.

Kratz, R. and Pfadenhauer, J. (2001). *Ökosystemmanagement für Niedermoore: Strategien und Verfahren zur Renaturierung*, Ulmer Verlag, Stuttgart.

Lamers, L., Smolders, A., Roelofs, J. (2002). The restoration of fens in the Netherlands. *Hydrobiologia*, **478**, 107–130.

LaRose, S., Price, J., Rochefort, L. (1997). Rewetting of a cutover peatland: hydrologic assessment. Wetlands, **17**, 416–423.

Lavoie, C., Grosvernier, P., Girard, M., Marcoux, K. (2003). Spontaneous revegetation of mined peatlands: a useful restoration tool? *Wetlands Ecology and Management*, **11**, 97–107.

Lavoie, C., Zimmermann, C., Pellerin, S. (2001). Peatland restoration in southern Québec (Canada): a paleoecological perspective. *Écoscience*, **8**, 247–258.

Lucchese, M., Waddington, J. M., Poulin, M., et al. (2010). Organic matter accumulation in a restored peatland: evaluating restoration success. *Ecological Engineering*, **36**, 482–488.

Mälson, K. and Rydin, H. (2007). The regeneration capabilities of bryophytes for rich fen restoration. *Biological Conservation*, **135**, 435–442.

Middleton, B. (1999). Revegetation alternatives. In B. Middleton, ed., *Wetland Restoration, flood pulsing, and disturbance dynamics*. New York, NY: Wiley, pp. 191–211.

Mitsch, W. J. and Gosselink, J. G. (2000). *Wetlands*. 3rd edn. New York, NY: Wiley.

Patzelt, A. (1998). Vegetationökologische und populationsbiologische Grundlagen für die Etablierung von Magerwiesen in Niedermooren. *Dissertationes Botanicae*, **297**, 1–215.

Pfadenhauer, J. and Grootjans, A. (1999). Wetland restoration in Central Europe: aims and methods. *Applied Vegetation Science*, **2**, 95–106.

Poulin, M., Rochefort, L., Quinty, F., Lavoie, C. (2005). Spontaneous revegetation of mined peatlands in eastern Canada. *Canadian Journal of Botany*, **83**, 539–557.

Price, J. S., Healthwaite, A. L., Baird, A. J. (2003). Hydrological processes in abandoned and restored peatlands: an overview of management approaches. *Wetlands Ecology and Management*, **11**, 65–83.

Price, J. S., Rochefort, L., Campeau, S. (2002). Use of shallow basins to restore cutover peatlands: hydrology. *Restoration Ecology*, **10**: 259–266.

Price, J. S., Rochefort, L., Quinty, F. (1998). Energy and moisture considerations on cutover peatlands: surface microtopography, mulch cover and Sphagnum regeneration. *Ecological Engineering*, **10**, 293–312.

Quinty, F. and Rochefort, L. (2000). Bare peat substrate instability in peatlands restoration: problems and solutions. In L. Rochefort and J. Y. Daigle, eds., *Sustaining our peatlands. Proceedings of the 11th International Peat Congress, vol. II*. Québec City, QC, International Peat Society, Jyväskylä, Finland, pp. 751–756.

Richert, M., Dietrich, O., Koppisch, D., Roth, S. (2000). The influence of rewetting on vegetation development and decomposition in a degraded fen. *Restoration Ecology*, **8**, 186–195.

Rochefort, L. (2000). Sphagnum – a keystone genus in habitat restoration. *Bryologist*, **103**, 503–508.

Rochefort, L. (2001). Restauration écologique. In S. Payette and L. Rochefort, eds., *Écologie des tourbières du Québec-Labrador*. Québec, QC: Les Presses de l'Université Laval, pp. 449–505.

Rochefort, L. and Campeau, S. (2002). Recovery of donor sites used in peatland restoration. In G. Schmilewski and L. Rochefort, eds., *Peat in Horticulture – Quality and Environmental Challenges: IPS Symposium Proceedings (Commissions II and V)*. Pärnu, Estonia, International Peat Society, Jyväskylä, pp. 244–251.

Rochefort, L. and Lode, E. (2006). Restoration of degraded boreal peatlands. In R. K. Wieder and D. H. Vitt, eds., *Boreal Peatland Ecosystems*. Vol. 188. Berlin: Springer-Verlag, pp. 381–423.

Rochefort, L., Quinty, F., Campeau, S., Johnson, K., Malterer, T. (2003). North American approach to the restoration of Sphagnum dominated peatlands. *Wetlands Ecology and Management*, **11**, 3–20.

Sagot, C. and Rochefort, L. (1996). Tolérance des sphaignes à la dessiccation. *Crytogamie, Bryologie et Lichénologie*, **17**, 171–183.

Salonen, V. (1987). Relationship between the seed rain and the establishment in two areas abandoned after peat harvesting. *Holarctic Ecology*, **10**, 171–174.

Schneider, R. and Dyer, S. (2006). Death by a Thousand Cuts: Impact of in Situ Oil Sands Development on Alberta's Boreal Forest. Edmonton, AB: The Pembina Institute Publications.

Sottocornola, M., Boudreau, S., Rochefort, L. (2007). Peat bog restoration: effects of phosphorus on plant re-establishment. *Ecological Engineering*, **31**, 29–40.

Tallis, J. H. (1987). Fire and flood at Holme Moss: erosion processes in an upland blanket mire. *Journal of Ecology*, **75**, 1099–1129.

Turchenek, L. W. (1990). Present and potential effects of anthropogenic activities on waters associated with peatland in Alberta. Environmental Research and Engineering Department, Alberta Research Council.

Turetsky, M. R. and St. Louis, V. L. (2006). Disturbance in boreal peatlands. In R. K. Wieder and D. H. Vitt, eds., *Boreal Peatland Ecosystems*. Berlin: Springer-Verlag, pp. 359–372.

van Breemen, N. (1995). How *Sphagnum* bogs down other plants. *Trends in Ecology and Evolution*, **10**, 270.

van der Valk, A. G., Bremholm, T. L., Gordon, E. (1999). The restoration of sedge meadows: seed viability, seed germination requirements, and seedling growth of *Carex* species. *Wetlands*, **19**, 756–764.

Vitt, D. H. (2000). Peatlands: ecosystems dominated by bryophytes. In A. J. Shaw and B. Goffinet, eds., *Bryophyte Biology*. Cambridge, UK: Cambridge University Press, pp. 312–343.

Waddington, J. M. and McNeil, P. (2002). Peat oxidation in an abandoned cutover peatland. *Canadian Journal of Soil Science*, **82**, 279–286.

Wheeler, B. D. and Shaw, S. C. (1995). A focus on fens-controls on the composition of fen vegetation in relation to restoration. In B. D. Wheeler, S. C. Shaw, W. J. Fojt, R. A. Robertson, eds., *Restoration of Temperate Wetlands*. West Sussex, UK: Wiley and Sons, pp. 49–72.

Wieder, R. K., Scott, K. D., Kamminga, K. (2009). Postfire carbon balance in boreal bogs of Alberta, Canada. *Global Change Biology*, **15**, 63–81.

Wind-Mulder, H. L., Rochefort, L., Vitt, D. H. (1996). Water and peat chemistry comparisons of natural and post-harvested peatlands across Canada and their relevance to peatland restoration. *Ecological Engineering*, **7**, 161–181.

Wind-Mulder, H. L. and Vitt, D. H. (2000). Comparison of water and peat chemistries of a post-harvested and undisturbed peatland with relevance to restoration. *Wetlands*, **20**, 616–628.

Zedler, J. B. and Kercher, S. (2004). Causes and consequences of invasive plants in wetlands: opportunities, opportunists, and outcomes. *Critical Reviews in Plant Sciences*, **23**, 431–452.

ROXANE ANDERSEN

13

Importance of microbes in peatland dynamics, restoration, and reclamation

INTRODUCTION

Boreal peatlands are estimated to store up to a third of all the terrestrial carbon (C) in the form of partially decomposed organic matter (Turetsky et al., 2002; Vitt et al., 2000). Nevertheless, they are also considered one of the largest sources of atmospheric methane (CH_4) (Crill et al., 1988). Although the vast majority of boreal peatlands are still in pristine condition in North America, extensive areas have been affected by anthropogenic activities or natural disturbances, shifting some of the systems from sinks to sources of CO_2 (Turetsky et al., 2002) and altering the microbial driven processes of CH_4 production and/or consumption patterns (Andersen et al., 2006; Basiliko et al., 2003; Glatzel et al., 2004; Strack et al., 2004). Large-scale restoration of cutover peatlands (Rochefort et al., 2003) and reclamation of fens in the oil sands-affected areas (Price et al., 2010) have been developed to bring back those systems to a self-sustainable state, which requires functional microbial communities. On the other hand, an increasing number of studies unequivocally show that peatlands and their associated microbial populations will be affected in various ways by global change (Davidson and Janssens, 2006; Dorrepaal et al., 2009; Freeman et al., 2004; Mastepanov et al., 2008). Understanding the effects of disturbances, restoration, and global change on carbon and nutrient dynamics in peatlands requires explicit consideration of the complex feedbacks that occur between belowground microbial communities, aboveground communities, and their environment. This chapter will: (1) review the diversity and roles of microorganisms in natural boreal

Restoration and Reclamation of Boreal Ecosystems, ed. Dale Vitt and Jagtar Bhatti. Published by Cambridge University Press. © Cambridge University Press 2012.

peatlands; (2) detail the impact of some natural and anthropogenic disturbances on microbial communities and the consequences on peatland dynamics; (3) discuss how microbial communities can be integrated into the monitoring of restored or reclaimed peatlands in North America; and (4) give an overview of anticipated effects of global changes on microbial communities in peatlands.

MICROBIAL COMMUNITIES IN NATURAL PEATLANDS

In a given ecosystem, microbial communities can be studied from the perspective of the processes they carry out through metabolic pathways and energy flows, the total quantity of organisms (biomass) and their turnover, or the relative abundance of particular species or functional groups (composition or structure) (Harris, 2003). Therefore, a range of techniques have been developed to study microbial communities, targeting those different properties (Table 13.1). In boreal peatlands, microorganisms are instrumental to various processes (Figure 13.1). The sequestration of C arises from the imbalance between input from primary productivity and loss, both to the atmosphere (CO_2 and CH_4) and as dissolved organic carbon (DOC) exports (Clymo et al., 1998), from microorganism-driven decomposition. Methane fluxes depend on anaerobic decomposition in the permanently waterlogged peat layers and on oxidation in periodically aerated horizons. Nutrient uptake, mineralization, and release are also controlled by microorganisms, and can feedback on plant productivity and overall ecosystem functioning (Bardgett et al., 2008; Van Der Heijden et al., 2008). At the same time, boreal peatlands have long been recognized to harbor large and unique microbial populations of wide metabolic diversity (Williams and Crawford, 1983). Nevertheless, most studies have focused on some particular functional groups (e.g., methanogens), on microbial groups as a whole without distinction of their different attributes (e.g., fungi), or on the fluxes resulting from their activity alone.

While there are still uncertainties about the relative contribution of each of the different microbial groups to decomposition and nutrient cycling processes, there is an agreement that it is carried out by a consortium of organisms with complementary enzymatic activities, interacting with each other and influenced by different environmental variables (Table 13.2). In addition, a range of heterotrophic protists and micrometazoa feeds on the microbiota, and thus adds another level of complexity to the system. Although heterotrophic protists and micrometazoa are a key component of the microbial loop, they have been excluded from this

Table 13.1. *Techniques used in microbial ecology and peatland research application*

Technique (reference)	Properties of the microbial community	Examples of studies using this technique in peatlands (references)
Fumigation-extraction (Vance et al., 1987)	Microbial biomass (total number of living microbial cells in a peat sample)	Impact of peat extraction on microbial communities (Croft et al., 2001) Microbial communities in restored peatlands (Andersen et al., 2006; Basiliko et al., 2007) Fate of nitrogen (N) in peatland mesocosms (Blodau et al., 2006)
Phospho-lipid fatty acids (Tunlid et al., 1989; Tunlid and White, 1990)	Microbial biomass (total number of living microbial cells in a peat sample) Microbial community structure	Microbial communities in restored peatlands (Andersen et al., 2010a) Response of microbial communities to long-term water table drawdown (Jaatinen et al., 2007; Jaatinen et al., 2008)
Incubation methods (e.g., substrate-induced respiration) (Anderson and Domsch, 1978)	Basal potential respiration rate Potential CO_2 or CH_4 production	Respiration and methane (CH_4) production potential following restoration (Andersen, 2006; Glatzel et al., 2004)
Cultivation – agar plates, tubes, etc.	Diversity Presence of functional groups of organisms using selective media (e.g., capacity to grow at a particular pH, salinity, with/without nutrients, etc.)	Saprobic characteristic of ericoid mycorrhizal taxa (Piercey et al., 2002) Isolation of methanotrophic strains unique to peatlands (Dedysh et al., 1998)
Biolog ™ (e.g., EcoPlates) (Garland, 1996)	Physiological diversity (also referred to as community level physiological profiles, CLPP) using cultivation-based approach	Microbial communities in restored peatlands (Andersen et al., 2010a) Physiological profiles of yeasts (Thormann et al., 2007)

(cont.)

Table 13.1 *(cont.)*

Technique (reference)	Properties of the microbial community	Examples of studies using this technique in peatlands (references)
MicroResp™ (Campbell et al., 2003)	Physiological diversity (also referred to as community level physiological profiles, CLPP) using whole soil	Turnover of carbon (C) in response to N additions (Currey et al., 2010) Variation of microbial communities with depth (Artz et al., 2006)
Enzymatic reactions	Microbial activity Potential capacity to perform a particular metabolical pathway	Effect of increased rainfall on microbial activity (Freeman et al., 1998) Turnover of C in response to N additions (Currey et al., 2010)
Stable Isotope Partitioning (SIP)	Pathways and activity, often combined with other methods, e.g., phospholipid fatty acids	CH$_4$ oxidation by symbiotic bacteria in mosses (Kip et al., 2010)
DNA extraction and PCR-based approaches (e.g., DGGE, T-RFLP)	Genetic diversity, comparison of genetic profiles Presence of organisms associated with specific genes	Characterization of Archeal communities (Cadillo-Quiroz et al., 2008b) Response of microbial communities to water level drawdown (Peltoniemi et al., 2009)
Cloning and sequencing	Diversity of operational taxonomic units (OTUs) Phylogeny and identification of organisms	Fungal communities' response to vegetation succession (Artz et al., 2007)
RT-PCR, mRNA	Functional diversity Transcription rates, and indication of activity	Diversity/activity of methanotrophic community (Chen et al., 2008) Methanotrophs and methane emissions (Freitag and Prosser, 2009; Freitag et al., 2010)
Next generation sequencing	Complete genome of organisms Relationships between phylogeny/functions	None published yet

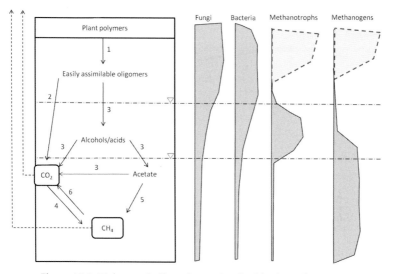

Figure 13.1. Main metabolic pathways involved in the carbon transformation in peatlands (left image) and schematic representation of depth distribution of major functional groups involved in the carbon transformation (right, shaded images). The metabolic pathways are: (1) hydrolysis via extracellular enzymes; (2) aerobic degradation of fresh organic matter and plant polymers; (3) anaerobic fermentation; (4) anaerobic degradation of formate (hydrogenotrophy); (5) anaerobic degradation of acetate (acetoclasty); and (6) oxidation of methane. (Modified from Artz, 2009.) The microorganisms associated with each metabolic pathway are detailed in Table 13.2. For the depth distribution of organisms, the light gray areas delimited by dashed lines for methanotrophs and methanogens represent flooded areas where these organisms may occur (e.g., in floating mats of *Sphagnum*).

chapter as they have recently been reviewed comprehensively by Gilbert and Mitchell (2006). In order to fully evaluate the role of peatlands on global C balance now and in the future, it is essential to deepen our understanding of the relative contributions of various groups of microorganisms to C cycling and organic matter transformations. To do so, we must elucidate how the functional and structural aspects of belowground communities relate to each other and identify the driving forces that shape them.

Vertical stratification of microbial communities and carbon cycling in peatlands

In peatlands, microbial communities and metabolic pathways are also vertically stratified with depth, as electron acceptors' availability (i.e.,

Table 13.2. *Common microorganisms found in peatlands and associated function in the carbon cycle*

	Group	Common organisms in peatlands (references)	Functions (pathways in Figure 13.1)
Fungi	Saprotrophic fungi	Ascomycetes, basidiomycetes, dark septate endophytes (Thormann et al., 2001b; 2004b; Thormann, 2006b; Thormann and Rice, 2007)	Hydrolysis via extracellular enzymes (1) Aerobic degradation of fresh organic matter and plant polymers (2)
	Ecto-mycorrhizal fungi (ECM)	Basidiomycetes including *Suillus* sp., *Cortinarius* sp., *Russula* sp. (Thormann et al., 1999)	Acquisition of N for trees, saprotrophic capacities (1,2)
	Ericoid mycorrhizal fungi (ErM)	Ascomycetes, such as *Rhizoscyphus ericae*, *Hymenoscyphus ericae*, *Oidiodendron maius*, *Myxotrichum arcticum*, *Phialocephala fortinii*, *Leptodontidium orchidicola* (Read et al., 2004; Thormann et al., 1999) Sebacinales (Selosse et al., 2007)	Acquisition of N for ericaceous shrubs, saprotrophic capacities (1,2)
	Vesicular-arbuscular mycorrhizal (VAM)	Glomales (Quilliam and Jones, 2010; Thormann et al., 1999)	Acquisition of P for herbaceous species
	Yeasts	Ascomycetous and basidiomycetous yeasts, such as *Cryptococcus*, *Candida*, *Pichia*, and *Rhodotorula* (Kachalkin et al., 2008; Thormann et al., 2007)	Aerobic degradation of fresh organic matter and plant polymers (2), anaerobic fermentation (3)
Bacteria	Heterotrophic bacteria	Gram+, such as *Bacillales* and *Firmicutes*, and Actinobacteria, such as *Streptomyces*, *Nocardia*, *Rhodococcus* Gram−, such as *Burkholderia*	Aerobic degradation of fresh organic matter and plant polymers (2), anaerobic fermentation (3)

Group	Common organisms in peatlands (references)	Functions (pathways in Figure 13.1)
	Other, such as *Acidobacteria, Plancotmycetes, Sphingobacteria* (Barkovskii et al., 2009; Belova et al., 2006; Croft et al., 2001; Dedysh et al., 2006; Dickinson, 1983; Hamberger et al., 2008; Juottonen et al., 2005; Morales et al., 2006; Opelt et al., 2007; Pankratov and Dedysh, 2009; Pankratov et al., 2006; Weber and Legge, 2010; Zadorina et al., 2009)	
Methanotrophs	type I *Gammaproteobacteria*, type II *Alphaproteobacteria*, such as *Methylocella sp., Methylocapsa sp.,* and *Methylocystis sp. Verrucomicrobia* (Chen et al., 2008; Chen and Murrell, 2010; Dedysh, 2002, 2009; Dedysh et al., 1998; Jaatinen et al., 2005; Op den Camp et al., 2009; Raghoebarsing et al., 2005; Sundh et al., 1995)	Oxidation of methane (6)
S-reducers	*Desulfovibrio*, deltaproteobacteria (Morales et al., 2006; Pester et al., 2010) *Clostridia*	Transformation of SO_4^{2-} in S^{2-}
N2-fixers	*Cyanobacteria, symbiotic actinobacteria (e.g., Frankia sp.)* (Belova et al., 2006)	Fixation of atmospheric N_2
Photosynthetic	*Cyanobacteria, Chloroflexi* (Dedysh et al., 2006; Gilbert et al., 1999)	Photosynthesis

(cont.)

Table 13.2 *(cont.)*

Group		Common organisms in peatlands (references)	Functions (pathways in Figure 13.1)
Archae	Methanogens	Hydrogenotrophic *Methanomicrobiales* Acetoclastic *Methanosarcinales*, *Methanosaetacea* (Basiliko et al., 2003; Bräuer et al., 2006; Cadillo-Quiroz et al., 2006, 2008b; Galand, 2004; Galand et al., 2002, 2005; Juottonen et al., 2005; Merilä et al., 2006; Rooney Varga et al., 2007)	Anaerobic degradation of formate (4; hydrogenotrophy) or acetate (5; acetoclasty), leading to formation of methane
	Other	Crenarchaeota (Cadillo-Quiroz et al., 2008a, 2008b; Juottonen, 2008; Putkinen et al., 2009; Rooney Varga et al., 2007)	Anaerobic fermentation (2), autotrophy

redox conditions) and C quality change, from the oxic upper layers (acrotelm) to the periodically anoxic horizons (mesotelm), and the permanently waterlogged, more decomposed horizons (catotelm) (Andersen et al., 2006; Morales et al., 2006; Sundh et al., 1995, 1997; Williams and Crawford, 1983) (Figure 13.1). Microbial biomass and activity are greatest in the acrotelm, where aerobic conditions prevail and fresh organic matter is found. As the organic matter becomes humified and increasingly recalcitrant with depth, more specialist species are involved in the decay process (Artz et al., 2006; Thormann et al., 2003), which is constrained by a combination of factors, such as availability of O_2 and alternative electron acceptors (Fe(III), SO_4^{3-}, NO_3^-), or low temperatures (see review by Artz, 2009). These constraints on decomposition and microbial communities make accumulation of organic matter and thus C sequestration possible in peatlands.

The dominant decomposition pathway in the acrotelm is aerobic, exoenzyme-driven polymer decomposition. In many terrestrial ecosystems, a succession of fungal species with different enzymatic capabilities and behaviors (Lumley et al., 2001) is generally observed as the organic matter is degraded from fresh litter to more recalcitrant compounds. In peatlands, this pattern has not been consistently observed; rather, species with a broader enzymatic profile seem to coexist (Artz et al., 2007; Thormann, 2006b; Thormann et al., 2003). To date, the most commonly isolated fungi from peatlands displayed a limited ability to degrade the most complex polymers (Thormann et al., 2001a, 2001b, 2003), which subsequently accumulate and increase in proportion with depth (Turetsky et al., 2000), forming the peat. However, most studies examining fungi contribution to polymer decomposition have used cultivation techniques, which might not give an accurate representation of the actual array of enzymatic capacities of the fungal mycota in peatlands. Fungal saprotrophs are generally thought to carry out a more important role than bacteria in the early stages of organic matter decomposition processes (Latter et al., 1967; Newell et al., 1995; Williams and Crawford, 1983), particularly in bogs, where the fungal biomass often predominates over bacteria (Golovchenko et al., 2007). Nevertheless, some data are contradictory (Gilbert et al., 1998) and a recent study by Winsborough and Basiliko (2009) demonstrated that bacterial activity was greater than fungal activity across peatland types–highlighting that the relationship between biomass and activity is not yet fully understood. Actinobacteria are another dominant microbial group involved in the early stages of decomposition, for which the community structure changes vertically as the organic matter quality decreases (Barkovskii et al., 2009).

The horizon where the water table fluctuates is generally anoxic, but is periodically partially or completely (depending on root penetration) aerated, and has been referred to as the mesotelm by Clymo and Bryant (2008). In the mesotelm, many microbial pathways exist, including aerobic respiration, fermentation, and methane oxidation. These processes involve a plethora of obligate and facultative anaerobic microorganisms. Aerobic respiration and fermentative pathways further the transformation of recent plant assimilates into volatile fatty acids and alcohols. Methane oxidation is carried out by methanotrophs, a key bacterial group that possesses a methane monooxygenase (MMO) enzyme, allowing them to convert methane to biomass and CO_2 in the presence of oxygen (Hanson and Hanson, 1996). Methanotrophs belong to two bacterial phyla, the Proteobacteria and the Verrucomicrobia (Hanson and Hanson, 1996; Op den Camp et al., 2009). Members of the Proteobacteria are divided into two groups: type I and type II, which belong to gamma- and alphaproteobacteria, respectively. The groups differ in not only cellular ultrastructure, but also their ecology in peatlands. For instance, type II methanotrophs have been shown to be more active in more acidic environments, such as *Sphagnum* peatlands, while type I are more active in high-pH environments. It is thought that a significant portion (10%–30%)

of the C in *Sphagnum* is derived from methane oxidized by endophytic methanotrophs associated with the mosses (Larmola et al., 2010).

The final pathway of anaerobic decomposition that predominates in permanently waterlogged and anoxic horizons is that of methanogenesis, which is carried out by a specialized group of Archaea, the methanogens. In peatlands, methanogens can occur in the bulk peat of deeper layers (catotelm) but also in the rhizosphere of plants in flooded areas. They utilize few substrates, most notably formate (HCO_2^-) and acetate ($CH_3CO_2^-$) (Zinder, 1993). Hydrogenotrophy (through which methane is derived from formate) is thought to be the main pathway for methane production in nutrient-poor peatlands, whereas the acetoclastic pathway (in which acetate is the precursor for methane) predominates in the surface layers of minerotrophic fens where *Carex* sedges grow (Kelly et al., 1992, Popp et al., 2000). Depth-related shifts from hydrogenotrophic to acetoclastic Archaea have been observed in various peatlands, and were more pronounced in bogs, where the peat composition ranges from overlying *Sphagnum* peat to deeper sedge peat, than in fens, where only sedge peat is present throughout the profile (Galand et al., 2002). Nevertheless, a recent study showed that both pathways may be significant in rich fens where acetoclastic (*Methanosaeta*) and hydrogenotrophic (*Methanomicrobiales*) species codominate (Cadillo-Quiroz et al., 2008a, 2008b). Thus far, the studies on Archaea inhabiting bogs, poor fens, and minerotrophic fens have revealed a large number of novel or uncultivated species with unique features (Bräuer et al., 2006, Cadillo-Quiroz et al., 2009; Galand, 2004; Juottonen et al., 2005).

Recycling of nitrogen, phosphorus, and sulfur by microorganisms in peatlands

The main pool of nitrogen (N) in peatlands resides in decayed organic matter; only a small fraction is stored in living organisms. As a result, bogs are generally regarded as efficient N sinks (Limpens et al., 2006). Similar to other microbially driven processes, N cycling in peatlands depends on the microorganisms present in the peat, but is also heavily influenced by the prevailing environmental conditions. For instance, all peatland types display a high diversity of N_2-fixing organisms including symbiotic actinobacteria, cyanobacteria, and free living bacteria (Dickinson, 1983; Zadorina et al., 2009). Nevertheless, nitrogen fixation is highly variable both spatially and temporally, with the highest rates reported for rich fens at lower latitudes (Waughman and Bellamy, 1980). Denitrification, the microbial reduction of NO_3^- to N_2O and N_2, takes place under anaerobic conditions and is constrained by pH and temperature. In bogs, denitrification is quantitatively unimportant both because the environmental conditions (cold and acidic) are unfavorable, and because NO_3^- is taken up by mosses, plants, and other microorganisms before it reaches anaerobic horizons. In fens, where conditions are more favorable, N_2O production may be higher when NO_3^- is not a limiting factor (Limpens et al., 2006; Verhoeven et al., 1996).

Phosphorus (P) is closely balanced and tightly conserved in boreal peatlands, especially in bogs, where the only input is from precipitation. It is found mostly in the upper horizons and the rooting zones (Walbridge and Navaratnam, 2006). In rich fens where groundwater inputs occur, P availability is improved and contributes to promoting the decomposition of organic matter (Moore and Bellamy, 1974; Walbridge and Navaratnam, 2006). Interestingly, although bogs and poor fens have a smaller total P pool, their P availability is similar to that of rich fens because of rapid cycling and efficient retention in the vegetation and microbial loop (Kellogg and Bridgham, 2003).

In peatlands, many different bacteria are also involved in sulfur (S) cycling processes. Sulfate (SO_4^{2-}) found in the acrotelm can be used by chemoheterotrophic sulfate-reducing bacteria as an electron acceptor for organic matter oxidation. The fate of the resulting S^{2-} depends on environmental conditions: it can form H_2S in anaerobic horizons and diffuse upwardly or be oxidized back to sulfate; alternatively, it can form FeS or FeS_2 (Wieder and Lang, 1988) or even HgS, which can be methylated (Galloway and Branfireun, 2004) into methyl sulfide. Most of the key organisms involved in sulfate reduction processes as well as their abundance remain unidentified in peatlands. Recently, a study showed that one species of sulfate reducer (*Desulfosporosinus* sp.), representing only 0.006% of the total active microbial population (estimated by *16SrRNA* genes), accounted for a significant part of sulfate reduction *in situ*, highlighting that biomass and activity were not necessarily related. It is important to appreciate that in peatlands, sulfate reducers compete with other microbial populations for organic C and electron acceptors, and can influence C mineralization pathways (Pester et al., 2010). Many studies have demonstrated reduction of methanogenesis in the presence of sulfate reducers (Vile et al., 2003; Wieder et al., 1990), as they divert the C flow from CH_4 to CO_2.

Microbial communities along the ombrotrophic–minerotrophic gradient

The differences in plant communities, pH, and nutrient levels between bogs (acidic, nutrient poor, and dominated by *Sphagnum* and ericaceous shrubs) and minerotrophic fens (higher pH and nutrient levels, dominated by brown mosses and sedges) also lead to clear distinctions in their microbial communities. In particular, studies have highlighted that communities of saprotrophic fungi (Thormann et al., 2004a, 2004b), mycorrhizal fungi (Thormann et al., 1999), yeast (Thormann et al., 2007), heterotrophic bacteria (Juottonen, 2008; Sundh et al., 1997), methanogens (Juottonen, 2008; Kim et al., 2008; Merilä et al., 2006), and methanotrophs (see review by Dedysh, 2009) varied across peatland types, either in composition, structure, biomass, or activity. Even within a peatland, small differences can lead to divergent microbial communities and associated decomposition rates; for example, microhabitats along the hollow–hummock microtopographic gradient in bogs (Belyea, 1996; Sundh et al., 1997).

Aboveground vegetation composition influences belowground microbial structure and function, either directly or indirectly. For instance, mycorrhizas and other endophytic or symbiotic microorganisms can be directly influenced by the life forms or even the species with which they are associated and that comprise aboveground vegetation assemblages. Mycorrhizas are mutualistic associations between fungi and the roots of higher plants, and provide access to nutrients that would otherwise be inaccessible for the plants in exchange for C from photosynthates. There are different groups of mycorrhizal associations, based on the type of structure that they develop with the roots of their host (Newman and Reddell, 1987). Ericoid mycorrhizal fungi (ErM) are common in N-limited systems and occur mostly in bogs, where they associate with the roots of ericaceous plant species (Read et al., 2004). Ectomycorrhizal fungi (ECM) are typically associated with trees and are therefore more abundant in forested peatlands (Thormann, 2006a; Thormann and Rice, 2007; Thormann et al., 1999). Both ErM and ECM are thought to have a certain saprotrophic potential in addition to their ability to acquire nutrients, and play an important regulatory role at the ecosystem level (Read et al., 2004). Vesicular-arbuscular mycorrhizal fungi (VAM) are a small but widely distributed group belonging to the Glomales (Zygomycota), who have a superior capacity to acquire P, but low saprotrophic abilities. They infect herbaceous species, and consequently, may not be of great significance in bogs (Thormann et al., 1999), and are likely more frequent in fens where host species occur.

Other than mycorrhiza, a certain number of endophytic species are associated with some particular peatland plant species to various degrees. For instance, a recent study demonstrated that the yeast communities of *Sphagnum* plants were different from the phylloplane population of other plant groups, including bog vascular plants and forest or meadow grasses

(Kachalkin et al., 2008), suggesting a species-specific association between yeast and plants. Partly, endophytic methanotrophs have been detected in the hyaline cells of leaves and stems in submerged *Sphagnum* mosses, the potential to consume CH_4 of which had been observed previously (Raghoebarsing et al., 2005, 2006; Young et al., 2010). These endophytic methanotrophs are mostly influenced by the water table level, and have been shown to move from one *Sphagnum* plant to another with the fluctuating water, displaying a rather loose symbiosis between the bacteria and the mosses (Larmola et al., 2010). *Burkholderia* sp., a dominant group of bacteria, is another microorganism directly associated with *Sphagnum* mosses that displays high host specificity (Belova et al., 2006).

Vegetation also has an indirect effect–in a chronosequence of peatlands at various successional stages, it was shown that the gradient in methanogenic microbial communities followed that of the vegetation, and that the diversity of methanogens was greater in fens than in bogs, reflecting aboveground diversity patterns (Merilä et al., 2006). Differences in litter and carbon quality are another indirect effect of vegetation on microbial processes; for instance, the hummock-forming *Sphagnum* species are intrinsically more resistant to decay than the hollow or lawn forming species (Belyea, 1996; Hogg, 1993; Johnson and Damman, 1991; Johnson et al., 1990). The effect of litter quality has been shown to exert a strong control on fungal community structure (Thormann et al., 2004b; Trinder et al., 2008, 2009). Rhizoexudate, and not only litter, also varies among plants and is reflected in the functional diversity of microorganisms in peat, measured as community level physiological profiles (CLPP) (Artz et al., 2006, 2008; Yan et al., 2008).

The combined influences of depth, nutrient status, aboveground vegetation, litter composition, and physicochemical conditions on microbial communities and on decomposition processes are complex, but also highly variable, both temporally and spatially. Understanding and appreciating this complexity is critical to improving our capacity to predict how microbial communities will respond to disturbance and global change.

DISTURBANCES AND MICROORGANISMS IN PEATLANDS

Disturbances, natural or anthropogenic, can have both direct and indirect effects on the microbial communities in peatlands (Figure 13.2). Direct physiological effects of stress on soil microbes can be seen in alteration of energy budgets; for example, shifting of resources otherwise allocated to growth and reproduction to maintenance and survival (Sibly and Calow,

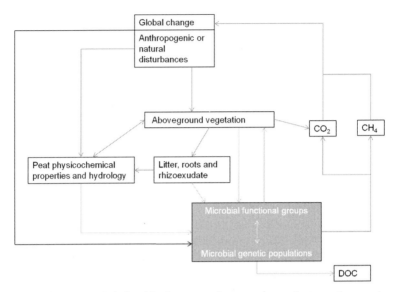

Figure 13.2. Relationships between microorganisms, plants, environment, and green house gases and feedback cycles under disturbances and/or global change. (Modified from Artz, 2009 and Bardgett et al., 2008.)

1989). On the other hand, any disturbance or dramatic event that leads to the physical erosion of the peat surface or to changes in the aboveground vegetation, the peat structure, hydrology, and/or chemistry will indirectly affect the microbial compartment. In peatlands, fire and peat extraction or mining are such disturbances, and can decrease microbial biomass and activity (Chapman et al., 2003; Croft et al., 2001) and lead to loss of certain specialized functional groups that have restrictive niches (Francez et al., 2000; Gilbert et al., 1998, 1999). Peatlands are resilient to fire or naturally occurring extreme events, and can recover from them, albeit slowly. Nevertheless, anthropogenic disturbances like extraction and mining modify the system beyond its limits and it will remain dysfunctional if no restorative or reclamation measures are taken.

Impact of fires on microorganisms in peatlands

Lightning-initiated fires are a prevalent natural disturbance affecting forested uplands and peatlands in continental western Canada and Alaska (Kasischke and Turetsky, 2006; Turetsky et al., 2002, 2004). Fire can alter controls on decomposition through changes in soil temperature and moisture (Kasischke and Johnstone, 2005; Kasischke et al., 1995;

Viereck, 1982; Zoltai et al., 1998), in microbial communities (Hart et al., 2005; Treseder et al., 2004), and/or in organic matter content and quality (see review by Certini, 2005). In upland forest ecosystems, fire has been shown to reduce the microbial biomass in near-surface soils, the colonization by ECM in roots, and the bacterial diversity (Hart et al., 2005; Treseder et al., 2004; Waldrop and Harden, 2008). In a boreal forest system, ergosterol, used as a proxy for fungi, was still absent from severely burnt plots after three years (Bergner et al., 2004), while the abundance of active bacteria had not been affected. Without fungi, the accumulation of organic C pools in soil could be compromised, and the colonization of mycorrhizal plants may be slow. In turn, the indirect effects of fire (i.e., change in quality of organic matter) on a microbial community have been shown to carry on for decades as succession proceeds in the aboveground communities and as hydrological conditions vary. In peatlands with discontinuous permafrost, severe fire events may contribute to permafrost melt, leading to more permanent vegetation changes (Kuhry, 1994; Myers-Smith et al., 2008). These events may also impact microbial composition and activity, notably affecting methanogen and methanotroph populations, and ultimately greenhouse gas balance in those peatlands.

Peat extraction and mining

In Canada, peat extraction affects as little as 0.01% of total peatland area; nevertheless, the activities are concentrated in particular areas, thus threatening regional diversity (Poulin et al., 2004). The extraction process, either block-cut or vacuum harvesting, necessitates the creation of drainage ditches and removal of vegetation and successive layers of peat, where the majority of the microbial biomass and nutrients are found. The physical removal of the biologically active layer translates into a two- to five-fold decrease in the microbial biomass in post-harvested sites, along with changes in bacterial (Andersen et al., 2006, 2010a; Croft et al., 2001) and fungal (Artz et al., 2007) community structure. In cutover peatlands, the catotelm peat that is exposed to the surface contains highly recalcitrant organic matter unsuitable for most decomposers, the microbiota becomes highly C-limited and less active, and generalist species tend to replace specialized organisms (Andersen et al., 2006; Francez et al., 2000; Gilbert et al., 1998). In addition, the large variations in hydrological regime found in post-harvested and cutover sites impair the establishment of stable methanogen and methanotroph populations (Andersen, 2006; Francez et al., 2000).

In the oil sands development areas in the Athabasca region (Alberta), another disturbance that can affect microbial communities in peatlands is the presence of contaminants in the water, such as high levels of sodium (Na), naphthenic acids (NAs, which are derived from bitumen), sulfate (SO_4), and ammonium (NH_4). The impact of increased salinity on a microbial community in peatlands is likely to depend on its ability to adapt to fluctuations in the osmolarity, and on the osmoadaptive coping strategies that it can develop (Welsh, 2000). On the other hand, NAs are toxic to certain organisms, and have been shown to alter microbial communities in soil. One study looking at wetlands in the Athabasca river basin showed that exposure to even slightly higher than naturally occurring levels of NAs shift the microbial community structure to one that is capable of metabolizing NA (Hadwin et al., 2006); however, clear patterns in functional diversity were not detected. Another study showed that long-term exposure to NAs could trigger shifts in the microbial population by increasing the populations of NA-degrading organisms while reducing overall diversity (Nyman, 1999), the impact of which is unclear at the ecosystem level. Similarly, exposure to high levels of sulfate could stimulate the growth of sulfate-reducers and alter methanogenic pathways as discussed in the previous section. Ammonia can be degraded by nitrifiers in the presence of high oxygen availability, but high concentrations of ammonia could unbalance nutrient ratios and create deficiencies, thereby altering microbial processes. Exposure to OSPW could thus trigger many different structural changes within the microbial communities, but could also modify processes like respiration (which would increase under stress per biomass unit), methane consumption or production patterns, and nutrient cycling.

INTEGRATING MICROBIAL COMMUNITIES IN THE MONITORING OF RESTORED PEATLANDS

Given the extent of disturbance due to horticultural exploitation and lack of spontaneous colonization by typical peatland species, ecological restoration targeting bog or fen species, depending on the initial conditions, has been considered the preferred option for *Sphagnum* peatlands that have been subjected to peat-harvesting. Over the last decades, the *Sphagnum* transfer technique, developed by the Peatland Ecology Research Group (PERG), has been successfully used for large scale restoration trials (Rochefort et al., 2003), and has been closely monitored. Most of the peatland reclamation is still at an embryonic stage in the oil sand affected areas (Price et al., 2010; Vitt et al., 2010, 2011), but the restored sites will need to be monitored to assess success–and microbial communities should not be left aside.

The restoration and reclamation of peatlands aims primarily to bring back a vegetation assemblage dominated by typical species in order to reset a self-sustainable system capable of sequestering C (Graf, 2009; Rochefort et al., 2003). Therefore, microbial communities are not directly targeted by restoration practices; nevertheless, they are an integral part of a system in which each element feeds back on the other. In fact, bringing back a healthy plant cover is not a guarantee that the C storage capacity of the system will be restored, as from a functional point of view, it is the imbalance between C input and output through decomposition that needs to be reestablished. Evaluating the success of restoration thus requires addressing belowground communities while simultaneously monitoring aboveground vegetation (Harris, 2003).

How bog restoration modifies microbial communities

From a belowground perspective, after peatland restoration, some changes persist in the upper layers that can hamper or delay a proper recovery of the microbial communities and associated decomposition processes (Andersen et al., 2006,2010b; Francez et al., 2000; Glatzel et al., 2004; Laggoun Défarge et al., 2008). The decomposed peat exposed by harvesting is a C- and nutrient-limited system where microbial activity is greatly reduced (Andersen et al., 2006; Fisk et al., 2003). With the addition of straw mulch and plants, coupled with the growth of those plants, there is a sudden input of fresh organic matter in the upper layers during restoration. At the same time, the water table continues to fluctuate, producing alternating periods of water-logging and aeration in a large portion of the profile for many years (Price et al., 2003). These conditions (fresh C and prolonged aeration) temporarily stimulate microbial activity, and could initially impede the recovery of C accumulation, or even increase C losses in comparison with cutover sites (Waddington et al., 2003). In a restored peatland in Eastern Canada, rapid increases in microbial biomass and turnover were observed within five years following restoration (Figure 13.3), coinciding with an increase in labile organic C leached from the new vegetation, as well as from the straw used as protecting mulch, and readily accessible for microorganisms (Andersen et al., 2006). The differences in biomass between natural, restored, and non-restored conditions were also strongly correlated with nutrient availability (Figure 13.4).

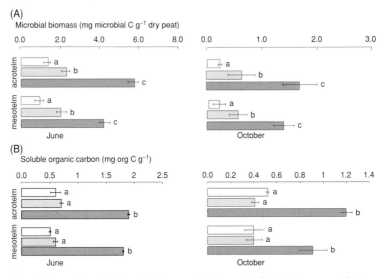

Figure 13.3. (**A**) Microbial biomass (estimated by fumigation extraction), and (**B**) soluble organic carbon (SOC) measured in the acrotelm and mesotelm of a natural (dark gray), a restored (light gray), and an unrestored (white) peatland in Eastern Canada (n = 6). The measures were taken in June and October 2003, three years after restoration.

Seven years after restoration, another study looked at differences in the microbial community structure (measured with PLFAs) and the catabolic diversity (measured by Biolog™ EcoPlates) at two points in the growing season (June and October) in five communities located at different depths (aerated surface or anaerobic horizon) along a disturbed-restored-natural gradient. The microbial community structure as evaluated by PLFAs differed between the beginning and the end of the growing season for a given type of sample, but was not significantly different among vegetation types or depths (Figure 13.5). On the other hand, catabolic diversity and decomposition potential were the highest beneath restored *Sphagnum* carpets (Figures 13.6); specifically, under aerobic conditions (surface). The surface samples of non-restored conditions, where C input is minimal, and the anaerobic horizons of the natural samples, where oxygen is limiting, had much lower potential for degrading various C sources (Andersen et al., 2010a). In contrast, decomposition rates *in situ* measured in the same restored peatland were uniform in all conditions for a given type of litter, but were significantly greater for fresh *Sphagnum* than for old peat (Andersen et al., 2010c). This might reflect the

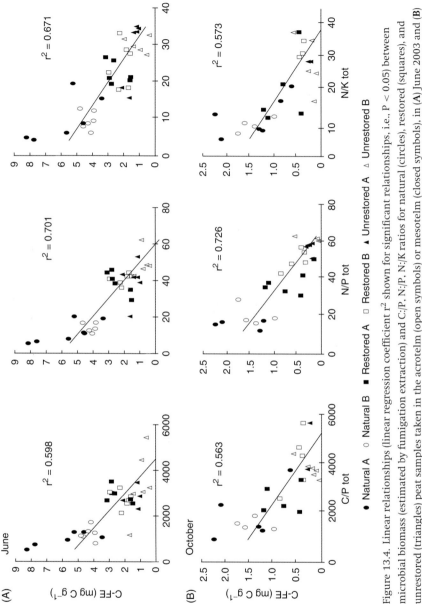

Figure 13.4. Linear relationships (linear regression coefficient r² shown for significant relationships, i.e., P < 0.05) between microbial biomass (estimated by fumigation extraction) and C:/P, N:/P, N:/K ratios for natural (circles), restored (squares), and unrestored (triangles) peat samples taken in the acrotelm (open symbols) or mesotelm (closed symbols), in (A) June 2003 and (B) October 2003, three years post-restoration. C, carbon; K, potassium; N, nitrogen; P, phosphorus;tot, total.

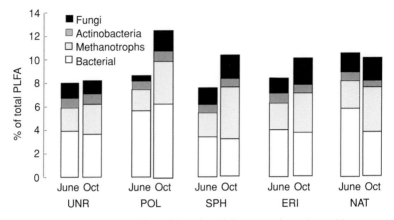

Figure 13.5. Composition of the microbial community estimated by phospholipid fatty acids (PLFAs) six years after restoration, in June and October. The samples (n = 9) were taken in the aerobic layers under bare peat communities found in unrestored conditions (UNR); *Polytrichum strictum* dominated communities in restored conditions (POL), *Sphagnum* sp. carpets in restored conditions (SPH), *Sphagnum* sp. mixed with ericaceous shrubs in restored conditions (ERI), and natural hummock communities in a reference peatland (NAT). PLFA markers were: i15:0, a15:0, i17:0, and a17:0 (bacteria); 18:1ω8 and 16:1ω8 (methanotrophs); 10Me16:0 and 10Me18:0 (actinobacteria), and 18:2ω6 (fungi).

importance of slow-growing fungi in the early stages of Sphagnum decomposition (Artz et al., 2008), which is not accounted for by methods like Biolog™ EcoPlates that are biased toward fast-growing bacteria. A further assessment of microbial functional diversity after 10 years of restoration using the MicroResp™ method (see Table 13.1), revealed that decomposition potential for the whole community followed a gradient: restored > natural > unrestored (with vegetation) > unrestored (bare peat), with significant differences still remaining between restored and natural reference conditions (Andersen, unpublished). Another study, comparing the effects of typical pioneer species on the functional response of the microbial community in a previously cutover peatland, demonstrated that new C inputs from plants colonizing an abandoned cutover peatland support communities of microorganisms that have functionally distinct roles in C turnover (Yan et al., 2008), highlighting once more the intricate relationships between plant and microorganisms. On the other hand, this finding also suggests that litter quality can potentially override the effects of site-specific environmental conditions (Thormann et al., 2004b).

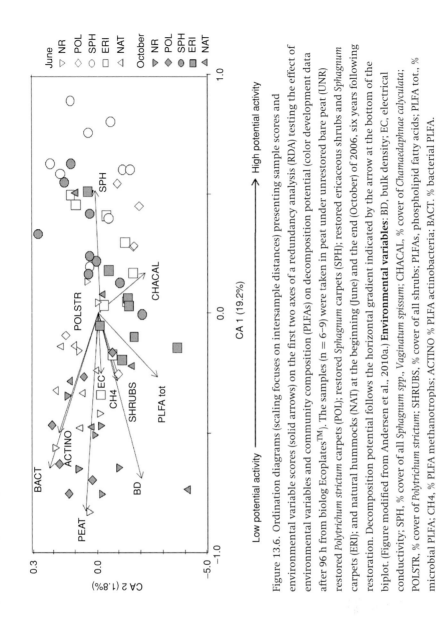

Figure 13.6. Ordination diagrams (scaling focuses on intersample distances) presenting sample scores and environmental variable scores (solid arrows) on the first two axes of a redundancy analysis (RDA) testing the effect of environmental variables and community composition (PLFAs) on decomposition potential (color development data after 96 h from biolog Ecoplates™). The samples (n = 6–9) were taken in peat under unrestored bare peat (UNR) restored *Polytrichum strictum* carpets (POL); restored *Sphagnum* carpets (SPH); restored ericaceous shrubs and *Sphagnum* carpets (ERI); and natural hummocks (NAT) at the beginning (June) and the end (October) of 2006, six years following restoration. Decomposition potential follows the horizontal gradient indicated by the arrow at the bottom of the biplot. (Figure modified from Andersen et al. 2010a.) **Environmental variables**: BD, bulk density; EC, electrical conductivity; SPH, % cover of all *Sphagnum spp.*, *Vaginatum spissum*; CHACAL, % cover of *Chamaedaphnae calyculata*; POLSTR, % cover of *Polytrichum strictum*; SHRUBS, % cover of all shrubs; PLFAs, phospholipid fatty acids; PLFA tot., % microbial PLFA; CH4, % PLFA methanotrophs; ACTINO % PLFA actinobacteria; BACT. % bacterial PLFA.

Microbial communities in the oil sand contaminated areas

Microorganisms with the potential to degrade N have been found in the rhizosphere of various wetland plants (Biryukova et al., 2007), in wetland sediments (Del Rio et al., 2006), and elsewhere (Whitby, 2010) and have been used for remediation in some cases. On the other hand, in natural systems exposed to contaminants, microbial communities have been found to experience nutrient limitation (N, P, or micronutrients) (Herman et al., 1994; Nyman, 1999), which could have important consequences on nutrient cycling and long-term sustainability of regenerating peatlands. The functional response of the microbial community to potential contamination by oil sands process water was studied in a preliminary greenhouse experiment using mesocosm filled with fen peat and supporting contrasting vegetation types (graminoids or mosses). Microorganisms under mosses were less active (lower CO_2 respiration rate for a given C source) and diverse (lower catabolic diversity) than those under graminoid plants, whose rhizosphere is comparatively well-developed and has been shown to increase the diversity of the microbial community (Grayston et al., 1998), thereby enhancing its capacity to metabolize various substrates (Degens et al., 2001). The vegetation type chosen for restoration is therefore likely to have a strong influence on the "restored" microbial communities.

The addition of contaminated water to C sources also had a significant effect on both plant species through modification of the C sources preferred by the community (Graf et al., 2009). This could be a consequence of the change in C:N ratio inherent to the addition of NAs. Other studies have also shown that the metabolism of microorganisms can be at least temporarily stimulated by crude oil extract (Nyman, 1999) and hydrocarbon (Greenwood et al., 2009). However, this could be a stress-related response wherein the microbial communities exposed to contaminated water allocate more energy to maintain basal function, and thus respire more than they likely would under unstressed conditions (Sibly and Calow, 1989). How microbial communities will develop in restored peatlands in the oil sand areas and how their development will affect processes at various scales remains unknown.

GLOBAL CHANGE AND MICROBIAL COMMUNITIES

Understanding the complexities of how climate and other global changes alter microbial communities and processes in peatland is difficult, because: (1) feedback mechanisms linking plant, microorganisms and their environment must be taken into account; (2) soil's microorganisms are inherently complex (Bardgett et al., 2008); and (3) current experiments do not adequately capture the responses of slow C pools (Pendall et al., 2004). This section will give a brief overview of some studies that have examined the impact of elevated CO_2, temperature, and increased atmospheric deposition, as well as changes in water table position due to reduced precipitation or permafrost melting.

Elevated carbon dioxide, temperatures, and atmospheric deposition

When CO_2 is elevated, the proportion of dissolved organic C derived from recently assimilated CO_2 is greatly increased (Freeman et al., 2004). It has been suggested that this shift explains the increase in the proportion of heterotrophic bacteria in peatlands exposed to stimulated high-CO_2 (Mitchell et al., 2003). Elevated CO_2 can also indirectly affect symbiotic organisms like mycorrhizas through changes in C allocation from host plants to fungi (Treseder and Allen, 2000). Nevertheless, the effects of elevated CO_2 on respiration, N mineralization, and microbial biomass are variable and remain difficult to predict, as they are also influenced by many other environmental conditions (see review by Zak et al., 2000).

Elevated temperatures can increase microbial activity–although not necessarily microbial biomass–in high-latitude soils, the effects of which on decomposition rates are undeniable (Davidson and Janssens, 2006). A study by Dorrepaal et al. (2009) estimated that climate warming of about 1°C over the next few decades could induce a global increase in heterotrophic respiration of 38–100 megatons of C per year. Other models suggest that a decrease in the fire return interval combined with increases in non-winter air temperature could transform the bogs of northern Alberta to a net C source (Wieder et al., 2009). On the other hand, soil warming experiments revealed that the effect of warming on respiration may be temporary, due to the depletion of labile pools of soluble organic C, or to the fact that soil microbial respiration thermally adapts to increased temperatures (Bradford et al., 2008; Davidson and Janssens, 2006; Kirschbaum, 2004; Knorr et al., 2005; Oechel et al., 2000), a phenomenon that may weaken the positive effect of warming on soil respiration rates. Thermal acclimation of respiration has been demonstrated for both ectomycorrhizal (Malcolm et al., 2008) and arbuscular mycorrhizal fungi in soils (Heinemeyer et al., 2006); however, those studies were not specific to peatlands.

Enhanced N and S deposition resulting from pollution and anthropogenic activities may directly affect microbial communities and decomposition rates in peatlands by increasing the availability of electron acceptors in the peat. For instance, increased SO_4 deposition from pollution could stimulate the growth of sulfate-reducing bacteria and alter pathways of methane production (Dise and Verry, 2001; Vile et al., 2003). Atmospheric deposition can also act indirectly on the belowground compartment through changes in vegetation composition and cover, most notably a shift to vascular cover at the expense of *Sphagnum* (Limpens et al., 2003). High levels of atmospheric N deposition have been shown to depress the extent of ericoid mycorrhizal infection of ericaceous (*Calluna vulgaris*) roots (Yesmin et al., 1996), which can have further repercussions on C cycling and plant nutrition. Increased N concentrations in soil have also been shown to correlate with decreases in ectomycorrhizal sporocarp production, and community diversity and composition (review by Cudlin et al., 2007).

Response of microbial communities to long- and short-term lowering of the water table position

Alteration in the position of the water table relative to the surface, or in the range of variation within the peat profile, is likely to impact the microbial community and associated processes. Nevertheless, there is a dearth of information relating changes in the water level to the decomposer communities (Laiho, 2006). To date, studies have demonstrated that the response of the microbial community to changes in hydrology depends on the extent and intensity of the change in time and space, as well as the type of peatland, and even of microform within the affected peatland (Jaatinen et al., 2007, 2008; Kim et al., 2008; Peltoniemi et al., 2009). The ecological niche of methanogens and methanotrophs is closely associated with the position of the water table, rendering them particularly susceptible to the effects of drainage. Methanogens require an anaerobic environment, thus lowering of the water table could push the populations deeper in the profile (Francez et al., 2000). Methanotroph sequences have been found at various depths in bog peat cores, albeit concentrated in particular regions, suggesting that under appropriate conditions, populations have the potential to become active and to grow (review by Dedysh, 2009). Persistent, progressive lowering of the water table could benefit fungi and certain Gram-negative bacteria, but could prove detrimental to certain Gram-positive bacteria in wet mesotrophic sites (Jaatinen et al., 2007, 2008). With increased aeration, some "old peat" would become available for aerobic decomposition, while at the same time, changes in the aboveground community, from herbs and grasses to trees and ericaceous vegetation, would reduce the quality of the litter. Therefore, recalcitrant substrates could favor fungi, which have a competitive advantage over certain bacteria, but could also promote the growth of Gram-negative bacteria, which can feed on simple monomers released by fungi (Jaatinen et al., 2008; Marilley and Aragno, 1999). Prolonged droughts could also be less detrimental to fungi, as they possess the ability to translocate nutrients and water from one part of the mycelium to another (Potila, 2004).

Short-term water table drawdowns (<1 month) during drought are not expected to trigger a shift in vegetation and their impact on the microbial community could be different. Kim et al. (2008) found that gene abundance (eubacteria, denitrifiers, and methanogens) would be more vulnerable than community composition or diversity in bogs and fens. They also suggest that following short-term drainage, small changes in environmental conditions could allow generalists and more common aerobes to colonize the peat, leading to an initial increase in diversity; however, in the long-term, repeated replacement of specialists by generalists could lead to decreased diversity.

While some peatlands are thought to experience drainage as a consequence of change in precipitation, approximately 2630 ± 105 km^2 of permafrost in peatlands has melted over the past ~100 yr in western Canada. Permafrost degradation continues today (Vitt et al., 1994), with an estimated 26.3 ± 1.1 km^2 of permafrost in peatlands melting annually as a consequence of global change in temperatures and radiative forcing. Changes in soil structure, hydrological regime, etc. resulting from this melting can influence the microbial community (e.g., shift in aerobic/anaerobic populations) but also the plant composition; for instance, a shift in plant community composition such as shrub expansion has already started to take place in Northern regions (Tape et al., 2006), where it could, for instance, alter the mycorrhizal and fungal communities and feedback on decomposition processes.

CONCLUSIONS AND FUTURE RESEARCH

Microorganisms play central roles in C and nutrient cycles in peatlands. They have the metabolic and genetic capability to adapt to changing environmental conditions on very short time scales, and thus constitute potentially interesting early indicators of ecosystem disturbances (Jassey et al., 2011). Although it is possible to calculate fluxes and assess if peatlands are sinks or sources of atmospheric C following disturbance or restoration, doing so will not allow us to identify the tipping points and key controls–the set of conditions, aboveground and belowground, that alter or reset C accumulation in a given context–and how to avoid or reach them more efficiently. The relationships linking aboveground and belowground must be considered in order to further our understanding of the processes, the drivers, and the interactions between the two that affect peatlands. Only by taking these complex factors into account can we accurately predict the fate of C in peatlands now and in the future. We emphasize that monitoring of microbial communities following restoration should be routinely implemented and coordinated with other measures and other disciplines (Laggoun Défarge et al., 2008), as it provides a unique opportunity to enhance our understanding of peatland functioning across various successional stages.

The development of new methods to study microbial communities in soil, such as RT-PCR, Stable-Isotope Probing, or high-throughput sequencing has broadened our understanding of soil organism diversity in recent years and raised new questions about the relationships between structure and function of the microbial communities. However, these questions have only recently been applied to peatlands. Putting microbial diversity into a broader relevant ecological context is one of the challenges that lie ahead for peatland microbiologists. At the same time, the individual effects of elevated CO_2, rising temperature, atmospheric deposition, drainage, or permafrost melt on peatlands have been examined in a number of experimental studies. Nevertheless, their combined effect on the microbial community and processes remains difficult to predict (Pendall et al., 2004), even more so in disturbed or restored peatlands, and thus represents a large gap in knowledge that needs to be addressed by future studies. Hypothesis-driven research making good use of new and promising technologies will hopefully help to unravel the intricacies of microbial diversity and its role in C and nutrient cycling under current and future climate and disturbance regimes.

REFERENCES

Andersen, R. (2006). Suivi de la restauration écologique des tourbières ombrotrophes: le point de vue microbiologique. *Le Naturaliste Canadien*, **130**, 25–31.
Andersen, R., Francez, A., Rochefort, L. (2006). The physicochemical and microbiological status of a restored bog in Québec: identification of relevant criteria to monitor success. *Soil Biology and Biochemistry*, **38**, 1375–1387.
Andersen, R., Grasset, L., Thormann, M., Rochefort, L., Francez, A. (2010a). Changes in microbial community structure and function following Sphagnum peatland restoration. *Soil Biology and Biochemistry*, **42**, 291–301.

Andersen, R., Pouliot, R., Rochefort, L., Francez, A., Artz, R. (2010b). Restoring the carbon accumulation function in cutover bogs: do micro-organisms matter? *Reclamation and Restoration of Boreal Peatland and Forest Ecosystems: Toward a Sustainable Future Meeting*, Edmonton, AB, March 25–27, 2010.

Andersen, R., Rochefort, L., Poulin, M. (2010c). Peat, water and plant tissue chemistry monitoring: a seven-year case-study in a restored peatland. *Wetlands*, **30**, 159–170.

Anderson, J. and Domsch, K. (1978). A physiological method for the quantitative measurement of microbial biomass in soils. *Soil Biology and Biochemistry*, **10**, 215–221.

Artz, R. (2009). Microbial community structure and carbon substrate use in northern peatlands. In A. J. Baird, L. R. Belya, X. Comas, A. S. Reeve, L. D. Slater, eds., *Carbon Cycling in Northern Peatlands*. Geophysical monograph series 184, American Geophysical Union, Washington, DC.

Artz, R., Anderson, I., Chapman, S., et al. (2007). Changes in fungal community composition in response to vegetational succession during the natural regeneration of cutover peatlands. *Microbial Ecology*, **54**, 508–522.

Artz, R., Chapman, S., Campbell, C. (2006). Substrate utilisation profiles of microbial communities in peat are depth dependent and correlate with whole soil FTIR profiles. *Soil Biology and Biochemistry*, **38**, 2958–2962.

Artz, R., Chapman, S., Siegenthaler, A., et al. (2008). Functional microbial diversity in regenerating cutover peatlands responds to vegetation succession. *Journal of Applied Ecology*, **45**, 1799–1809.

Bardgett, R. D., Freeman, C., Ostle, N. J. (2008). Microbial contributions to climate change through carbon cycle feedbacks. *The ISME Journal*, **2**, 805–814.

Barkovskii, A. L., Fukui, H., Lesien, J., et al. (2009). Rearrangement of bacterial community structure during peat diagenesis. *Soil Biology and Biochemistry*, **41**, 135–143.

Basiliko, N., Blodau, C., Roehm, C., Bengston, P., Moore, T. R. (2007). Regulation of decomposition and methane dynamics across natural, commercially mined, and restored northern peatlands. *Ecosystems*, **10**, 1148–1165.

Basiliko, N., Yavitt, J., Dees, P., Merkel, S. (2003). Methane biogeochemistry and methanogen communities in two northern peatland ecosystems, New York State. *Geomicrobiology Journal*, **20**, 563–577.

Belova, S., Pankratov, T., Dedysh, S. (2006). Bacteria of the genus Burkholderia as a typical component of the microbial community of Sphagnum peat bogs. *Microbiology*, **75**, 90–96.

Belyea, L. R. (1996). Separating the effects of litter quality and microenvironment on decomposition rates in a patterned peatland. *Oikos*, **77**, 529–539.

Bergner, B., Johnstone, J., Treseder, K. K. (2004). Experimental warming and burn severity alter soil CO_2 flux and soil functional groups in a recently burned boreal forest. *Global Change Biology*, **10**, 1996–2004.

Biryukova, O. V., Fedorak, P. M., Quideau, S. A. (2007). Biodegradation of naphthenic acids by rhizosphere microorganisms. *Chemosphere*, **67**, 2058–2064.

Blodau, C., Basiliko, N., Mayer, B., Moore, T. R. (2006). The fate of experimentally deposited nitrogen in mesocosms from two Canadian peatlands. *Science of the Total Environment*, **364**, 215–228.

Bradford, M. A., Davies, C. A., Frey, S. D., et al. (2008). Thermal adaptation of soil microbial respiration to elevated temperature. *Ecology Letters*, **11**, 1316–1327.

Bräuer, S. L., Cadillo-Quiroz, H., Yashiro, E., Yavitt, J. B., Zinder, S. H. (2006). Isolation of a novel acidiphilic methanogen from an acidic peat bog. *Nature*, **442**, 192–194.

Cadillo-Quiroz, H., Bräuer, S., Yashiro, E., et al. (2006). Vertical profiles of methanogenesis and methanogens in two contrasting acidic peatlands in central New York State, USA. *Environmental Microbiology*, **8**, 1428–1440.

Cadillo-Quiroz, H., Yashiro, E., Yavitt, J. B., Zinder, S. H. (2008a). Archaeal community in a minerotrophic fen and T-RFLP-directed isolation of a novel hydrogenotrophic methanogen. *Applied and Environmental Microbiology*, **74**, 2059–2068.

Cadillo-Quiroz, H., Yashiro, E., Yavitt, J. B., Zinder, S. H. (2008b). Characterization of the archaeal community in a minerotrophic fen and terminal restriction fragment length polymorphism-directed isolation of a novel hydrogenotrophic methanogen. *Applied and Environmental Microbiology*, **74**, 2059.

Cadillo-Quiroz, H., Yavitt, J. B., Zinder, S. H. (2009). *Methanosphaerula palustris* gen. nov., sp. nov., a hydrogenotrophic methanogen isolated from a minerotrophic fen peatland. *International Journal of Systematic and Evolutionary Microbiology*, **59**, 928.

Campbell, C. D., Chapman, S. J., Cameron, C. M., Davidson, M. S., Potts, J. M. (2003). A rapid microtiter plate method to measure carbon dioxide evolved from carbon substrate amendments so as to determine the physiological profiles of soil microbial communities by using whole soil. *Applied and Environmental Microbiology*, **69**, 3593.

Certini, G. (2005). Effects of fire on properties of forest soils: a review. *Oecologia*, **143**, 1–10.

Chapman, S., Buttler, A., Francez, A., et al. (2003). Exploitation of northern peatlands and biodiversity maintenance: a conflict between economy and ecology. *Frontiers in Ecology and the Environment*, **1**, 525–532.

Chen, Y., Dumont, M. G., McNamara, N. P., et al. (2008). Diversity of the active methanotrophic community in acidic peatlands as assessed by mRNA and SIP PLFA analyses. *Environmental Microbiology*, **10**, 446–459.

Chen, Y. and Murrell, J. C. (2010). Geomicrobiology: methanotrophs in moss. *Nature Geoscience*, **3**, 595–596.

Clymo, R. and Bryant, C. (2008). Diffusion and mass flow of dissolved carbon dioxide, methane, and dissolved organic carbon in a 7-m deep raised peat bog. *Geochimica et Cosmochimica Acta*, **72**, 2048–2066.

Clymo, R., Turunen, J., Tolonen, K. (1998). Carbon accumulation in peatland. *Oikos*, **81**, 368–388.

Crill, P., Bartlett, K., Harriss, R., et al. (1988). Methane flux from Minnesota peatlands. *Global Biogeochemical Cycles*, **2**, 371–384.

Croft, M., Rochefort, L., Beauchamp, C. J. (2001). Vacuum-extraction of peatlands disturbs bacterial population and microbial biomass carbon. *Applied Soil Ecology*, **18**, 1–12.

Cudlin, P., Kieliszewska-Rokicka, B., Rudawska, M., et al. (2007). Fine roots and ectomycorrhizas as indicators of environmental change. *Plant Biosystems– An International Journal Dealing with all Aspects of Plant Biology*, **141**, 406–425.

Currey, P. M., Johnson, D., Sheppard, L. J., et al. (2010). Turnover of labile and recalcitrant soil carbon differ in response to nitrate and ammonium deposition in an ombrotrophic peatland. *Global Change Biology*, **16**, 2307–2321.

Davidson, E. A. and Janssens, I. A. (2006). Temperature sensitivity of soil carbon decomposition and feedbacks to climate change. *Nature*, **440**, 165–173.

Dedysh, S. (2002). Methanotrophic bacteria of acidic Sphagnum peat bogs. *Microbiology*, **71**, 638–650.

Dedysh, S. (2009). Exploring methanotroph diversity in acidic northern wetlands: molecular and cultivation-based studies. *Microbiology*, **78**, 655–669.

Dedysh, S. N., Panikov, N. S., Tiedje, J. M. (1998). Acidophilic methanotrophic communities from Sphagnum peat bogs. *Applied and Environmental Microbiology*, **64**, 922.

Dedysh, S. N., Pankratrov, T. A., Belova, S. E., Kulichevskaya, I. S., Liesack, W. (2006). Phylogenetic analysis and in situ identification of bacteria community composition in an acidic Sphagnum peat bog. *Applied and Environmental Microbiology*, **72**, 2110.

Degens, B. P., Schipper, L. A., Sparling, G. P., Duncan, L. C. (2001). Is the microbial community in a soil with reduced catabolic diversity less resistant to stress or disturbance? *Soil Biology and Biochemistry*, **33**, 1143–1153.

Del Rio, L., Hadwin, A., Pinto, L., MacKinnon, M., Moore, M. (2006). Degradation of naphthenic acids by sediment micro organisms. *Journal of Applied Microbiology*, **101**, 1049–1061.

Dickinson, C. (1983). Micro-organisms in peatlands. In A. J. P. Gore, ed., *Ecosystems of the World*. New Haven, CT: Yale University Press.

Dise, N. B. and Verry, E. S. (2001). Suppression of peatland methane emission by cumulative sulfate deposition in simulated acid rain. *Biogeochemistry*, **53**, 143–160.

Dorrepaal, E., Toet, S., Van Logtestijn, R. S. P., et al. (2009). Carbon respiration from subsurface peat accelerated by climate warming in the subarctic. *Nature*, **460**, 616–619.

Fisk, M., Ruether, K., Yavitt, J. (2003). Microbial activity and functional composition among northern peatland ecosystems. *Soil Biology and Biochemistry*, **35**, 591–602.

Francez, A., Gogo, S., Josselin, N. (2000). Distribution of potential CO_2 and CH_4 productions, denitrification and microbial biomass C and N in the profile of a restored peatland in Brittany (France). *European Journal of Soil Biology*, **36**, 161–168.

Freeman, C., Fenner, N., Ostle, N., et al. (2004). Export of dissolved organic carbon from peatlands under elevated carbon dioxide levels. *Nature*, **430**, 195–198.

Freeman, C., Nevison, G., Hughes, S., Reynolds, B., Hudson, J. (1998). Enzymic involvement in the biogeochemical responses of a Welsh peatland to a rainfall enhancement manipulation. *Biology and Fertility of Soils*, **27**, 173–178.

Freitag, T. E. and Prosser, J. I. (2009). Correlation of methane production and functional gene transcriptional activity in a peat soil. *Applied and Environmental Microbiology*, **75**, 6679.

Freitag, T. E., Toet, S., Ineson, P., Prosser, J. I. (2010). Links between methane flux and transcriptional activities of methanogens and methane oxidizers in a blanket peat bog. *FEMS Microbiology Ecology*, **73**, 157–165.

Galand, P., Juottonen, H., Fritze, H., Yrjälä, K. (2005). Methanogen communities in a drained bog: effect of ash fertilization. *Microbial Ecology*, **49**, 209–217.

Galand, P. E. (2004). *Methanogenic Archaea in Boreal Peatlands*. Diss., University of Helsinki, Helsinki.

Galand, P. E., Saarnio, S., Fritze, H., Yrjälä, K. (2002). Depth related diversity of methanogen Archaea in Finnish oligotrophic fen. *FEMS Microbiology Ecology*, **42**, 441–449.

Galloway, M. and Branfireun, B. (2004). Mercury dynamics of a temperate forested wetland. *Science of The Total Environment*, **325**, 239–254.

Garland, J. L. (1996). Analytical approaches to the characterization of samples of microbial communities using patterns of potential C source utilization. *Soil Biology and Biochemistry*, **28**, 213–221.

Gilbert, D., Amblard, C., Bourdier, G., Francez, A. J. (1998). The microbial loop at the surface of a peatland: structure, function, and impact of nutrient input. *Microbial Ecology*, **35**, 83–93.

Gilbert, D., Francez, A. J., Amblard, C., Bourdier, G. (1999). The microbial communities at the surface of the Sphagnum peatlands: good indicators of human disturbances? *Ecologie*, **30**, 45–52.

Gilbert, D. and Mitchell, E. (2006). Microbial diversity in Sphagnum peatlands. In I. P. Martini, A. Matinez Cortizas, W. Chesworth, eds., *Peatlands: Basin Evolution and Depository of Records on Global Environmental and Climatic Changes*. Developments in Earth Surface Processes series. Amsterdam: Elsevier, pp. 287–318.

Glatzel, S., Basiliko, N., Moore, T. (2004). Carbon dioxide and methane production potentials of peats from natural, harvested and restored sites, Eastern Québec, QC. *Wetlands*, **24**, 261–267.

Golovchenko, A., Tikhonova, E. Y., Zvyagintsev, D. (2007). Abundance, biomass, structure, and activity of the microbial complexes of minerotrophic and ombrotrophic peatlands. *Microbiology*, **76**, 630–637.

Graf, M. D. (2009). Literature Review on the Restoration of Alberta's Boreal Wetlands Affected by Oil, Gas and *in situ* Oil Sands Development. Prepared for Ducks Unlimited, Canada.

Graf, M. D., Rezanezhad, F., Andersen, R., et al. (2009). Response of fen plants on peat contaminated with oil sands process-affected waters. Project funded by Suncor Energy Inc., 2009–2010.

Grayston, S. J., Wang, S., Campbell, C. D., Edwards, A. C. (1998). Selective influence of plant species on microbial diversity in the rhizosphere. *Soil Biology and Biochemistry*, **30**, 369–378.

Greenwood, P. F., Wibrow, S., George, S. J., Tibbett, M. (2009). Hydrocarbon biodegradation and soil microbial community response to repeated oil exposure. *Organic Geochemistry*, **40**, 293–300.

Hadwin, A. K. M., Del Rio, L. F., Pinto, L. J., et al. (2006). Microbial communities in wetlands of the Athabasca oil sands: genetic and metabolic characterization. *FEMS Microbiology Ecology*, **55**, 68–78.

Hamberger, A., Horn, M. A., Dumont, M. G., Murrell, J. C., Drake, H. L. (2008). Anaerobic consumers of monosaccharides in a moderately acidic fen. *Applied and Environmental Microbiology*, **74**, 3112.

Hanson, R. S. and Hanson, T. E. (1996). Methanotrophic bacteria. *Microbiology and Molecular Biology Reviews*, **60**, 439.

Harris, J. (2003). Measurements of the soil microbial community for estimating the success of restoration. *European Journal of Soil Science*, **54**, 801–808.

Hart, S. C., Deluca, T. H., Newman, G. S., MacKenzie, M. D., Boyle, S. I. (2005). Postfire vegetative dynamics as drivers of microbial community structure and function in forest soils. *Forest Ecology and Management*, **220**, 166–184.

Heinemeyer, A., Ineson, P., Ostle, N., Fitter, A. (2006). Respiration of the external mycelium in the arbuscular mycorrhizal symbiosis shows strong dependence on recent photosynthates and acclimation to temperature. *New Phytologist*, **171**, 159–170.

Herman, D. C., Fedorak, P. M., MacKinnon, M. D., Costerton, J. (1994). Biodegradation of naphthenic acids by microbial populations indigenous to oil sands tailings. *Canadian Journal of Microbiology*, **40**, 467–477.

Hogg, E. H. (1993). Decay potential of hummock and hollow Sphagnum peats at different depths in a Swedish raised bog. *Oikos*, 269–278.

Jaatinen, K., Fritze, H., Laine, J., Laiho, R. (2007). Effects of short and long term water level drawdown on the populations and activity of aerobic decomposers in a boreal peatland. *Global Change Biology*, **13**, 491–510.

Jaatinen, K., Laiho, R., Vuorenmaa, A., et al. (2008). Responses of aerobic microbial communities and soil respiration to water level drawdown in a northern boreal fen. *Environmental Microbiology*, **10**, 339–353.

Jaatinen, K., Tuittila, E. S., Laine, J., Yrjälä, K., Fritze, H. (2005). Methanotrophic bacteria in Finnish raised bog complex: effects of site fertility and drainage. *Pro Terra*, **22**, 40–41.

Jassey, V. E. J., Gilbert, D., Binet, P., Toussaint, M. L., Chiapusio, G. (2011). Effect of a temperature gradient on *Sphagnum fallax* and its associated living microbial communities: a study under controlled conditions. *Canadian Journal of Microbiology*, **57**, 226–235.

Johnson, L. C. and Damman, A. W. H. (1991). Species-controlled Sphagnum decay on a south Swedish raised bog. *Oikos*, **61**, 234–242.

Johnson, L. C., Damman, A. W. H., Malmer, N. (1990). Sphagnum macrostructure as an indicator of decay and compaction in peat cores from an ombrotrophic south Swedish peat-bog. *Journal of Ecology*, **78**, 633–647.

Juottonen, H. (2008). *Archaea, Bacteria, and Methane Production along Environmental Gradients in Fens and Bogs*. Ph.D. thesis, University of Helsinki, Helsinki.

Juottonen, H., Galand, P. E., Tuitilla, E. S., et al. (2005). Methanogen communities and bacteria along an ecohydrological gradient in a northern raised bog complex. *Environmental Microbiology*, **7**, 1547–1557.

Kachalkin, A., Glushakova, A., Yurkov, A., Chernov, I. Y. (2008). Characterization of yeast groupings in the phyllosphere of Sphagnum mosses. *Microbiology*, **77**, 474–481.

Kasischke, E. S., Christensen J. R. N., Stocks, B. J. (1995). Fire, global warming, and the carbon balance of boreal forests. *Ecological Applications*, **5**, 437–451.

Kasischke, E. S. and Johnstone, J. F. (2005). Variation in postfire organic layer thickness in a black spruce forest complex in interior Alaska and its effects on soil temperature and moisture. *Canadian Journal of Forest Research*, **35**, 2164–2177.

Kasischke, E. S. and Turetsky, M. R. (2006). Recent changes in the fire regime across the North American boreal region – spatial and temporal patterns of burning across Canada and Alaska. *Geophysical Research Letters*, **33**, L09703.

Kellogg, L. E. and Bridgham, S. D. (2003). Phosphorus retention and movement across an ombrotrophic-minerotrophic peatland gradient. *Biogeochemistry*, **63**, 299–315.

Kelly, C. A., Dise, N. B., Martens, C. S. (1992). Temporal variations in the stable carbon isotopic composition of methane emitted from Minnesota peatlands. *Global Biogeochemical Cycles*, **6**, 263–269.

Kim, S. Y., Lee, S. H., Freeman, C., Fenner, N., Kang, H. (2008). Comparative analysis of soil microbial communities and their responses to the short-term drought in bog, fen, and riparian wetlands. *Soil Biology and Biochemistry*, **40**, 2874–2880.

Kip, N., Van Winden, J. F., Pan, Y., et al. (2010). Global prevalence of methane oxidation by symbiotic bacteria in peat-moss ecosystems. *Nature Geoscience*, **3**, 617–621.

Kirschbaum, M. U. F. (2004). Soil respiration under prolonged soil warming: are rate reductions caused by acclimation or substrate loss? *Global Change Biology*, **10**, 1870–1877.

Knorr, W., Prentice, I. C., House, J. I., Holland, E. A. (2005). Long-term sensitivity of soil carbon turnover to warming. *Nature*, **433**, 298–301.

Kuhry, P. (1994). The role of fire in the development of Sphagnum-dominated peatlands in western boreal Canada. *Journal of Ecology*, **82**, 899–910.

Laggoun Défarge, F., Mitchell, E., Gilbert, D., et al. (2008). Cut over peatland regeneration assessment using organic matter and microbial indicators (bacteria and testate amoebae). *Journal of Applied Ecology*, **45**, 716–727.

Laiho, R. (2006). Decomposition in peatlands: reconciling seemingly contrasting results on the impacts of lowered water levels. *Soil Biology and Biochemistry*, **38**, 2011–2024.

Larmola, T., Tuittila, E. S., Tiirola, M., et al. (2010). The role of Sphagnum mosses in the methane cycling of a boreal mire. *Ecology*, **91**, 2356–2365.

Latter, P. M., Cragg, J., Heal, O. (1967). Comparative studies on the microbiology of four moorland soils in the northern Pennines. *Journal of Ecology*, **55**, 445–464.

Limpens, J., Berendse, F., Klees, H. (2003). N deposition affects N availability in interstitial water, growth of Sphagnum and invasion of vascular plants in bog vegetation. *New Phytologist*, **157**, 339–347.

Limpens, J., Heijmans, M. M. P. D., Berendse, F. (2006). The nitrogen cycle in boreal peatlands. *Boreal Peatland Ecosystems*, **188**, 195–230.

Lumley, T. C., Gignac, L. D., Currah, R. S. (2001). Microfungus communities of white spruce and trembling aspen logs at different stages of decay in disturbed and undisturbed sites in the boreal mixedwood region of Alberta. *Botany*, **79**, 76–92.

Malcolm, G. M., López-Gutiérrez, J. C., Koide, R. T., Eissenstat, D. M. (2008). Acclimation to temperature and temperature sensitivity of metabolism by ectomycorrhizal fungi. *Global Change Biology*, **14**, 1169–1180.

Marilley, L. and Aragno, M. (1999). Phylogenetic diversity of bacterial communities differing in degree of proximity of *Lolium perenne* and *Trifolium repens* roots. *Applied Soil Ecology*, **13**, 127–136.

Mastepanov, M., Sigsgaard, C., Dlugokencky, E. J., et al. (2008). Large tundra methane burst during onset of freezing. *Nature*, **456**, 628–630.

Merilä, P., Galand, P. E., Fritze, H., et al. (2006). Methanogen communities along a primary succession transect of mire ecosystems. *FEMS Microbiology Ecology*, **55**, 221–229.

Mitchell, E. A. D., Gilbert, D., Buttler, A., et al. (2003). Structure of microbial communities in Sphagnum peatlands and effect of atmospheric carbon dioxide enrichment. *Microbial Ecology*, **46**, 187–199.

Moore, P. and Bellamy, D. (1974). *Peatlands*. London, UK: Elek Science.

Morales, S. E., Mouser, P. J., Ward, N., et al. (2006). Comparison of bacterial communities in New England Sphagnum bogs using terminal restriction fragment length polymorphism (T-RFLP). *Microbial Ecology*, **52**, 34–44.

Myers-Smith, I., Harden, J., Wilmking, M., et al. (2008). Wetland succession in a permafrost collapse: interactions between fire and thermokarst. *Biogeosciences*, **5**, 1273–1286.

Newell, S., Moran, M., Wicks, R., Hodson, R. (1995). Productivities of microbial decomposers during early stages of decomposition of leaves of a freshwater sedge. *Freshwater Biology*, **34**, 135–148.

Newman, E. and Reddell, P. (1987). The distribution of mycorrhizas among families of vascular plants. *New Phytologist*, **106**, 745–751.

Nyman, J. (1999). Effect of crude oil and chemical additives on metabolic activity of mixed microbial populations in fresh marsh soils. *Microbial Ecology*, **37**, 152–162.

Oechel, W. C., Vourlitis, G. L., Hastings, S. J., et al. (2000). Acclimation of ecosystem CO_2 exchange in the Alaskan Arctic in response to decadal climate warming. *Nature*, **406**, 978–981.

Op Den Camp, H. J. M., Islam, T., Stott, M. B., et al. (2009). Environmental, genomic and taxonomic perspectives on methanotrophic Verrucomicrobia. *Environmental Microbiology Reports*, **1**, 293–306.

Opelt, K., Berg, C., Schönmann, S., Eberl, L., Berg, G. (2007). High specificity but contrasting biodiversity of Sphagnum-associated bacterial and plant communities in bog ecosystems independent of the geographical region. *ISME Journal*, **1**, 502–516.

Pankratov, T. and Dedysh, S. (2009). Cellulolytic streptomycetes from Sphagnum peat bogs and factors controlling their activity. *Microbiology*, **78**, 227–233.

Pankratov, T. A., Kulichevskaya, I. S., Liesack, W., Dedysh, S. N. (2006). Isolation of aerobic, gliding, xylanolytic and laminarinolytic bacteria from acidic Sphagnum peatlands and emended description of *Chitinophaga arvensicola* Kampfer et al., 2006. *International Journal of Systematic and Evolutionary Microbiology*, **56**, 2761–2764.

Peltoniemi, K., Fritze, H., Laiho, R. (2009). Response of fungal and actinobacterial communities to water-level drawdown in boreal peatland sites. *Soil Biology and Biochemistry*, **41**, 1902–1914.

Pendall, E., Bridgham, S., Hanson, P. J., et al. (2004). Below ground process responses to elevated CO2 and temperature: a discussion of observations, measurement methods, and models. *New Phytologist*, **162**, 311–322.

Pester, M., Bittner, N., Deevong, P., Wagner, M., Loy, A. (2010). A 'rare biosphere' microorganism contributes to sulfate reduction in a peatland. *ISME Journal*, **4**, 1591–1602.

Piercey, M., Thormann, M., Currah, R. (2002). Saprobic characteristics of three fungal taxa from ericalean roots and their association with the roots of *Rhododendron groenlandicum* and *Picea mariana* in culture. *Mycorrhiza*, **12**, 175–180.

Popp, T. J., Chanton, J. P., Whiting, G. J., Grant, N. (2000). Evaluation of methane oxidation in the rhizosphere of a Carex dominated fen in northcentral Alberta, Canada. *Biogeochemistry*, **51**, 259–281.

Potila, H. (2004). *Mycorrhizal Fungi and Nitrogen Dynamics in Drained Peatland.* Ph.D. thesis, University of Helsinki, Helsinki.

Poulin, M., Rochefort, L., Pellerin, S., Thibault, J. (2004). Threats and protection for peatlands in Eastern Canada. *Géocarrefour*, **79**, 331–344.

Price, J., Heathwaite, A., Baird, A. (2003). Hydrological processes in abandoned and restored peatlands: an overview of management approaches. *Wetlands Ecology and Management*, **11**, 65–83.

Price, J. S., McClaren, R. G., Rudolph, D. L. (2010). Landscape restoration after oil sands mining: conceptual design and hydrological modelling for fen reconstruction. *International Journal of Mining, Reclamation and Environment*, **24**, 109–123.

Putkinen, A., Juottonen, H., Juutinen, S., et al. (2009). Archaeal rRNA diversity and methane production in deep boreal peat. *FEMS Microbiology Ecology*, **70**, 87–98.

Quilliam, R. S. and Jones, D. L. (2010). Fungal root endophytes of the carnivorous plant *Drosera rotundifolia*. *Mycorrhiza*, **20**, 341–348.

Raghoebarsing, A. A., Pol, A., Van De Pas-Schoonen, K. T., et al. (2006). A microbial consortium couples anaerobic methane oxidation to denitrification. *Nature*, **440**, 918–921.

Raghoebarsing, A. A., Smolders, A. J. P., Schmid, M. C., et al. (2005). Methanotrophic symbionts provide carbon for photosynthesis in peat bogs. *Nature*, **436**, 1153–1156.

Read, D. J., Leake, J. R., Perez-Moreno, J. (2004). Mycorrhizal fungi as drivers of ecosystem processes in heathland and boreal forest biomes. *Botany*, **82**, 1243–1263.

Rochefort, L., Quinty, F., Campeau, S., Johnson, K., Malterer, T. (2003). North American approach to the restoration of Sphagnum dominated peatlands. *Wetlands Ecology and Management*, **11**, 3–20.

Rooney Varga, J. N., Giewat, M. W., Duddleston, K. N., Chanton, J. P., Hines, M. E. (2007). Links between archaeal community structure, vegetation type and methanogenic pathway in Alaskan peatlands. *FEMS Microbiology Ecology*, **60**, 240–251.

Selosse, M. A., Setaro, S., Glatard, F., et al. (2007). Sebacinales are common mycorrhizal associates of Ericaceae. *New Phytologist*, **174**, 864–878.

Sibly, R. M. and Calow, P. (1989). A life-cycle theory of responses to stress. *Biological Journal of the Linnean Society*, **37**, 101–116.

Strack, M., Waddington, J., Tuittila, E. S. (2004). Effect of water table drawdown on northern peatland methane dynamics: implications for climate change. *Global Biogeochemical Cycles*, **18**, GB4003.

Sundh, I., Borgå, P., Nilsson, M., Svensson, B. H. (1995). Estimation of cell numbers of methanotrophic bacteria in boreal peatlands based on analysis of specific phospholipid fatty acids. *FEMS Microbiology Ecology*, **18**, 103–112.

Sundh, I., Nilsson, M., Borga, P. (1997). Variation in microbial community structure in two boreal peatlands as determined by analysis of phospholipid fatty acid profiles. *Applied and Environmental Microbiology*, **63**, 1476.

Tape, K., Sturm, M., Racine, C. (2006). The evidence for shrub expansion in Northern Alaska and the Pan-Arctic. *Global Change Biology*, **12**, 686–702.

Thormann, M. (2006a). The role of fungi in boreal peatlands. *Boreal Peatland Ecosystems*, **188**, 101–123.

Thormann, M. and Rice, A. (2007). Fungi from peatlands. *Fungal Diversity*, **24**, 241–299.

Thormann, M. N. (2006b). Diversity and function of fungi in peatlands: a carbon cycling perspective. *Canadian Journal of Soil Science*, **86**, 281.

Thormann, M. N., Bayley, S. E., Currah, R. S. (2001a). Comparison of decomposition of belowground and aboveground plant litters in peatlands of boreal Alberta, Canada. *Botany*, **79**, 9–22.

Thormann, M. N., Bayley, S. E., Currah, R. S. (2004a). Microcosm tests of the effects of temperature and microbial species number on the decomposition of *Carex aquatilis* and *Sphagnum fuscum* litter from southern boreal peatlands. *Canadian Journal of Microbiology*, **50**, 793–802.

Thormann, M. N., Currah, R. S., Bayley, S. E. (1999). The mycorrhizal status of the dominant vegetation along a peatland gradient in southern boreal Alberta, Canada. *Wetlands*, **19**, 438–450.

Thormann, M. N., Currah, R. S., Bayley, S. E. (2001b). Microfungi isolated from *Sphagnum fuscum* from a southern boreal bog in Alberta, Canada. *Bryologist*, **104**, 548–559.

Thormann, M. N., Currah, R. S., Bayley, S. E. (2003). Succession of microfungal assemblages in decomposing peatland plants. *Plant and Soil*, **250**, 323–333.

Thormann, M. N., Currah, R. S., Bayley, S. E. (2004b). Patterns of distribution of microfungi in decomposing bog and fen plants. *Botany*, **82**, 710–720.

Thormann, M. N., Rice, A. V., Beilman, D. W. (2007). Yeasts in peatlands: a review of richness and roles in peat decomposition. *Wetlands*, **27**, 761–773.

Treseder, K. and Allen, M. (2000). Mycorrhizal fungi have a potential role in soil carbon storage under elevated CO_2 and nitrogen deposition. *New Phytologist*, **147**, 189–200.

Treseder, K. K., Mack, M. C., Cross, A. (2004). Relationships among fires, fungi, and soil dynamics in Alaskan boreal forests. *Ecological Applications*, **14**, 1826–1838.

Trinder, C., Johnson, D., Artz, R. (2009). Litter type, but not plant cover, regulates initial litter decomposition and fungal community structure in a recolonising cutover peatland. *Soil Biology and Biochemistry*, **41**, 651–655.

Trinder, C. J., Johnson, D., Artz, R. R. E. (2008). Interactions among fungal community structure, litter decomposition and depth of water table in a cutover peatland. *FEMS Microbiology Ecology*, **64**, 433–448.

Tunlid, A., Ringelberg, D., Phelps, T., Low, C., White, D. (1989). Measurement of phospholipid fatty acids at picomolar concentrations in biofilms and deep subsurface sediments using gas chromatography and chemical ionization mass spectrometry. *Journal of Microbiological Methods*, **10**, 139–153.

Tunlid, A. and White, D. C. (1990). Use of lipid biomarkers in environmental samples. In A. Fox, S. L. Morgan, L. Larsson, G. Odham, eds., *Analytical Microbiology Methods: Chromatography and Mass Spectrometry*. New York, NY: Plemun Press, pp. 259–274.

Turetsky, M., Amiro, B., Bosch, E., Bhatti, J. (2004). Historical burn area in western Canadian peatlands and its relationship to fire weather indices. *Global Biogeochemical Cycles*, **18**, GB4014.

Turetsky, M., Wieder, K., Halsey, L., Vitt, D. (2002). Current disturbance and the diminishing peatland carbon sink. *Geophysical Research Letters*, **29**, 21–1.

Turetsky, M., Wieder, R., Williams, C., Vitt, D. (2000). Organic matter accumulation, peat chemistry, and permafrost melting in peatlands of boreal Alberta. *Ecoscience*, **7**, 379–392.

Van Der Heijden, M. G. A., Bardgett, R. D., Van Straalen, N. M. (2008). The unseen majority: soil microbes as drivers of plant diversity and productivity in terrestrial ecosystems. *Ecology Letters*, **11**, 296–310.

Vance, E., Brookes, P., Jenkinson, D. (1987). An extraction method for measuring soil microbial biomass C. *Soil Biology and Biochemistry*, **19**, 703–707.

Verhoeven, J. T. A., Keuter, A., Van Logtestijn, R., Van Kerkhoven, M. B., Wassen, M. (1996). Control of local nutrient dynamics in mires by regional and climatic factors: a comparison of Dutch and Polish sites. *Journal of Ecology*, **84**, 647–656.

Viereck, L. A. (1982). Effects of fire and firelines on active layer thickness and soil temperatures in interior Alaska. US Forest Service.

Vile, M. A., Bridgham, S. D., Wieder, R. K., Novák, M. (2003). Atmospheric sulfur deposition alters pathways of gaseous carbon production in peatlands. *Global Biogeochemical Cycles*, **17**, 1058.

Vitt, D., Halsey, L., Bauer, I., Campbell, C. (2000). Spatial and temporal trends in carbon storage of peatlands of continental western Canada through the Holocene. *Canadian Journal of Earth Sciences*, **37**, 683–693.

Vitt, D. H., Halsey, L. A., Zoltai, S. C. (1994). The bog landforms of continental western Canada in relation to climate and permafrost patterns. *Arctic and Alpine Research*, **26**, 1–13.

Vitt, D., Koropchak, S., Xu, B., et al. (2010). Rebuilding Peatlands on Mineral Soils Utilizing Lessons Learned from Past Peatland Initiation. *Reclamation and Restoration of Boreal Peatland and Forest Ecosystems: Toward a Sustainable Future*. Southern Illinois University, Carbondale, IL.

Vitt, D. H., Wieder, R. K., Xu, B., Kaskie, M., Koropchak, S. (2011). Peatland establishment on mineral soils: effects of water level, amendments, and species after two growing seasons. *Ecological Engineering*, **37**, 354–363.

Waddington, J., Greenwood, M., Petrone, R., Price, J. (2003). Mulch decomposition impedes recovery of net carbon sink function in a restored peatland. *Ecological Engineering*, **20**, 199–210.

Walbridge, M. R. and Navaratnam, J. A. (2006). Phosphorous in boreal peatlands. *Boreal Peatland Ecosystems*, **188**, 231–258.

Waldrop, M. P. and Harden, J. W. (2008). Interactive effects of wildfire and permafrost on microbial communities and soil processes in an Alaskan black spruce forest. *Global Change Biology*, **14**, 2591–2602.

Waughman, G. and Bellamy, D. (1980). Nitrogen fixation and the nitrogen balance in peatland ecosystems. *Ecology*, **61**, 1185–1198.

Weber, K. P. and Legge, R. L. (2010). Dynamics in the bacterial community-level physiological profiles and hydrological characteristics of constructed wetland mesocosms during start-up. *Ecological Engineering*, **37**, 666–677.

Welsh, D. T. (2000). Ecological significance of compatible solute accumulation by micro organisms: from single cells to global climate. *FEMS Microbiology Reviews*, **24**, 263–290.

Whitby, C. (2010). Microbial naphthenic acid degradation. *Advances in Applied Microbiology*, **70**, 93–125.

Wieder, R. K. and Lang, G. E. (1988). Cycling of inorganic and organic sulfur in peat from Big Run Bog, West Virginia. *Biogeochemistry*, **5**, 221–242.

Wieder, R. K., Scott, K. D., Kamminga, K., et al. (2009). Postfire carbon balance in boreal bogs of Alberta, Canada. *Global Change Biology*, **15**, 63–81.

Wieder, R. K., Yavitt, J. B., Lang, G. E. (1990). Methane production and sulfate reduction in two Appalachian peatlands. *Biogeochemistry*, **10**, 81–104.

Williams, R. T. and Crawford, R. L. (1983). Microbial diversity of Minnesota peatlands. *Microbial ecology*, **9**, 201–214.

Winsborough, C. and Basiliko, N. (2009). Bacterial and Fungal Activities of Northern Peatland Ecosystems. *Eos Transactions, American Geophysical Union*, **90**, B73A-15.

Yan, W., Artz, R. R. E. and Johnson, D. (2008). Species-specific effects of plants colonising cutover peatlands on patterns of carbon source utilisation by soil microorganisms. *Soil Biology and Biochemistry*, **40**, 544–549.

Yesmin, L., Gammack, S. M., Cresser, M. S. (1996). Effects of atmospheric nitrogen deposition on ericoid mycorrhizal infection of *Calluna vulgaris* growing in peat soils. *Applied Soil Ecology*, **4**, 49–60.

Young, B., Varner, R., Larmola, T., Bubier, J. (2010). The role of sphagnum mosses in methane cycling of a temperate fen. Abstract 0292, presented at 2010 Fall Meeting, American Geophysical Union, San Francisco, CA.

Zadorina, E., Slobodova, N., Boulygina, E., et al. (2009). Analysis of the diversity of diazotrophic bacteria in peat soil by cloning of the nifH gene. *Microbiology*, **78**, 218–226.

Zak, D. R., Pegitzer, K. S., King, J. S., Holmes, W. E. (2000). Elevated atmospheric CO_2, fine roots and the response of soil microorganisms: a review and hypothesis. *New Phytologist*, **147**, 201–222.

Zinder, S. H. (1993). Physiological ecology of methanogens. In J. G. Ferry, ed., *Methanogenesis: Ecology, Physiology, Biochemistry and Genetics*. New York, NY: Chapman and Hall, pp. 128–206.

Zoltai, S., Morrissey, L., Livingston, G., Groot, W. (1998). Effects of fires on carbon cycling in North American boreal peatlands. *Environmental Reviews*, **6**, 13–24.

Part III   Carbon in the boreal forest

14

Carbon and nitrogen stocks in western boreal forest ecosystems

INTRODUCTION

Approximately half of the total Canadian landmass (410 Mha) is covered by forest (Natural Resources Canada, 2004), with boreal forests as the dominant forest type, spanning the entire width of the country. Forest biomass, detritus, and soil are the three major pools of carbon (C) in forest ecosystems. Aboveground and belowground biomass, forest floor, and mineral soils in Canadian boreal forests contain approximately 200 Pg of C (excluding peat), which represents approximately 15% of the total amount of C stored in the terrestrial biosphere (Bhatti and Tarnocai, 2009; Goodale et al., 2002). Understanding the factors controlling these pools and the exchange of C among them and the atmosphere is critical for estimating the role of forests in the global C cycle (Bond-Lamberty et al., 2007; Bonan, 2008; Kurz et al. 2008; Sun et al., 2008). Changes in forest ecosystem C pools are driven primarily by the dynamics of the living biomass. The C stocks in the forest floor and soil change substantially with respect to both natural (fire, insects) and anthropogenic (harvesting, landuse change, oil and gas development) disturbances. Land-use change in northern Alberta, with widespread construction of roads, pipelines, seismic lines, power transmission lines, and well pads (Jordaan et al., 2009) for oil, gas, and *in situ* oil sands development, has altered the balance of both hydrological and C cycles on all scales (Yeh et al., 2010). Disturbances transfer biomass C to detritus and soil C pools, where it decomposes at various rates over the years following the disturbance (Seedre et al., 2011). Soil C stocks are characterized by long residence times relative to other biological C pools. This is particularly true in boreal and cold

Restoration and Reclamation of Boreal Ecosystems, ed. Dale Vitt and Jagtar Bhatti. Published by Cambridge University Press. © Cambridge University Press 2012.

temperate zones where the soils have high C contents (Wang et al., 2003). Linear disturbances may contribute to or accelerate the effects of climate change by acting as starting points for contagious processes (Turetsky and St. Louis, 2006).

The type of disturbance, along with climate, soil moisture, temperature, nutrient availability, and soil texture controls the primary processes of production and decomposition, which in turn regulate net ecosystem C dynamics (Kurz et al., 2008; Seedre et al., 2011). Accumulation of biomass C is affected by site-specific factors and by disturbance patterns. Through disturbance, there is direct release of C to the atmosphere, as well as transfer to the forest floor and soil pool, and indirect release of C resulting from modifications to site factors (Bond-Lamberty et al., 2004; Howard et al., 2004). This feedback of disturbance effects on site factors influences the accumulation, transfer, and release of C and is particularly important. Interactions between climate change and altered disturbance regimes, for example, or cumulative impacts arising from the joint action of climatic and anthropogenic change, might alter the C balance significantly. Therefore, there is a strong need for across-scale and across-ecosystem studies to assess the overall change on the landscape level. Our understanding of these changes in landscape can be informed by empirical data on stand-level C and nitrogen (N) stocks. In this paper, C and N pools data have been summarized, both regionally and at the stand level. Site variables are also assessed and related to stand growth and C and N distribution.

METHODS

Total C and N storage were estimated from two different sources (Shaw et al., 2005; Siltanen et al., 1997) .

Description of the databases

The Ecosystem Carbon Database for Canadian Forests (ECD) comprises data from 706 plots across Canada, with 494 of these located in the western boreal forest. Depending upon site conditions, the main tree species of the western boreal plots include trembling aspen (*Populus tremuloides*), black spruce (*Picea mariana*), jack pine (*Pinus banksiana*), lodgepole pine (*Pinus contorta*), white spruce (*Picea glauca*), balsam fir (*Abies balsamea*), and mixedwood. Field-observed data from Shaw et al. (2005) provided both tree biomass and site and soil information, such as: site characteristics, soil drainage class, forest floor thickness, bulk density, total N content,

C content, mineral soil horizon thickness, % clay content, and % silt content. Siltanen et al. (1997) include 374 sites in the western boreal, with the majority located in Alberta, Saskatchewan, and Manitoba. From this database, 82 sites were excluded due to missing data. This database does not have aboveground biomass information, but does have information on soil drainage class, forest floor thickness, bulk density, total N and C content, mineral soil horizon thickness, % clay content, and % silt content. The dominant plant species on these sites included aspen (*Populus tremuloides*), black spruce (*Picea mariana*), jack pine (*Pinus banksiana*), and white spruce (*Picea glauca*).

For further analysis, data from 142 plots included in the ECDCF, all located in the oil sand region of Alberta (between 51°23′–59°50′N latitude and 110°00′–115°59′W longitude), were used in the present study. Data for tree biomass, forest floor, and soil C were compiled from 11 aspen (*Populus tremuloides*) stands, 16 black spruce (*Picea mariana*) stands, 8 jack pine (*Pinus banksiana*) stands, 43 lodgepole pine (*Pinus contorta)* stands, and 57 white spruce (*Picea glauca*) stands. For this report, jack pine and lodgepole pine data points were combined. Regression analyses were used to ascertain the relationship between aboveground biomass with clay content and total N in relation to forest floor C content. The best regression equation was chosen based on the adjusted r^2. Soil C from 142 sites was also related to different drainage classes.

Annual biomass increment estimate

Plots from the ECD located in the oil sands region of Alberta were also used to analyze annual aboveground biomass increment (MBI) for each forest species (aspen, white spruce, pines, and black spruce) using the equation:

Field-estimated MBI (tons ha^{-1} yr^{-1})

$$= \text{total aboveground tree biomass age}^{-1}. \qquad [14.1]$$

For this equation, C stocks were first estimated by multiplying the aboveground biomass by a factor of 0.5 (carbon fraction) (IPCC 2003), and their values were then used to further analyze the relationships.

Estimation of aboveground net primary productivity

Increment cores were collected from nine dominant trees of jack pine and black spruce from fixed area tree mensuration sample plots located near

Anzac, AB, in the oil sand region. Tree ring data were used to reconstruct historical tree diameters and heights, using regional species-specific relationships. These historical tree dimensions were used in conjunction with published biomass functions and/or local site-specific functions to calculate historical tree biomass and (by difference) changes in biomass. Change in biomass was averaged across the nine stand trees and scaled by proportion to the entire stand (of which the biomass was estimated using mensuration data and biomass functions).

Forest litterfall was collected over a three-year period (2007–2010) using a combination of buckets and open mesh screens. Each site incorporated 16 plastic buckets (20.3 cm in diameter by 20 cm tall, with an aluminum window screen bottom) for collecting leaves, needles, bark, cones, and twigs smaller than 10 cm in length. The screened bottoms ensured that the buckets and their contents dried out as quickly as possible after a rainfall and minimized environmental degradation. Because the openings on the buckets were too small to allow random collection of larger litter, each site also included four plastic open-mesh screen quadrats (0.83 m^2 surface area) staked out on the forest floor, where twigs larger than 10 cm long were collected.

The annual litterfall weights were added to the stand-level changes in tree biomass to yield aboveground net primary productivity (ANPP) for each site. This method of ANPP estimation incorporates those components that constitute the largest proportion of ANPP (i.e., tree biomass increment and foliar production) (Comeau and Kimmins, 1989) and is commonly used as a simple, direct measurement of forest productivity (Smith et al., 2002). It does not, however, include belowground NPP, and disregards other components that contribute to total ANPP, namely tree mortality and biomass lost to herbivory. Tree mortality effects are usually only a few percent over a short term, and herbivory usually accounts for 1.5 to 2.5% of NPP under non-infestation conditions (Gower et al., 1999); thus both errors were effectively ignored in our ANPP estimates.

RESULTS AND DISCUSSION

Aboveground biomass, biomass increment, and aboveground net primary productivity

Aboveground biomass in the western boreal forest varied between 22 and 187 Mg ha^{-1}. Conversion of biomass to C indicates that C storage in these boreal forests ranges from 31 to 177 Mg C ha^{-1} for well-drained sites and from 20 to 143 Mg C ha^{-1} for poorly drained sites. Further analysis of the

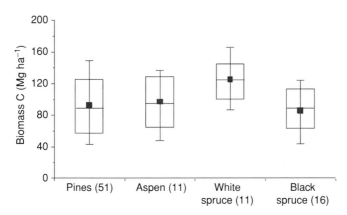

Figure 14.1. Carbon (C) content in aboveground biomass for trembling aspen (*Populus tremuloides*), pines (jack pine [*Pinus banksiana*] and lodgepole pine [*Pinus contorta*]), white spruce (*Picea glauca*), and black spruce (*Picea mariana*). Numbers in parentheses denote the number of stands in the database for each forest type.

data for the oil stand region of Alberta shows that tree biomass strongly depended upon the tree species (Figure 14.1). Black spruce and pines had lower biomass C as compared to white spruce. These values are similar to values for biomass C reported by Banfield et al. (2002); Chertov et al. (2009); and Wang et al. (2003) for the boreal forests of Canada.

Several factors influence the variability of biomass C across the landscape, including climatic conditions, disturbance history, successional stage, vegetation distribution, and site factors. The aboveground biomass in the boreal zone was related to the soil clay content for upland forests (Figure 14.2). The results are consistent with those of Banfield et al. (2002) for the same range of clay content in the west central Alberta. The significance of the relationship between soil clay content and aboveground biomass suggests that soil clay content plays a major role in providing both soil nutrients and the physical environment for plant growth. Aboveground biomass increases with increasing clay content over an initial range, but then decreases rapidly. Indeed, clay content above a threshold of about 45% appears to limit biomass growth, potentially due to restriction of soil rooting volume and poor aeration.

Average biomass increments for different species ranges from 0.82 Mg /ha^{-1} /yr^{-1} for black spruce, 0.96 Mg /ha^{-1} yr^{-1} for pines, 1.11 Mg ha^{-1} yr^{-1} for aspen, and 1.29 Mg ha^{-1}yr^{-1} for white spruce growing in moderately well-drained conditions. These estimates were within the range of values observed for coniferous species. The mean biomass increment

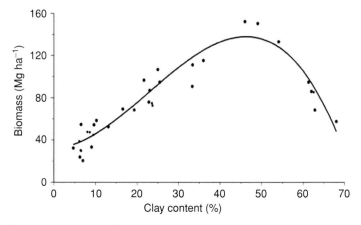

Figure 14.2. Relationship between percentage clay content and aboveground biomass under well-drained and moderately well-drained mature jack pine and lodgepole pine stands ($Y = 3.19 + 0.20^*X + 0.14^*X^2 - 0.0021^*X^3$; $r^2 = 0.89$; $n = 34$).

was estimated to be 0.8 Mg ha^{-1}yr^{-1} for forests younger than 20 years, and 1.5 Mg ha^{-1}yr^{-1} for forests older than 20 years. The mean annual increment for white spruce varies between 1.15 and 1.29 Mg ha^{-1}yr^{-1} depending upon the soil drainage conditions, signifying that soil moisture availability is an important factor in tree productivity in the oil sand region of Alberta. These results are consistent with the conclusions of Hogg et al. (2005), who found that interannual variation in regional-scale aspen growth could be explained by two important factors: the climate moisture index (precipitation − potential evapotranspiration) and insect defoliation. Further analysis of the impact of various climate variables on stem C increment is recommended to help determine what factors influence the interannual variability for different species in the region.

In the oil sands region, ANPP was estimated for jack pine and black spruce. The average ANPP over the last 20 years (1988−1908) was 1.14 Mg C ha^{-1} yr^{-1} and 0.65 Mg C ha^{-1} yr^{-1} for black spruce and jack pine, respectively (Figure 14.3). There was a general increase in black spruce ANPP, while jack pine remained the same. These observations are from a limited number of stands (two black spruce and two jack pine) in the area. As past mortality was not considered in the estimation of tree productivity over these last 20 years, the upward trend observed with the increase in black spruce could be an artifact. However, observed ANPP values in this study are within previously reported ranges for boreal forests (Gower et al., 2001). Based on data documented in boreal forest research

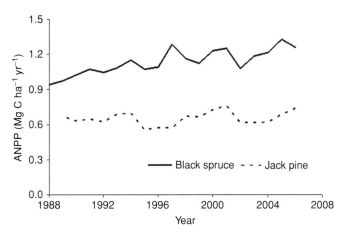

Figure 14.3. Aboveground net primary productivity of black spruce (*Picea mariana*) and jack pine (*Pinus banksiana*) stands near Anzac, AB, from 1988 to 2006. ANPP, aboveground net primary productivity.

published in the United States, Canada, Finland, Sweden, and China, Gower et al. (2001) estimated an average belowground ANPP of 1.1 and 1.0 Mg C ha^{-1} yr^{-1} for deciduous and evergreen boreal forests, respectively, which are relatively consistent with the field measurements. Additionally, Bond-Lamberty et al. (2004) observed a significant increase in ANPP (from 1.24 to 1.45 Mg C ha^{-1} yr^{-1}) for the black spruce stand in Thompson, MB, between 1993 and 2002.

Forest floor carbon and nitrogen stocks

The forest floor C in western boreal forest soils (litter fermentation humus [LFH] plus litter humus [LH]) was observed to vary about an average of 37 Mg ha^{-1}, with values between 16 Mg ha^{-1} and 50 Mg ha^{-1}. Nitrogen concentrations ranged from 0.24% to 2.34%, with an average of 1.14% in the western boreal forest. The observed variability in C and N content could be due to changeability of three variables, namely the concentration of C or N, the soil bulk density, and the depth of the forest floor. The mean values of forest floor organic C are close to the 33 Mg C ha^{-1} reported by Norris et al. (2009) and Preston et al. (2006) for the boreal forest, and to the 16–37 Mg C ha^{-1} reported by Hunt et al. (2010), but differ significantly from the estimated surface soil organic C contents of 118 Mg ha^{-1} reported by Tarnocai (1998). However, the higher level of C reported by Tarnocai (1998) is likely due to the inclusion of organic soils, agricultural soils, and other soil types along with the upland forested soils in the

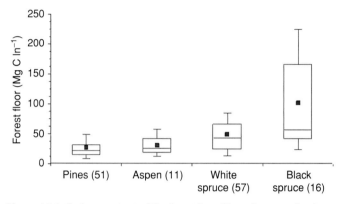

Figure 14.4. Carbon content of the forest floor (litter fermentation humus horizon) for trembling aspen (*Populus tremuloides*), pines (jack pine [*Pinus banksiana*] and lodgepole pine [*Pinus contorta*]), white spruce (*Picea glauca*), and black spruce (*Picea mariana*). Numbers in parentheses denote the number of stands in the database for each forest type.

estimation of C in the boreal zone. Our values are also much lower than the average of 83 Mg C ha^{-1} in southeast Alaska (Alexander et al., 1989), but higher than the 20 Mg C ha^{-1} for the mountainous region of Oregon (Homann et al., 1997), and the 17 Mg C ha^{-1} in Minnesota, Wisconsin, and Michigan forests (Grigal and Ohmann, 1992).

Forest floor C is part of the active portion of the forest C cycle. The forest floor is also a major nutrient-rich pool, thus forest floor organic C content is also significantly related to the N concentration (Figure 14.4). However, this relationship is not linear; as N concentration increases, there does not appear to be a direct increase in the forest floor organic C content. These relationships indicate that organic C within the forest floor saturates at an N concentration above 1.3%. It appears that there is a threshold level, or a limiting process, above which no further accumulation of forest floor organic C takes place. This would suggest that at litter N concentrations above 1.3%, the decomposition of forest floor C is not limited by the N supply, and there will be net mineralization. Nitrogen dynamics in soils are generally more conservative than C dynamics, and the high N percentage is simply an expression of achieving a more humified material, which suggests that the leftover C is due to more resilient C–N bonding in humified organic matter rather than N becoming more easily leached (Smith et al., 2011). Because the forest floor is at

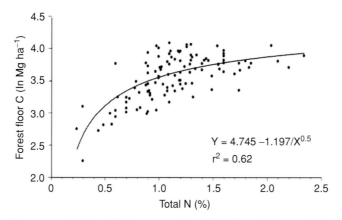

Figure 14.5. Relationship between carbon (C) and total nitrogen (N) in the forest floor horizons (litter fermentation humus) $(Y = 4.75 - 1.20/X^{0.5}$; $r^2 = 0.62)$ in boreal forest soils.

the surface, forest floor C is also more sensitive to fluctuations in temperature and moisture (Khomik et al., 2006). Van Cleve et al. (1986) studied a range of forest site types in interior Alaska and concluded that forest floor N concentration had a strong influence on soil N mineralization rates. Similarly, Zhang et al. (2007) reported that litter decomposition is mainly driven by climate variability across Canada, while rates of N-mineralization depend on the initial N concentration forest type.

Analyses of boreal forest stands in the oil sands country of Alberta also indicate that the C content is related to the forest floor thickness, and is the single most important site variable among the stand types. The average C content associated with black spruce stands was 102 Mg ha^{-1} (Figure 14.5), followed by 47 Mg ha^{-1} for white spruce and 30 Mg ha^{-1} for aspen stands, while the well-drained pine stands had the least, with 26 Mg ha^{-1} of C content (Figure 14.5). These observations were similar to those reported by Yu et al. (2002), who documented forest floor C contents of 26 Mg ha^{-1} for aspen (with a range of 5.8–38 Mg ha^{-1}), 19 Mg ha^{-1} for jack pine (with a range of 5–49 Mg ha^{-1}), and 44 Mg ha^{-1}, with the largest variation (range of 13–147 Mg ha^{-1}), for black spruce. Nalder and Wein (1999) found that forest floor C was strongly related to tree species and forest types. Similarly, Bond-Lamberty et al. (2004) found that in boreal forests, forest floor C content varies strongly among forest tree species, as litter production may be a more important factor than litter decomposition in determining the forest floor C dynamics.

Soil carbon and nitrogen content

The boreal forest soils showed more variability in C content of the mineral soil (top 50 cm) than in the litter layers of the forest floor. For the mineral soil, the average C content was 55 Mg C ha^{-1}, with a range from 9–231 Mg C ha^{-1}. The average N content was 1210 kg ha^{-1}, with a range from 18–5860 kg ha^{-1}. These results therefore indicate that upland boreal forests retain significant amounts of N along with C. This agrees with Melillo (1996) who determined that the soil was a major sink of N in forest ecosystems of the northeastern United States. The amount of C measured in this study is comparable to the organic C in mineral soils (up to 100 cm) of 111–190 Mg C ha^{-1} reported by Post et al. (1985) for the boreal forest, globally. Similarly, the average C content for 169 forest sites in Minnesota, Wisconsin, and Michigan was 105 Mg C ha^{-1} (Grigal and Ohmann, 1992), and 107 Mg C ha^{-1} in Manitoba (Rapalee et al., 1998). The average for 149 forest profiles in southeast Alaska was 185 Mg C ha^{-1}, with some profiles extending to a depth of 150 cm (Alexander et al., 1989). Variability in all soil-forming factors, including climate, vegetation, parent material, topography, and especially moisture regime (Goulden et al., 1998), likely contribute to these differences. Elevational differences of only a few meters in the western boreal forest often separate upland forests from the poorly drained forests.

Total soil C content in western boreal forest soils ranged from 78 to 492 Mg C ha^{-1} for the total soil column. These determinations are within the range of soil C content reported for forested ecosystems in central Canada (Bhatti et al., 2002), for Canadian soils (Hunt et al., 2010; Tarnocai et al., 2007), global boreal forests (Post et al., 1985), and for North American boreal forests. The world average for all soils is 117 Mg C ha^{-1} to 100 cm depth (Eswaran et al., 1993).

Site variables such as forest type also have a strong influence on soil C storage in the oil sands of Alberta. For example, the pine stand had the least amount and least variable soil C storage, followed by aspen and white spruce (Figure 14.6). There was large variability in soil C observed under black spruce. These differences are generally related to soil drainage, texture, slope, and aspect. The greater capacity for C storage under black spruce forest is primarily because of high soil moisture and low soil temperature conditions, which results in slow decomposition rates. The insulative properties of thick moss carpets (especially *Sphagnum*) add to the prevalence of the high moisture and low temperature conditions (Bonan and Van Cleve, 1992).

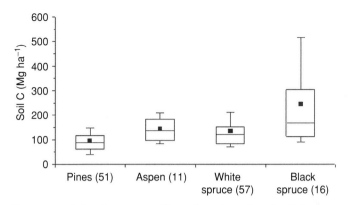

Figure 14.6. Soil carbon content (forest floor plus mineral soil) for trembling aspen (*Populus tremuloides*), pines (jack pine [*Pinus banksiana*] and lodgepole pine [*Pinus contorta*]), white spruce (*Picea glauca*), and black spruce (*Picea mariana*). Numbers in parentheses denote the number of stands in the database for each forest type.

Relations between soil organic C and edaphic conditions (Jenny, 1980) have been studied extensively at both local and regional levels. In a literature review, Martin and Haider (1986) concluded that mineral soil C increases with an increase in the amount of clay in the soil. Typically, clay enhances the formation of organomineral complexes and soil aggregates (Oades, 1988), thus physically protecting the soil C from mineral degradation through polyvalent cations. Polyvalent cations such as Al^{3+} and Fe^{3+} also stabilize soil C compounds by a number of mechanisms, including electrostatic cation bridging of organic colloids, and through specific adsorption onto Fe and Al hydrous oxide surfaces (Oades, 1988; Torn et al., 1997). The reaction between N and soil C is important as well; nonbiological condensation reactions of phenols with ammonium contribute to the production of stable humus (Johnson 1992), while binding with mineral colloids protects soil S against microbial attack (Torn et al., 1997).

Soil texture also determines the drainage condition; clay soils yield poor drainage conditions and therefore reduce decomposition rates, which influences the soil organic C content (Figure 14.7). Hence, as drainage classes go from rapid to moderately well drained, soil C increases. However, under imperfect to poor drainage classes, soil C contents decrease again. This decrease is due to lower root penetration, and therefore lower soil biomass productivity (Labrecque et al., 1994).

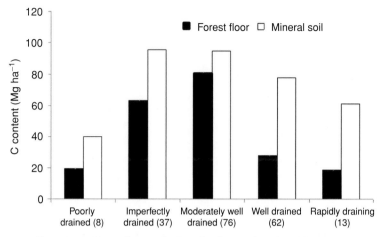

Figure 14.7. Forest floor and mineral soil organic carbon (C) content (Mg C ha^{-1}) in relation to drainage classes for upland boreal forest.

In poorly drained sites in western Canadian boreal forests, poor soil aeration is commonly associated with lower productivity (Startsev and McNabb, 2009), with a reduced litter production rate resulting in lower soil C stocks.

Implications for severe disturbances and climate change

Western boreal forest ecosystems are a long-term source or sink of C, depending upon the type and history of disturbances (Kurz et al., 2008). Disturbance type, disturbance frequency, size and severity, forest types, and site properties are some of the important variables contributing to the C dynamic in the forest ecosystems. Stand replacement disturbances have a large effect on the ecosystem C stocks at a given site. Forest biomass and forest floor C increase with stand development. Soil C pools decline immediately after disturbance and begin increasing later with stand development. With surface mining, all live vegetation is destroyed, while detritus and soil C pools in stockpiled material experience an increased rate of decomposition, thereby leading to net losses from the soil C pool. Because the C:N ratio of surface soil material, such as the organic forest floor, is particularly high (Post et al., 1985), a large amount of CO_2 will be released through decomposition of C, while some of the accompanying N will mineralize and leach.

With site revegetation of overburden landform, biomass accumulation in both roots and shoots of vegetation will start from zero level.

Initially, the site will be colonized by understory vegetation grasses, shrubs, herbs, mosses, lichens, and understory trees (Hart and Chen, 2006). Similarly, tree establishment and biomass accumulation on a given site will depend on climate, site quality, soil moisture, and nutrient regime. As tree and shrub cover increases, there will be an exponential increase in accumulation and storage in the aboveground C biomass pool, resulting in increased annual needle, leaf, and root input to the soil pool. Along with nutrient cycling, soil processes will increase in microbial activity, nutrient availability, and soil aggregation to restore the ecosystem function (Drozdowski et al., 2010). Enhancing soil fertility through the addition of organic materials to soil generally stimulates microbial activity, promotes N transformation and nutrient cycling, and could accelerate the ecosystem recovery. The use of natural organic soil materials like mucks, mulches, soil stabilizers, and amendments reduces erosion and improves soil health, and thereby increases biomass productivity–a major goal of restoring ecosystem function (Whitford, 1988). Climate-related stresses such as low moisture content in the western boreal ecosystems result in lower forest productivity (Zoltai et al., 1998), and ultimately lower ecosystem C accumulation.

Large areas in northern Alberta have been disturbed by construction of roads, pipelines, seismic lines, and well pads for oil, gas, and *in situ* oil sands development, but the long-term effects of these disturbances on C dynamics are not well understood. Research techniques (e.g., long-term eddy covariance, modeling, and ecological studies) must be used to estimate the ecosystem C balance. Post-reclamation assessment of C balance is critical to our understanding of C sink capacity and identification of practices that can increase the ecosystem C storage. Carbon storage could be increased by adopting: (1) recommended reclamation techniques, (2) recommended soil and vegetation management practices, (3) enhancing soil fertility, (4) employing land-use practices to improve nutrient cycling by returning biomass to the soil, and (5) planting fast-growing tree species that are able to establish quickly. Therefore, careful and well-planned research is needed to obtain inventories of fluxes and pools of C. Several critical knowledge gaps must be filled in order to better understand the C balance for this oil sands region on site- and stand-levels, as well as on the boreal forest landscape.

REFERENCES

Alexander, E. B., Kissinger, E., Huecker, R. H., Cullen P. (1989). Soils of southeast Alaska as sinks for organic carbon fixed from atmospheric carbon-dioxide.

In E. B. Alexander, ed., *Proceedings of Watershed '89: a Conference on the Stewardship of Soil, Air, and Water Resources.* Juneau, AK: USDA Forest Service, pp. 203–210.

Banfield, G. E., Bhatti, J. S., Jiang, H., Apps, M. J. (2002). Variability in regional scale estimates of carbon stocks in boreal forest ecosystems: results from West-Central Alberta. *Forest Ecology and Management*, **169**, 15–27.

Bhatti, J. S., Apps, M. J., Tarnocai, C. (2002). Estimates of soil organic carbon stocks in central Canada using three different approaches. *Canadian Journal of Forest Research*, **32**, 805–812.

Bhatti, J. S. and Tarnocai, C. (2009). Influence of climate and land-use change on carbon in agriculture, forest, and peatland ecosystems across Canada. In R. Lal and R. Follett, eds., *Soil Carbon Sequestration and the Greenhouse Effect.* 2nd edn. Madison, WI: Soil Science Society of America, pp. 47–70.

Bonan, G. B. (2008). Forests and climate change: forcings, feedbacks, and the climate benefits of forests. *Science*, **320**, 1444–1449.

Bonan, G. B. and Van Cleve, K. (1992). Soil temperature, nitrogen mineralization, and carbon source-sink relationships in boreal forests. *Canadian Journal of Forest Research*, **22**, 629–639.

Bond-Lamberty, B., Peckham, S. D., Ahl, D. E., Gower, S. T. (2007). Fire and the dominant driver of central Canadian boreal forest carbon balance. *Nature*, **450**, 89–93.

Bond-Lamberty, B., Wang, C. K., Gower, S. T. (2004). Net primary production and net ecosystem production of a boreal black spruce wildfire chronosequence. *Global Change Biology*, **10**, 473–487.

Chertov, O., Bhatti, J. S., Komarov, A., et al. (2009). Use the EFIMOD model to study the influence of climate change, fire and harvest on the carbon dynamics for black spruce in central Canada. *Forest Ecology and Management*, **257**, 941–950.

Comeau, P. G. and Kimmins, J. P. (1989). Above- and below-ground biomass and production of lodgepole pine on sites with differing soil moisture regimes. *Canadian Journal of Forest Research*, **19**, 447–454.

Drozdowski, B. L., Macyk, T. M., Faught, R. L., Vassov, R. J. (2010). Carbon storage in landscape affected by oil sands mining in Alberta's northern boreal forest. *National Meeting of the American Society of Mining and Reclamation, Pittsburgh, PA: Bridging Reclamation, Science and the Community*, R. I. Barnhisel, ed. Lexington, KY: ASMR.

Eswaran, H., van den Berg, E., Reoch, P. (1993). Organic carbon in soils of the world. *Soil Science Society of America Journal*, **57**, 192–194.

Goodale, C. L, Apps, M. J., Birdsey, R. A., et al. (2002). Forest carbon sinks in the Northern Hemisphere. *Ecological Applications*, **12**, 891–899.

Goulden, M. L., Wofsy, S. C., Harden, J. W. et al. (1998). Sensitivity of boreal forest carbon balance to soil thaw. *Science*, **279**, 214–217.

Gower, S. T., Krankina, O., Olson, R. J. et al. (2001). Net primary production and carbon allocation patterns of boreal forest ecosystems. *Ecological Applications*, **11**, 1395–1411.

Gower, S. T., Kucharik, C. J., Norman, J. M. (1999). Direct and indirect estimation of leaf area index, $fAPAR$, and net primary production of terrestrial ecosystems. *Remote Sensing of Environment*, **70**, 29–51.

Grigal, D. F. and Ohmann, L. F. (1992). Carbon storage in upland forests of the Lake States. *Soil Science Society of America Journal*, **56**, 935–943.

Hart, S. A. and Chen, H. Y. H. (2006). Understory vegetation dynamics of North American boreal forests. *Critical Reviews in Plant Sciences*, **25**, 381–397.

Hogg, E. H., Brandt, J. P., Kochtubajda, B. (2005). Factors affecting interannual variation in growth of western Canadian aspen forests during 1951–2000. *Canadian Journal of Forest Research*, **35**, 610–622.

Homann, P. S., Sollins, P., Chappell, H. N., Stangenberger, A. G. (1997). Soil organic carbon in a mountainous forested region: relation to site characteristics. *Soil Science Society of America Journal*, **59**, 1468–1475.

Howard, E. A., Gower, S. T., Foley, J. A., Kucharik, C. J. (2004). Effects of logging on carbon dynamics of a jack pine forest in Saskatchewan, Canada. *Globe Change Biology*, **10**, 1267–1284.

Hunt, S. L., Gordon, A. M., Morris, D. M. (2010). Carbon stocks in managed conifer forests in northern Ontario, Canada. *Silva Fennica*, **44**, 563–582.

Intergovernmental Panel on Climate Change [IPCC]. (2003). Good Practice Guidance for Land-use, Land-Use Change and Forestry. Address: http://www.ipcc-ggip.iges.or.jp/public/

Jenny, H. (1980). *The Soil Resources*. New York, NY: Spring-Verlag.

Johnson, D. W. (1992). Effects of forest management on soil carbon storage. *Water, Air, and Soil Pollution*, **64**, 83–120.

Jordaan, S. M., Keith, D. W., Stelfox, B. (2009). Quantifying land-use of oil sands production: a life cycle perspective. *Environmental Research Letters*, **4**, 024004.

Khomik, M., Arain, M. A., McCaughey, J. H. (2006). Temporal and spatial variability of soil respiration in a boreal mixedwood forest. *Agricultural and Forest Meteorology*, **140**, 244–256.

Kurz, W. A., Stinson, G., Rampley, G. J., Dymond, C. C., Neilson, E. T. (2008). Risk of natural disturbances makes future contribution of Canada's forests to the global carbon cycle highly uncertain. *Proceedings of the National Academy of Sciences*, **105**, 1551–1555.

Labrecque, M., Teodorescu, T. I., Babeux, P., Cogliastro, A., Daigle, S. (1994). Impact of herbaceous competition and drainage conditions on the early productivity of willows under short-rotation intensive culture. *Canadian Journal of Forest Research*, **24**, 493–501.

Martin, J. P. and Haider, K. (1986). Influence of mineral colloids on turnover rates of soil organic carbon. In P. M. Huang and M. Schnitzer, eds. *Interactions of Soil Minerals with Natural Organics and Microbes*. SSSA Spec. Publ. 17, 284–304. SSSA, Madison, WI.

Melillo, J. M. (1996). Carbon and nitrogen interactions in the terrestrial biosphere. In B. Walker and W. Steffen, eds., *Global Change and Terrestrial Ecosystems*. Cambridge, UK: Cambridge Univ. Press, pp. 431–450.

Nalder, I. A. and Wein, R. W. (1999). Long-term forest floor carbon dynamics after fire in upland boreal forests of western Canada. *Global Biogeochemical Cycles*, **13**, 951–968.

Natural Resources Canada. (2004). The State of Canada's Forests 2003–2004. Ottawa, ON: Natural Resources Canada.

Norris, C. E., Quideau, S. A., Bhatti, J. S., Wasylishen, R. E. (2009). Soil carbon stabilization in jack pine stands along the Boreal Forest Transect Case Study. *Global Change Biology*, **17**, 480–494.

Oades, J. M. (1988). The retention of organic matter in soils. *Biogeochemistry*, **5**, 35–70.

Post, W. M., Pastor, J., Zinke, P. J., Stangenberger, A. G. (1985). Global patterns of soil nitrogen storage. *Nature*, **317**, 613–616.

Preston, C. M., Bhatti, J. S., Flanagan, L. B., Norris, C. (2006). Stocks, chemistry, and sensitivity to climate change of dead organic matter along the Canadian Boreal Forest Transect case study. *Climatic Change*, **74**, 223–251.

Rapalee, G., Trumbore, S. E., Davidson, E. A., Harden, J. W., Veldhuis, H. (1998). Soil carbon stocks and their rates of accumulation and loss in a boreal forest landscape. *Global Biogeochemical Cycles*, **12**, 687–701.

Seedre, M., Shrestha, B. M., Chen, H. Y. H., Colombo, S., Jõgist, K. (2011). Carbon dynamics of North American boreal forest after stand replacing wildfire and clearcut logging. *Journal of Forest Research*, **16**, 168–183.

Shaw, C. H., Bhatti, J. S., Sabourin, K. (2005). An ecosystem carbon database for Canadian forests. Northern Forestry Centre, Edmonton, AB: Natural Resources Canada, Canadian Forest Service. Information report NOR-X-403.

Siltanen, R. M., Apps, M. J., Zoltai, S. C., Mair, R. M., Strong, W. L. (1997). A soil profile and organic carbon data base for Canadian forest and tundra mineral soils. Northern Forestry Centre, Edmonton, AB: Natural Resources Canada, Canadian Forest Service. Information report Fo42-271/1997E.

Smith, A. C., Bhatti, J. S., Hua, C., Harmon, M. E., Arp, P. A. (2011). Modelling mass loss and N dynamics in wooden dowels (LIDET) placed across North America. *Ecological Modelling*, **222**, 2276–2290.

Smith, M., Ollinger, S. V., Martin, M. E., et al. (2002). Direct estimation of above-ground forest productivity through hyperspectral remote sensing of canopy nitrogen. *Ecological Applications*, **12**, 1286–1302.

Startsev, A. D. and McNabb, D. H. (2009). Effects of compaction on aeration and morphology of boreal forest soils in Alberta, Canada. *Canadian Journal of Soil Science*, **89**, 45–56.

Sun, J., Peng, C., McCaughey, H., et al. (2008). Simulating carbon exchange of Canadian boreal forests II. Comparing the carbon budgets of a boreal mixedwood stand to a black spruce forest stand. *Ecological Modeling*, **219**, 276–286.

Tarnocai, C. (1998). The amount of organic carbon in various soil orders and ecoprovinces in Canada. In R. Lal, J. Kimbla, R. F. Follett, B. A. Stewart, eds., *Soil Processes and the Carbon Cycle*. Boca Raton, FL: CRC Press, pp. 81–92.

Tarnocai, C., Ping, C. L., Kimble, J. (2007). Carbon cycles in the permafrost region of North America. In A. W. King, L. Dilling, D. F. Fairman, et al., eds., *The First State of the Carbon Cycle Report (SOCCR): the North American Carbon Budget and Implications for the Global Carbon Cycle*. A Report by the U.S. Climate Change Science Program and the Subcommittee on Global Change Research. Silver Spring, MD: National Oceanic and Atmospheric Administration, Climate Program Office, pp. 101–112.

Torn, M. S., Trumbore, S. T., Chardwick, O. A., Vitousek, P. M., Hendricks D. M. (1997). Mineral control of soil organic carbon storage and turnover. *Nature*, **389**, 170–173.

Turetsky, M. R. and St. Louis, V. (2006). Disturbance in boreal peatlands. In R. K. Wieder and D. H. Vitt, eds., *Boreal Peatlands Ecosystems*. New York, NY: Springer-Verlag, pp. 359–379.

Van Cleve, K., Heal, O. W., Roberts, D. (1986). Bioassay of forest floor nitrogen supply to plant growth. *Canadian Journal of Forest Research*, **16**, 1320–1326.

Wang, C., Bond-Lamberty, B., Gower, S. T. (2003). Carbon distribution of a well- and poorly-drained black spruce fire chronosequence. *Global Change Biology*, **9**, 1066–1079.

Whitford, W. G. (1988). Decomposition and nutrient cycling in disturbed arid ecosystems. In E. B. Allen, ed., *The Reconstruction of Disturbed Arid Lands: an Ecological Approach*. New York, NY: Westview Press, pp. 136–161.

Yeh, S., Jordaan, S. M., Brandt, A., et al. (2010). Land-use greenhouse gas emissions from conventional and unconventional oil production. *Environmental Science and Technology*, **44**, 8766–8772.

Yu, Z., Apps, M. J., Bhatti, J. S. (2002). Implications of floristic and environmental variation for carbon cycle dynamics in boreal forest ecosystems of central Canada. *Journal of Vegetation Science*, **13**, 327–340.

Zhang, C. F., Meng, F. R., Trofymow, J. A., Arp, P. A. (2007). Modelling mass and nitrogen remaining in litterbags for Canadian forest and climate conditions. *Canadian Journal of Soil Science*, **87**, 413–432.

Zoltai, S. C., Morrissey, L. A., Livingston, G. P., de Groot, W. J. (1998). Effects of fire on carbon cycling in North American boreal peatlands. *Environmental Reviews*, **6**, 13–24.

15

Projected patterns of carbon storage in upland forests reclaimed after oil sands mining

INTRODUCTION

Under Alberta's Environmental Protection and Enhancement Act (EPEA), land disturbed through oil sands mine operations must be reclaimed, with "the objective ... to return the specified land to an equivalent capability." Equivalent land capability is defined within the EPEA as "the ability of the land to support various land uses after ... reclamation is similar to the ability that existed prior to an activity being conducted on the land, but that the individual land uses will not necessarily be identical." Upland areas disturbed by mining are reclaimed by capping with a mixture of organic peat and mineral soil (typically 50% each by volume) that is over-stripped from low-lying areas prior to mining (Alberta Environment, 2010). This mix constitutes the rooting matrix for the terrestrial reclaimed plant community. Following application of the capping material, a plant community is established consisting of tree seedlings and minor vegetation that are appropriate to site conditions and representative of locally common ecosystems.

While the intensity of oil sands carbon (C) emissions can be mitigated through technological and process innovations, reclamation is the only mining-related activity that directly removes atmospheric CO_2, as a result of the C fixed through growth and development of the reclaimed plant community. However, another important consideration is the C stored in the peat:mineral mix used as capping material. Loss of this material through microbial decomposition will generate a release of CO_2 through aerobic respiration. Given that the cap constitutes a large pool of

Restoration and Reclamation of Boreal Ecosystems, ed. Dale Vitt and Jagtar Bhatti. Published by Cambridge University Press. © Cambridge University Press 2012.

stored C (Welham, 2004, 2005a, b), one possibility is that respiratory losses exceed the C fixed through plant growth, leading to a net atmospheric emission. To date, however, the actual C balance associated with reclamation has not been calculated. Net ecosystem storage from reclamation that occurs during active mining would count as a deduction from the overall emissions profile, whereas a net emission adds to the profile.

Here we use an ecosystem model, FORECAST, to simulate the C balance associated with the proposed reclamation schedule for Imperial Oil Ltd.'s Kearl Lake oil sands mining project, located approximately 70 km north of Ft. McMurray, Alberta. A basic description of the model has been provided elsewhere in this volume (see Chapter 15) (Kimmins et al., 1999, 2010; Seely et al., 2008). FORECAST has been applied to oil sands mine reclamation for more than a decade. In this regard, model output has been used to derive multipliers and nutrient regime classes factoring into a landscape capability classification system (Welham, 2004); factors include the depth (Welham, 2005a, b) and type (Welham, 2005b, 2006) of the capping material; nitrogen deposition (Welham, unpublished); subsoil organic matter content (Welham, 2006); species mixes (Welham, 2005a), planting densities (Welham, 2005a, 2006), understory dynamics (Welham, 2005a, b, 2006), and dead organic matter dynamics (specifically snags) (Welham, 2005b), all within the context of growth and yield.

One important application of the FORECAST model in reclamation was to examine the long-term implications of different peat decomposition rates for forest productivity (Welham, 2005a, b, 2006). As the basis for the rooting matrix in reclamation soils, the biogeochemical properties of the peat material are a key feature of its ability to support the growth and development of a boreal mixedwood forest. Peat biogeochemistry, decomposition, and nutrient release are the subject of a comprehensive research program within the Alberta oil sands (Hemstock et al., 2010; MacKenzie and Quideau, 2010; Turcotte et al., 2009). Unfortunately, many years will have elapsed before results can be considered conclusive and thus sufficiently reliable as a guide to reclamation practices and assessing outcomes. Models such as FORECAST that can represent the basic features associated with the peat:mineral mix and the developing forest floor are thus a requirement if projections of C balance are to be meaningful.

The specific objectives of this chapter include the following:

1.   compare FORECAST's projections of C accrual in an aspen-dominated stand with empirical measures. This step serves to establish the suitability of the model in simulating the C balance in natural stands within the region;

2.   compare FORECAST's projections of C accrual in a reclaimed aspen-dominated stand and its natural analogue;

3.   project the C balance associated with progressive reclamation across the Kearl Lake mine footprint over the period of active mining.

METHODS

Objective 1: compare FORECAST's projections of carbon accrual in an aspen-dominated stand with empirical measures

To assess the efficacy of the model in generating reliable C estimates, a comparative analysis was conducted, as follows. FORECAST's capability to represent the C balance in local forest ecosystems was evaluated by calibrating the model for an aspen (*Populus tremuloides*)-dominated stand that originated from a stand-replacing fire at a starting density of 2500 stems ha^{-1}, and included an understory plant community. Details regarding the construction of a calibration dataset for aspen are reported in Welham et al. (2002, 2007). Model output was then compared to literature values derived from plots located in fire-origin aspen-dominated stands within the region (Arevalo et al., 2009; Fitzsimmons et al., 2004; Martin et al., 2005). It should be noted that none of the data used to evaluate model output were incorporated into the calibration dataset.

Objective 2: compare FORECAST's projections of carbon accrual in a reclaimed aspen-dominated stand and its natural analogue

Using the same calibration dataset as in Objective 1, FORECAST was used to simulate a generalized reclamation scenario applicable to tailings sand, on "good-" to "fair"-quality non-saline-sodic overburden. (For a basic description of these materials and general principles associated with their reclamation, see Alberta Environment (2006, 2010, respectively). In brief, large volumes of upland overburden and tailings sand are generated from the mining process. These materials have a low water storage capacity, nutrient status, and organic C content. They are therefore capped with a cover soil mixture of organic peat and mineral soil (typically 50% each by volume) (Alberta Environment, 2010). This peat:mineral mix constitutes the rooting matrix for the terrestrial reclaimed plant community.

In the model simulations, the cover soil was represented as a 50 cm-deep peat:mineral mix layer, with an initial consistency of 100 t C ha^{-1}

and 4200 kg N ha^{-1}. Long-term trends in peat decomposition are not well understood; therefore two general patterns were simulated in FORECAST, termed fast and slow decomposition (further details are discussed later). The sequence of events in the simulated reclamation event was: year 1, apply cover soil; year 2, plant aspen (2500 stems ha^{-1}) at a starting site index = 16[1]; year 3, establish an understory community at a density of 800 stems ha^{-1}.

Objective 3: project the carbon balance associated with progressive reclamation across the Kearl Lake mine footprint

Details of mine development and associated reclamation plans were derived from the Kearl Lake Environmental Impact Assessment (EIA) documents, available from the Canadian Environmental Assessment Agency (www.ceaa-acee.gc.ca). The development consists of four open pits that will be mined over the period 2010 to 2060. Mining operations and progressive reclamation will continue until 2060, followed by final reclamation to year 2065. The Kearl project will eventually occupy about 230 km^2 of land although with progressive reclamation, the actual active footprint may be much smaller at any one time. The modeling exercise was conducted in three steps. First, Kearl Lake EIA documents were used to obtain information on reclamation practices from mine initiation to closure with respect to application of the peat:mineral mix, which ecosite phases[2] were to be established, the time periods when each phase was to be reclaimed, and how much area a given phase was expected to occupy during a given reclamation event. For practical purposes, application of the peat:mineral mix was assumed to occur over nine discrete periods beginning in 2016, with a final event in 2060. Community establishment (i.e., a given ecosite phase) was initiated in the year following, as described in in this section. An illustration of the progress of reclamation on the Kearl Lake mine site is shown in Figure 15.1. Second, a series of FORECAST runs was conducted to simulate the productivity (expressed in units of C accrual) in each of the proposed ecosites in accordance with

[1] Note that in FORECAST, site index is not treated as a site property. Hence, the starting site index is used only at the beginning of a simulation. Thereafter, the model adjusts tree productivity (and, hence, site index) in relation to resource availability (see Kimmins et al. 1999, for further details).

[2] Ecosites are ecological units that develop under similar environmental influences (climate, moisture, and nutrient regime). They consist of groups of one or more ecosite phases, where a given ecosite phase is defined by the dominant tree species in the canopy (see Beckingham and Archibald, 1996 for details).

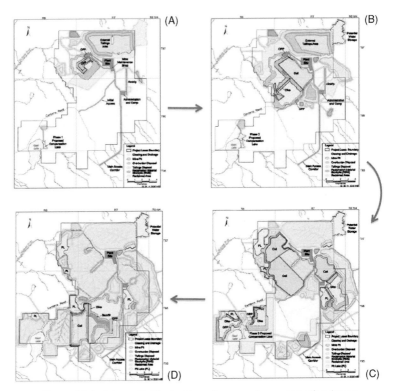

Figure 15.1. Schematic illustration of progressive reclamation (green areas) on the Kearl Lake mine footprint for the periods 2012–2016 (**A**), 2022–2026 (**B**), 2032–2041 (**C**), and 2052–2060 (**D**). (See color plate section for colored image.)

the expected pattern of progressive reclamation. In contrast to Objective 2, a peat decomposition rate intermediate between "fast" and "slow" was used for these simulations. Finally, total ecosystem C accrual was then calculated across the Kearl Lake footprint. Further details on how the reclamation plan described in the EIA documents was represented within the FORECAST model are described elsewhere in this volume (see Chapter 15).

RESULTS

Objective 1: compare FORECAST's projections of carbon accrual in an aspen-dominated stand with empirical measures

A comparison of predicted and measured live pools is shown in Figure 15.2, for total aboveground wood (comprised of stemwood and branch C),

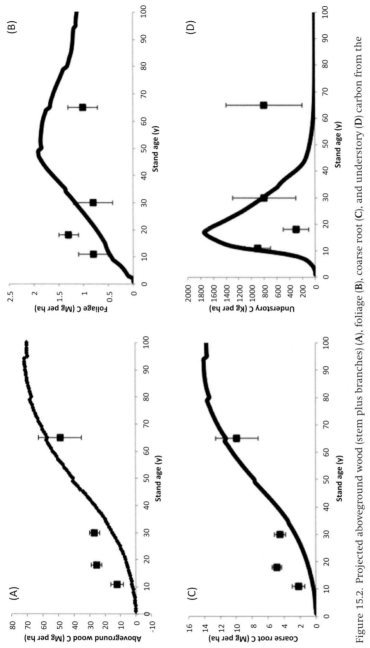

Figure 15.2. Projected aboveground wood (stem plus branches) (A), foliage (B), coarse root (C), and understory (D) carbon from the FORECAST model for a natural aspen stand. Squares are measured values from field plots (±SE).

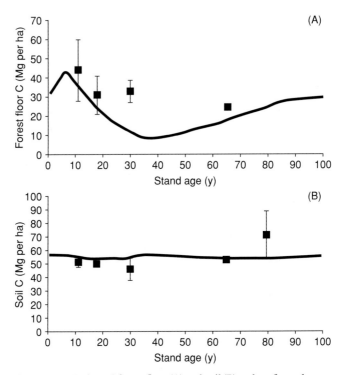

Figure 15.3. Projected forest floor (**A**) and soil (**B**) carbon from the FORECAST model for a natural aspen stand. Squares are measured values from field plots (±SE).

foliage, coarse root, and understory C (Figures 15.2A-D, respectively). It should be noted that a value of 31.6 Mg C ha^{-1} reported for coarse root biomass by Arevalo et al. (2009) in an 80-year-old aspen stand was not included in Figure 15.2C. This value far exceeds (by 37%) reported total root biomass for similar-aged aspen stands in Alberta, as reported in Peterson and Peterson (1992, Table 18). Furthermore, when the allometric equation reported in Li et al. (2003; equation 5) for predicting total root biomass in hardwoods was used in conjunction with the reported value for aboveground biomass of 49.2 Mg ha^{-1} (Figure 15.2A), the predicted value (17.3 Mg C ha^{-1}) was 45% lower than the value reported in Arevalo et al. (2009), despite the fact that the latter only included coarse root biomass. Figure 15.3 shows comparative values of dead organic matter (DOM) for forest floor (Figure 15.3A) and soil C (Figure 15.3B).

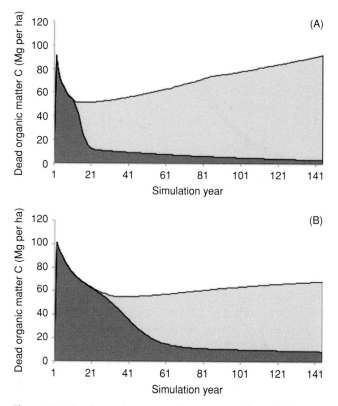

Figure 15.4. Dead organic matter carbon content of peat (dark gray) and material derived from onsite litterfall (light gray) in relation to time since deposition, for fast (**A**) and slow (**B**) rates of peat decomposition, as projected from the FORECAST model.

Objective 2: compare FORECAST's projections of carbon accrual in a reclaimed aspen-dominated stand and its natural analogue

The mass of peat remaining in the cover soil associated with differences in peat decomposition rate is shown in Figure 15.4. When peat decomposition was fast, more than 80% of the material had decomposed over the first 20 years of the simulation (Figure 15.4A). At a slow rate of decomposition, however, about 60 years would elapse before there was a similar amount remaining (Figure 15.4B). Aboveground wood C production in aspen showed similar trends on reclaimed and natural sites when peat decomposition was fast (Figure 15.5). Although production on reclaimed

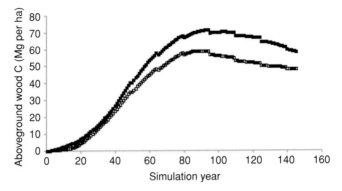

Figure 15.5. Aboveground wood (stem plus branches) carbon from a natural (solid symbols) and reclaimed (open symbols) aspen stand, as projected from the FORECAST model.

sites was consistently lower, values were generally within about 20% of those derived from natural sites (Figure 15.6A). There were similar trends for DOM (Figure 15.6B) and total net ecosystem C (Figure 15.6C). Similarly, DOM C with slow peat decomposition was generally within 20% of the value simulated from natural sites (Figure 15.7B), and thus values were similar to those when peat decomposition was fast (Figures 15.6B and 15.7B). Aboveground wood C production in the reclaimed stand, however, was very low compared to the natural stand when peat decomposition was slow (Figure 15.7A). The types of material constituting the DOM pools were generally different between the two rates of peat decomposition. With fast decomposition, 20 years or more after the beginning of the simulation, the DOM pool comprised largely biomass derived from living plant material (Figure 15.4A). With slow peat decomposition, at least 60 years had elapsed before this component came to dominate the DOM pool (Figure 15.4B). Overall, total net ecosystem C with slow peat decomposition declined to about 50% of that found in a natural aspen-dominated forest (Figure 15.7C).

Objective 3: project the carbon balance associated with progressive reclamation across the Kearl Lake mine footprint

During the working life of the mine (2010 to 2065), the change in total net ecosystem C was positive with each deposition event of peat:mineral mix but was negative during the intervening years (Figure 15.8A). Total

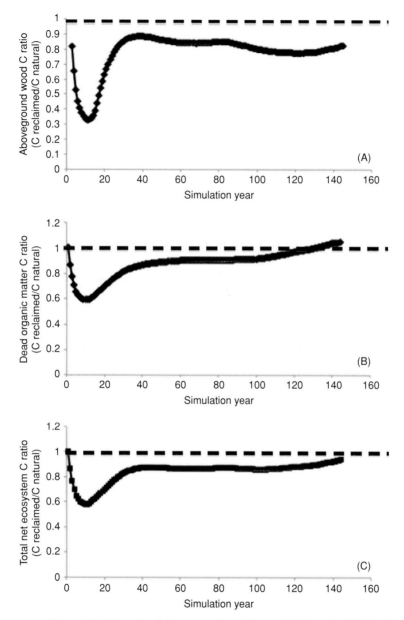

Figure 15.6. The ratio of aboveground wood (stem plus branches) (**A**), dead organic matter (**B**), and total net ecosystem (**C**) carbon between a natural and reclaimed aspen stand. The horizontal broken line denotes the ratio at unity. Data were derived from projections made by the FORECAST model. The reclaimed stand was simulated using a fast peat decomposition rate.

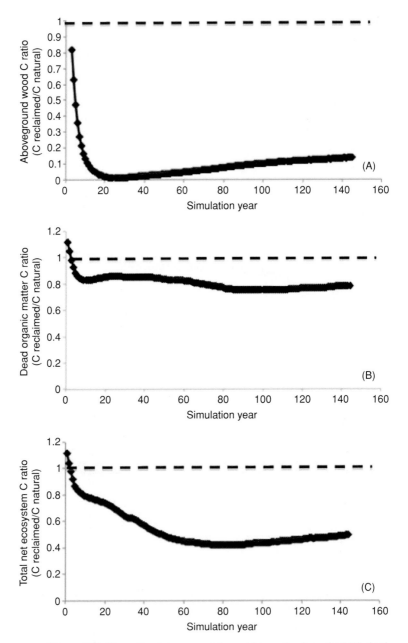

Figure 15.7. The ratio of aboveground wood (stem plus branches) (**A**), dead organic matter (**B**), and total net ecosystem (**C**) carbon between a natural and reclaimed aspen stand. The horizontal broken line denotes the ratio at unity. Data were derived from projections made by the FORECAST model. The reclaimed stand was simulated using a slow peat decomposition rate.

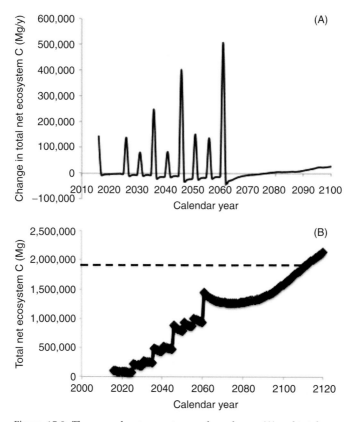

Figure 15.8. The annual net ecosystem carbon change (**A**) and total accumulated net ecosystem carbon (**B**) across the Kearl Lake mine footprint. The broken line indicates the point at which total carbon added from the deposition of peat–mineral mix is equivalent to the total accumulated net ecosystem carbon.

net ecosystem C accumulated to a maximum of about 1.4 million Mg at the last deposition event in year 2060 and declined thereafter until it reached a minimum value of 1,262,000 Mg in year 2075 (Figure 15.8B). Summed across all deposition events, the C added from the peat:mineral mix alone totaled about 1,917,000 Mg, which suggests that up to year 2075, reclamation activities resulted in total net C emissions of about 655,000 Mg. After 2075, sequestration from plant growth exceeded C losses from decomposition, but total net ecosystem C storage did not exceed the amount of C deposited from the peat:mineral mix until year 2111 (Figure 15.8B).

DISCUSSION

Comparing FORECAST's projections of carbon accrual in an aspen-dominated stand with empirical measures

A key feature of any modeling exercise is to ensure that model construction and parameterization provide a reasonable representation of the system of interest. The best means of assessing model performance is by comparison of predictions with empirical measures. Unfortunately, there are no long-term datasets available for reclaimed sites. The FORECAST model has been validated against five separate published datasets from natural stands (Kimmins et al., 2010). Although a comparative exercise was undertaken against the standard yield curves for Alberta mixedwoods (Welham, unpublished), the analysis conducted here is the first comparison that uses published data. Overall, model predictions matched the empirical measures reasonably well, although there were minor discrepancies (Figures 15.2 and 15.3). This is not surprising given that the empirical values were derived from three different sources (Figures 15.2 and 15.3), two of which sampled from multiple stands (Fitzsimmons et al., 2004; Martin et al., 2005). Differences among stands in, for example, disturbance history (such as fire intensity), and overstory and understory establishment densities, can generate considerable variation in aboveground biomass C (Peterson and Peterson, 1992), although soil C tends to be relatively stable (Figure 15.3B).

Empirical estimates of aboveground wood (stem plus branches) and coarse root C in younger stands (30 years or less; derived from Martin et al., 2005) were consistently higher than predicted from the FORECAST model. Coarse root biomass was not calculated directly, but instead was estimated using an average percentage of total biomass (18.3 %; Martin et al., 2005). A similar approach is employed in the FORECAST model, although the ratio varies by tree size. This indicates that the source of the discrepancy was in the aboveground C component. One possibility is that following the last harvest event (Martin et al., 2005) new stems in the natural stand originated from vegetative reproduction (principally suckering). Vegetative reproduction is very common in aspen (Peterson and Peterson, 1992). These stems are supported initially by the parent root system and early growth is rapid compared to stems that develop from seed. In the FORECAST simulations, aspen was assumed to establish from seed (although FORECAST can represent vegetative reproduction), which could explain the lower predictions for aboveground C accumulation.

Comparing FORECAST's projections of carbon accrual in a reclaimed aspen-dominated stand and its natural analogue

In previous FORECAST simulations, peat decomposition rate was a critical determinant of yield (expressed as volume) on reclaimed ecosites (Welham, 2005a, b, 2006). Results from these simulations indicate that aboveground wood C production in reclaimed aspen-dominated stands will be similar to the values for simulated natural stands only if peat decomposes at the fast rate (or higher) (Figures 15.6A and 15.7A). With fast peat decomposition, aboveground wood C accrual on the reclaimed site declined over the first 10 years of the simulation (in relative terms) before increasing to within about 20% of the values expected from a natural aspen stand. The initial decline in aboveground wood C is a consequence of a brief period when nitrogen availability was limiting to plant growth due to microbial immobilization (data not shown) (Kimmins et al., 1999). Short-term (i.e., less than one year) peat decomposition data from laboratory incubations appear to be closer to the high than the low rate (MacKenzie and Quideau, unpublished). However, these rates were derived under optimal conditions, suggesting that *in situ* rates may be lower (Hemstock et al., 2010), possibly somewhere between the high and low rates. If this were the case, then aboveground wood C production on reclaimed sites would be intermediate between the two trend lines simulated here, and somewhat less than occurs on natural sites.

The DOM C accrual for an aspen stand on a reclaimed site with fast decomposition showed a trend similar to its natural analogue (Figure 15.6B). As with aboveground wood C, there was an initial decline in the relative size of the DOM C pool in the reclaimed stand resulting from the rapid loss of peat biomass from decomposition (Figure 15.4A). Although the developing plant community represents a source for new DOM C (e.g., from leaf litter and stem mortality), early growth was not sufficient to provide enough new DOM C to offset the decline in peat biomass C (Figure 15.4A). With slow peat decomposition, there was also an initial loss of DOM C relative to the natural site over the first 10 years of the simulation, but thereafter the ratio was relatively constant (Figure 15.7B). In this case, mass loss from decomposition was less pronounced (Figure 15.4B), which resulted in a relatively even transition from the peat to a litter-based DOM C pool. Hence, despite differences in the relative contribution of each source of DOM C (peat versus live biomass), the size of this ecosystem pool over the long-term remained constant as compared to its natural analogue, regardless of the peat decomposition rate.

At the fast peat decomposition rate, total net ecosystem C was similar to the projections for a natural aspen stand (Figure 15.6C). As with both aboveground wood and DOM C, there was an initial decline in this measure during early stand development. This is not unexpected as total net ecosystem C is derived from the sum of the other two C pools. This phenomenon has been documented in natural stands where fire (Rothstein et al., 2004) or removal of live biomass from logging (Fredeen et al., 2007) has resulted in decomposition of residual dead biomass exceeding the C fixed in the early stages of new plant growth. This pattern also occurred in the natural stand simulations conducted for this report (data not shown). The simulation results indicate, however, that this decline was more pronounced and of longer duration on the reclaimed versus the natural stand.

Total net ecosystem C was substantially reduced when peat decomposition was slow, as compared to when it was fast (Figures 15.6C and 15.7C). Because DOM C stock was not affected by the peat decomposition rate, this was due largely to the comparatively low rate of aboveground wood C production. If peat decomposition rates are indeed closer to the slow rate, then efforts at promoting C storage on upland reclaimed sites should thus target the enhancement of vegetation development and growth. One option is to implement a fertilizer program. Fertilizer is applied to most reclaimed sites during the first several years after planting to promote stand establishment. Whether there are benefits, in terms of C sequestration, to extending this program has not been determined, either empirically or through modeling (see following discussion). Another important consideration is to ensure that the full growth potential is realized by planting reclaimed areas with species appropriate to site conditions. The most recent edition of the oil sands revegetation manual provides considerable guidance in this regard (Alberta Environment, 2010).

Projecting the carbon balance across the Kearl Lake mine footprint

Two competing processes determine the pattern of C accumulation associated with progressive reclamation within a given year. The first is the loss of C from the peat:mineral mix as a consequence of decomposition, which is balanced against the C that accrues from growth of the reclaimed plant communities. The general relationship between these two processes can be ascertained by considering the period after the final deposition of the peat:mineral mix (in 2060). As was the case following all deposition events, total net ecosystem C declined immediately after the final event (Figure 15.8B). However, the two processes were approximately equivalent 15 years following the last deposition (in year 2075), after which the C stored in new growth exceeded losses from decomposition (Figure 15.8B). Given that the peat:mineral mix was almost always deposited on only 10-year intervals (Figure 15.8B), this explains why during the intervening periods the C accrued from growth of the reclaimed plant communities was not sufficient to offset losses from peat decomposition (Figure 15.8A). The increase in total net ecosystem C during the period of active mining (to year 2065) was thus driven exclusively by deposition of the peat:mineral mix. It should be noted that the 15-year interval required to achieve C neutrality following the final deposition event is a conservative estimate. Because a majority of the mine footprint had already been reclaimed prior to the last deposition event in 2060, (Figure 15.8), the peat on these preexisting reclaimed sites will have already been subject to varying degrees of decomposition (Figure 15.4). Many of these ecosystems will have thus transitioned to a positive C balance, which would help to balance out the losses from decomposition that will occur following the final deposition event.

In terms of an overall C balance associated with reclamation, the simulation results indicated that up to year 2075, reclamation activities resulted in total net C emissions of about 655,000 Mg. After year 2075, net storage (i.e., C accrued from growth minus decomposition losses) does not reach a level equivalent to the total C deposited from peat:mineral deposition until 2111, over 50 years after the last deposition event (Figure 15.8B).

Taken together, these results suggest that the schedule for reclamation has important implications for the impact of oil sands mining on the C balance on the mine footprint. For example, delaying reclamation until the last 10 years of active mining may be a favored option by industry because it defers the associated financial costs. This would generate an abrupt and very large increase in storage with deposition of the peat:mineral capping layer, which would then be followed immediately by a protracted post-mining interval of carbon emissions from decomposition before both net storage became positive and the total net ecosystem C balance exceeded the sum of all emissions from peat decomposition. Although delaying reclamation would not change the total C balance (assuming the same depth and density of peat is applied as was simulated here), an additional consideration is the C emissions that will occur from decomposition when the peat is stockpiled or remains *in situ* on drained sites, prior to its deployment (Kong et al., 1980). Presumably, this "lost" peat would have to be recovered from elsewhere to restore the total amount of peat to its original mass. Thus, from a reclamation perspective, emissions from storage constitute a lost opportunity because they are not linked to plant growth. Hence, the greater the extent to which reclamation occurs in the early life of a mine, the more favorable its impact on the overall C balance, as the period of peat storage prior to deployment is minimized and the period of C fixation through forest growth is extended.

The peat decomposition rate had a significant impact on projections of plant growth (Figures 15.6A and 15.7A). As noted in the previous section, one option for increasing C storage on the mine footprint, particularly if peat decomposes only very slowly, might be to promote growth through fertilization. Although fertilizer is applied during the first few years of stand establishment, extending this period for several decades or more would serve to increase storage in live biomass and also to increase the size of the DOM C pools derived from live biomass, thereby increasing total ecosystem C storage. There is evidence from peatlands demonstrating greater live plant biomass in areas with high nitrogen deposition (Turunen et al., 2004; Vitt et al., 2003). However, additional emissions of greenhouse gases (example.g., N_2O, NO_x) (Kim and Dale, 2008) from the fertilizer itself should be considered. In addition, any benefit from fertilization will not be realized if the productivity of reclaimed upland areas is more limited by moisture availability than by nutrients, or if added fertilizer also increases the peat decomposition rate. Evidence on the latter point suggests otherwise, however. Turunen et al. (2004) indicated that peat decomposition declined with nitrogen addition, and Maas and Adamson (1975) added nitrogen to peat and recorded a decrease in mass loss rate in three cases, although the result was significant in only two of them.

An important uncertainty in projections of C dynamics is the role of climate change and its impact on ecosystem processes. Current and future bioclimatic conditions are subject to anthropogenic influences (nitrogen deposition and leaching, CO_2 fluxes) that are altering the survival and growth potential of extant species in ways that we have not experienced previously and do not yet fully understand. Furthermore, the impact of anthropogenically driven climate change is projected to increase through this century (see Barrow and Yu, 2005, for projections specific to Alberta). By 2050, the mean temperature across the prairies is expected to increase by at least 2–4°C, compared with the 1961–1990 climate norms (Sauchyn and Kulshreshtha, 2007). Although precipitation is projected to increase, particularly in northeastern Alberta, conditions will actually be drier during the growing season because of the evaporative effects of increased heating (Schindler and Donahue, 2006). Forests in the oil sands region often incur growing season moisture deficits even under today's climate regime. If projected climate trends are reasonable, this suggests that tree growth may be much lower than projected from the simulations used here, leading to reduced rates of C sequestration. Another possibility is that the species currently planted may be replaced by species better adapted to prevailing conditions (Schneider et al., 2009), in which case climate change may have relatively little impact on C sequestration. In contrast, drier conditions can impair microbial activity and hence decomposition, which would then help to maintain this C pool. While this may depress plant growth, ecosystem C storage could remain relatively stable as much of the peat will remain *in situ*, a situation comparable to the slow peat decomposition simulations. These are important issues for oil sands reclamation and warrant further attention. They can be addressed with process models that explicitly simulate climate effects and climate change (e.g., the FORECAST Climate model; Welham et al,. unpublished).

SUMMARY

Reclamation is the only mining-related activity that directly removes atmospheric CO_2, a result of the C fixed through growth and development of a reclaimed plant community. Despite the gain in sequestered C from plant growth, however, it is possible that other factors could lead to a release of C in excess of this gain, resulting in a net loss. One important consideration is the C stored in the peat:mineral mix used as capping material in upland sites. Loss of this material through microbial decomposition will generate a release of CO_2 through aerobic respiration; respiratory losses could exceed the C fixed through plant growth, leading to a net atmospheric emission. To date, however, the actual C balance associated with reclamation has not been calculated. Here we use an ecosystem model, FORECAST, to simulate the C balance associated with the proposed reclamation schedule for Imperial Oil Ltd.'s Kearl Lake oil sands mining project, located approximately 70 km north of Ft. McMurray, Alberta.

FORECAST's projections of C accrual in fire-origin aspen-dominated stands showed a good overall fit with empirical measures of aboveground (stem plus branches) live and dead organic matter C pools, establishing the suitability of this model in simulating the C balance in natural stands within the region. Simulations of plant community development on aspen-dominated reclaimed sites were conducted with FORECAST using two peat decomposition rates, termed fast and slow. Aspen aboveground C production and total net ecosystem C showed similar trends on reclaimed and natural sites when peat decomposition was fast, but not when it was slow (in the latter case, C storage was lower on reclaimed sites). The DOM C showed similar trends on reclaimed and natural sites when peat decomposition was either fast or slow, but the types of material constituting the DOM pools generally differed between the two decomposition rates. With fast peat decomposition, 20 years or more after the beginning of the simulation, the DOM C pool was composed largely of biomass derived from onsite litterfall. With slow peat decomposition, at least 60 years had elapsed before this component came to dominate the DOM C pool.

During the working life of the mine (2010 to 2065), the change in total net ecosystem C was positive with each deposition event of the peat:mineral mix, but was negative during the intervening years. Total net ecosystem C accumulated to a maximum of about 1.4 million Mg at the last deposition event in year 2060 and declined thereafter until it reached a minimum value of 1,262,000 Mg in year 2075. Summed across all deposition events, the C added from the peat:mineral mix alone totaled about 1,917,000 Mg, which suggests that up to year 2075, reclamation activities resulted in total net C emissions of about 655,000 Mg. After 2075, sequestration from plant growth exceeded C losses from decomposition, but total net ecosystem C storage did not exceed the amount of C deposited from the peat:mineral mix until year 2111.

Efforts at improving the C balance associated with reclamation might include: (a) establishing plant communities as early as possible during the period of active mining, thereby minimizing the period when peat is stored, and (b) applying fertilizer over long periods to improve plant growth. Finally, climate change could have a significant impact on the C balance in reclaimed ecosystems and thus warrants consideration in future analyses.

ACKNOWLEDGMENTS

Special thanks to Drs. Caroline Bampfylde and Brett Purdy of Alberta Environment for their support and input into the project. This work was supported by the Oil Sands and Clean Energy Policy Branch, Alberta Environment, Grant 09-GROF02, and administered by the Oil Sands Information Research Network, University of Alberta.

REFERENCES

Alberta Environment. (2006). *Land Capability Classification System for Forest Ecosystems in the Oil Sands*, 3rd edn. Volume 1: Field manual for land capability determination. Prepared for Alberta Environment by the Cumulative Environmental Management Association, Fort McMurray, AB.

Alberta Environment. (2010). *Guidelines for Reclamation to Forest Vegetation in the Athabasca Oil Sands Region*, 2nd edn. Prepared by the Terrestrial Subgroup of the Reclamation Working Group of the Cumulative Environmental Management Association, Fort McMurray, AB.

Arevalo, C. B. M, Bhatti, J. S., Chang, S. X., Sidders, D. (2009). Ecosystem carbon stocks and distribution under different land-uses in north central Alberta, Canada. *Forest Ecology and Management*, **257**, 1776–1785.

Barrow, E. and Yu, G. (2005). *Climate Change Scenarios for Alberta*. A report prepared for the Prairie Adaptation Research Collaborative (PARC) in co-operation with Alberta Environment. Regina, SK: Climate Research Services and Prairie Adaptation Research Collaborative.

Beckingham, J. D. and Archibald, J. H. (1996). *Field Guide to Ecosites of Northern Alberta*. Edmonton, AB: Canadian Forest Service, Northwest Region, Northern Forestry Centre, Spec. Rep. 5.

Fitzsimmons, M. J., Pennock, D. J., Thorpe, J. (2004). Effects of deforestation on ecosystem carbon densities in central Saskatchewan, Canada. *Forest Ecology and Management*, **188**, 349–361.

Fredeen, A., Waughtal, J. D., Pypker, T. G. (2007). When do replanted sub-boreal clearcuts become net sinks for CO2? *Forest Ecology and Management*, **239**, 210–216.

Hemstock, S., Quideau, S. A., Chanasyk, D. S. (2010). Nitrogen availability from peat amendments used in boreal oil sands reclamation. *Canadian Journal of Soil Science*, **90**, 165–175.

Kim, S. and Dale, B. (2008). Effects of nitrogen fertilizer application on greenhouse gas emissions and economics of corn. *Environmental Science and Technology*, **42**, 6028–6033.

Kimmins, J. P., Blanco, J. A., Seely, B., Welham, C., Scoullar, K. (2010). *Forecasting Forest Futures: a Hybrid Modelling Approach to the Assessment of Sustainability of Forest Ecosystems and their Values*, Earthscan UK.

Kimmins, J. P., Mailly, D., Seely, B. (1999). Modelling forest ecosystem net primary production: the hybrid simulation approach used in FORECAST. *Ecological Modeling*, **122**, 195–224.

Kong, K., Lindsay, J. D., McGill, W. B. (1980). *Characterization of Stored Peat in the Alberta Oil Sands Area*. Prepared for the Alberta Oil Sands Environmental Research Program by Research Council of Alberta, Soils Division, and Department of Soil Science, University of Alberta. AOSERP Rep. 91.

Li, Z., Kurz, W. A., Apps, M. J., Beukema, S. J. (2003). Belowground biomass dynamics in the Carbon Budget Model of the Canadian Forest Sector: recent improvements and implications for the estimation of NPP and NEP. *Canadian Journal of Forest Research*, **33**, 126–136.

Maas, E. F. and Adamson, R. M. (1975). Peat, bark and sawdust mixtures for nursery substrates. *Acta Horticulturae*, **50**, 147–151.

MacKenzie, D. M. and Quideau, S. A. (2010). Microbial community structure and nutrient availability in oilsands reclaimed boreal soils. *Applied Soil Ecology*, **44**, 32–41.

Martin, J. L., Gower, S. T., Plaut, J., Holmes, B. (2005). Carbon pools in a boreal mixedwood logging chronosequence. *Global Change Biology*, **11**, 1883–1894.

Peterson, E. B. and Peterson, N. M. (1992). *Ecology, Management, and Use of Aspen and Balsam Poplar in the Prairie Provinces, Canada*. Edmonton, AB, Canadian Forest Service, Northwest Region, Northern Forestry Centre. Spec. Rep. 1.

Rothstein, D. E., Yermakov, Z., Buell, A. L. (2004). Loss and recovery of ecosystem carbon pools following stand-replacing wildfire in Michigan jack pine forests. *Canadian Journal of Forest Research*, **34**, 1908–1918.

Sauchyn, D. and Kulshreshtha, S. (2007). Prairies. In D. S. Lemmen, F. J. Warren, J. Lacroix, E. Bush, eds., *From Impacts to Adaptation: Canada in a Changing Climate*. Ottawa, ON: Government of Canada, pp. 275–328.

Schindler, D. W. and Donahue, W. F. (2006). An impending water crisis in Canada's western prairie provinces. *Proceedings of the National Academy of Science*, **103**, 7210–7216.

Schneider, R. R., Hamann, A., Farr, D., Wang, X., Boutin, S. (2009). Potential effects of climate change on ecosystem distribution in Alberta. *Canadian Journal of Forest Research*, **39**, 1001–1010.

Seely, B., Hawkins, C., Blanco J. A., Welham, C., Kimmins, J. P. (2008). Evaluation of an ecosystem-based approach to mixedwood modelling. *Forest Chronicle*, **84**, 181–193.

Turcotte, I., Quideau, S. A., Oh, S. W. (2009). Organic matter quality in reclaimed boreal forest soils following oilsands mining. *Organic Geochemistry*, **40**, 510–519.

Turunen, J., Roulet, N. T., Moore, T. R., Richard, P. J. H. (2004). Nitrogen deposition and increased carbon accumulation in ombrotrophic peatlands in eastern Canada. *Global Biogeochemical Cycles*, **18**, GB3002.

Vitt, D. H., Wieder, K., Halsey, L. A., Turetsky, M. (2003). Response of *Sphagnum fuscum* to nitrogen deposition: a case study of ombrogenous peatlands in Alberta, Canada. *Bryologist*, **106**, 235–245.

Welham, C. (2004). *Deriving Multipliers And Nutrient Regime Classes for the Land Capability Classification System using the Ecosystem Simulation Model, FORECAST*. Final report in partial fulfillment of CEMA Contract No. 2003–0007. Ft.McMurray, AB: Cumulative Environmental Management Association.

Welham, C. (2005a). *Evaluating a Prescriptive Approach to Creating Target Ecosites using D-Ecosites as a Test Case*. Final report in partial fulfillment of CEMA Contract No. 2004–0014. Ft.McMurray, AB: Cumulative Environmental Management Association.

Welham, C. (2005b). *Evaluating Existing Prescriptions for Creating Target Ecosites using the Ecosystem Simulation Model, FORECAST: Implications for Ecosystem Productivity and Community Composition*. Final report in partial fulfillment of CEMA Contract No. 2005–0025. Ft.McMurray, AB: Cumulative Environmental Management Association.

Welham, C. (2006). *Evaluating Existing Prescriptions for Creating Target Ecosites using the Ecosystem Simulation Model, FORECAST: Implications for Ecosystem Productivity and Community Composition in Reclaimed Overburden*. Final report in partial fulfillment of CEMA Contract No. 2006–0030. Ft.McMurray, AB: Cumulative Environmental Management Association.

Welham, C., Seely, B. and Kimmins, H. (2002). The utility of the two-pass harvesting system: an analysis using the ecosystem simulation model FORECAST. *Canadian Journal of Forest Research*, **32**, 1071–1079.

Welham, C., Van Rees, K., Seely, B., Kimmins, H. (2007). Projected long-term productivity in Saskatchewan hybrid poplar plantations: weed competition and fertilizer effects. *Canadian Journal of Forest Research*, **37**, 356–370.

16

The business of carbon

INTRODUCTION

Terrestrial ecosystems are one of the world's largest sinks for carbon and (along with the oceans) are the only large scale "technology" capable of actively removing existing greenhouse gases (GHG) from the atmosphere. At the same time, terrestrial ecosystems are also one of the largest sources of man-caused GHG emissions through the development or destruction of forests, grasslands, and wetlands. Ecosystems simultaneously provide large-scale opportunities to sequester existing GHG emissions and to avoid GHG emissions. Some 12% of man-made global emissions are the result of land use change (e.g., deforestation and wetland drainage). Forests also sequester some 27% of these emissions each year. In addition, ecosystems provide a low-cost mechanism to achieve GHG emission reductions and sequestration in comparison to most other technological changes.

This chapter will take a practical look at how and why markets for carbon offsets have been developing, and then examine the details of ecosystem-based carbon project development and the business opportunities within carbon offset project development.

THE UNDERPINNINGS OF A CARBON MARKET

Creating a market for carbon

One of the most challenging features of the climate change issue is the scale of the problem, and therefore the scale of the solutions necessary

Restoration and Reclamation of Boreal Ecosystems, ed. Dale Vitt and Jagtar Bhatti. Published by Cambridge University Press. © Cambridge University Press 2012.

to even put a dent in reducing the risk of catastrophic change. Enkvist et al. (2007) estimated that to achieve a 450 ppm atmosphere in 2030, the world economy would need to reduce emissions by 26 gigatons CO_2e, at a cost of 500–1100 billion euros. There are many potential sources of emissions abatement, some of which are even financially beneficial regardless of carbon (i.e., building efficiency changes). Forestry and land use changes account for a significant portion of the lower cost emission abatement activities potential. Enkvist et al. (2007) calculated forestry had the highest potential for low-cost emissions abatement of any sector– 25.1% of the total, higher than opportunities in power, manufacturing, transportation, buildings, or agriculture.

The question has been how to force or enable significant actions in any of these abatement activities at the necessary economy-wide, not to mention global, scale.

As atmospheric pollution is a "tragedy of the commons," or externality cost, one logical approach is to rely on direct government action to enforce or incentivize large-scale emission reductions through mechanisms such as carbon taxation, direct source emission regulation, or direct government investment in sequestration or other offsetting activities. These government-led actions (e.g., British Columbia's revenue neutral carbon tax supplements, the pending British Columbia cap and trade program, and Ontario reportedly phasing out coal power plans by government mandate), although still part of the solution, are politically very difficult, particularly when looking at the level of tax or regulatory burden that would be required to force the large-scale technological and societal change necessary to match the scale of the emissions problem. True to form, over the past 10–20 years large scale, direct government action related to managing emissions has proven very difficult in most major global economies (with the exception of the EU, where a market-based cap and trade exists) within the limited political and financial capital of governments, and the current state of the economy and level of ongoing divisive political debate in general (particularly in the U.S. and Canada) makes this unlikely to change any time soon.

For example, in Canada, GHG emissions have actually increased by 17% from 1990–2009, since the signing of the Kyoto protocol, which called for significant economy-wide reductions by 2012 (5% below 1990 levels). In 2009, Canada signed the Copenhagen Protocol, making the commitment to reduce GHG emissions by 17% from the period of 2005–2020. Environment Canada (Fig. 16.1) (Environment Canada, 2011) reported that all of the currently planned collective action of governments across Canada is projected to reduce emissions by 65 $MtCO_2e$ by 2020, which

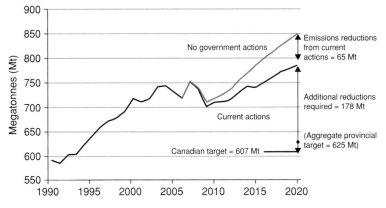

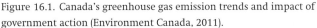

Figure 16.1. Canada's greenhouse gas emission trends and impact of government action (Environment Canada, 2011).

is 25% of the necessary reduction to meet the Copenhagen 2020 target. In 2010 alone, all government action is projected to amount to an annual reduction of 8 $MtCO_2e$ (718 Mt to 710 Mt), or a reduction impact of 1.1% of total emissions. Two key points are (using Canada as an example): first, direct government actions have not been effective at large scale emissions reductions; and second, the scale of the emissions reductions required are quite staggering: a 17% reduction in Canada is 243 $MtCO_2e$ or 24.3 $MtCO_2e$ yr^{-1}–and this is only a fraction of the typical global target of reducing emission by 80% by 2050.

The alternative to direct government action is to enable market-based solutions, where the powers of business and the capital markets are used to rapidly scale up cost-effective economy-wide GHG emissions action. In the simplest terms, financial markets have the greatest capability to mobilize immense amounts of capital and resources to effect change–that is, when there is an opportunity to make money.

Tradable carbon units

Although there are various formal definitions, carbon offsets are fundamentally created through measuring carbon emissions reductions and sequestration related to a specific activity (or change in activity), and translating these changes into measurable and trackable units. For the purposes of this chapter and for simplicity, carbon offsets, credits, allowances, and other terms for tradable carbon units are treated similarly as "carbon offsets." In reality, allowances are tradable units within capped economic sectors, while offsets or credits are units from emission reductions within non-capped sectors. Offsets provide a quantifiable and comparable "currency" around which market transactions can occur between entities that make changes to reduce emissions or sequester carbon, and entities that want or need to reduce their emissions impact beyond their current internal levels.

Within a market-based emissions reduction system, carbon offsets can play a significant role in incentivizing emissions reductions or sequestration across a broad set of abatement activities, both as part of a regulatory system, or on a voluntary basis. Essentially carbon offsets create a mechanism to place a value on emissions reductions and sequestration, and then let businesses and entrepreneurs find the best solutions–buyers demand the type of desired credits at the lowest cost, while suppliers will overturn every stone looking for ways to create marketable offsets to sell, and a "market" starts to develop.

Government policy and markets for carbon

The global carbon market can develop (and has developed, in some cases) as a purely voluntary market without government involvement and with independently developed standards and quality controls. However, this voluntary market is limited in scale and scope to the most progressive leading companies, consumers, and regions. It appears unlikely that a global market for carbon will develop voluntarily at the scale and timeline of necessary abatement to avoid serious climate change. Governments therefore have a critical role to develop policy that further enables and accelerates the deployment of capital into a carbon market. Government can play a key role in removing barriers and uncertainty in project eligibility and standards requirements, but perhaps most significantly, government can drive economy-wide demand for emissions reductions through policy, which puts a price on carbon and creates a market-based trading system, such as a cap and trade.

Cap and trade, where the government sets and enforces a set of emissions caps by industry, is a critically important step toward rapidly reaching the scale required to reduce economy-wide emissions. Without such a regulatory system, carbon offsets and trading will continue and grow, but only at the pace that progressive businesses (and customer demand) are willing to voluntarily lead change. Without some form of mandatory emissions limits, much of mainstream business will not participate in reducing what is currently a free external cost (i.e., emissions are free) until a tipping point is reached due to public demand.

Unregulated, such a point is difficult to reach–business is business and much of it follows the cheapest path until forced to do otherwise.

There are a series of variations on cap and trade, but the starting point is that the government sets mandatory participation and mandatory emissions "caps" that decline over time, reducing emissions even in the face of industry growth. Left at this, these are purely regulatory costs on businesses and industries that would be very expensive and costly to the economy, and in reality, practically impossible to enact politically. The key then is the addition of the "trade" component, where the government can enable market-based solutions that radically lower the business and societal costs of large-scale emissions reductions. By creating the ability for businesses to choose to invest in their own emission reductions (i.e., by changing their technology or processes), or buy the surplus emissions reductions or offsets from others, it allows participants to choose the best solutions for their business, depending on the options available to them (and the costs thereof), in comparison to the costs of acquiring offsets from other market participants. Businesses, industries, and financial capital can all find the most efficient way to reduce emissions–and as the emissions caps are lowered, the supply and demand for allowances, offsets, and technological changes will direct all market capital into the most efficient solutions.

At its essence, the cap forces the change, but the trade allows flexibility for the market to find the best solutions and keep the costs of the required changes minimized. Once there is a demand for carbon, a mechanism to trade, and the ability to set a price, then the business opportunities within carbon begin to emerge at scale. In particular, this creates the environment to put a value on ecosystems to retain and sequester carbon, which changes the entire paradigm for how we value natural resources and ecosystems as a whole.

The benefits of ecosystem-based carbon offsets

As noted, ecosystem-based carbon plays a significant role in emissions and sequestration of carbon, and therefore can logically play a major role in the carbon offsets market(s). In particular, ecosystem-based abatement strategies are one of the few opportunities with the project-level scale to provide large quantities of carbon emissions reductions and sequestration at relatively low cost.

As noted by Enkvist et al. (2007), global forests and ecosystems provide the largest cost-effective opportunity for emissions abatement. At a project scale, ecosystem-based projects are by far the largest opportunity

for emissions reductions and sequestration as compared to other potential project types and abatement activities. For example, implementing
the negative-cost building efficiency opportunities across economies and
at a large scale is difficult at best–the timelines to change building codes
and convert standing building stock one at a time is a significant under-
taking (although theoretically, if there were a price on carbon, the market
would incentivize this change). For example, the average state of the art
LEED-certified green building reduces emissions by 350 tCO2e yr^{-1} as
compared to an average conventional building, and buildings typically
have lifespans of 50–100 years and refurbishment cycles of 20–30 years.
In comparison, large forestry-based carbon projects are simpler to scale
up–the largest forest carbon project in North America to date (outlined
in more detail in the case study at the end of this chapter) created net
emission reduction offsets of about 300,000 tCO_2e yr^{-1} off 55,000 ha
of land base. Developing 25 additional, similar projects across Canada
could match all of the currently projected emission reductions from government policies across Canada with a fraction of the effort.

As another example of the relative importance of forest-based carbon offsets in the market, Barclays Capital (2010) projected that forest-
based carbon offsets would have accounted for the majority of the potential aggregate offset supply under a U.S. national capital and trade
system–of a projected offset supply from all project types or sources,
forest carbon would account for 62% of the domestic offset supply from
2012–2020. Over those eight years, forestry offset projects were expected
to produce about 944 million tCO_2e of carbon offsets.

The key point is that although all types of emissions abatements
will be necessary, ecosystem-based carbon projects will be in particular
demand due to the relative simplicity, scaleability, and effectiveness in
achieving low-cost and large-scale emission reductions.

In addition to real abatement scale, ecosystem-based carbon
projects are generally likely to create additional, significant co-benefits in
protection of water, biodiversity, and other ecosystem services by maintaining or restoring the ecosystem.

Putting a price on ecosystem carbon

The key outcome of market-based GHG emissions solutions is the creation
of a market value for the carbon held or sequestered in ecosystems, which
creates:

1.   a paradigm shift in the valuation of land and ecosystems due to
      the opportunity to monetize (i.e., sell) carbon. Previously, land

management choices were essentially dichotomous: either to develop and extract the resource to make money, or conserve the resource and lose the economic opportunity. With the ability to sell carbon, the second alternative becomes to conserve the resource or reduce extraction, and make money from ecosystem carbon;

2.   real business opportunities to retain and sequester carbon in ecosystems. A key point to this chapter is the fact that carbon offsets are becoming valuable within very large and potentially rapidly growing markets, and therefore are becoming an interesting investment for financial return. In other words, saleable carbon offsets from ecosystems have moved from theory into business reality;

3.   the potential for market-driven solutions for large-scale emission abatement. As the markets for carbon and the business case for ecosystem-based carbon offsets develop, significant amounts of capital can be mobilized into ecosystem management for carbon.

CARBON OFFSET MARKETS AND THE BUYERS OF CARBON

Market categories

In general, the carbon offset market is broken down into three categories.

Voluntary market

The voluntary carbon market, as the name implies, is made up of private over-the-counter (OTC) sales of carbon offsets to buyers who voluntarily purchase offsets. Voluntary buyers are typically corporations, government entities, or even retail individuals who are taking independent action to voluntarily offset their GHG emissions. These buyers may be driven by:

- Concern for the environment and climate change.
- Concern for corporate reputation or corporate sustainability (CSR).
- Desire to build new environmental credentials into products and marketing.
- Management or shareholder concerns over business risks related to climate change.

Examples:

- A European natural gas retailer/distributor branded their retail product as "climate friendly," and uses voluntary carbon credits to offset the emissions related to the use of their natural gas product in homes and buildings. This product branding allowed this company to gain market share and build market reputation.

- Many airlines and car rental companies now offer an option to their customers to offset the emissions related to their travel at minimal cost. It is unclear if this is a marketing advantage or has become a market minimum requirement. For example, Air Canada offers carbon offsets as an add-on for most flights–domestic flight offsets generally cost less than $5.00 per flight.

- 178 municipalities in British Columbia have agreed to voluntarily become carbon neutral using emission reductions and offsets by 2012.

Regulatory/compliance market

The regulatory carbon market is created by mandatory emission reduction requirements through regulations, policy, or even international agreements. These emission reductions requirements can be applied economy-wide, within targeted industrial sectors, or within particular industries or jurisdictions.

Examples:

- The European Union Emissions Trading System (EU-ETS) is an economy-wide cap and trade program that is currently deployed across a wide range of industries, with a planned expansion across more sectors of the economy over time. This system has even begun to extend to international industries directly involved in the EU, including the controversial inclusion of mandatory emission reductions on international airlines flying into the EU.

- British Columbia has enacted GHG reduction legislation, including the BC Emissions Offset Regulation. This province-wide cap and trade program is designed to rollout across various industrial and commercial segments over the next decade. This program has started by requiring that all government operations be climate neutral by 2010, and has led to the purchase of over 750,000 tCO_2e to meet this offset need. Owing to the early stage of this program, the purchases used to meet regulatory objectives were made from the voluntary market; however, in the future, British Columbia expects to have a regulatory market for emissions reductions and carbon offsets.

- Alberta enacted one of the first comprehensive mandatory cap and trade programs (Alberta Greenhouse Gas Reduction Program) that is based on capping large scale emissions on an emission intensity basis (i.e., emission per unit production–as compared to absolute emission reductions proposed or existing in other cap and trade systems). Emitters have the choice of paying into a fund at a pre-determined carbon offset price (i.e., $15.00 tCO$_2$e^{-1} in 2010), or allowing participants to purchase carbon offsets within certain approved project types and methodologies.

- Additional regulatory systems are developing or have been deployed, including national systems in New Zealand, Australia, and regional systems in California (ARB), the Western Climate Initiative (WCI), and the Regional Greenhouse Gas Initiative (RGGI).

A more detailed review of the current status of various global regulatory markets can be found in the World Bank State and Trends of the Carbon Market 2011 (www.worldbank.org).

Pre-compliance market

The "pre-compliance" market is a hybrid between the voluntary and compliance markets where companies are entering into the carbon market in advance of pending or anticipated future regulations. These are technically voluntary buyers; however, their motivation is generally to prepare for future legal requirements. The key expectation of the pre-compliance market is that any offsets acquired will be fundable in future regulatory markets.

Examples:

Several large oil and gas firms in Canada have begun to investigate and invest in projects from the voluntary carbon market in order to gain skills, market insight, and expertise for use in future regulatory markets. In addition, some companies are looking to acquire lower-cost carbon projects or carbon rights for use in expected future emissions caps on some or all of their operating units.

- Carbon brokerage companies around the globe continue to acquire offsets for pre-compliance portfolios. Of particular interest recently is pre-compliance market activity in advance of the expected start of the California cap and trade system (scheduled to start in 2013).

Current carbon offset market scale

According to Bloomberg New Energy Finance and Ecosystem Marketplace analysis (Peters-Stanley et al., 2010), the global market for carbon offsets reached US$124 billion in 2010 (up 5% from 2009) on a traded volume of 6.7 billion tCO_2e. Despite the recent global economic recession, carbon policy uncertainties, and inaction in major economies such as the U.S., Japan, and Canada, the carbon market is continuing to grow into a significant global commodity market. In fact, analysts at Barclay Capital have estimated the global carbon market has the potential to become the largest traded commodity market in the world (est. $2–3 trillion by 2020) (Kantor, 2007).

The global voluntary market continues to grow, up from 55 million tCO_2e (2009) to 69 million tCO_2e (2010), worth in excess of $413 million (excluding transactions related to the Chicago Climate Exchange (CCX), which added voluntary volumes of 55–69 million tCO_2e prior to closing in 2010). In 2010, approximately 42% of the voluntary market was made up of forest-based carbon offsets (24 million tCO_2e). These forest carbon offsets are being sold to compliance, pre-compliance, and voluntary markets. The bottom line is that the market for carbon is substantial and growing (even in the face of a major international economic downturn), and staged for substantial upside growth if local, regional, national, or even international cap and trade regulations are implemented.

What is driving current market demand?

There are a host of factors driving the current market demand for carbon, all of which are driving increasing awareness and recognition of carbon across all sectors of the economy:

1. marketing/public relations/corporate sustainability
   - Corporate sustainability reporting goals.
   - Product differentiation and marketing.
   - Reaction to competitors.

Carbon impact is increasingly becoming a potential product, brand, or reputational attribute that can provide a competitive advantage in the marketplace. Companies, brands, and products are increasingly using carbon impact as a marketing tool to differentiate their operations or specific products as environmentally friendly, or some form of "climate-friendly." Generally, these are voluntary buyers, where the quality of the carbon offsets projects and related storyline is important.

This also relates to increasing demand for transparency into the impacts of company operations or products in the world. Consumers are increasingly demanding more environmentally friendly options (or at least "less bad" products); businesses are demanding more transparency and reporting from across their supply chain; and investors and financiers are increasingly scrutinizing investment risks (and opportunities) related to carbon emissions and climate change. Voluntary markets provide a method for companies to demonstrate early action and assure consumers and investors they are taking action to mitigate their carbon impact and risk.

2. Pending or existing regulations, reporting, and carbon risk

- Current regulations: some jurisdictions have begun to implement regulations to restrict carbon emissions within particular sectors of the economy. This is particularly concerning to businesses with multi-jurisdictional operations and interests, as they can become subject to a complex patchwork of regulatory emissions requirements that are difficult to manage across business lines. Further, these regulations can be implemented to direct the emissions liability to different places in the supply chain, so one jurisdiction might restrict emissions at the retailer level; others might be leveled at the source of the product.

- Pending or potential for future regulations: it is clear that a broad set of government jurisdictions are considering emissions reduction regulations, or may well do so at some point in the business planning and investment cycles of emitter businesses. Increasingly, forward thinking businesses are not only monitoring and evaluating these risks, but also acting to begin to develop the resources and expertise in carbon emissions reductions and trading in advance. Some companies are beginning to invest considerable resources and capital into the voluntary carbon market with the speculation that market experience and voluntary offsets will reduce the risk of future regulatory market liabilities and uncertainty.

- Emerging supply chain emissions reporting and reductions: major global companies are increasingly analyzing and reporting on environment metrics such as GHG emissions across their entire global supply chains. For example, Wal-Mart has announced a goal of eliminating 20 million tCO_2e from its global supply chain by 2015 (http://walmartstores.com/Sustainability/8141.aspx). As one of the largest companies in the world, Wal-Mart's voluntary action has serious ramifications for thousands of suppliers across the globe. Tesco is labeling the carbon footprint by product for consumers across their entire product selection. Companies such as Nike, PandG, Puma, Whole Foods, and a host of others are making similar movements.

- Emerging corporate carbon financial liabilities and shareholder action: companies are also faced with emerging shareholder demands to disclose carbon liabilities. In fact, the U.S. Securities and Exchange Commission (SEC) recently issued guidance that all listed public companies should be reporting on potential carbon liabilities within their public filings. The Carbon Disclosure Project is another indicator, where 551 investors representing $71 trillion in investment capital asked the Global 500 to begin reporting on carbon and related strategies–81% of the Global 500 responded.

The bottom line is that corporations are beginning to have to recognize, report, and mitigate real or potential carbon emission liabilities. Carbon is moving beyond the sustainability and marketing departments to reach the level of corporate risk management, capital acquisition and deployment planning, shareholder relations, customer requirements, etc.

In addition, as corporations begin to track and report emissions, they are recognizing the need to develop mitigation and adaptation strategies and also seeing the potential scale of the problem for those with large emission profiles. Progressive companies are looking to develop experience, understanding, and expertise in the carbon market in advance of reporting.

Although diverse and fragmented, these events and initiatives are creating a set of increasingly interested buyers for carbon offsets in a generally voluntary capacity, which creates a set of diverse markets for carbon offsets that exist today and are evolving and emerging rapidly. As regulatory markets continue to develop in various jurisdictions, the markets for carbon are becoming larger, more stable, and more transparent.

FOREST CARBON PROJECTS AS EMERGING BUSINESS AND INVESTMENT OPPORTUNITIES

At the carbon offset project level, 3GreenTree has found that some private forests can generate better risk-adjusted financial returns from carbon than timber. Some of our partners have found markets for carbon offsets from forest restoration activities worth millions of dollars; others have generated significant internal funding from carbon offsets properties acquired for conservation purposes. Simply put, creating and monetizing carbon offsets from ecosystems is possible today, and is looking to be even better in the future.

In theory, retaining or sequestering ecosystem carbon is worth something–potentially, a great deal. However, designing and developing high quality carbon projects and reaching these diverse markets can be complex, with a multitude of current and emerging project types and protocol choices, a labyrinth of existing and emerging market scenarios, and the need to match long-duration projects to moving goal posts in the realm of market, policy, and rules.

In reality, it is harder than it looks to get the right project, with the right characteristics, to the right market.

What makes a carbon offset marketable or saleable?

The emergence of the market for ecosystem-based carbon offsets has been hampered by the lack of methods and specific rules and requirements to design carbon projects. This has changed very rapidly in the last two years, and high quality protocols and methodologies are now available for forest carbon projects, and are under development for reclamation and wetlands. Virtually all carbon standards require third party independent auditing, many with very robust auditor accreditation standards. These carbon standards have further evolved to include the issuance of serialized (i.e., numbered and tracked) offset credits on registries, which track credits by project over their lifespan and further assure buyers of the source and pedigree of purchased offsets.

All carbon standards utilize a common set of underlying principles (adapted from the VCS program documents):

1. real–all GHG emission reductions and removals and the projects that generate them must be proven to have genuinely taken place;
2. measurable–all GHG emission reductions and removals must be quantifiable using recognized measurement tools (including adjustments for uncertainty and leakage) against a credible emissions baseline;
3. additional–project-based GHG emission reductions and removals must be additional to what would have happened under a business-as-usual scenario if the project had not been carried out;
4. permanent–where GHG emission reductions or removals are generated by projects that carry a risk of reversibility, adequate safeguards must be in place to ensure that the risk of reversal is minimized and that, should any reversal occur, a mechanism is in

place that guarantees the reductions or removals will be replaced or compensated;

5.   verifiable–all GHG emission reductions and removals must be verified to a reasonable level of assurance by an independent accredited validation or verification audit body with the expertise necessary in both the country and sector in which the project is taking place;

6.   unique–VCU must be unique and must only be associated with a single GHG emission reduction or removal activity. There must be no double counting or double claiming of the environmental benefit, in respect of the GHG emission reductions or removals.

Forest carbon offset project types

Currently, various protocols exist to develop projects related to ecosystems, including (but not limited to):

1.   afforestation–establishing forests on land previously devoid of forests;

2.   reforestation–reestablishing forests on areas not normally reforested;

3.   avoided deforestation (i.e., reduced emissions from deforestation [RED] or reduced emissions from deforestation and degradation [REDD])–avoiding the conversion of forest areas to non-forested land use;

4.   improved forest management (extended rotations, reduced impact logging, avoided logging)–changing forest management practices to increase the net carbon within the forest;

5.   wetland management (rewetting peatlands, avoided drainage, avoided conversion)–retaining or improving the net carbon content of wetland areas.

Several protocols exist relating to various forms of agricultural carbon offset projects (some of which could be included here as "ecosystem-based" projects, while others are more industrial production related). Finally, additional protocols and methodologies are being or could be,developed to cover an even wider range of possible ecosystem-based project situations.

The key is clearly establishing a change in land use, land management, or operating practices that retains carbon already existing in biological systems and/or sequesters additional carbon over time. At its simplest, a carbon offset is the difference in the carbon storage between the baseline or business-as-usual scenario and the scenario in which a carbon project is implemented; however, within the constraints of a given carbon protocol and/or methodology, there are many potential carbon offset project design options. It is also important to recognize that a carbon offset project can be designed within other developments. In other words, carbon and resource development are not always mutually exclusive–with innovative project planning and practices, carbon can be retained and then sold as carbon offsets. In some cases, an entire area might be set aside and managed solely for carbon, but in other cases carbon might only play a supplemental role to pay for improved or innovative practices, which increase the net carbon content of a site, or anything in between. Thus, clear and widely accepted protocols and methodologies are important to enabling carbon offset projects, but design at the individual project level is also critical to success.

Carbon standards

A key to reaching the carbon offset market is the use of a widely recognized, high-quality carbon standard or protocol with independent third party project validation and verification. Simply put, validation is confirmation that the project meets all of the requirements of the carbon standard, while verification is confirmation that the carbon accounting and quantification is done correctly prior to offsets being issued for sale.

Currently, there are four leading North American voluntary carbon standards:

- Verified Carbon Standard (VCS – formerly: Voluntary Carbon Standard).
- Climate Action Reserve (CAR).
- American Climate Registry (ACR).
- Climate, Biodiversity Association (CCBA).

There are a series of other global voluntary carbon standards available with varying applicability regionally or by project type.

Regulatory market carbon standards are at different levels of development, depending on the jurisdiction.

- Alberta is developing an internal set of protocols or methodologies, including currently, draft materials for various forestry project types.
- British Columbia Forest Offsets Protocol–currently a voluntary standard expected to develop as a methodology in the future British

Columbia cap and trade program. British Columbia currently also accepts VCS and other standards as alternatives, although this may change.

- California–at this point, the California Air Resources Board has adopted four protocols from the Climate Action Reserve voluntary standard, including forestry and urban forestry.
- Outside of North America, there are multiple regulatory markets with standards relating to forest-based carbon projects, including:
  - CDM–allows afforestation or reforestation from certain developing countries;
  - New Zealand–has extensive forestry protocols;
  - Australia–is adopting various agricultural and forestry protocols;
  - China–is developing a set of carbon protocols.

There continues to be ongoing discussion about the acceptance of voluntary carbon standards and methodologies within developing regulatory markets around the globe.

Financial opportunities in ecosystem-based carbon projects

The emergence of both voluntary and regulatory carbon markets is creating the opportunity for carbon to play a significant role in ecosystem management finance. Depending on the project type and design, financial returns from carbon can produce the following.

- Funding for restoration and ongoing restoration management, in whole or in part.
- Fund changes in management practices to enhance ecosystem protection or function, or to achieve other land use objectives such as conservation, recreation, or cultural use.
- Supplemental income to extractive resources such as timber.
- Investment-grade financial returns on investment in place of, or in combination with, timber and other resource extraction.

The magnitude and impact of revenues from carbon on any of these activities is highly variable; however, it is clear that carbon offsets can be used to extract value from changes in management practices, and hence can become a new tool in the toolbox for all land managers and investors to research and develop.

Carbon prices

Carbon prices are another key variable in the business of carbon. Currently, carbon pricing has been relatively nontransparent outside the key regulatory markets such as the EU-ETS. In addition, the lack of policy certainty has clearly hampered price discovery. Therefore, it is difficult to monitor current prices, and forward looking carbon prices are relatively speculative.

In 2010, VCS voluntary carbon offsets were typically selling for $5.00–$7.50 tCO_2e^{-1}. California ARB allowance contracts for 2013 delivery are pricing at $16.00–$19.00 tCO_2e^{-1} (and offsets should trade at a discount to this). EU-ETS allowances trade at €15.00–€20.00 tCO_2e^{-1}, while CDM offsets trade at a $3.00–$5.00 discount to this. In Alberta, emitters can choose between paying into a fund at $15.00 tCO_2e^{-1} or buying offsets, which indicates that offsets should trade below this threshold.

Speculation and projection on future carbon prices is, frankly, all over the map. For example, the Pacific Carbon Trust in British Columbia is, by regulation, paid $25.00 tCO_2e^{-1} by government organizations and, while this does not relate to the prices paid by PCT to project offsets, it is instructive of early government expectations of carbon price ranges. Barclays Capital has estimated California market prices to rise to $30.00–$35.00 tCO_2e^{-1} by 2017. Point Carbon estimates (based on supply and demand projections) that the California market will reach $75.00 tCO_2e^{-1} by 2020.

In summary, current carbon pricing is not transparent, and forward looking prices are subject to uncertainty in the markets and tend to vary significantly depending on the market development assumptions used.

Challenges

Prior to 2010, the primary barrier to carbon project development was a lack of protocols and methodologies for most types of ecosystem-based carbon projects. By 2010, however, several key carbon protocols were stable and applicable across a rapidly growing set of jurisdictions, and actual methodologies were being approved for a variety of project types (particularly forest carbon projects). By late 2010 and early 2011, forest carbon projects had gained the carbon standard certainty to fully develop a wide range of projects (at least within the voluntary market).

However, key challenges and barriers still exist for carbon projects.

Ownership

A key criterion for any carbon project is demonstrating ownership rights over the carbon and/or related land use for the duration of the carbon project. On fee-simple private land, this can be relatively easily established (although not immune to complexity due to title restrictions, multiple owners, separated title rights, and future change of ownership issues).

On publicly owned lands, however, ownership becomes complicated and can present a barrier to private project development. Public lands are subject to existing and future resource-use agreements (for aboveground and subsurface rights, often simultaneously), First Nations title and rights claims, and perhaps most importantly, government land use policy.

Moving goalposts in carbon standards and government policy

On both private and public lands, carbon projects are subject to the specifics of the carbon standards and methodologies the project has chosen, along with changes in government policy. Carbon standards are new and undergoing change and development that can significantly affect existing and developing projects, sometimes in unintended ways. Government policy and laws or regulations also have the potential to shift markets or affect projects, sometimes in unintended ways. For example, new laws or land use requirements can change the baseline scenarios for future projects. Policies can change what standards or methodologies are accepted in compliance markets, what projects are eligible, or even what sectors of the economy can participate (e.g., international agreements such as Kyoto or others can have all sorts of unintended project level implications).

Attracting capital to uncertainty

Generally, carbon projects require financial capital to either acquire the carbon rights (i.e., land acquisition, etc.), or to fund the development and approval of the project prior to carbon offset credits being issued for sale. The uncertainties in the carbon market, carbon prices, government policy, and even carbon standards serve to create uncertainties for investors and capital providers.

Planning and commitment time horizon

The objective of carbon projects is to remove and/or keep GHG emissions out of the atmosphere for very long timeframes. Although the target timelines for carbon removal are still controversial, it is increasingly apparent that the general consensus is emerging by which the most conservative approach of a target project timeline should be 100 years (although some standards require less, or in some cases more). On the theoretical side, 100 years seems generally beyond our societal capacity to plan for and commit to. We can model ecosystems and carbon at 100 years and beyond, but our ability to create lasting policy and contractual commitments is challenging. On the practical side, the 100-year time frame provides a considerable disincentive for private landowners and governments to participate.

Market or pricing uncertainty

One of the key challenges to carbon project development is the uncertainty in the development path for carbon offset markets, and the resulting carbon offset pricing expectations. There is uncertainty about which of the carbon standards will be accepted in what markets, and how fungible and transferable credits from different standards will be. This is multiplied by the lack of certainty on price expectations within different markets and between different carbon standards, particularly when looking at the mid- to long-term.

In summary, although there has been tremendous improvement in carbon standards, markets, and buyer demands, it is still an emerging business field with the risks, uncertainties, and opportunities of a leading edge emerging market.

CASE STUDY

The Darkwoods Carbon Project: carbon as conservation asset financing

Starting in 2010, 3GreenTree Ecosystem Services Ltd. developed the largest forest carbon project in North America. In addition, 3GreenTree began to assess the financial implications of forest carbon opportunities on timberland investment for private forest properties.

Background

The Nature Conservancy of Canada undertook the largest conservation-based private land acquisition in Canadian history with an imbedded carbon project as a key revenue source on the 55,000 ha Darkwoods property in southeastern British Columbia. Fundamentally, the project created carbon offsets through the avoidance of emissions related to logging in the baseline scenario that was based on independent land valuation appraisal scenarios and relevant common practices in surrounding managed forests that had been put up for sale. The NCC acquired the land and reduced the logging to low levels for conservation and ecological management purposes as part of a 100-year carbon project and other ecological management objectives. The project underwent a full VCS validation and verification for the first three years of the project, including double independent auditor reviews of detailed permanence risk assessments. The project includes full dynamic carbon flow accounting through all carbon pools; net downs for project activities, leakage risk, and uncertainty risk; and contributes a portion of credits to the VCS pooled permanence buffer account (which serves as all-cause insurance against any unanticipated future emissions reversals)[1]. The project followed the VCS methodology VM0012[2]. The project is additional primarily because there is no revenue or business model from the conservation activities of the project without the carbon project, and hence there is no market or investment rationale to acquire and set aside these types of commercial properties.

Development timeline

The Darkwoods carbon project was ground-breaking, and hence required a significant amount of extra time and costs to develop brand new and untested methods. However, as one of the first approved and fully operational forest carbon projects, the timelines, costs, and revenue streams are instructive for similar project types. The development of a new VCS carbon methodology and approval through the robust VCS double-approval process took approximately nine months. This was undertaken on an accelerated schedule; however, as one of the first methodologies undertaken for a forestry project of this kind, the process was longer than those for subsequent methodologies will be. The development of the project and project design document (PDD or PD) was undertaken simultaneously with the methodology development, and took approximately six months.

The project monitoring plan development was undertaken simultaneously with the PDD development, and implementation has been

---

[1] The Darkwoods project details are available at: http://www.vcsprojectdatabase.org/.
[2] Methodology available at: http://www.v-c-s.org/methodologies/VM0012.

ongoing for the six-month field season post-PDD approval. Although project specific, the development of the full monitoring plan on the property will be ongoing over the first two to three project years, and then continue as a remeasurement process annually for the project duration.

Although highly variable, based on the project scenario and situation, a new project should consider:

- Methodology development and approval:
  - Development of a brand new methodology through approval: 8–12 months.
  - Revision or modification of an existing methodology: substantially shorter–minimum 1–2 months, depending on the level of revision.
- Development of the project design and related documents:
  - 4–6 months if a new project type,
  - 2–4 months if developing a new project of an existing type.

Development costs

The Darkwoods project was potentially unique due to its ground-breaking position and the disjointed acquisition and project development timelines; therefore, the generalized results outlined here are not necessarily directly comparable or representative of other similar project situations. However, we can look at the timelines, costs and revenues as an indicator, or single data points, for comparison.

In terms of the carbon project itself (not including property acquisition and related costs, property management and overheads, taxes, or other non-carbon project related costs), the actual costs are difficult to isolate due to multiple processes being undertaken simultaneously, and the unique nature of the property level data at Darkwoods. In addition, note that the operating posture on Darkwoods was set up to verify and issue carbon offsets annually; but the minimum or committed project cost liability is a fraction of the following if they choose to operate at the minimum requirements. In terms of estimates:

- Methodology development: $100,000–$155,000
  - These costs should decline as developers become more experienced and have more approved methodologies to work from.
  - Includes costs of VCS double auditor costs ($45,000–$65,000).
- PD development: $50,000–$100,000

- Highly dependent on project scale, complexity, and level of starting data available.
  - Reasonable estimate for other timberland projects: $5–$10.00/ha ($2–$4.00 acre^{-1}).
- Monitoring development: $125,000–$175,000 yr^{-1} for the first three years, declining to $50,000 yr^{-1}, ongoing.
  - Darkwoods started with an excellent timber inventory, but no carbon or biomass plots or other carbon project monitoring tools.
  - Reasonable estimate for other projects: $0.50–$1.25 acre^{-1} yr^{-1}.

Revenues

The sales pricing and strategies at Darkwoods are confidential; however, a reasonable proxy can be created from general voluntary market price ranges and Darkwoods issuance volumes.

- Project carbon offset volumes: approximately 810,000 tCO$_2$e in the first three years; then variable, but averaging 200,000 tCO$_2$e yr^{-1}, ongoing.
- Carbon pricing (2009–2010, source: Ecosystem Marketplace State of the Carbon Markets and 3GreenTree market intelligence), range $5.50–$7.50 tCO$_2$e^{-1}.
  - Estimated Initial Project Revenue
  - Low end: 810,000 tCO$_2$e (first three years verified) @ $5.50 tCO$_2$e^{-1} = $4.45 million,
  - High end: 810,000 tCO$_2$e (first three years verified) @ $7.50 tCO$_2$e^{-1} = $6.08 million,
- Estimated Ongoing Project Revenue (example carbon pricing only, real basis)
  - Low end: 200,000 tCO$_2$e yr^{-1} @ $10.00 tCO$_2$e^{-1} = $2.0 million yr^{-1},
  - High end: 200,000 tCO$_2$e yr^{-1} @ $30.00 tCO$_2$e^{-1} = $6.0 million yr^{-1}.

Note that voluntary OTC carbon pricing is not transparent; however, we are beginning to get indications of carbon offset pricing from other markets as well, in the EU-ETS, offsets trade at a discount to allowances, and in 2010 have ranged around €10–€12.00 tCO$_2$e^{-1}. The first one-year contracts on California market allowances traded in mid-2010 at $17–$18.00 tCO$_2$e^{-1} (offsets will likely participate at a discount to this, estimated at \$9–\$15.00 tCO_2e^{-1} at the market start). The Alberta default market price for carbon offsets is presumably near \$15.00 tCO_2e^{-1} based on the option in that system to contribute to a fund at that rate. The key message is the current voluntary market prices–and those used in this project example estimate–are low in context with the existing regulatory market evidence, and presumably will rise in future years as certainty in the regulatory markets improves.

Financial returns

The Darkwoods project was not undertaken on a purely financially driven basis, and details of the Darkwoods acquisition scenario and costs were unique and proprietary to NCC. However, we can use comparable property valuations, costs, and revenues to provide a reasonable proxy of the financial returns possible within such a project.

1.   Key metrics

- Estimated scaled comparable property valuation: \$45.0 million (approx. \$820 ha^{-1} or \$2080 $acre^{-1}$ [3]).
- First sale (first three years carbon–from estimates above): \$4.45–\$6.08 million.
- Ongoing sales (200,000 tCO_2e yr^{-1} for 30 years @ \$20.00 tCO_2e^{-1} real): \$4.0 million yr^{-1} revenue.
- EBITDA margins near 80%.

2.   Key financial results

- First sale generated revenue equal to 10%–13.5% of the acquisition cost.
- Expected IRR: 10.2%.[4]
- Returns are primarily annualized cash returns (cash yields of 3%–5% per year).

---

[3] Note that this is an example valuation based on similar properties at current market, and modified to reflect the substantial areas of the property that are steep, non-merchantable, alpine, and/or previously logged. Therefore, the land value on a per hectare basis is representative for example purposes only, but the results are reflective of other comparable properties and project results.

[4] Calculated on unleveraged EBITDA returns, using the US EPA floor carbon price curve past 2012, 100-year discounted cash flow model (i.e., imbedded terminal value due to the 100-year model), retrieving initial capital investment on a real basis at year 100 (zero land value appreciation), full project, land, and sales management costs included, with 3.5% inflation rate, and 8% real cost of capital/discount rate.

Summary

As a case study, the Darkwoods Carbon Project demonstrates that forest carbon projects are fully feasible and cost-effective, with a high operating margin for the project itself. The carbon project would not have provided up-front financing or acquisition capital within a typical not-for-profit context, and in fact, included substantial up-front time and costs to develop after the acquisition costs. However, the project will be capable of fully funding itself and the ongoing property management costs throughout its lifespan, while also contributing operating capital back into the mission of the project proponent. The bottom line is that this is a game changing development in the world of conservation, where business-like returns are now possible within a conservation-based framework.

When expanded to create a proxy for an investment-driven project, it can be seen that with reasonable acquisition costs and carbon market pricing, a similar project situation is capable of providing interesting investment returns from carbon that are competitive with the comparable timber returns.

Variations on this case study

In addition, 3GreenTree has evaluated (and is developing) forest carbon projects with:

- Carbon as the revenue driver on acquired private industrial forestland for comparison to investment returns from timber management.
- Mixed portfolios of carbon and timber (or carbon, timber, and other ecosystem services) which seek to optimize the risk and returns from timberland investment.

The carbon development activities and costs within these types of business models are similar to the Darkwoods Carbon Project outlined previously; however, rather than focusing on conservation financing for not-for-profit organizations, it is targeted toward generating superior returns on investment for timberland investors using market capital.

What we have found is, in a broad set of timberland properties:

- At carbon offset prices of approximately $5.00–$8.00 tCO_2e^{-1}, growing at 2%–5% above inflation, a carbon-led project will produce marginally competitive returns in comparison to the baseline logging returns.

- At prices from $8.00–$15.00 tCO_2e^{-1}, carbon can become directly comparable in return performance to timberland, with lower risk and a substantially improved upside potential.
- At prices starting at $12–$15 tCO_2e^{-1} and growing at the low end of many industry carbon market predictions, the carbon project can outperform the timber asset financially in cash returns, and has substantially higher additional upside potential.

Perhaps most importantly, within a properly designed project and business model (and within a supporting policy and market context), carbon can provide important diversifying revenue within a timberland business model to reduce investment risk and improve returns while providing a substantial new upside potential to financial returns, and while maintaining the downside risk protection of timber as an investment asset class. This presents a paradigm shift in terms of financial evaluations of timberland, with carbon presenting a viable financial alternative to timber.

In particular, if there is a competitive financial return from forest carbon projects, then:

1. it creates the potential to bring the full weight of market capital to bear on investment into ecosystem-based carbon projects to scale emission abatement opportunities rapidly;
2. it changes the implications of land use policies and carbon policies significantly, and the possibility of returns from carbon can create opportunities for progressive new land use policies to benefit society in the face of development pressure;
3. it radically changes the toolbox available to land managers to achieve financial, ecological, and other objectives on forestlands. Carbon can provide important diversifying revenue; it opens a completely different set of management options and decisions;
4. it creates a clear impetus to explore various types of project design options and financial objectives across a broad set of ecosystem-based carbon opportunities. Not all projects will provide investment-grade returns, but even margin carbon revenue may alter management decisions and investment in many different ecosystem types and situations.

IMPLICATIONS FOR PEATLAND AND WETLAND RECLAMATION

Carbon project methodologies and protocols are a step behind for wetlands and other complex ecosystem reclamation or avoided development projects. However, the fundamental concepts and carbon project development frameworks are the same as for upland forests. The Verified Carbon Standard has already published protocols for avoided wetland conversion and peatland rewetting, and new methodologies and variations can be developed relatively easily with government policy and market support.

Opportunities are emerging to evaluate the implications of a market value on carbon on:

- Avoiding wetland development and/or disturbance, in whole or in part.
- Accelerating or enhancing reclamation activities beyond current practices.

For example, by putting a value on the carbon retained in current wetland ecosystems and future sequestration in these systems, it opens new opportunities to offset the lost development revenue or increased development costs created when protecting key ecosystem components surrounding or within development areas. It is conceivable that mining or oil sands developers could develop alternative mine planning methods to protect key habitat, riparian or other biodiversity systems and future sequestration in these, which would strongly enhance future reclamation success. Carbon within the retained features could play a role in offsetting the increased operational costs. These will not be simple or easy changes to implement in planning and operational practices, but the fact is that carbon revenue can play a (potentially significant) role in reducing the net costs and risks to new innovative development approaches to reduce short- and long-term ecosystem impact. Furthermore, market opportunities in carbon provide incentives for developers to be proactive in identifying potentially radically different operating practices to avoid even stronger regulations, future development limitations, and/or negative public and market issues.

Carbon revenue can also play a significant role in offsetting the costs of enhancing current reclamation operations beyond current common practices. For example, there are very likely significant enhancements in terms of recontouring and shaping (particularly for larger scale hydrological features), addition of off-site organic matter, improved native species planting (i.e., increased planting density or diversity versus seeding), and numerous other improvements that experts can identify that are not currently undertaken due to extra costs over current business-as-usual. Carbon (and other monetizable ecosystem services) can play a role in offsetting these costs over time. It may be that these types of carbon projects are not self-sufficient from carbon revenue, but there are other innovative opportunities to gain value, whether it is to generate public relations improvements, or additional "social license," or even to generate carbon credits to offset operator emissions directly; at base, value can be retrieved from carbon enhancement.

The key point is that carbon offsets can be developed for a wide range of activities related to development operational planning and post-development reclamation, and the financial returns from carbon offsets can offset increased costs in whole or in part, or even present new business opportunities within industrial extraction operations over the short or longer term, and this should be fully explored.

OTHER ECOSYSTEM SERVICES

Carbon is the first of many emerging ecosystem services assets that potentially can be monetized, primarily because the units of measurement, demand from existing or pending government regulation, other market drivers, and protocols are all in place. However, the concepts and methods can and are being expanded to consider monetizing and marketing "offsets" or other monetizable units for biodiversity, water quality and/or quantity, and other ecosystem components. In the United States, wetland, nutrient, and endangered species banking have all become established regulated ecosystem services market mechanisms. Similarly, multiple global jurisdictions have established various forms of endangered species banking, which have become established habitat-offsetting options for developers. Biodiversity offset credits are being developed and registered for sale on global environmental offset registries as a voluntary credit with a value (i.e., the Malua BioBank, for example, sells Biodiversity Conservation Certificates to protect orangutan habitat in SE Asia).

Thus, although this chapter has covered the business of carbon, the concepts can quickly be extended to the business of ecosystem services. Upland, wetland, and riparian ecosystems all contain a suite or portfolio of ecosystem services that can be described, measured, and monetized. When real financial returns are ascribed to these services, it fundamentally changes the land management options for development businesses, conservation organizations, and policy makers. Developers have a suite of new options to develop land differently to improve their environmental and reclamation performance voluntarily, or offset their impacts with similar or equivalent ecosystem protections. In this new paradigm, ecosystem-system based management decisions can find competitive business models to conventional extractive industries, and policymakers have new elements that change the cost structure of imposing new requirements on developers to better protect and manage public resources.

SUMMARY

A market-based carbon offset program can be a low-cost, large-scale mechanism for jurisdictions to reduce GHG emissions and increase carbon sequestration. Offsets provide a market-based mechanism to price carbon, and provide vital flexibility and time for emitting industries to develop and deploy technological GHG emission reductions. Ecosystem-based carbon offset projects provide large-scale opportunities to reduce GHG emissions and one of the only technological mechanisms to remove existing carbon from the atmosphere. In addition, ecosystem-based carbon projects have remarkable synergies with other ecosystem attributes desired by society, including the conservation or restoration of full ecosystem function, and related biodiversity, water, along with other benefits. The development of carbon projects, offset markets, and capital investment require supporting government policy that simultaneously provides assurance and stability for long-term project development and investment along with operational flexibility to develop financially attractive business opportunities. Policymakers must now consider both the implications of land use policies in restricting market opportunities from carbon and other ecosystem services, as well as the ability to leverage these markets to achieve the policy goal.

As of 2010, the protocols and standards for carbon are sufficient to develop high quality ecosystem-based projects, and the carbon markets, although new and variable, are established and growing rapidly. Pending regional regulations are moving rapidly toward the establishment of large-scale compliance markets where ecosystem-based carbon offsets will be accepted. Within this context, interesting real world business opportunities are emerging for financial returns from carbon offsets. The returns from carbon can provide significant funding to restoration or changes in land management practices. In some cases, the returns from carbon are providing a compelling investment business model that may provide a superior risk or return profile in comparison to typical resource extraction (e.g., as compared to logging).

In the end, carbon is shifting the playing field for ecosystem management by putting a real-world, monetizable value on the retention, enhancement, and reclamation of ecosystems. Carbon is now a viable business asset that should be considered by all land management entities–there is indeed "a business of carbon."

REFERENCES

Barclays Capital. (2010). *Carbon Flash: US Offset Supply*. Commodities Research-Energy, London, UK.

Enkvist, P., Naucier, T., Rosander, J. (2007). A cost curve for greenhouse gas reduction. *The McKinsey Quarterly*, **1**, 35–45.

Environment Canada. (2011). *Canada's Emissions Trends*. Ottawa, ON: Ministry of Environment.

Kantor, J. (2007). In London's Financial World, Carbon Trading is the New Big Thing. *New York Times*, July 6.

Peters-Stanley, M., Hamilton, K., Marcello, T., Sjardin, M. (2010). *Back to the Future-State of the Voluntary Carbon Markets 2011*. Washington, DC: Ecosystem Marketplace/Forest Trends, Bloomberg New Energy Finance.

17

Effects of peat extraction and restoration on greenhouse gas exchange from Canadian peatlands

INTRODUCTION

Peat extraction for human use has occurred throughout the last few centuries and continues today across North America, Europe, and Russia. In Canada, peat is extracted predominantly for horticultural purposes, although some small scale use as fuel has recently developed. Approximately 24,000 ha of peatland has been drained for horticultural use in Canada, with 14,000 ha currently under active extraction (Environment Canada, 2010). Although this represents only 0.02% of Canada's estimated 120 million ha of peatland area (Tarnocai, 2006), in some regions up to 70% of peatland area has been affected (Laframboise, 1987, as referenced in Lavoie and Rochefort, 1996). Peat extraction severely alters the ecohydrological conditions of the ecosystem, resulting in massive releases of carbon dioxide (CO_2) (Waddington et al., 2002) and hindering recolonization by *Sphagnum* mosses following extraction (Poulin et al., 2005). In fact, even decades after extraction ceases and the peatland is abandoned, revegetation on ombrotrophic peat remains limited (Poulin et al., 2005). In order to return peatland ecosystem function to these sites, active restoration is required. Intensive research programs over the last two decades have resulted in the development of the North American peatland restoration guide (Quinty and Rochefort, 2003). Application of this restoration strategy can result in the return of a plant community that is dominated by species characteristic of wetland ecosystems in general, and peatlands, specifically. Moreover, the emerging plant community and altered hydrology resulting from restoration should also help to return greenhouse gas (GHG) dynamics to those more similar to

Restoration and Reclamation of Boreal Ecosystems, ed. Dale Vitt and Jagtar Bhatti. Published by Cambridge University Press. © Cambridge University Press 2012.

undisturbed peatland. Given the continuing pressure to report GHG exchange related to land-use change on a variety of ecosystem types (IPCC, 2006), understanding the impact of peat extraction and restoration on peatland GHG fluxes is critical not only for meeting reporting requirements, but also for the development of strategies to reduce emissions associated with land-use change.

GREENHOUSE GAS EMISSIONS ACCOUNTING FOR PEAT EXTRACTION ACTIVITIES

In order to evaluate GHG emissions from peat extraction for horticultural or fuel use, emissions from all activities related to its extraction and use should be considered using a life cycle analysis (LCA) approach. Emissions may arise from land-use change, fuel used by machinery to prepare the site and extract the peat, and the combustion or decomposition of the peat itself. Using this method, emissions associated with land-use change are determined by comparing the GHG balance of the ecosystem during and following extraction to that of the ecosystem prior to extraction activities. When peat is extracted from previously undisturbed sites, the baseline GHG balance is considered to be that of a natural peatland, although values will likely vary regionally and between peatland types. However, few long-term ecosystem-scale GHG balances have been measured in undisturbed northern peatlands (Koehler et al., 2011; Nilsson et al., 2008; Roulet et al., 2007), thus it is unclear what baseline values should be applied in this situation. Attempts have been made to collect literature values of peatland GHG exchange to constrain this baseline. Saarnio et al. (2007) report annual CO_2 flux of 85 to -67 and 101 to -98 g C m^{-2} yr^{-1} and annual fluxes of methane (CH_4) of 0.2–16 and 0.1–42 g C m^{-2} yr^{-1} for ombrotrophic and minerotrophic peatland, respectively, where negative values indicate uptake by the ecosystem from the atmosphere. Variability in values is related to local hydrology, peatland chemistry, latitude, and likely interannual variability in climatic conditions, indicating a need for monitoring of GHG balances across a range of peatland types over lengthy (e.g., 6–10 yr) study periods. In Canada, monitoring of carbon balance for six years at Mer Bleue bog near Ottawa, ON (45.41°N, 75.48°W) revealed an average rate of carbon (C) accumulation of 21.5±39.0 g m^{-2} yr^{-1}, with an average long-term carbon accumulation rate determined from peat cores of 21.9±2.8 g m^{-2} yr^{-1} (Roulet et al., 2007). In western Canada, Wieder et al. (2009) measured carbon accumulation in ombrotrophic bogs along a fire chronosequence and reported exchange rates of C, as CO_2, from a source of 107 g m^{-2} yr^{-1} during the first year following fire, to a peak accumulation of 221 g m^{-2} yr^{-1} at 75 years after fire, falling to 122.4 g m^{-2} yr^{-1} 100 years post-fire. Considering the fire return interval for the region and average annual burn area, they estimate that average carbon accumulation for ombrotrophic bogs in this region is 76.8±27.6 g m^{-2} yr^{-1} (Wieder et al., 2009). While more research is needed to determine the appropriate baseline value of GHG exchange for undisturbed peatland, the remainder of this chapter will focus on emissions resulting from peat extraction activities.

Kirkinen et al. (2007) conducted LCA to compare GHG emissions from peat fuel extraction to those arising from the use of fossil fuels and determined that emissions from most peat fuel utilization chains were similar to those from coal. However, in addition to comparing peat and fossil fuels, the LCA also allowed for the investigation of shifts in emissions when peat was extracted from different initial peat types and subjected to a variety of after-uses. In fact, Kirkinen et al. (2007) determined that the extraction of peat from previously cultivated peatlands, where initial GHG emissions were high, followed by an after-use of afforestation reduced the radiative forcing of peat fuel utilization to only one-quarter that of coal over 300 years. Given that the same amount of fuel is combusted in each scenario, shifts in net GHG emissions arose from land-use decisions. Similarly, Cleary et al. (2005) presented LCA results for the Canadian horticultural peat industry. Although the largest source of GHG emissions (71%) resulted from decomposition of the extracted peat, 15% of all emissions were attributed to land-use change. This suggests that not only is it important to account for land-use change emissions, but that reduction of emissions during land-use change can have a significant impact on total GHG emissions related to peat extraction.

According to guidance provided by the IPCC (2006) for GHG emissions reporting, accounting of managed peatlands falls under land use, land use change, and forestry, and GHG emissions should be determined during land conversion for peat extraction, active extraction, and abandonment. There is currently no default methodology for accounting on restored sites. The default methodology of IPCC for reporting emissions from peat soils in different land-use categories is to multiply a land-use-specific emission factor by the area affected (Lapveteläinen and Pipatti, 2008). If region- or country-specific research results are available, emission factors may be derived or process-based models may be developed for higher-level accounting (Lapveteläinen and Pipatti, 2008).

According to Canada's 2008 National Inventory Report for GHG sources and sinks (Environment Canada, 2010), estimates of CO$_2$ emissions from peatlands were limited to those affected by horticultural peat extraction. Emissions from vegetation clearing and decomposition, decay of soil organic matter from drained peatlands, fields currently being extracted, peat stockpiles, abandoned peat fields, and restored peatlands were estimated. Values and methods used to estimate emissions are detailed in the National Inventory Report. To summarize, the emission factors for newly drained peat fields and production areas are 351 and 1019 g CO_2-C m^{-2} yr^{-1}. It is assumed that the emissions of CO_2 from fields decreases with time post-abandonment at a rate of 15 g CO_2-C m^{-2} yr^{-1} for block-cut peatlands and 35 g CO_2-C m^{-2} yr^{-1} for vacuum-extracted (extraction techniques are described in detail in the next section). Following restoration, emissions are initially assigned a value of 1753 g CO_2-C m^{-2} yr^{-1} although within five years post-restoration the site is assumed to be a sink of CO_2 at a rate of 80 g CO_2-C m^{-2} yr^{-1}. Ongoing research on peatland GHG exchange throughout the extraction process will continue to constrain and evaluate the validity of these emission factors and guide future reporting methodology.

EFFECT OF PEAT EXTRACTION ON GREENHOUSE GAS EXCHANGE

Peat has been extracted in Canada over the last century, using a variety of methods. Prior to the 1960s, peat was extracted by hand using the block-cutting method (Girard et al., 2002). The peatland was drained by a series of ditches and peat extracted by hand-cutting in trenches. The surface vegetation and peat were cut off and put aside, and blocks of deeper, more decomposed peat were cut out until trenches were 3–4 m wide and approximately 60 cm deep. Surface peat and vegetation would then be pushed back into the trench and a new trench opened, resulting in a topography consisting of successive baulks and trenches that remained after site abandonment. Given that vegetation remained on the baulks and a seed bank was available in discarded surface material, many of these block-cut peatlands spontaneously revegetated with species typical of bogs (Lavoie et al., 2003).

Since the 1960s, and continuing today, most peat is extracted using the vacuum extraction technique. In vacuum extraction, the peatland is drained by a series of ditches, usually 30 m apart (Waddington and Price, 2000), and the surface vegetation is removed and discarded offsite (Cagampan and Waddington, 2008). The surface of the peatland is milled and the dry peat is then collected several millimeters at a time by large vacuums drawn across the surface. This can continue for decades until a depth of peat several meters thick has been extracted. Abandonment often occurs when the mineral surface is reached or the composition of the peat becomes unsuitable for horticultural use (Waddington and Price, 2000). As this is currently the most commonly used peat extraction mechanism in Canada, this chapter will focus on GHG emissions associated with this process.

Finally, some horticultural operations and emerging peat fuel operations in Canada have proposed the use of the peat-block replacement (also called acrotelm-transplant or wet extraction) method of peat extraction (Waddington et al., 2009; Wilhelm et al., unpublished). For this method, a deep ditch is created adjacent to the area to be extracted. The surface vegetation and upper peat are carefully removed and placed on the undisturbed peat surface. Several meters depth of wet peat are then mechanically removed and sent to be dried in the operations' processing facilities. The upper peat layer and vegetation (the so-called peat blocks) are then replaced on the exposed, lower peat surface and the next section is harvested in a similar manner, until a large area of peat has been extracted. This peat-block replacement (PBR) method provides "immediate" restoration following extraction and thus has the potential to reduce land-use change GHG emissions, as will be discussed later.

During active vacuum extraction, a deep water table position allows aeration of the peat profile, resulting in organic matter decomposition and large emissions of CO_2. Waddington et al. (2002) reported CO_2 emissions as high as 112 g C m^{-2} between May and August of a wet year, rising to over 300 g C m^{-2} during a dry summer. They found no significant differences in CO_2 emissions between sites open for 2–3 years and those open for 7–8, suggesting that peat extraction areas remain a large source of atmospheric CO_2 throughout the 20–30 years (Waddington and Price, 2000) that they are active.

Methane emissions from active peat extraction areas are often considered negligible (Environment Canada, 2010), as deep water tables limit the zone of production and allow for oxidation of any CH_4 produced as it diffuses through the peat column. In fact, CH_4 fluxes measured on extracted or abandoned bare peat fields are greatly reduced compared to neighboring undisturbed peatlands (Figure 17.1). Considering a series of natural, abandoned, and restored peatlands across Canada, it appears that the mean growing season CH_4 flux is very low at any location where the average summer water table position is deeper than 20 cm (Figure 17.2) and in these situations it may be fair to consider CH_4 emissions as negligible. However, CH_4 fluxes from drainage ditches can remain high (Maljanen et al., 2010; Waddington and Day, 2007). Comparing CH_4 flux estimates based on peat field values alone to those when fluxes are

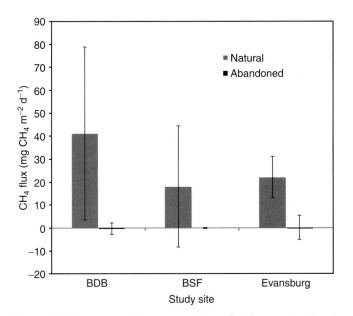

Figure 17.1. Average growing season methane flux from a natural and neighboring vacuum-extracted, abandoned, peat field. Estimates are based on daily average values assuming a 150-day growing season. Error bars give standard deviations. BDB, Bois-des-Bel, Quebec (47°53′N, 69°27′W); BSF, Bic-St. Fabien, Quebec (48°18′N, 68°52′W); Evansburg, Evansburg North, AB (53°38′N, 115°06′W), Canada.

area-weighted to include ditches can shift the site from a small sink of CH_4 to a source of up to 0.8 g CH_4-C m^{-2} during the growing season (Figure 17.3).

GREENHOUSE GAS EMISSIONS FROM ABANDONED PEATLANDS

As stated earlier, abandoned block-cut peatlands are often spontaneously recolonized by peatland species. However, they often remain GHG sources. For example, growing season CO_2 emissions were found to be 363 and 397 g C m^{-2}, and CH_4 emissions 1.2 and 0.3 g C m^{-2} at block-cut peatlands abandoned for two and seven years, respectively (Waddington and Price, 2000). Although this study was conducted in a relatively dry summer, in which a nearby undisturbed peatland emitted 138 g C m^{-2} as CO_2 and 2.5 g C m^{-2} as CH_4, the abandoned site GHG emissions remained

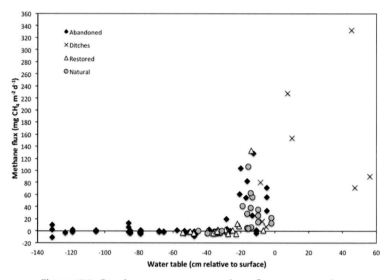

Figure 17.2. Growing season average methane flux versus growing season average water table position from a series of Canadian abandoned, restored, and natural peatlands.

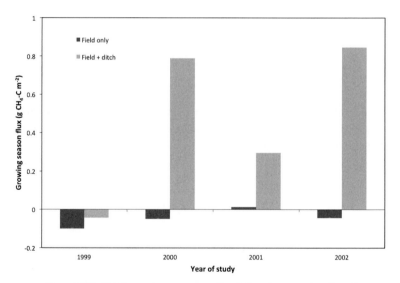

Figure 17.3. Total growing season methane flux from an abandoned section of the Bois-des-Bel peatland in Quebec, Canada (47°53′N, 69°27′W), considering the entire peatland area as a peat field (peat field only) and including the contribution of ditches, accounting for their areal coverage (peat field plus ditch).

more than double those of the undisturbed site (Waddington and Price, 2000).

At abandoned vacuum extracted sites with ombrotrophic residual peat, recolonization by vegetation can be poor (Poulin et al., 2005), and sites remain persistent GHG sources. For example, 20 years following abandonment, the vacuum extracted portion of the Bois-des-Bel peatland in southern Quebec had less than 20% plant cover and emitted between 76 and 263 g C m^{-2} as CO_2 during the growing season between 1999 and 2001 (Waddington et al., 2010). Similar results have been reported for abandoned cutover peatlands in Finland, with growing season CO_2 emissions of 112–164 g C m^{-2} (Tuittila et al., 1999). Despite the suggestion that CO_2 emissions will decline over time as residual peat becomes increasingly recalcitrant (e.g., Basiliko et al., 2007), high rates of peat oxidation maintained for two decades (Waddington and McNeil, 2002) suggest that these sites can remain persistent sources of CO_2. As discussed, emissions of CH_4 from abandoned peat fields remain low (Waddington and Day, 2007); however, ditch CH_4 efflux can be significant and may increase if ditches are colonized by vegetation, particularly cattails, Typha spp., which can provide fresh substrate for CH_4 production and vent CH_4 to the atmosphere (Mahmood and Strack, 2011).

In some cases peat extraction exposes minerotrophic peat and spontaneous revegetation on these sites, once abandoned, can be more widespread (Graf et al., 2008). Graf et al. (2008) reported an average vegetation cover of 70%, 50%, and 25% on minerotrophic abandoned peatlands on bulldozer-extracted, undrained vacuumed, and drained vacuum-extracted sites, respectively. While reduced vegetation cover on vacuum-extracted sites where active drainage systems remain is likely linked to lower water table position, the vacuum-extracted sites had also been abandoned for significantly less time than the bulldozer-extracted sites (Graf et al., 2008). This suggests that the lower vegetation cover may simply be linked to a shorter period of colonization. In fact, vegetation cover increased from 5% in 2005, five years after abandonment, to 25% in 2009 on an abandoned vacuum-extracted peatland in central Alberta (Graf et al., 2009).

These spontaneously recolonizing communities can play an important role in GHG exchange on abandoned peatlands. For CO_2 exchange, these communities will take up CO_2 through gross photosynthesis and may start to return the ecosystem to a net carbon sink. Higher peat accumulation potential was measured for recolonizing species on an abandoned fen than for those on a natural fen (Graf and Rochefort, 2009). Mahmood (2011) reported net growing season CO_2 uptake for

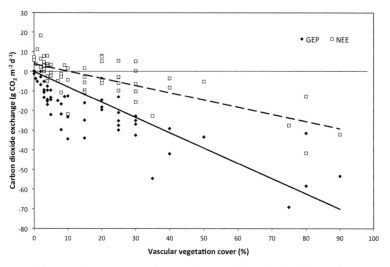

Figure 17.4. Gross ecosystem photosynthesis (GEP) and net ecosystem carbon dioxide (CO_2) exchange (NEE) under full light conditions versus vascular vegetation cover at Evansburg North abandoned, vacuum-extracted peatland in Alberta, Canada (53°38′N, 115°06′W). Negative values indicate uptake of CO_2 by the ecosystem. Regression lines shown are: GEP $= -0.58$*vascular cover $- 10.21$ (F $= 57.0$, P < 0.001, $r^2 = 0.69$); NEE $= -0.39$*vascular cover $+ 4.72$ (F $= 65.1$, P < 0.001, $r^2 = 0.57$).

spontaneously recolonizing communities dominated by *Carex aquatilis*, *Eriophorum vaginatum*, *Typha latifolia*, and *Scirpus atrocinctus*. Although not all communities act as annual net CO_2 sinks, vegetation cover was found to be the strongest predictor, under full light conditions, of both rates of gross photosynthesis and net ecosystem exchange of CO_2 on an abandoned peatland in central Alberta (Figure 17.4) (Graf et al., 2009)).

Revegetation can also impact CH_4 emissions. Vascular plants can increase CH_4 efflux by providing fresh substrate for CH_4 production and transporting CH_4 from below the water table to the atmosphere through porous aerenchyma tissue (Popp et al., 1999). Transportation of oxygen below the water table, also through aerenchyma, can promote CH_4 oxidation, thereby reducing emission (Popp et al., 1999); however, most studies have found a positive effect of vascular plants, particularly sedges, on CH_4 flux (Popp et al., 1999; Waddington et al., 1996). High CH_4 efflux has been reported from numerous abandoned peatlands from *E. vaginatum* tussocks within the range of 5.5–64.6 mg CH_4 m^{-2} d^{-1}, or approximately 0.6–7.2 g CH_4-C m^{-2} over a 150 day growing season (Mahmood and Strack, 2011; Marinier et al., 2004; Samaritani et al., 2011; Tuittila et al., 2000;

Waddington and Day, 2007). Other species may also impact CH_4 emissions on abandoned peatlands, although few studies exist. Mahmood and Strack (2011) found a significant correlation between vegetation volume and CH_4 efflux across a series of recolonizing communities on an abandoned minerotrophic peatland in southeastern Quebec. Fluxes from *T. latifolia*, *C. aquatilis*, and *E. vaginatum* were significantly greater than those from *Equisetum arvense*, *S. atrocinctus*, *Calamagrostis canadensis*, bare peat, and the neighboring undisturbed fen.

EFFECT OF PEATLAND RESTORATION ON GREEN HOUSE GAS EXCHANGE

Restoration techniques differ between Europe and North America. Most European restoration techniques for extracted peatlands involve only rewetting through blocking of active drainage ditches, but this often appears to return the ecosystem to a net GHG sink within several decades. Tuittila et al. (1999) report the return of CO_2 sink function to a rewetted cutover peatland within three years, as the higher water table position reduced peat oxidation and rewetting encouraged the establishment of dense *E. vaginatum* cover. Both the higher water table and the presence of *Eriophorum* increased growing season CH_4 flux, which rose from 0.03–0.14 g CH_4-C m^{-2} before to 0.40–0.95 g CH_4-C m^{-2} after rewetting (Tuittila et al., 2000). Yli-Pëtays et al. (2007) measured C exchange in several communities in a revegetated block-cut peatland in Finland and reported an annual CO_2 balance between a sink of 74 g C m^{-2} and source of 22 g C m^{-2}. The same site had annual CH_4 emissions of ~11–34 g C m^{-2}. In contrast, rewetting of a cutover peatland in Ireland, resulting in the creation of a lake, resulted in continued GHG emissions. Wilson et al. (2007b) report annual emissions of CO_2 of between 163 and 760 g C m^{-2}, varying between plant communities and study years; CH_4 emissions were also high from revegetated areas at 29–39, 18–31, and 3–4 g C m^{-2} from *Typha*, *Phalaris*, and *Eriophorum* and/or *Carex* communities, while a small annual uptake of 0.07 g CH_4-C m^{-2} was measured on the remaining bare peat areas (Wilson et al., 2007a).

In North America, restoration involves not only ditch blocking, but also the introduction of donor vegetation material and protection with mulch (see Chapter 14 for details). The application of straw mulch is critical in the early stages of restoration to stabilize the surface against frost heaving and to create a microclimate suitable for *Sphagnum* moss establishment (Price et al., 1998). However, this mulch represents a labile C source that rapidly decomposes over the first three years post-restoration, releasing a pulse of CO_2. Waddington et al. (2003) determined that in the first two years following restoration, annual CO_2 exchange on a restored peatland could be a release of up to 465 g C m^{-2}, with straw decomposition accounting for 17%–30% of this flux in the first year and 2%–6% in the second year.

In contrast, active restoration also encourages the establishment of vegetation resulting in uptake of CO_2 through photosynthesis. Ecosystem scale restoration of 7.2 ha of vacuum-harvested peatland at Bois-des-Bel resulted in a shift from >60% bare peat areas to ∼90% vegetation cover three years post-restoration, with mosses accounting for about half of the total vegetated area (Waddington et al., 2010). Not only did CO_2 uptake increase due to a large vegetated area, but also because both moss- and vascular-dominated communities had increased rates of gross photosynthesis at restored areas compared to a paired, unrestored site (Waddington et al., 2010). Moreover, a shallower water table resulting from ditch blocking reduced respiration rates at the restored site and helped to convert it to a net sink of CO_2 during the growing season in the second year post-restoration, storing 20 g CO_2-C m^{-2}, while the unrestored area released 76 g CO_2-C m^{-2} over the same period. As observed in European studies, restoration also increased CH_4 efflux, particularly from areas colonized by *E. vaginatum*, remnant ditches, and ponds created during restoration to increase habitat diversity (Waddington and Day, 2007). During the third growing season post-restoration, CH_4 flux accounted for a release of 0.7 g C m^{-2} and 3.1 g C m^{-2} at the unrestored and restored sites, respectively.

Despite the promising early results at Bois-des-Bel, even 10 years post-restoration, GHG fluxes remain significantly different from a nearby natural bog. While the natural bog acted as a small sink of CO_2 over the growing season, the restored site acted as a source of CO_2, although a much smaller source than the unrestored area (Zuback, 2011). Furthermore, CH_4 efflux remained much lower than the natural bog except for efflux from ditches and ponds (Zuback and Strack, 2011). These differences likely remain because, despite the accumulation of 10–20 cm of fresh organic material post-restoration, the water table at the restored site continues to fluctuate in the residual, catotelmic peat that remained following peat extraction (McCarter and Price, 2011). It has been hypothesized that the development of a surface layer of newly accumulated, poorly decomposed *Sphagnum*, in which water table fluctuations occur, is required for the restored peatland to begin functioning hydrologically as an undisturbed site. Lucchese et al. (2010) examined organic matter accumulation rates, peat properties, and site water balance and suggested that this functional surface would develop within ∼20 years following restoration. Investigations 10 years post-restoration indicate that water table fluctuations are not yet isolated within the newly accumulated peat layer and that this non-natural hydrology directly impacts GHG exchange.

POTENTIAL METHODS FOR REDUCING LAND-USE GREENHOUSE GAS EMISSIONS

Northern peatlands have accumulated organic matter throughout the Holocene, locking atmospheric CO_2 into a long-term store as peat, and despite continued release of CH_4, accounting for a radiative forcing of -0.22 to -0.56 W m^{-2} (Frolking and Roulet, 2007). Any removal of this organic matter from the peatland, and its subsequent conversion to CO_2 via combustion or decomposition, will result in a release of GHG to the atmosphere. Once the decision is made to manage peat areas for peat extraction, this release is unavoidable; however, GHG emissions associated with land-use change caused by peat extraction can be mitigated through wise land management practices.

Most simply, much GHG release could be avoided by restoring peat areas as soon as they are abandoned. As mentioned earlier, Environment Canada (2010) reports that 24,000 ha of peatland have been disturbed by peat extraction activities, with 14,000 ha of peatland currently under active horticultural extraction. At least 750 ha have been restored (Peatland Ecology Research Group, personal communication), leaving potentially over 9000 ha of unrestored abandoned peat area in Canada. Given that abandoned peatland can release up to 400 g C m^{-2} (4 t ha^{-1}) as CO_2, restoring currently unused areas could prevent the release of up to 36 kt C yr^{-1}.

Considering the large GHG emissions associated with actively extracted and abandoned peat fields, management strategies that reduce the time that peat fields are drained and non-vegetated should reduce land-use GHG emissions associated with peat extraction. One strategy could be the use of the PBR approach introduced in a previous section. The goal of PBR is to build restoration or reclamation directly into the extraction method. As described above, only the limited area about to be extracted is drained, and following removal of the peat, the vegetation and near-surface peat layer is replaced on the residual peat column, resulting in rapid restoration of the site. As indicated by Waddington et al. (2009), PBR completely eliminates open active peat fields, limits ditch and drained peatland areas, and restores the peatland immediately, eliminating any time spent as an abandoned peat field. Accordingly, land-use change GHG emissions from PBR were calculated as accounting for only 1.6% and 4.9% of the total land-use change emissions associated with block-cut and vacuum-extraction methods, respectively (Waddington et al., 2009).

The replacement of the vegetation and near-surface peat on the extracted area may also speed the return of C sink function in peatlands extracted using PBR, although few studies have quantified the success of these restored areas. Cagampan and Waddington (2008) studied a pilot project in eastern Quebec and determined that even in the first season after peat block placement, vegetation was productive, although gross ecosystem photosynthesis was significantly lower than that of undisturbed peatland. Despite a reduction in ecosystem respiration at the restored area, these plots were net sources of CO_2 over the growing season, while the undisturbed peatland was a sink. This was likely linked to damage incurred by the vegetation during removal and replacement (Cagampan and Waddington, 2008). Wilhelm et al. (unpublished) reported similar results for a PBR test plot for peat fuel extraction in northern Ontario. Mosses on the replaced peat survived the removal and replacement while most of the vascular plants died. As a result, the restored plot was a net source of CO_2 to the atmosphere while a nearby undisturbed site was a small CO_2 sink at hummocks and near neutral at hollows. Methane flux was also measured at the Ontario site and significantly higher fluxes were observed at the restored plot compared to the undisturbed peatland. Because peat had been extracted and the vegetation replaced on the residual, lower peat level, the restored site was wetter, resulting in high CH_4 flux. Using global warming potential methodology (IPCC, 2001), the undisturbed site was almost neutral, with GHG exchange between an uptake of 1.0 g CO_2-e m^{-2} d^{-1} and release of 0.2 g CO_2-e m^{-2} d^{-1} during the two years of the study, while the restored site was a source in both years of 11.7–11.9 g CO_2-e m^{-2} d^{-1}. Thus, while PBR clearly reduces GHG emissions during the extraction phase, care must be taken to avoid shallow water tables or flooding following vegetation replacement in order to avoid large GHG emissions associated with CH_4 release.

CONCLUSIONS

Extraction of peat for horticulture or fuel use will result in a release of GHG. Organic matter present as peat represents stored C that has accumulated slowly over thousands of years and combustion or decomposition of this organic matter results in its release as atmospheric CO_2. This is an unavoidable consequence of peat extraction.

In addition, land-use change associated with peat extraction converts the ecosystem from a GHG sink to a source by removing the

Table 17.1. *Greenhouse gas emissions associated with stages of peat extraction[a]*

Land use		CO_2 exchange g CO_2-C m^{-2}	CH_4 exchange g CH_4-C m^{-2}
Extraction	Peat field	110–300[b]	−0.03–0.1[c]
	Ditch	110–350[d]	1.2–18[c]
Abandonment	Peat field (block-cut)	360–400[e]	0.3–1.2
	Peat field (vacuum–bare)	76–260[d,f]	−0.03–0.1[b]
	Peat field (vacuum–revegetated)	−470–570[f]	0.8–4.7[g]
	Ditch	110–350[d]	1.2–18[b]
Restoration	Restored field	−56[d]	0–1.3[c]
	Remnant ditch	110–164[d]; −120[f] (vegetated)	1.3–53[c,g]
Peat block replacement	Restored field	78–310[h,i]	0.5–1.1[i]

[a] Reported fluxes are for the growing season only. Values were taken as a growing season total when reported in the literature. In all other cases, seasonal averages were used to determine seasonal total flux by multiplying by 150 days. Positive values indicate a release of greenhouse gas from the ecosystem to the atmosphere. In many cases error estimates are not provided in the original references. Waddington et al. (2010) cite an estimated error of ±25% and this is likely reasonable for most values;

[b] Waddington et al., 2002;

[c] Waddington and Day, 2007. This study measured fluxes in an abandoned and restored vacuum-harvested peatland. Abandoned site values have been used as estimates for extraction;

[d] Waddington et al., 2010. This study measured fluxes in an abandoned and restored vacuum-harvested peatland. Abandoned site values have been used as estimates for extraction. The restored value is two years post-restoration;

[e] Waddington and Price, 2000;

[f] Mahmood, 2011;

[g] Mahmood and Strack, 2011;

[h] Cagampan and Waddington, 2008;

[i] Wilhelm et al., unpublished.

photosynthesizing vegetation layer and lowering water tables through drainage, thereby increasing oxidation of the remaining peat. Large emissions of CO_2 occur from active extraction areas and abandoned peat fields, with drainage ditches acting as sources of CO_2 and CH_4 (Table 17.1). Although many abandoned peat fields have limited spontaneous revegetation, more minerotrophic peat deposits may be recolonized, and this revegetation can begin to restore the carbon accumulation function of these sites. Active restoration will further encourage a return of the GHG balance to that of undisturbed peatland, although this may take 10–20 years and requires the return of hydrology to conditions similar to those pre-disturbance.

Some of the GHG emissions associated with land-use change can be mitigated by reducing the time spent under extraction and abandonment. Restoring sites currently abandoned and restoring those currently being extracted immediately upon completion of activities will reduce GHG emissions from abandoned peatlands. The peat block replacement method of extraction, which incorporates restoration into the extraction process, may also help to reduce GHG emissions, but care must be taken to avoid large CH_4 emissions from the restored site (Table 17.1).

As this chapter has focused on GHG exchange, hydrologic exports of C have not been addressed. However, it is clear that peatlands are sources of particulate and dissolved C and that peat extraction increases concentrations (Glatzel et al., 2003) and export (Waddington et al., 2008). The fate of these hydrologic exports is unclear, but microbial degradation in downstream ecosystems likely results in emission of CO_2 and CH_4, and these GHG fluxes should also be associated with extraction activities. More research is needed to determine the fate of hydrologically exported C once it leaves the peatland, and policy must be put in place to assign responsibility for any GHG emitted as a result.

REFERENCES

Basiliko, N., Blodau, C., Roehm, C., Bengtson, P., Moore, T. R. (2007). Regulation of decomposition and methane dynamics across natural, commercially mined, and restored northern peatlands. *Ecosystems*, **10**, 1148–1165.

Cagampan, J. P. and Waddington, J. M. (2008). Net ecosystem CO_2 exchange of a cutover peatland rehabilitated with a transplanted acrotelm. *Écoscience*, **15**, 258–267.

Cleary, J., Roulet, N. T, Moore, T. R. (2005). Greenhouse gas emissions from Canadian peat extraction, 1990–2000: a life-cycle analysis. *Ambio*, **34**, 456–461.

Environment Canada. (2010). *Greenhouse Gas Sources and Sinks in Canada*. National Inventory Report 1990–2008: Government of Canada. Address: http://www.ec.gc.ca/ges-ghg/default.asp?/lang=En&n=1357A041-1.

Frolking, S. and Roulet, N. T. (2007). Holocene radiative forcing impact of northern peatland carbon accumulation and methane emission. *Global Change Biology*, **13**, 1079–1088.

Girard, M., Lavoie, C., Thériault, M. (2002). The regeneration of a highly disturbed ecosystem: a mined peatland in southern Québec. *Ecosystems*, **5**, 274–288.

Glatzel, S., Kalbitz, K., Dalva, M., Moore, T. (2003). Dissolved organic matter properties and their relationship to carbon dioxide efflux from restored peat bogs. *Geoderma*, **113**, 397–411.

Graf, M. D. and Rochefort, L. (2009). Examining the peat-accumulating potential of fen vegetation in the context of fen restoration of harvested peatlands. *Écoscience*, **16**, 158–166.

Graf, M. D., Rochefort, L., Poulin, M. (2008). Spontaneous revegetation of cutaway peatlands of North America. *Wetlands*, **28**, 28–39.

Graf, M.D., Strack, M., Critchley, D., Rochefort, L. (2009). *Restoring Peatlands in Alberta: a Case Study of Evansburg North*. Report prepared for Sun Gro Horticulture.

IPCC. (2001). *Climate Change 2001: Synthesis Report*. New York, NY: Cambridge University Press.

IPCC. (2006). *2006 IPCC Guidelines for National Greenhouse Gas Inventories*. IPCC and IGES, Hayama. Address: http://www.ipcc-nggip.iges.or.jp/public/2006gl/index.htm.

Kirkinen, J., Minkkinen, K., Penttilä, T., et al. (2007). Greenhouse impact due to different peat fuel utilisation chains in Finland – a life-cycle approach. *Boreal Environment Research*, **12**, 211–223.

Koehler, A. K., Sottocornola, M., Gerard, K. (2011). How strong is the current carbon sequestration of an Atlantic blanket bog. *Global Change Biology*, **17**, 309–319.

Lapveteläinen, T. and Pipatti R. (2008). Peat in international climate change conventions. In M. Strack, ed., *Peatlands and Climate Change*. Saarijärven Offset Oy, Saarijärvi, Finland: International Peat Society, pp. 211–223.

Lavoie, C., Grosvernier, P., Girard, M., Marcoux, K. (2003). Spontaneous revegetation of mined peatlands: a useful restoration tool? *Wetlands Ecology and Management*, **11**, 97–107.

Lavoie, C. and Rochefort, L. (1996). The natural revegetation of a harvested peatland in southern Québec: a spatial and dendroecological analysis. *Écoscience*, **3**, 101–111.

Lucchese, M. C., Waddington, J. M., Poulin, M., et al. (2010). Organic matter accumulation in a restored peatland: evaluating restoration success. *Ecological Engineering*, **36**, 482–488.

Mahmood, Md. S. (2011). Carbon dynamics of recolonized cutover minerotrophic peatland: implications for restoration. M.Sc. thesis, University of Calgary, Calgary, AB.

Mahmood, Md. S. and Strack, M. (2011). Methane dynamics of recolonized cutover minerotrophic peatland: implications for restoration, *Ecological Engineering*, **37**, 1859–1868.

Maljanen, M., Sigurdsson, B. D., Guomundsson, J., et al. (2010). Greenhouse gas balances of managed peatlands in the Nordic countries – present knowledge and gaps. *Biogeosciences*, **7**, 2711–2738.

Marinier, M., Glatzel, S., Moore, T. R. (2004). The role of cotton-grass (*Eriophorum vaginatum*) in the exchange of CO2 and CH4 at two restored peatlands, eastern Canada. *Écoscience*, **11**, 141–149.

McCarter, C. and Price, J. (2011). Hydrological assessment of restoration of the Bois-des-Bel peatland, Quebec: a decade later. International Symposium on Responsible Peatland Management and Growing Media Production, Quebec City, QC.

Nilsson, M., Sagefors, J., Buffam, I., et al. (2008). Contemporary carbon accumulation in a boreal oligotrophic minerogenic mire – a significant sink after accounting for all C-fluxes. *Global Change Biology*, **14**, 2317–2332.

Popp, T. J., Chanton, J. P., Whiting, G. J., Grant, N. (1999). Methane stable isotope distribution at a *Carex* dominated fen in north central Alberta. *Global Biogeochemical Cycles*, **13**, 1063–1077.

Poulin, M., Rochefort, L., Quinty, F., Lavoie, C. (2005). Spontaneous revegetation of mined peatlands in eastern Canada. *Canadian Journal of Botany*, **83**, 539–557.

Price, J. S., Rochefort, L., Quinty, F. (1998). Energy and moisture considerations on cutover peatlands: surface microtopography, mulch cover and *Sphagnum* regeneration. *Ecological Engineering*, **10**, 293–312.

Quinty, F. and Rochefort, L. (2003). *Peatland Restoration Guide*, 2nd edn.. Canadian Sphagnum Peat Moss Association and New Brunswick Department of Natural Resources and Energy.

Roulet, N. T., Lafleur, P. M., Richard, P. J. H., et al. (2007). Contemporary carbon balance and late Holocene carbon accumulation in a northern peatland. *Global Change Biology*, **13**, 297–411.

Saarnio, S., Morero, M., Shurpali, N. J., et al. (2007). Annual CO_2 and CH_4 fluxes of pristine boreal mires as a background for the lifecycle analyses of peat energy. *Boreal Environment Research*, **12**, 101–113.

Samaritani, E., Siegenthaler, A., Yli-Pëtays, M., et al. (2011). Seasonal net ecosystem carbon exchange of a regenerating cutaway bog: how long does it take to restore the C-sequestration function? *Restoration Ecology*, **19**, 480–489.

Tarnocai, C. (2006). The effect of climate change on carbon in Canadian peatlands. *Global and Planetary Change*, **53**, 222–232.

Tuittila, E.-S., Komulainen, V.-M., Vasander, H., et al. (2000). Methane dynamics of a restored cut-away peatland. *Global Change Biology*, **6**, 569–581.

Tuittila, E.-S., Komulainen, V.-M., Vasander, H., Laine, J. (1999). Restored cut-away peatland as a sink for atmospheric CO_2. *Oecologia*, **120**, 563–574.

Waddington, J. M. and Day, S. M. (2007). Methane emissions from a peatland following restoration. *Journal of Geophysical Research*, **112**, G03018.

Waddington, J. M., Greenwood, M. J., Petrone, R. M., Price, J. S. (2003). Mulch decomposition impedes recovery of net carbon sink function in a restored peatland. *Ecological Engineering*, **20**, 199–210.

Waddington, J. M. and McNeil, P. (2002). Peat oxidation in an abandoned cutover peatland. *Canadian Journal of Soil Science*, **82**, 279–286.

Waddington, J. M., Plach, J., Cagampan, J. P., Lucchese, M., Strack, M. (2009). Reducing the carbon footprint of Canadian peat extraction and restoration. *Ambio*, **38**, 194–200.

Waddington, J. M. and Price, J. S. (2000). Effect of peatland drainage, harvesting, and restoration on atmospheric water and carbon exchange. *Physical Geography*, **21**, 433–451.

Waddington, J. M., Roulet, N. T., Swanson, R. V. (1996). Water table control of CH_4 emission enhancement by vascular plants in boreal peatlands. *Journal of Geophysical Research*, **101**, 22775–22785.

Waddington, J. M., Strack, M., Greenwood, M. J. (2010). Toward restoring the net carbon sink function of degraded peatlands: short-term response in CO_2 exchange to ecosystem-scale restoration. *Journal of Geophysical Research*, **115**, G01008.

Waddington, J. M., Tóth, K., Bourbonniere, R. (2008). Dissolved organic carbon export from a cutover and restored peatland. *Hydrological Processes*, **22**, 2215–2224.

Waddington, J. M., Warner, K. D., Kennedy, G. W. (2002). Cutover peatlands: a persistent source of atmospheric CO_2. *Global Biogeochemical Cycles*, **16**, 1002.

Wieder, R. K, Scott, K. D., Kamminga, K., et al. (2009). Postfire carbon balance in boreal bogs of Alberta, Canada. *Global Change Biology*, **15**, 63–81.

Wilson, D., Alm, J., Laine, J., et al. (2007a). Rewetting of cutaway peatlands: are we creating hot spots of methane emissions? *Restoration Ecology*, **17**, 796–806.

Wilson, D., Tuittila, E.-S., Alm, J., et al. (2007b). Carbon dioxide dynamics of a restored maritime peatland. *Écoscience*, **14**, 71–80.

Yli-Petäys, M., Laine, J., Vasander, H., Tuittila, E.-S. (2007). Carbon gas exchange of a re-vegetated cut-away peatland five decades after abandonment. *Boreal Environment Research*, **12**, 177–190.

Zuback, Y. C. A. (2011). Carbon biogeochemistry after peatland restoration: carbon dioxide exchange and dissolved organic carbon dynamics. M.Sc. thesis, University of Calgary, Calgary, AB.

Zuback, Y. C. A. and Strack, M. (2011). *Carbon dynamics at Bois-des-Bel: 10 years post restoration*. International Symposium on Responsible Peatland Management and Growing Media Production, Quebec City, QC.

Index